AF478273

Global Competitive Strategies in the New World Economy

NEW HORIZONS IN INTERNATIONAL BUSINESS

General Editor: Peter J. Buckley
Centre for International Business,
University of Leeds (CIBUL), UK

The New Horizons in International Business series has established itself as the world's leading forum for the presentation of new ideas in international business research. It offers pre-eminent contributions in the areas of multinational enterprise – including foreign direct investment, business strategy and corporate alliances, global competitive strategies, and entrepreneurship. In short, this series constitutes essential reading for academics, business strategists and policy makers alike.

Titles in the series include:

Managing the Multinationals
An International Study of Control Mechanisms
Anne-Wil Käthe Harzing

The Origins of the International Competitiveness of Firms
The Impact of Location and Ownership in the Professional Service Industries
Lilach Nachum

Deepening Integration in the Pacific Economies
Corporate Alliances, Contestable Markets and Free Trade
Edited by Alan M. Rugman and Gavin Boyd

The Global Integration of Europe and East Asia
Studies of International Trade and Investment
Edited by Sang-Gon Lee and Pierre-Bruno Ruffini

Foreign Direct Investment and Economic Growth in China
Edited by Yanrui Wu

Multinationals, Technology and National Competitiveness
Marina Papanastassiou and Robert Pearce

Globalizing America
The USA in World Integration
Edited by Thomas L. Brewer and Gavin Boyd

Information Technology in Multinational Enterprises
Edited by Edward Mozley Roche and Michael James Blaine

A Yen for Real Estate
Japanese Real Estate Investment Abroad – From Boom to Bust
Roger Simon Farrell

Corporate Governance and Globalization
Long Range Planning Issues
Edited by Stephen S. Cohen and Gavin Boyd

The European Union and Globalisation
Towards Global Democratic Governance
Edited by Brigid Gavin

Global Competitive Strategies in the New World Economy

Multilateralism, Regionalization
and the Transnational Firm

Edited by
Hafiz Mirza

Professor of International Business, University of Bradford, UK

NEW HORIZONS IN INTERNATIONAL BUSINESS

Edward Elgar

Cheltenham, UK • Northampton, MA, USA

Published by
Edward Elgar Publishing Limited
Glensanda House
Montpellier Parade
Cheltenham
Glos GL50 1UA
UK

Edward Elgar Publishing, Inc.
136 West Street
Suite 202
Northampton
Massachusetts 01060
USA

Reprinted 2001

A catalogue record for this book is available from the British Library

Library of Congress Cataloging-in-Publication Data
Global competitive strategies in the new world economy:
    multilateralism, regionalization, and the transnational firm/
    edited by Hafiz Mirza.
        (New Horizons in international business series)
        Includes bibliographical references.
        1. International economic integration. 2. International business
    enterprises. 3. Competition, International. I. Mirza, Hafiz.
    II. Series: New horizons in international business.
    HF1418.5.G57   1998
    658'.049—dc21   97–45219
                                                                 CIP

ISBN 1 85898 136 0

Printed and bound in Great Britain by Biddles Ltd, Guildford and King's Lynn

Contents

List of figures   vii
List of tables   ix
List of contributors   xiii

PART 1   OVERVIEW

1   Globalization and regionalization: an introduction
    Hafiz Mirza   3
2   A perspective on the emerging world economy: protectionism,
    regionalization and competitiveness
    Peter J. Buckley   12
3   Samsung's views on global regionalization strategies
    Kirsty O'Neil   22

PART 2   REGIONALISM AND EUROPE

4   Global competitive strategies for the European domestic market
    B. Nino Kumar   29
5   Regional headquarters in Europe: a new Japanese management
    initiative?
    John B. Kidd   49
6   Japanese multinationals' strategies towards the process of European
    regionalization, with special reference to former socialist countries:
    an empirical study (1990–1992) on Japanese multinationals'
    activities in Berlin and Eastern Germany
    Sung-Jo Park, Heike H. Rudolph and
    Natascha Haehling von Lanzenauer   64
7   Investment strategies of Japanese firms in the new Federal States
    Dieter Beschorner and Christine Müller   77

PART 3   REGIONALISM AND NORTH AMERICA

8   Regional economic agreements and multinational firms:
    the investment provisions of the NAFTA
    Edward M. Graham and Christopher Wilkie   97

9   Canada, the Free Trade Agreement and US trade actions:
    the implications for business
    Mary-Anne Stevens   119
10 The NAFTA and the Single European Market: an empirical study
    of Canadian and UK companies' trade and investment strategies
    Christopher L. Pass, Kate Prescott and Peter J. Buckley   131
11 Overseas production activities of Toyota Motor Corporation
    Hiroshi Kumon   143
12 Toshiba's overseas production activities: seven large plants in
    the USA, Mexico, the UK, Germany and France
    Tetsuo Abo   157

PART 4   REGIONALISM AND ASIA

13 Growth triangles: a new approach to Asian economic co-operation
    Min Tang   187
14 The ASEAN Free Trade Area: attractive for international business?
    Jacques Pelkmans and Annette Balaoing   199
15 Japanese international investment in the regions of East Asia and
    the Pacific: a horizontal division of labour?
    Shigeki Tejima   214
16 Taiwanese outward FDI: the response to regionalization
    Michael McDermott   243
17 The characteristics of successful firms in strategic alliances:
    a study of the Notebook PC Consortium in Taiwan
    Po-Young Chu, Charles Trappey and David Lee   258
18 The opening of Taiwan's financial markets in the current period
    of protectionism
    Henry Lo   269
19 Political risk management: a case study of Turkish companies
    in Central Asia and Russia
    Mehmet Demirbag, Recep Gunes and Hafiz Mirza   283

PART 5   INTEGRATION STRATEGIES

20 Integration within MNCs: from multidomestic to global and
    transnational firms?
    Anne-Wil Harzing   313

Index   327

Figures

1.1	Tendencies towards regionalization: some examples	5
2.1	Internationalization of firms – conflict of markets	13
2.2	Aspects of competitiveness	15
2.3	Measuring competitiveness in a global market place	16
3.1	Samsung's overseas estimated figures for 1995 by region	26
4.1	Direct investment (DI) and globalization strategy from the perspective of strategic management	31
4.2	Variants of globalization strategies	35
4.3	Globalization strategies of the sample firms in the EC region	40
5.1	Comparisons of total Japanese foreign direct investment (FDI) by numbers of firms	50
5.2	FDI in production subsidiaries in Europe	51
5.3	The roof over a roof issue	53
5.4	Single- and double-loop learning: following Hampden-Turner	56
5.5	National differences	60
6.1	Location factors of Greater Berlin	73
7.1	Japanese direct investment in Europe: regional distribution, cumulative from 1951–1990 in million US$	78
7.2	Reasons why Japanese companies have not invested in the new federal states	84
7.3	Biggest problems for investors in the new federal states	85
13.1	Growth triangles in Asia	189
15.1	Transaction cost and internalization cost (convex: TAC max < ICC max)	226
15.2	Transaction cost and internalization cost (convex: TAC max << ICC max)	228
15.3	Transaction cost and internalization cost (convex: TAC max >> ICC max)	228
15.4	Transaction cost and internalization cost (concave: TAC max < ICC max)	229
15.5	Transaction cost and internalization cost (concave: TAC max > ICC max)	231
17.1	The Notebook PC Consortium analysis framework	261
20.1	Three different organizational models of MNCs	316

Tables

3.1 Structure of Samsung Group 23

4.1 Exchange relationship as an indicator of co-ordination in the
EC region 38

4.2 Personnel socialization as an indicator of co-ordination in the
EC region 38

4.3 Centralization of decision making as an indicator of
co-ordination in the EC region 39

4.4 Local adaptation in the EC region 39

4.5 Degree of satisfaction with the activity of the EC subsidiaries 41

4.6 Variants of globalization strategies and success 41

4.7 Corporate skills of the companies (in comparison to competitors) 42

4.8 Significance of location factors for the operation of the EC
subsidiaries 43

4.9 Significance of EC promotional measures as location factor for
investment in the EC region 43

4.10 Characteristics of direct investment in the European Domestic
Market 44

4.11 Analysis of success factors of globalization in the European
Domestic Market 44

4.12 Significant relations between characteristics of direct
investment and globalization strategies (success factors) 45

5.1 Characteristics of 'world class' plants versus 'other' plants 52

10.1 Classification of sample companies 132

10.2 UK firms: foreign market servicing modes in the Canadian
and USA markets 134

10.3 Canadian firms: foreign market servicing modes in the UK
and the EU 138

11.1 Start up of overseas production plants of three Japanese
automobile firms by country 145

11.2 Profile of Toyota's four automobile plants in North America
and Taiwan 148

11.3 Four aspects evaluation of the hybrid model for
Japanese-affiliated plants in North America 149

11.4   Four aspects evaluation of the hybrid model for
        Japanese-affiliated automobile plants in Taiwan   150
12.1   Overseas production activities of Japanese consumer electronics
        companies   159
12.2   A comparison of Toshiba's seven large plants abroad
        (1989–1991)   160
12.3   'Hybrid ratios' of Toshiba's seven overseas plants   162
12.4   Four perspectives evaluation of the 'hybrid ratios' of Toshiba's
        overseas plants   165
13.1   Regional co-operation in Asian and Pacific developing countries 191
14.1   Summary of lists of product inclusions and exclusions   208
14.2   Winners and losers in the 'fast track' sectors   209
14.3   Winners and losers by country   210
15.1   Recent trends of Japanese FDI   217
15.2   Changes in motivation for medium term FDI
        (FY 1990 and 1996 survey)   218
15.3   The most important customers for existing production bases
        (FY1991 survey)   221
15.4   The most important customers for existing production bases
        (FY1992 survey)   221
15.5   The most important customers for existing production bases
        (FY1993 survey)   222
15.6   The most important customers for existing production bases
        (FY1994 survey)   222
15.7   Contents of products of existing production bases for all
        industries   234
15.8   Contents of products of existing production bases for electrical
        machinery   234
15.9   Contents of products of future investment plans for all
        industries   234
15.10   Contents of products of future investment plans for electrical
        machinery   235
15.11   Contents of products of each existing production base by market 236
15.12   Contents of products of each existing production base by
        markets (electrical machinery industry)   238
17.1   Detailed list of firm's attributes   262
19.1   Turkish Eximbank credits for C.A.R. (31 August 1993)   286
19.2   Turkey's direct investment by country   287
19.3   Distribution of the sample firms' operations by country of
        origin   289
19.4   Distribution of the sample firms' operations by organization
        type   290

19.5	Problems faced by Turkish investors in Newly Independent Central Asian Republics (qualitative assessment)	291
19.6	Risk factors related to production and distribution	292
19.7	Factor analysis: underlying dimensions of production and distribution related risk factors	293
19.8	Risk factors related to financing and macroeconomic management	294
19.9	Factor analysis: underlying dimensions of finance and macroeconomic management related factors	296
19.10	Risk factors related to the host countries' social and political aspects	297
19.11	Factor analysis: underlying dimensions of social and political aspects	298
19.12	Risk factors related to the host countries' legal and administrative aspects	301
19.13	Factor analysis: underlying dimensions of legal and administrative aspects	302
19.14	Risk assessment methods used for operations in the Central Asian Republics and Russia by Turkish firms	303
19.15	Assessment of strategies for management of political risk	304
19.16	Factor analysis: underlying dimensions of social and political aspects	305
19.17	Advantages perceived by Turkish firms in managing political risk	307
20.1	Number of respondents by industry, subsidiary country and headquarters country	318
20.2	Product and people flows in different types of MNCs	320
20.3	Level of intra-firm trade in eight industries, 1982 and 1994	322

Contributors

Tetsuo Abo is Professor of Economics at the Institute of Social Science, University of Tokyo, Japan.

Annette Balaoing is Assistant Professor of Economics, DeLaSalle University, Manila, the Philippines.

Dieter Beschorner is Professor and Deputy Head of the Department of Business Planning, Mathematics and Economics, Universität Ulm, Germany.

Peter J. Buckley is Professor of International Business and Director of the Centre of International Business, University of Leeds, UK. He is also Visiting Professor at the Universities of Reading, Paris 1, Panthéon: Sorbonne, and Rennes 1, France.

Po-Young Chu is Professor of Management Science at the National Chiao-Tung University (NCTU) in Hsinchu, Taiwan, Republic of China.

Mehmet Demirbag is Associate Professor at the Faculty of Economics and Administrative Sciences, Inönü University, Malatya, Turkey.

Edward M. Graham is Senior Fellow at the Institute for International Economics in Washington, USA. He has previously held faculty positions at MIT and the University of North Carolina and, additionally, has served in the US Government.

Recep Gunes is Assistant Professor at the Faculty of Economics and Administrative Sciences, Inönü University, Malatya, Turkey.

Natascha Haehling von Lanzenauer is a Lecturer in Japanese Media and Marketing at the East Asian Institute, Free University of Berlin, Germany.

Anne-Wil Harzing is Lecturer in International Management at the University of Bradford Management Centre.

John B. Kidd is Lecturer in Operations and Information Management at the University of Aston Business School, UK.

B. Nino Kumar is Professor and Chair of Business Economics and International Management, Universität Erlangen-Nürnberg, Germany.

Hiroshi Kumon is Professor of Economics at the Faculty of Sociology, Hosei University, Japan.

David Lee is Industrial Analyst at the Market Intelligence Center, the Institute for Information Industry, Taiwan, Republic of China.

Henry Lo is Associate Professor at the Department of Finance, National Sun Yat-Sen University, Kaohsiung, Taiwan, Republic of China.

Michael McDermott is Senior Lecturer in International Business and Marketing at the University of Strathclyde, UK.

Hafiz Mirza is Professor of International Business and Chair of the Asia-Pacific Business and Development Research Unit, University of Bradford Management Centre.

Christine Müller is a Revenue Analyst at Avis European Headquarters, Bracknell, UK, and was formerly at the Universität Ulm, Germany.

Kirsty O'Neil is a Manager in the Global Operations Division of Samsung Electronics, Asia and Middle East Team.

Sung-Jo Park is Professor of Economics at the East Asian Institute and Professor of Political Science at the Free University, both in Berlin, Germany. He is also President of the Euro-Asia Management Studies Association.

Christopher L. Pass is Reader in Comparative Industrial Economics at the University of Bradford Management Centre, UK.

Jacques Pelkmans is Professor of European Economic Integration, Maastricht University, the Netherlands, and Senior Research Fellow at the Centre for European Policy Studies, Brussels, Belgium.

Kate Prescott is Lecturer in International Business at the University of Bradford Management Centre.

Heike H. Rudolph is a freelance researcher at a number of German organizations.

Mary-Anne Stevens is Area Director of The Ontario Legal Aid Plan, Windsor, Ontario, Canada.

Min Tang is an Economist at the Asian Development Bank, Manila, the Philippines.

Shigeki Tejima is Deputy Director General of the Research Institute for International Investment and Development at the Export-Import Bank of Japan (Japan EXIM). He is responsible for Japan EXIM's Annual Survey of Japanese Foreign Direct Investment.

Charles Trappey is Professor of Management Science at the National Chiao Tung University in Hsinchu, Taiwan, Republic of China.

Christopher Wilkie is Senior Policy Analyst, International Investment and Services Policy, Industry Canada in Ottawa, Canada. His current focus is on investment policy and international agreements such as NAFTA, APEC, WTO and the Multilateral Agreement on Investment (MAI) at the OECD.

PART 1

Overview

1. Globalization and regionalization: an introduction

Hafiz Mirza

Both globalization and regionalization are deceptive concepts: they are widely used, but varying definitions mean that they retain a degree of ambiguity. The definition of globalization used in a recent IMF publication is common:

> Globalization refers to the growing economic interdependencies of countries worldwide through the increasing volume and variety of cross-border transactions in goods and services and of international capital flows, and also through the rapid and widespread diffusion of technology. (International Monetary Fund 1997, p. 45)

At one level this definition is self-evident and uncontroversial. For example, the ratio of trade to world output has doubled since the end of World War II (IMF 1997, p. 46); and the ratio of foreign direct investment (FDI) to domestic investment similarly doubled between 1980 and 1994 (UNCTAD 1996, p. 16). Moreover it is increasingly argued that post-war globalization is a resumption of trends already inherent in the world economy prior to 1913 (IMF 1997, historical annex) and that the process will lead to wider global prosperity. On the other hand, Bairoch and Kozul-Wright (1996) argue that, 'the issues surrounding globalization involve much more than measuring the extent of cross-border economic exchanges and linkages (p. 25)' and question accepted views on globalization, especially those related to its historical genesis and evolution (in their view globalization is not inevitable and there are distinct differences between the pre-1913 and post-1945 periods), the role of the state (significant in both 'globalizing' and 'non-globalizing' periods) and its implications (globalization can reinforce uneven development, leading to *both* richer and poorer countries and regions in the world economy). Another set of issues relate to *what* is being globalized – companies, products, 'business culture', the realm of ideas, or all of these; and the consequences: will there be an inevitable *convergence* between economies? At a cultural level Huntington (1996, p. 68) argues that globalization will exacerbate civilizational, societal and ethnic self-consciousness, and lead to a 'clash of civilizations', although this argument is

                                    Overview

somewhat overdrawn (Mirza 1997). At yet another level, what precisely is the relationship between globalization and regionalization?

Interpretations of 'regionalization' (at an *inter*national) level are even more nebulous than those surrounding 'globalization' (Figure 1.1). Sometimes 'regions' are treated as arising from particular types of international institutional agreements between countries; examples include the European Union (EU), the North American Free Trade Agreement (NAFTA), and the Association of South East Asian Nations (ASEAN). It is worth noting that these agreements differ markedly, ranging from customs unions to full-fledged political unions. Sub-regions (a grouping of parts of countries) are also sometimes referred to as 'regions'. Instances include the ASEAN growth triangles (for example, parts of Malaysia, Thailand and Indonesia comprise the North ASEAN Growth Triangle); the Tumen River Area Development (parts of Russia, China and North Korea); and the Karpotok-Tisza Agreement (the 'Carpathian Common Market' which comprises provinces from Hungary, Slovakia, Poland, the Ukraine and Romania). In addition, the literature frequently treats cross-border 'growth zones' such as the USA-Mexican border or Greater China (China, Hong Kong and Taiwan) as regions, although it is not clear what defines a growth zone; nor are growth zones conterminous with regions defined by political agreement or treaty. Finally, it is worth mentioning that although companies will be influenced by these types of regions, their geographical divisions will be determined by a wider set of factors and objectives. For instance, electronic companies may locate in a region such as ASEAN in order to take advantage of the regional division of labour, whereas petrochemical firms may establish a regional headquarters in Singapore or Malaysia (both ASEAN members) in order to supply countries as far afield as Australia, South Korea and Pakistan. So, for an electronics corporation ASEAN may be a 'natural' region, while for a petrochemicals firm the region may be Asia.

Furthermore, the precise nature and direction of regionalization is unclear, as is its likely ultimate impact on multilateralism. This can be illustrated by a quotation from a recent speech by Renato Ruggiero, Director-General of the World Trade Organization (WTO),

> The regional liberalising impulse is not in itself a cause for alarm among the upholders of the multilateral system … At the most basic level the real split is between liberalization, at whatever level, and protectionism. However the sheer size and ambition of recent regional initiatives means we can no longer take this complementarity for granted. We need a clear statement of principles … to ensure that regional schemes do not act as a centrifugal force, pulling the multilateral system apart. The answer is to be found … in the principle which some of the newer regional groupings have enunciated – Open Regionalism. [But this may not be enough.] Of course, we need to be clear about what open regionalism means. Among the different possibilities, I see two basic alternatives.

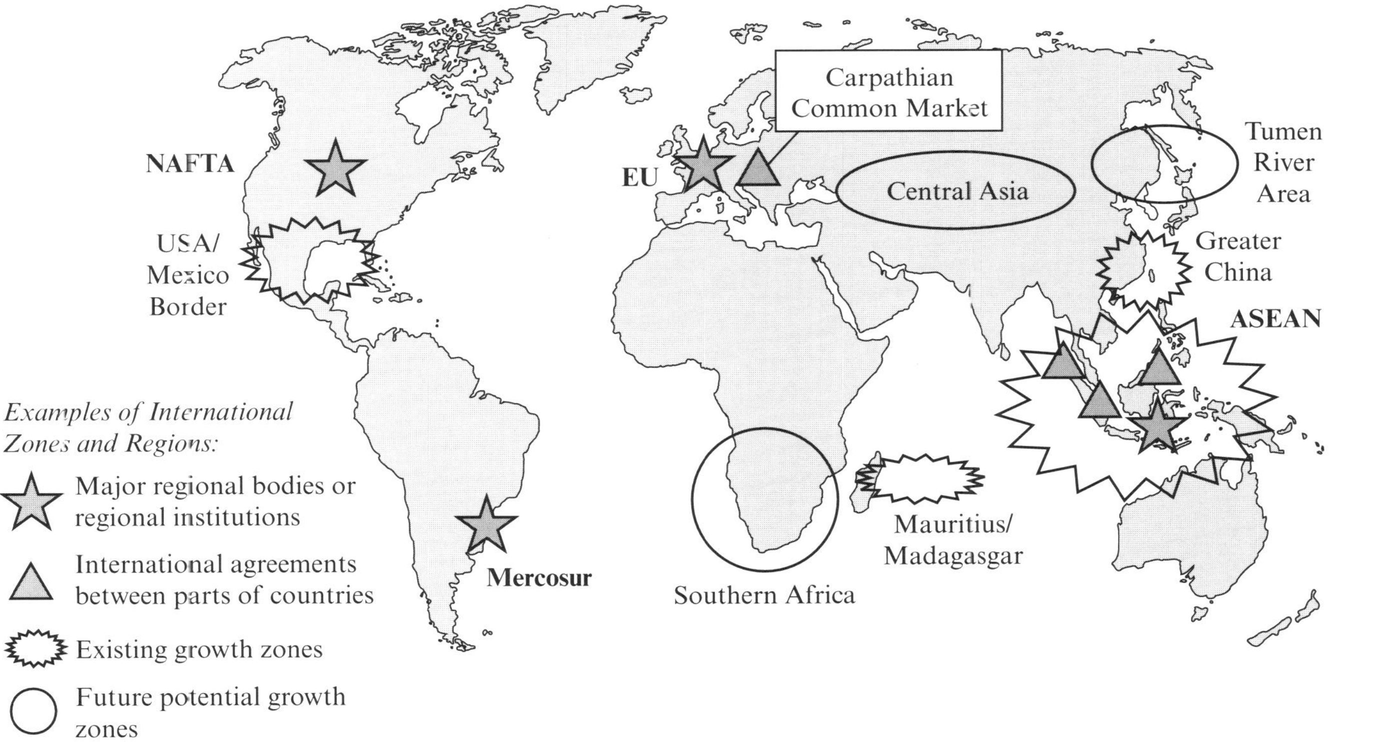

Figure 1.1   Tendencies towards regionalization: some examples

The first is to ensure that any preferential area under consideration will be consistent with the legal requirements of the multilateral system. The existing provisions mean that such areas could at the same time be legally compatible with the WTO's rules and preferential in their nature ... [Such exceptions within the rules[1] were] conceived in a completely different time and situation. Today, with the proliferation of regional groupings, the exception could become the rule, and this would risk changing completely the nature of the system.

The second interpretation of open regionalism is the one I hear from a number of governments including some members of APEC[2] or Mercosur. In this scenario, the gradual elimination of internal barriers to trade within a regional grouping will be implemented at more or less the same rate and on the same timetable as the lowering of barriers towards non-members ...

The choice between these alternatives is a critical one ... In the first case, the point at which we would arrive in no more than 20 or 25 years would be a division of the trading world into two or three intercontinental preferential areas, each with its own rules and with free trade inside the area, but with external barriers still existing among the blocs ... imagine the consequences of this vision in terms of world stability and security ... where, for example, would China and Russia be in such a world? The second alternative, on the other hand, points towards the gradual convergence of regionalisms and multilateralism on the basis of shared aims and principles ... (Ruggiero 1996).

There is no need to dwell on these, admittedly stark, alternatives any further, save to mention two things. First, the choice made will affect (and be affected by) the operations of transnational corporations (TNCs)[3] directly and to a considerable extent. Secondly, although the general tendency appears to be towards a convergence of regions and multilateralism, there is little in the agreements underlying institutions such as the EU, NAFTA and ASEAN to ensure completely that they will comply with the spirit, as well as the letter, of the rules and regulations enshrined in the WTO charter.

TOWARDS A GENERAL THEORY OF GRAVITY

What of the relationship between 'Globalization' and 'Regionalization'? One way of analysing this would be as an elaboration of the *gravity model* which can be used to explain the extent of trade between countries. The model was first developed by Tinbergen (1962) to explain the extent of bilateral trade by measuring the trade potential of any two economies and examining factors encouraging 'resistance' to this trade. The model has been further developed by others, including Linnemann (1966), Wolf and Weinschrott (1973), Ceraci and Prewo (1977) and Chia and Lee (1992). Factors or variables used in the various studies utilising the gravity model include GNP, population, comparative advantage, economies of scale (all generally potential trade variables), relative geographic distance, transportation costs, membership of preferential trade areas and social-psychic distance (generally resistance variables). Without going into the results here,[4] it is clear that such issues are relevant in explaining growth zones and regionalization (this is further discussed below). However, these factors are also relevant in explaining global trade (or indeed trade between a country's sub-regions) and in this sense, it should be possible to construct both a general (global) gravity theory and a special (regional) one.

Globalization and regionalization may thus, arguably, be seen as being a part of the same phenomenon; any apparent differences lie at the level of observation, not in the fundamental forces at work. In consequence, the earlier IMF definition of globalization can be readily adapted to encompass regionalization (in terms of growth zones):

> *Growth Zones* refer to the growing economic interdependencies of countries *regionally* through the increasing volume and variety of cross-border transactions in goods and services and of international capital flows, and also through the rapid and widespread diffusion of technology.

There are nevertheless qualitative differences in the *growing economic interdependence of countries* between the regional and global levels and these can be largely defined in terms of the actions of governments[5] and companies (especially TNCs) – and their complex interaction. For example, the relationship between transnational firms, governments and regionalization can be divided conceptually into four types:

- Economic development and proximal expansion (across borders) leading to integration between countries (France and Germany, say) and regional growth zones (for instance, the USA/Mexico border). This is essentially a 'spillover' model with obvious similarities to the 'potential' half of the gravity model. The extent to which 'spillovers' are regional as opposed to global can be explained in terms of growth pole and location theories (Hansen 1972), relative 'resistances' (as in the gravity theory), as well as other contingencies including government policies and TNC strategies.
- A regional impulse might be imparted or intensified by a variety of corporate strategies, for instance, (i) TNC expansion to growth zones (some of the large inflow of FDI to 'greater China' in recent years has been of a 'me too' character); (ii) initial foreign direct investment in countries such as Singapore and Hong Kong, often driven by government incentives, can create the conditions for later 'spillover' into nearby countries; and (iii) North American, Japanese and Asian investment in Europe from the mid-1980s – because of fears of a 'Fortress Europe' after the EU's decision to establish a Single European Market (SEM) – has helped to accelerate the industrial and economic integration of the European Union.

- Regional tendencies might be created or intensified by more specific regionalization strategies of transnational corporations. For example, economies of scale may lead to 'spillover' because the size of the national market is insufficient for efficient operations (though these do not need to be confined to the regional level). Similarly, many TNCs take advantage of regional divisions of labour; in South East Asia, for example, electronic firms such as Matsushita are utilising the variable factor endowments, competencies and markets of countries such as Malaysia, Singapore, the Philippines, Vietnam and Indonesia (Mirza, Bartels and Hiley 1997). Regional strategic alliances, for example between European companies in the face of foreign competition are also a case in point.

- Finally, government policies, some deliberately designed to encourage regionalization, are also important. A number of (non-exhaustive) examples can be given. For instance, the establishment of customs unions, free trade areas, regional institutions and incentives etc. can help create or formalize growth zones. Mercosur is a good recent example of 'creation', and NAFTA of 'formalization'. Creation or intensification is not a foregone conclusion: for instance the southern ASEAN growth triangle (parts of Malaysia, Singapore and Indonesia) has been successful because it further extends an existing growth region – Singapore and Johore in Malaysia. On the other hand, the eastern ASEAN growth triangle (Brunei and parts of the Philippines, Malaysia and Indonesia) is less successful because it lacks an obvious industrial or corporate motor for growth. International organizations can also get into the act. For example, the gravity model partly underlies the Asian Development Bank's (ADB) policy of encouraging growth through mega-dollar infrastructural development in the 'Greater Mekong Sub-region' (a territory comprising Cambodia, Laos, Myanmar, Thailand, Vietnam and Yunnan Province of China, with a population of a quarter billion people). The idea is that infrastructural development will play a catalytic role in encouraging corporate activity in the region by both local and foreign firms. Governments and companies also co-operate directly in regional activities, an instance being the close collaboration between these entities in both East Asia and the European Union in encouraging trade and investment links *between* the regions as part of the ASEM (Asia Europe Meeting) process. ASEM began at a meeting in Bangkok during March 1996 because of the relatively weak links between Europe and East Asia (as opposed to their respective links with North America); the process has continued through a variety of initiatives, including two reports (EC and UNCTAD-DTCI (1996) and UNCTAD-DITE (1996)), whose recommendations require TNCs and governments to work very closely in order to further future investment, trade and other technology, capital and labour flows in, and between, the two regions. The proposed Multilateral Agreement on Investment (MAI) will also influence international investment and trade – the globalization and regionalization implications depending on its provisions (Sauvé and Schwanen 1996).

THE STRUCTURE OF THE BOOK

The four above-mentioned types of interaction between governments, TNCs and other social, economic and political forces in the process of regionalization (and globalization) are themselves interrelated, and the discussion could be even more wide-ranging. There are interesting implications arising, for example, from Kobrin's (1995) view that regions are essentially national markets writ large. The same can be said about Petri's (1994) contention that 'intense regional ties are spearheaded by trade, and more distant ones by investment'. It is worth recalling that the gravity model is primarily a trade model; a more refined version, including foreign direct investment, other international flows and the role of government, would undoubtedly illuminate the many issues related to the globalization–regionalization dialectic.

The book should be seen in this context. It is not the last word in understanding business activity in the new world economy; rather it is part of a wider research effort seeking to understand the strategies of transnational firms in an evolving international environment in which issues such as globalization, regionalism and multilateralism are to the fore. No single approach has been imposed on the authors, and the chapters seek to represent a range of perspectives on the topic, as viewed by academics, policymakers and business people. Apart from this chapter, the first section includes two overviews of the subject, one by a leading academic (Peter Buckley), the other by Kirsty O'Neil on behalf of a major transnational corporation, Samsung. Samsung's visionary attitude towards the new world economy is interesting because the company is both 'non-Western' and has only recently arrived among the ranks of the largest TNCs.

The remaining chapters examine themes related to TNC strategy in Europe, North America and Asia, the three areas of the world where globalization and regionalization have proceeded the furthest; essentially these are the old triad countries (the USA, Western Europe and Japan) in a newer, wider form and potentially, they are the core of the three intercontinental preferential trading blocs which Ruggiero (1996) fears may arise if the spirit of multilateralism is not kept alive. Apart from the EU, NAFTA and ASEAN, a number of chapters examine TNC strategies in 'new' regions, including Eastern Europe (the chapter by Park et al.), Central Asia (Demirbag et al.) and various parts of East Asia (Tang). The implications of specific policy regimes and agreements for international business are assessed (for example, in the chapter by Graham and

Wilkie and that by Pelkmans and Balaoing); they also look at the strategies of particular companies arising from these regimes. There is particular stress on the strategies of East Asian corporations (for example, in the chapters by Kumon, Abo, Tejima and McDermott) because less is known about these than their European and North American counterparts. The particular themes explored include global competition in regional markets (Kumar), headquarters location (Kidd), inter-regional strategies (Prescott and Pass), political risk management (Demirbag et al.), the strategies of smaller TNCs (Stevens and Chu et al.) and production/management transplants (Kumon and Abo). A final chapter by Harzing examines the integration strategies being pursued by TNCS, with their consequent implications for regionalization and globalization.

NOTES

1. See World Trade Organization (1995) for a full discussion of the relevant provisions of the GATT/WTO.
2. The Asia Pacific Economic Cooperation, a group with no *binding* regional agreements as such, but nevertheless a significant forum for discussion of international trade and investment matters. Its membership includes countries from the Americas (among them, the USA, Canada, Chile), the Pacific Basin (Australia, New Zealand) and East Asia (the ASEAN Nations, Japan, South Korea and so on).
3. The definition of a transnational corporation (or company or firm) used in this book is that used by the United Nations: *'Transnational corporations are incorporated or unincorporated enterprises comprising parent enterprises and their foreign affiliates. A parent enterprise is defined as an enterprise that controls assets of other entities in countries other than its home country, usually by owning a certain equity capital stake. A foreign affiliate is an incorporated or unincorporated enterprise in which an investor, who is resident in another economy, owns a stake that permits a lasting interest in the management of that enterprise (an equity stake of 10 percent for an incorporated enterprise or its equivalent for an unincorporated enterprise). Subsidiary enterprises, associate enterprises and branches are all referred to as foreign affiliates'* (UNCTAD 1996). Multinational companies (MNCs) can mostly be treated as equivalent to transnational corporations (TNCs), but a clear distinction is drawn in Chapter 20 for methodological reasons.
4. For a fuller discussion of contributions to the gravity model see Drysdale and Garnaut (1994), which also discusses a 'close cousin', the intensity approach.
5. Including intergovernmental organizations (such as the WTO, the EU, ASEAN and the OECD).

REFERENCES

Bairoch, P. and R. Kozul-Wright (1996) *Globalization Myths: Some Historical Reflections on Integration, Industrialization and Growth in the World Economy,* UNCTAD Discussion Papers, No. 113, Geneva: UNCTAD.

Ceraci, V.J. and W. Prewo (1977) 'Bilateral Trade Flows and Transport Costs', *Review of Economics and Statistics,* **59** (1).

Chia, S.Y. and T.Y. Lee (1992) 'Subregional Economic Zones: A New Motive Force in Asia-Pacific Development', a paper presented at the *20th Pacific Trade and Development Conference*, Washington, September.

Drysdale, P. and R. Garnaut (1994) 'Trade Intensities and the Analysis of Bilateral Trade Flows in a Many-Country World', in Garnaut and Drysdale (1994).

European Commission and UNCTAD-DTCI (1996), *Investing in Asia's Dynamism: European Direct Investment in Asia*, Luxembourg: Office for Official Publications of the European Communities.

Garnaut, R. and P. Drysdale (1994) *Asia Pacific Regionalism: Readings in International Economic Relations*, Pymble: Harper International.

Hansen, N.M. (ed.) (1972) *Growth Centres in Regional Economic Development*, New York: The Free Press.

Huntington, S.P. (1996) *The Clash of Civilizations and the Remaking of World Order*, New York: Simon and Schuster.

International Monetary Fund (1997) *World Economic Outlook, May 1997: Globalization – Opportunities and Challenges*, Washington: IMF.

Kobrin, S.J. (1995) 'Regional Integration in a Globally Net-Worked Economy', *Transnational Corporations*, **4** (2).

Linnemann, H. (1966) *An Econometric Study of World Trade Flows*, Amsterdam: North-Holland.

Mirza, H. (1997) 'The Emerging Cultures of Capitalism', paper presented at the 14th Sino-European Conference, *Civilizations, National Powers and Economics: Convergence or Clash?*, Geneva, 23–24 September (co-organised by the Modern Asia Research Centre, University of Geneva and the Institute of International Relations, National Chengchi University, Taipei).

Mirza, H., F. Bartels and M. Hiley (1997) *The Promotion of Foreign Direct Investment Into and Within ASEAN: Towards the Establishment of an ASEAN Investment Area*, Jakarta: ASEAN Secretariat.

Petri, P.A. (1994) 'The Regional Clustering of Foreign Direct Investment and Trade', *Transnational Corporations*, **3** (3).

Ruggiero, R. (1996), *The Road Ahead: International Trade Policy in the Era of the WTO*, The Fourth Annual Sylvia Ostry Lecture, Ottawa, 28 May.

Sauvé, P. and D. Schwanen (1996) *Investment Rules for the Global Economy: Enhancing Access to Markets*, Toronto: C.D. Howe Institute.

Tinbergen, J. (1962) *Shaping the World Economy – Suggestions for an International Economic Policy*, New York: Twentieth Century Fund.

UNCTAD (1996) *World Investment Report 1996: Investment, Trade and International Policy Arrangements*, New York and Geneva: United Nations.

UNCTAD-DITE (1996) *Sharing Asia's Dynamism: Asian Direct Investment in the European Union*, New York and Geneva: United Nations.

Wolf, C. Jr. and D. Weinschrott (1973) 'International Transactions and Regionalism: Distinguishing "Insiders" from "Outsiders"', *American Economic Review*, **63** (2).

World Trade Organization (1995) *Regionalism and the World Trading System*, Geneva: WTO.

2. A perspective on the emerging world economy: protectionism, regionalization and competitiveness

Peter J. Buckley[1]

The continent (Europe) is being overtaken by the East. This is assumed to be a matter of economics, but it is not. It is a matter of cultural cohesion and self belief, a matter, you might say, of faith.
Bryan Appleyard 'Give us faith, in something' *Independent*, London, 3 August 1994, p. 15.

The notion of cultural competition, initially among nations and now among (real and imagined) trade blocs, is an idea whose time appears to have come. This chapter examines the ideas of competitiveness and cultural competitiveness in the context of the world economy as we approach the 21st century. In so doing, it includes digressions on the nature of development, the reality of trade blocs and different attitudes to free trade and investment amongst interest groups. The chapter examines the complex relationship between conflict and co-operation that characterizes firms, nation states and supranational groupings.

COMPETITIVENESS

The notion of competitiveness has been examined extensively in recent intellectual history. Notable models have been produced by Porter (1992) and by Buckley, Pass and Prescott (1992). Many empirical studies exist (see for instance Kogut 1993). This concern for competitiveness is often driven by the perceived relative success of Japan, Japanese industry, or Japanese firms and groupings of firms (Keiretsu).

Trade, and trade-based measures are no longer good analogues for competitiveness. This is because trade flows are intimately bound up with other transnational flows – notably flows of technology, personal and capital. It is little exaggeration to say that 'straight trade' or 'pure trade' hardly exists in the modern world economy. Trade flows are invariably bound up with technology and increasingly with capital flows. This leads to a major theme of this chapter – the centrality of capital flows. John Dunning (1994) estimates the amount of trade directly or indirectly connected to foreign direct investment (FDI) at 60 to 70%. He calls this trade 'connected transactions'. Estimates suggest that fully 50% of world trade flows are intra-firm, which puts control of prices within the compass of multinational firms. This has profound implications for the location of economic activity, the distribution of the gains from trade, and the effectiveness of national revenue authorities in protecting their tax-base. A further proposition is that 'investment blocs' are likely to be more cohesive than 'free trade areas'. Thus regions such as the European Union (EU) are likely to be more effective than bodies such as EFTA (European Free Trade Area) which exist to remove barriers to trade.

We can thus envisage a world economy configured as in Figure 2.1. Overlaying the world economy is an international capital market. Below this are a series of more or less coherent regional groupings attempting to harmonize movements of goods and services (and to administer a common external tariff) and to integrate and harmonize regulations and create a 'single market'. Below this, national governments attempt (forlornly) to regulate labour markets in conditions where capital flows are determined by international differences in interest rates (or rates of return on FDI) and goods markets are increasingly regulated at the regional level. This leads to a conflict of management of the world economy. Attempts to regulate unemployment rates and rates of inflation at the national level are thus fraught with difficulty.

The response of many national governments is an attempt to improve 'competitiveness'. This may be considered to be analagous to the struggle for

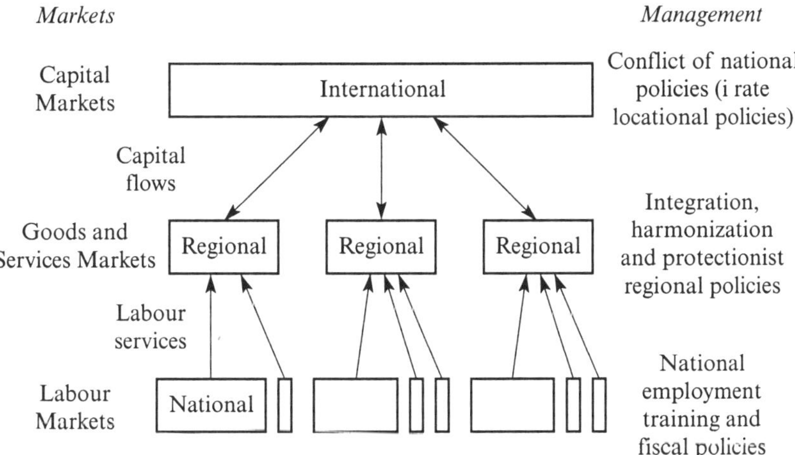

Figure 2.1   Internationalization of firms – conflict of markets

the world product. In many national settings this is translated as reducing real wages relative to competitors. Many of the prescriptions for success in Eastern and Central Europe are of this kind (Casson 1994). Advanced capitalist countries such as the USA and UK are explicitly following other types of policy prescription following a presumed causal mechanism which runs:

'reduce (relative) real wages → improve 'competitiveness' → increase share of world trade (or product) → increase growth and living standards'.

The issue of competitiveness is thus central to current thinking on international political economy.

What is Competitiveness?

The literature on competitiveness yields a vast array of potential measures, but this literature is problematical. There is the question of the level of analysis – is competitiveness to be measured at the level of the firm, the nation or the sub-firm (product) level? A vast array of measures is possible (Buckley, Pass and Prescott 1988) but any single measure is likely to miss some of the essence of competitiveness. First, competitiveness is a wider issue than efficiency – it includes *both* efficiency (reaching goals at the least possible cost) and effectiveness (having the right goals). Second, competitiveness is a relative concept – it must be defined in opposition to another state of the world. The possible comparators are: (1) relative to a different historical point of time (raising the issue of a loss of competitiveness); (2) relative to a different point of economic space (such as paired national firms or groups of firms, or two different divisions of the same firm); (3) relative to a well-defined counter factual position. Third, as mentioned above, trade performance is a poor surrogate for competitiveness. Exports are only one means of reaching foreign markets, and even net exports fail to account for technology and investment flows (Buckley and Prescott 1989). Fourth, all performance measures ignore the time dimension and dynamics. Some measures of creating future potential and managing the competitive process are essential to overcome crude, point of time measures.

Thus competitiveness is best conceived as a *process*. There are three key dimensions to the concept: competitive *performance*, competitive *potential* and the management *process* of competitiveness. Thus it is possible to define three empty boxes as shown in Figure 2.2. These boxes can be filled with the most appropriate measures in the circumstances (Buckley Pass and Prescott 1990 and 1992). The essence of the model is the need for managing the balance between performance (achievement today) and potential (investing in future achievement). As an example, consider the competitiveness of an individual firm. If it goes all out to achieve current performance, it will underinvest in the

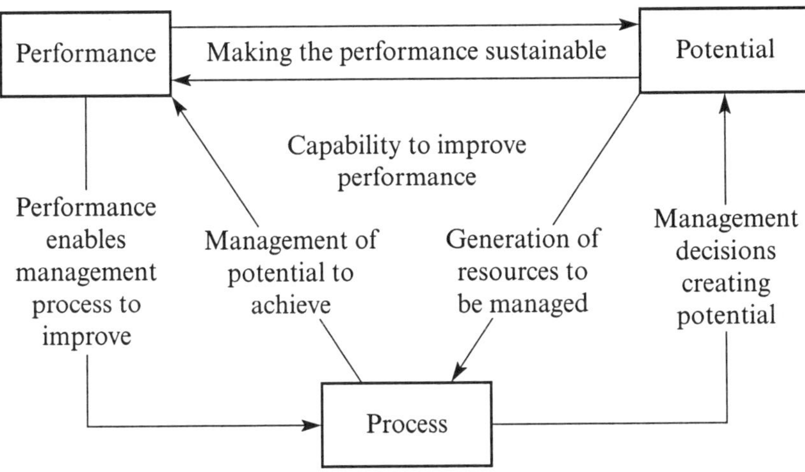

Figure 2.2 Aspects of competitiveness

future and 'burn out'. If it invests all its resources in the future, it will underperform today and will go bust or be vulnerable to take-over. The management of the process is crucial.

Management of competitiveness is also important at the level of the national economy on exactly analogous principles. There is at least one major complication which is germane to this paper – the dissonance between the competitiveness of the country and the competitiveness of multinational firms owned by agents of the country. Figure 2.3 shows the measurement of competitiveness of a global firm. In assessing the competitiveness of such a firm all its activities need to be accounted for. This means assessing its total world sales (exports plus licensed sales plus sales financed by direct investment), world profits, world assets, its overall global competitive potential (including all its foreign research and development and training facilities) and its international management processes (its global managerial cadres and its relationships between headquarters and subsidiaries). The dissonance between the competitiveness of the firm and the country arises in many ways. One example is that, in order to improve the competitiveness of the firm, the correct policy prescription may be to invest in foreign R & D facilities. Is this policy prescription likely to contribute to the competitive potential of the home country? Probably not.

This discussion of the nature of competitiveness thus leads to the key issue of the role of the state in global competition. The role of the state is a controversial one in global political economy – in particular, there is an ongoing argument as to whether the success of the newly industrialising countries of East Asia is owed to laissez-faire or state support for industry.

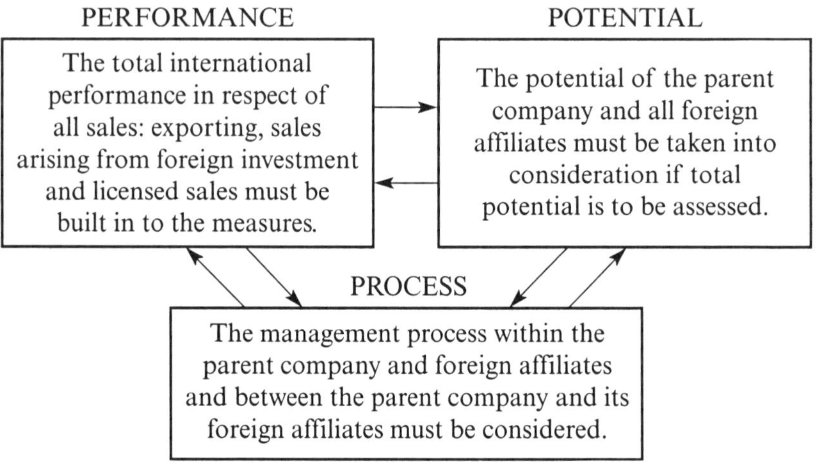

Figure 2.3   Measuring competitiveness in a global market place

THE STATE AND GLOBAL COMPETITION

This paper draws a parallel between the economic theory of the multinational enterprise and a theory of the nation state. The economic theory of the multinational enterprise was the earliest and most successful application (Buckley and Casson 1976) of Coasian 'new institutional economics' (Coase 1937, Williamson 1991). Multinational enterprises (MNEs) are treated in this theory as profit maximizing institutions whose evolution is endogenized within a model. The crucial driving forces in the growth of MNEs are the increasing supply of proprietary technologies and the growing difficulties of using licenses and cartels to exploit these technologies to the full.

This approach can be contrasted with the usual treatment of institutions as exogenous sources of power whose emergence is simply explained by history. However, the analogy between the evolution of the MNE and the evolution of the state is already well established in the work of Douglass North (1990) and Mancur Olsen (1965). The 'median voter' 'owns' a state in much the same way as a majority shareholder owns a foreign subsidiary. The principals delegate respectively to politicians and managers, both of whom require entrepreneurial skills. Politicians and bureaucrats allocate resources in the public sector as managers do in the private sector.

There are a number of key differences though. The first is that corporate rivalry takes place within a framework of law made by politicians, whereas international political rivalry takes place under a fairly weak legal framework in which recourse to force (violence, terrorism, war) is not uncommon. The second is that firms generate revenue from sales whereas politicians generate revenues from taxation. The third is that corporate objectives are relatively easy to specify (profits), whereas the objective function of the state is more complex.

However, progress can be made by comparing the functions performed by firms and states. Both can be conceived as solutions to the incentive problems described by non-co-operative game theory. Both attempt to overcome these problems by inviting individuals to join organizations in which they surrender some autonomy in return for the opportunity to improve the co-ordination of their own actions with those of other people. The most efficient organization is the one which minimises transaction costs. Such an organization needs to motivate its leadership well. Each organization thus rests power in owners, whose own rewards are linked to its overall performance. Both can, in principle at least, remove its leadership and replace it with one whose potential is judged to be greater.

Context

The discussion of the economic theory of the state takes place in a context in which markets and institutions are responding to change. Crudely put, the globalization of capital markets and the regionalization of markets for products and services are becoming increasingly dissonant with labour markets which remain almost exclusively national. Adjustments in national labour markets are required in response to globalization as represented by the activities of the MNE, and regionalization as represented by economic integration (the European Union, NAFTA and so on). This reaction can be conceptualized in two ways. First, by an argument which runs from trade and investment to labour markets, in which the state (by default) co-ordinates responses to increasing (national) inequalities and the displacement of relatively unskilled labour. Conversely, the causality can run the other way. On this view, education, vocational training, fiscal and other policies create new areas of specialization of national resources which result in enhanced competitiveness and comparative advantage. The state can be seen as residual solver of problems caused by changes in the relations between its economic agents and the rest of the world, or as a dynamic innovator and creator of enhanced competitive abilities of its national agents versus the rest.

The Origins of the State

'It is by the adoption of a common historical purpose that a group of human beings becomes a nation. It is then that history begins as the history of a nation'

(Bultmann 1956, p. 103). The Greek view of the state was that it allowed human beings to be insulated from the mysterious forces of the natural environment so that man could (to some extent) control his own destiny. The main means of this control was the law. Law represented the greatest good of the citizens. By being bound to the law, citizens gained their freedom. Freedom did not mean that every man could do as he pleased, but that the individual found his dignity in political responsibility. Freedom was the ability to do one's duty to the State. Greece's 'free citizens' were contrasted with the State of the East ('masses ruled by despots').[2] The Greek was always ready to die for his city. To be expelled from it meant ostracism from society, from all that gave man justice and dignity, and to expose him to the uncanny character of nature. The move of law from divine sanction to contract clearly devalues much of this force.

Parallels have been drawn between the method of Coase and Thomas Hobbes' *Leviathan* (Shepherd, Silberston and Strange (1985)). Coase's definition of the firm as the institution which minimizes transaction costs prevalent in markets can be seen to be congruent with Hobbes' view of government as the institution arising out of the failures of a 'state of nature'. Hobbes explains the existence of government as the result of a voluntary contract between citizens and a protective sovereign in which citizens agree to submit to governmental authority in return for relief from anarchy and the threat of war which would prevail in the absence of government. Both views are not historical descriptions of the growth of firms and governments, but are clarifications of the functions of institutions set against an 'alternative position' or 'null hypothesis' in which the institution under analysis did not exist. Frank Knight's (1921) view of the firm is as a response to risks present in a world of pervasive uncertainty.

DEVELOPING COUNTRIES IN THE WORLD SYSTEM

'There's no point in expecting someone who's warm to understand someone who's cold' (Solzhenitsyn 1970 p. 24).

Much of the foregoing discussion omits the role of developing countries. Their role in the world economy has recently undergone radical reappraisal (Buckley and Clegg 1991). Even categorizing developing countries is fraught with difficulty – there is no such thing as an average (even a representative) developing country. The increased dynamism of East Asian economies in various waves of growth has focused attention upon their success. Crudely the 'waves' may be characterized as (1) Japan, (2) Hong Kong, Taiwan, South Korea and Singapore (the four little tigers), (3) the newly industrializing economies including Malaysia, Thailand, Indonesia, (4) China and (5) the transitional economies, including Vietnam and Laos. This view of tranches of economies achieving dynamism is of course a gross caricature. However, if we accept this view, the awkward question remains: What about the rest? Is Africa in particular to be written off? Are the large dynamic, but dual economies of South America to remain in limbo, with rapidly developing pole cities surrounded by poor, crime- and drug-ridden *favela* and a passive countryside? Uneven development appears to be endemic: across the globe, within regions, within countries, within provinces and within cities.

To add a further twist to the tale, much is currently being made of exogenous growth theory – the view that the key to growth lies outside normal market processes. The determinants of growth on this reading might be technological accumulation, an increase in the labour force and cultural factors. Whilst these forms of theorizing have their attractiveness, they are best treated as adjuncts to endogenous growth theory. Combining the analysis of growth with exogenous factors has its difficulties, however.

The two key issues of this development are the role of culture and the role of the state. Buckley and Casson (1991) attempted to combine culture, geography and economic factors in their analysis of multinational enterprises (MNEs) in less developed countries (LDCs). This paper took the view that interactions between MNEs and LDCs represented a clash of cultures in which the highly entrepreneurial culture of the MNE potentially clashed with a traditional element in LDCs. The interaction between cultures is generally acknowledged to play a role in the location of economic success but it is difficult to conceptualize and operationalize (Casson 1991). Ways forward might be to pay more attention to the literature of social anthropology (Geertz 1975, Inkeles and Smith 1974, Foster 1962), although its combination with economics is at best awkward (Buckley and Chapman 1996). Paying more serious attention to 'native categories' – the ways in which the people under investigation conceptualize the world – may lead to some progress (Buckley and Chapman 1994).

Earlier parts of this paper have shown that it is possible to integrate an economic theory of the state with growth theory.

CONCLUSION

'The race is not to the swift nor the battle to the strong, neither yet bread to the wise, nor yet riches to men of understanding, nor yet favour to men of skill, but time and chance happeneth to them all' (Ecclesiastes ix,11) – but Damon Runyan added 'that's the way to bet'! The underlying motivation for trade blocs is to create big batallions to allow the maximum exploration of economies of scale and to go beyond shallow integration into the deep integration which results from links arising through the activities of multinational firms. These activities include not only foreign direct investment, but also strategic alliances and other forms of network activity. Indeed, a parallel phenomenon to trade blocs is 'alliance competition', where groups of countries pursue harmonized (or at best parallel) policies, and groups of firms co-operate as alliances. This promises to make the study of global political economy extremely complex and fascinating as we enter the next millennium.

NOTES

1. I was asked to deliver, and to write, a speculative piece. In this respect, at least; it will not disappoint.
2. Herodotus has Demaratus say to Xerxes of the Spartans: 'For though they be freemen, they are not in all respects free; Law is the master whom they own; and this master they fear more than their subjects fear thee' (Herodotus VII p. 104, Rawlinson translation).

BIBLIOGRAPHY

Buckley, Peter J. and Mark Casson (1976) *The Future of the Multinational Enterprise,* London: Macmillan.

Buckley, Peter J. and Mark Casson (1991) 'Multinational Enterprises in Less Developed Countries: Cultural and Economic Interactions' in Peter J. Buckley and Jeremy Clegg (eds), *Multinational Enterprises in Less Developed Countries*, London: Macmillan.

Buckley, Peter J. and Malcolm Chapman (1996) 'Economics and Social Anthropology: Reconciling Differences', *Human Relations* **49** (2), pp. 1123–50.

Buckley, Peter J. and Malcolm Chapman (1994) *The Use of 'Native Categories' in Management Research*, paper presented at the British Academy of Management Conference, Lancaster, July.

Buckley, Peter J. and Jeremy Clegg (1991) *Multinational Enterprises in Less Developed Countries*, London: Macmillan.

Buckley, Peter J. and Pervez N. Ghauri (eds) (1994) *The Economics of Change in East and Central Europe*, London: Academic Press.

Buckley, Peter J., C.L. Pass and Kate Prescott (1988) 'Measures of International Competitiveness: A Critical Survey', *Journal of Marketing Management*, **4** (2), Winter pp. 175–200.

Buckley, Peter J., C.L. Pass and Kate Prescott (1990) 'Measures of International Competitiveness: Empirical Findings from British Manufacturing Industry', *Journal of Marketing Management*, **6** (1), Summer, pp. 1–14.

Buckley, Peter J., C.L. Pass and Kate Prescott (1992) 'Measures of International Competitiveness: Empirical Findings from British Banks, Building Societies and Insurance companies' in Peter Barrar and Cary Cooper (eds), *Managing Organizations in 1992*, London: Routledge.

Buckley Peter J. and Kate Prescott (1989) 'The Structure of British Industry's Sales in Foreign Markets' *Managerial and Decision Economics*, **10** (3), September, pp. 189–208.

Bultmann, Rudolf (1956) *Primitive Christianity in its contemporary setting*, London: Thames & Hudson.

Casson, Mark (1991) *The Economics of Business Culture,* Oxford: Clarendon Press.

Casson, Mark (1994) 'Enterprise Culture and institutional change in Eastern Europe', in Peter J. Buckley and Pervez N. Ghauri (eds) *The Economics of Change in East and Central Europe*, London: Academic Press.
Coase, Ronald (1937) 'The Nature of the Firm' *Economica*, **4**, pp. 386–405.
Dunning, John H. (1994) *What's Wrong – and Right – with Trade Theory* University of Reading, *Mimeo*.
Foster, George M. (1962) *Traditional Cultures: and the Impact of Technological Change* New York: Harper and Row.
Geertz, Clifford (1975) *The Interpretation of Cultures*, London: Hutchinson.
Inkeles, Alex and David H. Smith (1974) *Becoming Modern: Individual Change in Six Developing Countries*, London: Heinemann.
Knight, Frank H (1921) *Risk, Uncertainty and Profit*, Chicago: University of Chicago Press.
Kogut, Bruce (ed) (1993) *Country Competitiveness*, Oxford: Oxford University Press.
Olsen, Mancur (1965) *The Logic of Collective Action*, Cambridge, MA: Harvard University Press.
Porter, Michael E. (1992) *The Competitive Advantage of Nations*, New York: Free Press.
Shepherd, David; Silberston, Aubrey and Roger Strange (1988) *British Manufacturing Overseas*, London: Methuen.
Solzhenitsyn, Alexander (1970) *Ivan Denisovich*, London: Sphere Books (first published 1962).
Williamson, Oliver E. (1996) *The Mechanics of Governance*, Oxford: Oxford University Press.

3. Samsung's views on global regionalization strategies

Kirsty O'Neil

Samsung Group views the most likely scenario for regionalization tendencies as the continuation and expansion of existing trade blocs for both now and the mid-term, despite the 1995 inauguration of the World Trade Organization (WTO). The trade blocs with the largest influence on Samsung are NAFTA, the EU, and ASEAN. It follows that Samsung's global business policies are developed with the continuation and strengthening of these economic blocs in mind. The effect of these blocs has contributed to Samsung's decision to develop its own corporate regionalization. From the commencement of 1995, Samsung Group established its own five regional headquarters and three regional manufacturing complexes. Also discussed in this paper are Samsung's views on the development of an East Asian Caucus (EAC) as proposed by Dr Mahathir, Prime Minister of Malaysia, and finally, the possibility of the development of an East Asia bloc consisting of Japan, Korea and China.

Samsung Group is divided into five subgroups (see Table 3.1). Samsung Electronics Co. Ltd. and Samsung Trading Corporation led Samsung Group in its expansion overseas during the 1970s and 80s, but in the 1990s, overseas growth by many of Samsung's companies, combined with other external factors such as regionalization tendencies, forced the Group to rethink and restructure its overseas operations and strategy.

In 1994 Samsung Group's overseas manufacturing facilities produced US $2.5 billion. This figure was 10% of all overseas sales and 3% of total group sales. Samsung's goal for the year 2000 is to increase overseas manufacturing facilities to 20% of total group sales, and overseas sales to $60 billion of total Group sales. To achieve this the group has recognized the need for corporate regionalization. This involves setting up a regional headquarters, regional manufacturing facilities, development and design centres, training facilities and marketing facilities; and developing the working process culture (Samsung corporate culture combined with the local culture). Within each region all Samsung companies and manufacturing facilities will be operated as entirely local entities. To meet this regionalization need, five regional headquarters were

Table 3.1　Structure of Samsung Group

Sub group	No. of companies	No. of people	1994 sales (US$ billion)
Electronics	7	77 386	18.2
Machinery	3	17 900	3.6
Chemicals	4	2 582	1.2
Finance & Insurance	4	76 707	14.7
Other Companies	13	31 832	25.8

Note:　1 billion = 1 thousand million

established in Europe, North America, China, SE Asia and Japan, at the beginning of 1995. Alongside these, three manufacturing complexes were established, the first in Cleveland in the UK, the second in Tijuana in Mexico, and the third in Tianjing in China. 'Getting on the inside' of the EU and NAFTA was one of the key factors in deciding where to establish manufacturing bases in Europe and North America. ASEAN has only recently increased its strategic economic importance for Samsung. The introduction of the CEPT (Common Effective Preferential Tariffs) since January 1993 is the most consolidated effort by the ASEAN members to become a regional economic strength so far. Further the recent admission of Vietnam to ASEAN, combined with the push to hasten the tariff reduction process, have recently greatly increased the importance of ASEAN at Samsung. Therefore, while ASEAN in 1994 did not greatly influence Samsung's decision on where to establish the regional manufacturing complex in Asia, the economic bloc will certainly have a lot greater impact on decision making in the future.

Another co-related key factor motivating Samsung's corporate regionalization is the belief that the customer is number one. In order to satisfy the customer to the best of each company's ability, processes such as manufacturing, delivery time, local tastes for the product, and sales and marketing, need to be fully accommodated. The only people fully equipped for this are the local employees. Head office considers that unless each Samsung company becomes fully localized we cannot be competitive in that country. For Samsung, regionalization has become synonymous with localization.

Each of the five regional headquarters is responsible to head office for all the Samsung companies in that region, and it is also the base from which regionalization will develop. It is still early days, but the overall plan is for these regional headquarters to operate with increasing autonomy from head office. As previously explained, three of the regions have their own large-scale manufacturing complexes. There are also a number of manufacturing facilities already established throughout SE Asia, Mexico and various parts of Europe.

Three of Samsung's five regional headquarters are in Asia. This is because Samsung places great importance on the economic growth of Asia both now and in the future. Samsung divides Asia into the following categories:

* ASEAN, China & Taiwan
* Cambodia, Laos, Myanmar, Bangladesh (new markets)
* Hong Kong and Singapore (city states)
* India (under the jurisdiction of South East Asian HQ)
* Japan (separate due to the high level of economic development)
* Korea (head office).

The most important and potentially advantageous markets are ASEAN, China and India. These countries hold the most investment and market growth potential, and have the fastest economic growth. They also have cultures that are easier to match with Samsung's culture, which eases communication and market penetration; and they have a GNP per capita of US $1000–5000, and can therefore afford Samsung's products.

Other regional groups which are expected to grow in importance in and around the Asian area are South Asia, Central Asia and the Middle East. The principal countries in South Asia are Bangladesh, India, Sri Lanka and Pakistan. However, South Asia is yet to become a consolidated economic regional group, and is not expected to in the near future. There are still too many political instabilities and insurgencies that prevent development. India is the exception and is seen as having the greatest potential, due to recent deregulation and privatization initiatives by the government, combined with increased economic growth, greater stability and increased foreign investor confidence. The importance of India is illustrated by the fact that it has been labeled as one of Samsung's primary emerging markets.

Central Asia is considered part of the Commonwealth of Independent States (CIS) and all operations and strategies by Samsung Group are planned accordingly. At this stage the CIS comes under the jurisdiction of the European regional headquarters. Samsung anticipates that as sales increase within the CIS region, it may be necessary to separate the CIS and Europe into two regional groups. However, it will be quite some time before Central Asia will be considered as a separate regional group from the CIS.

The Middle East and Africa are two separate regions combined together for more efficient operational purposes. The Middle East is presently in the initial stages of developing an economic regional group, but it is expected to take some years before it becomes a strong economic force. Both the Middle East and Africa have not traditionally been regarded as strong potential growth areas, but in 1995,

Samsung Electronics Co., always the leader of Samsung companies abroad, established a subsidiary in Dubai to service both the Middle East and Africa. In particular, rising incomes, a growing generation of young people and political stability are the factors that make the Middle East a promising region. In 1995, the Middle East and Africa regions are one of Samsung Group's smallest markets. For Samsung Electronics Co., sales turnover amounted to US $400 million. However the electronics company aims to have a sales turnover of US $1 billion by the year 2000. South Africa, Egypt, Turkey and Saudi Arabia are considered to be the major markets in the two regions at present.

FUTURE ECONOMIC REGIONAL BLOCS IN THE ASIAN REGION

The East Asian Caucus proposed by Dr Mahathir of Malaysia is similar to APEC, but is an economic bloc rather than a political bloc. It involves countries from NE Asia and SE Asia, but excludes some Asia-Pacific rim countries such as the US and Australia. Samsung does not view such a bloc as very likely due to the different levels of economic development and competing comparative advantages, the wide range in levels of political stability within the region, the geographical enormity of the proposed area, and the differences in religions, cultures, languages and beliefs. ASEAN as an economic bloc has not been a good precedent for the EAC because of a lack of economic unity, competitive economies, the maintenance of trade barriers, and a lack of co-development. ASEAN came together during the 1960s, but did not really have much economic weight until the 1990s.

There has also been, to a much lesser extent, speculation about the formation of a NE Asian economic bloc. Likely core candidates would be Japan, Korea and China. Taiwan is an unlikely candidate because of the One China Policy. Benefits of such a bloc would be manufacturing, technological co-operation, and a large market. However again Samsung does not view this as a likely scenario in the immediate and short-term future.

SAMSUNG'S ESTIMATED FIGURES FOR 1995

1995 is the first year that Samsung Group broke down its sales figures overseas by region. Samsung Group's total sales for 1995 including overseas sales and domestic sales in Korea, were estimated to be US $75 billion. This is broken down to US $24.8 billion for overseas sales and US $48.2 billion for domestic sales. There is a remaining difference of $2 billion, which comes from sources such as direct sales overseas.

Overseas sales are broken down into the following regions: Americas, China, Europe, Japan and SE Asia (see Figure 3.1).

These regions are expected to undergo fast growth over the five years from 1995, particularly the emerging economies in Asia, Latin America and Eastern Europe. Samsung Group aims to have US $60 billion in overseas sales and $200 billion in total Group sales by the year 2000.

To the casual observer it may seem that Samsung Group has been very slow to recognize the importance of the overseas markets beyond mere sales, and to formulate the Group's strategy accordingly. However, the nature of the domestic Korean market during the 1970s and 1980s has meant that Samsung could grow at an astonishing pace without focusing greatly on overseas markets. The Korean government provided a completely protected environment, supplying subsidies and keeping out all foreign competition, while at the same time producing unprecedented economic growth. The acknowledgment that Samsung's rapid sales growth can no longer rely just on the growth of the domestic Korean market is now well and truly entrenched at HQ in Seoul. Further, the onset of the WTO ensures that the Korean government can no longer protect the Korean market and keep out aggressive foreign competition.

The formation and consolidation of economic regional blocs around the globe has contributed to the Group's decision to develop its own corporate regionalization, seen through the establishment of five regional headquarters. Moreover, this corporate regionalization is all part of a larger globalization plan through which Samsung aims to meet its goal of becoming a truly global Group in the 21st century.

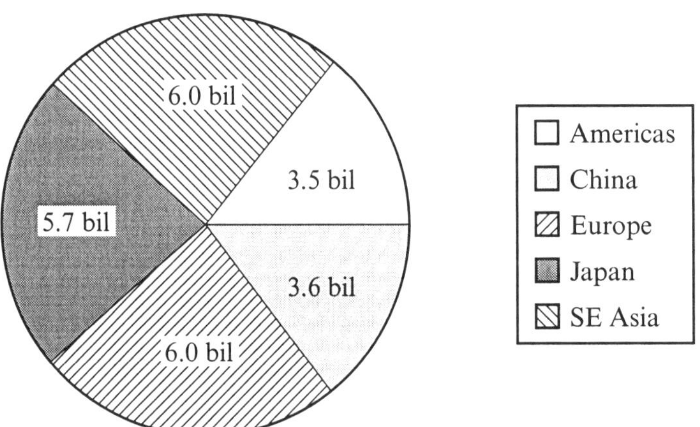

Figure 3.1   Samsung's overseas estimated figures for 1995 by region

PART 2

Regionalism and Europe

4. Global competitive strategies for the European domestic market

B. Nino Kumar

OBJECTIVE OF CHAPTER

In the European Union, companies in member countries must prepare for competition within the European Domestic Market. Since competitive strategies cover Europe, the globalization paradigm offers a suitable concept for investigation. The objectives of this chapter are as follows:

1. What are the major characteristics of corporate global competitive strategies in the European Domestic Market? What is the pattern of these strategies? What are the main influencing factors?
2. Which special type of globalization strategy is effective and successful? What are the success factors and problems of implementation?
3. Do the employed globalization strategies comply with the requirements of the European Domestic Market? Where do opportunities and constraints lie?

The information for this chapter is based on empirical research carried out by the author in early 1992. The method of research and the composition of the sample check will be discussed later.

GENERAL OVERVIEW

Two Theoretical Streams

The theoretical concept of this problem is developed in connection with the theory of international corporations. In the Anglo-American and German literature, two main theoretical streams of thought can be identified. These themes reflect the complementary paradigms in the field of international business, but differ in their approaches. First, there is the *theory of direct investment*. This theory attempts to explain international production and the development and growth of international business. Second, in contrast, the *concept of globalization* focuses on the forms and strategies of international activity, that is, how a company organizes its foreign activities.

The Integration of These Streams: a Strategic Perspective

In literature, these two streams are more or less treated separately from one another. The theory of direct investment developed from a macroeconomics background, while the globalization concept was initiated in connection with problems of management and marketing in overseas operations. Thus, the traditional direct investment theories, for example, Hymer (1960), Vernon (1966), Knickerbocker (1973), Buckley and Casson (1976), do not refer to the problem of globalization. On the other hand, globalization theories hardly incorporate issues of direct investment, for example in Doz and Prahalad (1984), Wiechmann (1974), Bartlett and Ghoshal (1989), and Levitt (1984). Only recently have integrative approaches been considered (for example, Kobrin 1991 and Kogut 1989). In the following chapter both approaches are integrated into the conceptual framework. Globalization strategies in the European Domestic Market are analysed in interconnection with direct investment in the European Community countries. The integration paradigm is provided by the concept of strategic management and strategic planning. With this, both streams of theory are brought together in one integrated, coherent model.

Based on the standard model of strategic planning (as in Steinmann and Schreyögg, 1997; Christensen et al., 1982; Hinterhuber, 1992), direct investment is conceived as a strategic option which relates to both the main lines of business and to relevant markets. The strategy of direct investment emerges in connection with a set of influencing factors defined by the theory of direct investment. These determinants comply with the influences of 'environment' and 'corporate characteristics' within the general framework of strategy formulation. Globalization strategy, on the other hand, is the concept of strategy implementation defining the frame for strategic programmes.

This basic model integrates the two main international business theory streams into one uniform strategy-based concept. The unified perspective has the advantage that the determinants of direct investment which hitherto were dealt with on a macroeconomic perspective can now be treated on a strategy level. In this way, it is possible to integrate their influence on globalization strategy. Compatibility between the two defines the basis for success in compliance with the 'fit' model in the general framework of strategy formulation (as in Christensen et al., 1982; Hinterhuber, 1992).

THEORY OF DIRECT INVESTMENT: THE STRATEGIC DETERMINANTS

Strategic Determinants

Since Hymer's (1960) pioneering work, several concepts have been proposed for explaining direct investments. Depending on the main focus of the chapter and analysis, the theories have a macroeconomic or microeconomic approach. Based on the market-failure paradigm, direct investment is considered a strategic behaviour of firms in imperfect competition. The influencing variables thereby draw on different theories, such as the theory of industrial organization, institutional economics, and trade theory (as in Kogut, 1983; Caves, 1982).

For the purpose of this chapter, Dunning's (1988) *eclectic paradigm* is chosen as the conceptual basis. Three major variables explain international production through direct investment:

1. Ownership of business-specific advantages,
2. Internalization and transaction cost advantages, and
3. Location advantages.

Influence of ownership and internalization advantages

These two variables can be analysed within the strategic perspective (Figure 4.1) in terms of strengths and weaknesses combined in the corporate characteristics. The influence of ownership advantages has been discussed extensively in

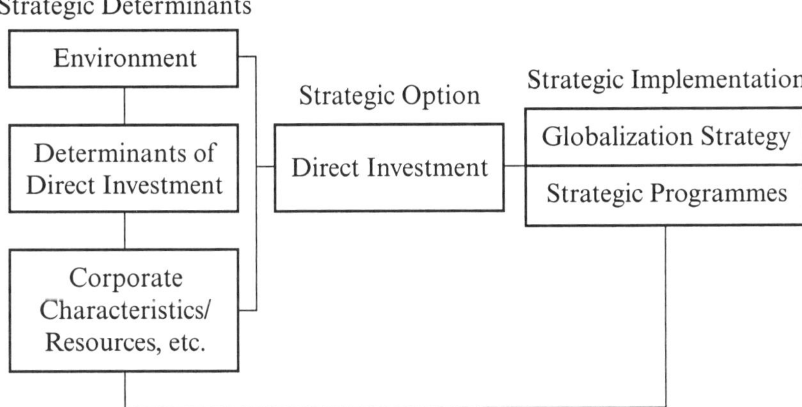

Figure 4.1   Direct investment (DI) and globalization strategy from the perspective of strategic management

theory (for example, Hymer, 1960; Knickerbocker, 1973; Porter, 1989), as has been the effect of internalization in connection with exploiting competitive advantages abroad (Buckley and Casson, 1976).

According to Buckley, Pass and Prescott (1988), these strategic capabilities must be determined as comparative competitive advantages within the respective industries in both the home as well as the host country. The following factors can be seen as proxy for these ownership advantages (Buckley, Pass and Prescott 1988; Nohria and Garcia-Pont, 1991):

1. The relative position of the company in its branch of industry with respect to, for example, research and development, technology, marketing, and so on; a positive gap indicates greater competitive advantages.
2. The relationship of labour costs to the total cost in industry average. The smaller the relationship, the larger the labour productivity and the ability of the firm to manage labour-intensive production.
3. The breadth of the product line. Firms that operate in a larger number of market segments possess more diversity and flexibility than companies specializing in only a few market segments.

Influence of location advantages

The third element of the eclectic paradigm is supported by the traditional location theory. Businesses undertake direct investment in a foreign country because they expect a more cost-effective production based on location advantages. These environmental influences can be related to market factors as well as administrative support. Accordingly, it is important to ascertain two points:

1. The significance of the location factors, such as labour costs, for the operations of the foreign subsidiary in the host country. The larger the importance, the higher the presumed influence on the investment decision.
2. The significance of the administrative policies, such as measures by governments to support the setting up of operations. The greater the importance and the more companies avail of such measures, the higher the presumed influence on the investment decision.

Strategic Options

Direct investments are connected with the transfer of material and immaterial resources and the establishment of the firm's own sales and production subsidiaries, which can also be in the form of co-operative ventures. The structural features of direct investment in connection with the influencing factors (Figure 4.1) are:

1. The number of foreign subsidiaries (the extent of direct investment). This number reflects the potential to exploit the competitive and location advantages abroad.
2. The number of foreign subsidiaries which are integrated into the value chain (the type of direct investment). This is an indicator of the firm's potential to take advantage of internalization.
3. The ownership of the foreign subsidiaries (type of direct investment). Firms have a choice between 100 per cent subsidiaries and joint ventures with local partners. Ownership reflects the possibility of control over the foreign subsidiary and, therefore, the potential for the exploitation of the competitive and internalization advantages.

THE CONCEPT OF GLOBALIZATION STRATEGY

The Theoretical Dimensions

The implementation of direct investment follows within the frame of globalization strategy (Figure 4.1). Two basic elements define globalization: (1) local adaptation and (2) (global) co-ordination.

In connection with the geographic dispersion of the company's activity, the need for differentiation and adaptation with respect to the local environment in the host-country also increases (Welge and Böttcher, 1991; Kumar, 1987). The following points can be considered as proxy for geographic dispersion and adaptation:

1. The number of countries in which the firm is established. This shows the environmental diversity, and therefore the adaptation demands on the firm. In the context of the European Domestic Market, diversity is perhaps low due to institutional harmonization within the Community. Nevertheless, the cultural and sociodemographic characteristics remain very much different in many areas, such as the food market (Maucher and Brabeck-Lemathe, 1991).
2. The importance of the foreign subsidiaries within the company. On this basis, the firm's motivation and commitment to fulfil the (adaptation) requirements in the foreign country can be estimated. The share of sales achieved in this particular market as a portion of total sales is considered an indicator. The higher the share, the larger the significance of this market, and therefore the higher the presumed commitment to carry the cost of adaptation demands.
3. Finally, the degree of adaptation can be established through two complementary indicators:

- the number of market segments served abroad that have no significance at home, and
- the share of sales in the foreign subsidiaries that accrue from products developed solely for that particular market.

With global co-ordination, one addresses the issue that it is economically meaningful to integrate dispersed world-wide activities in order to profit from the synergies resulting from economies of scale, exchange relations, and so on. (Welge and Böttcher, 1991; Meffert, 1989; Bartlett and Ghoshal, 1989; Kobrin, 1991). It is clear that an effective (global) co-ordination is possible only to the extent that dispersed activities are uniform or standardized. The greater the standardization, the more effectively co-ordination and integration can be achieved. Since standardization means imposing parent company norms and skills on foreign subsidiaries, co-ordination stands in contrast to local adaptation, which abides by local influences.

Indicators of global co-ordination are:

1. Exchange relations. These are, according to Kobrin (1991), the most reliable indicators for existing co-ordination:
   - the share of intersubsidiary trade in relation to the total foreign trade of the company,
   - the share of trade between foreign subsidiaries and the parent company,
   - the intensity of the financial and technological transactions among the subsidiaries themselves and between them and the parent organization. For each indicator the following applies: the larger the share, the more intense the relationship, and therefore the higher the presumed co-ordination.
2. Centralization and socialization. According to Bartlett and Ghoshal (1989), the following points reflect the means of co-ordination.
   - Regarding centralization, an important measure is the distribution of the locus of decision-making between the parent and the subsidiaries (Goehle, 1980; Kumar, 1987; Wiechmann, 1974). Decision making which is more strongly anchored in the parent indicates greater centralization and also greater co-ordination potential.
   - The criterion 'socialization' aims at creating a shared consciousness for the common goals and policies throughout the world-wide business. This makes it easier to implement co-ordination (Bartlett and Ghoshal, 1989). Foreign personnel assignments are a reliable measure for socialization of co-workers in foreign subsidiaries (Kumar and Karlshaus, 1992). The more intensive the exchange of persons, the greater the socialization, and also the greater the co-ordination potential.

Variants of global strategy

The problem in globalization and of global competitive strategies lies in finding the right balance between co-ordination and local adaptation. Companies must search for a compromise with respect to the given situation and the functional areas (Meffert, 1990). Within the frame of co-ordination and local adaptation four strategy variants can be identified (Figure 4.2). Each variant represents a type of strategy of globalization which defines how within the frame of 'global co-ordination' and 'local adaptation', direct investment can be implemented. In literature, the basic strategy types are described as follows (Welge and Böttcher, 1991; Bartlett and Ghoshal, 1989):

- 'International' strategies are characterized by a centralized management concept. Successful structures and processes of the parent company are transferred to the branch without any changes.
- 'Multinational' strategies take into account the knowledge that the host environment places special demands on management. Structures and processes in the foreign subsidiaries are adapted to the needs of the particular host countries, and there is little communication between the subsidiaries.
- 'Global' strategies aim at achieving global efficiency in the world market. Structures and processes in the foreign subsidiaries are co-ordinated in alignment with the common goals of the firm.

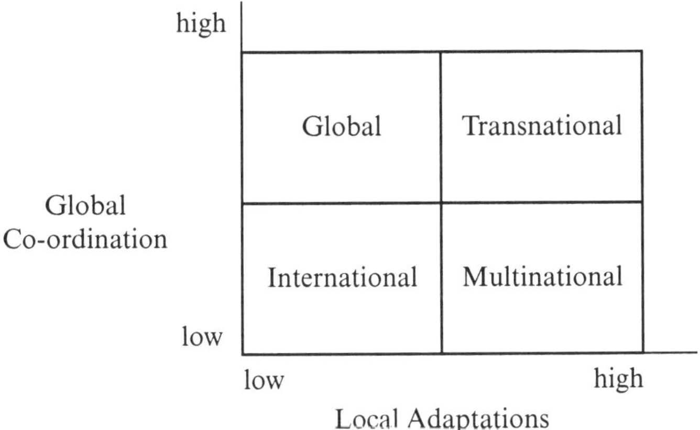

Figure 4.2   Variants of globalization strategies

- 'Transnational' strategies are conceived in the knowledge that advantages are achieved through differentiation as well as co-ordination (standardization). These strategies fully take into account the demands of the host countries while at the same time taking into consideration the central goals and skills.

SUCCESSFUL GLOBALIZATION STRATEGIES

The Success Concept

According to this concept (see Figure 4.1), successful globalization can be expected if a 'fit' exists between the influencing factors of direct investment and the globalization strategy. The 'fit' must be achieved in context of the real situation of the host country. For example, the intersubsidiary trade and co-ordination will also depend on the foreign trade laws in the host country and the transportation means available there. By the same token, local adaptation can be easy or difficult depending on how big the problems of differing cultural influences in the host countries are. Also in the European Domestic Market there are contextual influences which support co-ordination, and others that impede it and require local adaptation. Moreover, the 'optimal mix' between co-ordination and adaptation will also depend on the individual firm, its size and line of business (Figure 4.1).

Hypotheses for Success

According to the success concept, several hypotheses can be formulated. A general guiding hypothesis is that firms whose globalization strategies and globalization dimensions 'fit' with the determinants and characteristics of direct investment will be more successful than businesses where this is not the case. Success of globalization is expressed in active exploitation of opportunities in global markets and is indicated in *total satisfaction* with regard to the foreign subsidiaries' activity.

Hypotheses on testing for compatibility and 'fit':

1. The globalization dimension *'global co-ordination'* is connected with ownership advantages and transaction costs. Businesses which possess relatively large potential in competitive advantage co-ordinate their foreign activities more closely in contrast to businesses where such competencies do not exist or only exist in small measures.
2. The globalization dimension *'local adaptation'* is connected with location advantages. Businesses, whose activities are more dispersed as a function

of location advantage, must adapt more intensively to the local conditions than businesses with a smaller geographic dispersion.
3. The globalization strategies are connected with the number of foreign subsidiaries, the degree of vertical integration and the ownership strategy pursued in the host country. Businesses with a large number of subsidiaries, a small degree of vertical integration and with more joint ventures than 100% owned subsidiaries will pursue more intensely the strategies of local adaptation, and vice versa.

EMPIRICAL SURVEY

This chapter is based on an empirical survey conducted by the author in early 1992. Questionnaires were sent to firms in the greater Hamburg area which maintained direct investment in production and sales subsidiaries (100% ownership and joint ventures) in the European Community. The questionnaire survey was supplemented by interviews in some firms. In total, 27 firms (21%) responded.

The composition of the sample according to industry and size of the business is as follows: 21 (78%) firms belong to the investment and capital goods sector (for example, machine tool, construction and installation industries), and 6 (22%) to the consumer goods sector (such as the foods industry). Of the 27 businesses, 17 (63%) employ less than 1000 workers in the German parent company (small to medium-sized enterprises), and 10 (37%) over 1000 (large enterprises).

The objective of the survey was to find out what globalization strategies are pursued by businesses currently operating in the European Community.

THE FINDINGS

The Pattern of Globalization Strategies within the European Union

Global co-ordination

The exchange relations (Table 4.1), in general, vary. Intersubsidiary exchange within the EC subsidiaries is relatively small, while exchange between the EC subsidiaries and the parent company is substantial. The strongest exchange relation established is maintained between EC subsidiaries and the German parent company with regard to know-how. This relationship indicates a strong degree of co-ordination.

Table 4.1   Exchange relationship as an indicator of co-ordination in the EC region (N = 27)

Characteristics of intersubsidiary exchange relations	Intensity: average on a 5-point scale*
Exchange of goods among EC subsidiaries	1.360[1]
Exchange of goods between the EC subsidiaries and the German parent company	2.04[2]
Exchange of finances among the EC subsidiaries	1.26
Exchange of finances between the EC subsidiaries and the German parent company	3.20
Exchange of know-how (technology, etc.) among the EC subsidiaries	1.87
Exchange of know-how between the EC subsidiaries and the German parent company	3.92
Total value of intersubsidiary exchange relations	2.27

Notes:
*   the higher the value, the more intense the co-ordination or exchange
1.   under 20% of the total foreign trade value
2.   between 20 and 40% of the total foreign trade value

Exchange of personnel, which indicates co-ordination through socialization, scarcely exists among the EC subsidiaries. However, again, in relation to the German parent company, this exchange is developed more strongly (Table 4.2).

Table 4.2   Personnel socialization as an indicator of co-ordination in the EC region (N = 27)

Characteristics of socialization	Intensity: average on a 5-point scale*
Personnel assignment and exchange among the EC subsidiaries	1.478
Personnel assignment and exchange between the EC subsidiaries and the German parent company	2.32
Total value	1.90

Notes: *   1 = overall none; 5 = very frequent

According to the findings, businesses implement the co-ordination of their activities in the EC region quite strongly through centralization of decision making (Table 4.3). The function 'Research and Development' is centralized the most and 'Sales' and 'Personnel' the least.

Table 4.3   Centralization of decision making as an indicator of co-ordination in the EC region (N = 27)

Fields of centralization	Intensity: average on a 5-point scale*
Purchasing	3.125
Production	3.591
Sales	2.250
R & D	4.208
Personnel	2.250
Investment	3.167
Finance	3.625
Total value	3.209

Notes:
*   1 = responsibility lies only with the EC subsidiaries
      5 = responsibility lies only with the German parent company

Table 4.4   Local adaptation in the EC region (N = 27)

Characteristics of local adaptation	Value: average on a 5-point scale*
Number of foreign countries where firms have operations	1.89[1]
Share of EC sales (excluding Germany) to total sales	3.63[2]
Share of EC sales from market segments that Germany does not serve	1.259[2]
Share of EC sales with products developed specifically for the EC market	1.852[2]
Total value (share of sales)	2.253

Notes.
*   the higher the value, the larger the geographic dispersion and local adaptation
1 = 1 EC country, 2 = 2 EC countries, etc.
1 = < 20%; 2 = 20–40%; 3 = 41–60%; 4 = 61–80%; 5 = > 80%

Local adaptation: According to the findings, geographic dispersion and local adaptation of activities of the investigated firms within the EC region is moderate (Table 4.4). On average, the companies have operations in one or two EC countries, where they play quite a substantial role with respect to the share of sales to total company turnover. The adaptation efforts of the business are, however, small when the share of sales achieved from the specific domestic market segments and with special edition products is examined.

Based on the results, Figure 4.3 shows the configuration of co-ordination and adaptation and the corresponding types of globalization strategies as adopted by the sample firms.

A stringent division of strategy types according to the four variants is, of course, not possible, because the borders are not established theoretically. Nevertheless,

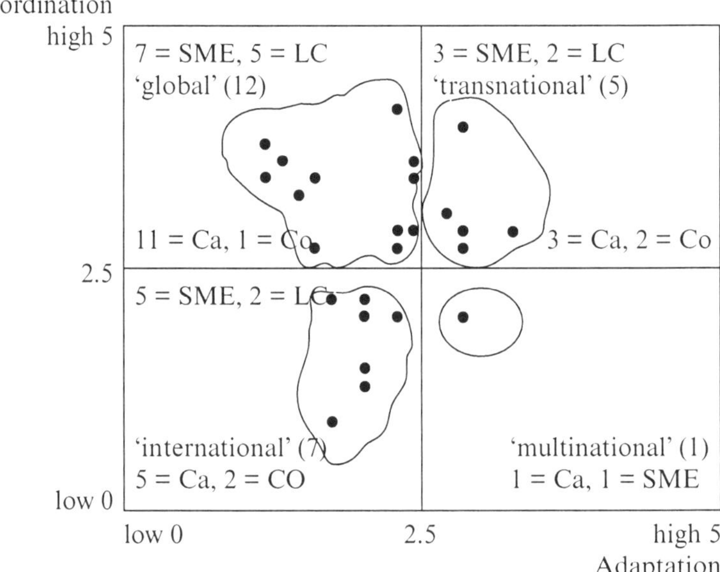

Figure 4.3   Globalization strategies of the sample firms in the EC region (number of businesses, N = 25)

one can draw the lines on a heuristic basis and divide the field into four equal quadrants. The pursued strategies can be put together in a cluster diagram and interpreted accordingly.

The majority of the investigated companies are located in the variant of 'global' strategy. The businesses in the investment and capital goods sectors are more strongly represented in this area than the consumer goods industry, which is based more in the field of 'transnational strategy'. The overall pattern of globalization strategy indicates that firms concentrate their activities on a few key markets in the EC region and keep their adaptation relatively small. Obviously that is possible only on the basis of advanced harmonization of markets and standardization of products. Apparently, this type of strategy is easier for small and medium-sized enterprises as can be seen by the concentration in the area of 'global' strategy. Interestingly, a relatively large portion of small and medium-sized companies also follows the 'transnational' strategy, which is most demanding.

Success of Globalization

Our findings show that the investigated businesses on average are quite satisfied with their present activity in the EC region (Table 4.5). This success varies according to the globalization strategy (Table 4.6).

Table 4.5   Degree of satisfaction with the activity of the EC subsidiaries (N = 27)

	Average on a 5-point scale*
Have your expectations placed in the EC subsidiaries been met?	3.560

Notes: *   1 = overall not met; 5 = fully and completely met

Table 4.6   Variants of globalization strategies and success (N = 27)

	Globalization strategy			
Success criteria	'International'	'Global'	'Multinational'	'Transnational'
Satisfaction with EC subsidiaries	3.57 *	3.25 *	4.0 *	4.0 *

Notes: *   average on a 5-point scale: 1 = overall no; 5 = full and complete.

Firms with the 'transnational' and 'multinational' strategies are the ones most satisfied with the results, followed by businesses with the 'international' strategy. The 'global' strategy is on average less successful. Keeping the characteristics of this variant in mind, it seems that the one-sided co-ordination of activities without paying much attention to adaptation in the European Domestic Market becomes dysfunctional.

The Influencing Factors

Influencing factors of direct investment

As Table 4.7 shows, the investigated firms assess their corporate skills and activities quite positively or even superior in comparison to competition. Only in the case of labour productivity is the situation not so good, although quite comparable to the average local company.

Table 4.7   Corporate skills of the companies (in comparison to competitors) (N = 27)

Business skills	Value: Average on a 5 point scale*
Production technology	3.708 [1]
Product technology	3.760[1]
Productivity	3.269[1]
Work climate	3.840[1]
Research and Development	3.538[1]
Marketing	3.423[1]
Relationship of the labour costs to total cost in comparison to branch averages (Labour prod.)	2.875[2]
Breadth of product line in comparison to the branch average	3.259[3]
Total value of competitive advantages (in comparison to competition)	3.459

Notes:
*   the higher the value, the larger the competitive advantage
1.   Scale: 1 = we are below competition; 5 = we are much better
2.   Scale: 1 = we are much higher; 5 = we are far below
3.   Scale: 1 = we are set up much smaller; 5 = we are much wider

The role which location factors play in the operation of the EC subsidiaries is shown in Table 4.8. The biggest importance is attributed to the local market. Also, the labour costs are of some significance.

Table 4.8   Significance of location factors for the operation of the EC subsidiaries (N = 27)

Characteristics of location advantages	Value: average on a 5-point scale*
Significance of location factors for EC operations	2.670
Labour costs	2.720
Access to local market	4.480
Access to raw materials	1.560
Access to third markets	1.920

Note: *   the higher the value, the larger the significance

Promotional measures of the EC for boosting direct investments play almost no role at all as a location factor (Table 4.9).

Table 4.9   Significance of EC promotional measures as location factor for investment in the EC region

Significance of promotion measures of EC for investment in the EC region	Assessment: average on a 5-point scale
Extent of utilization of EC promotion programme	1.56
Significance of EC promotion programmes for investment decisions	1.0
Total	1.29

Note: *   1 = no significance; 5 = very great significance

Characteristics of direct investment

According to this concept, globalization must also be matched with the characteristics of direct investment. Table 4.10 indicates the path of direct investment in the European Domestic Market as followed by the sample firms. The majority of EC subsidiaries is fully-owned. On average, firms maintain three EC subsidiaries. However, not all are active as vertically-integrated suppliers in the companies' value chain.

Table 4.10   Characteristics of direct investment in the European Domestic Market (N = 27)

Characteristics of direct investment	
Average number of owned EC subsidiaries (direct investment projects) in the EC region (excluding Germany)	3.1
Average number of vertically integrated EC subsidiaries	2.218
Average proportion of 100% owned subsidiaries in the EC to total number of EC subsidiaries	5.0[1]

Note: 1.   Scale: 1 = under 20%; 2 = 20 – under 30%; 3 = 30 – under 40%; 4 = 40 – under 50%; 5 = over 50%.

Success Factors

According to this concept, success factors are based on 'fit' between direct investment and globalization. These success factors must be identified in connection with firms which followed the 'multinational' and 'transnational' globalization strategies, which proved to be the most satisfactory in the European Domestic Market. Table 4.11 shows the correlations and 'fit' between the characteristics of direct investment and the characteristics of the globalization strategies mentioned.

Table 4.11   Analysis of success factors of globalization in the European Domestic Market

Success factors of DI	International		Multinational°		Global		Transnational°	
	C	LA	C	LA	C	LA	C	LA
Business competence		*	*				*	*
Location advantages		*	*				*	*
Promotiona lmeasures		*	*				*	*
Av. no. of owned EC-subsidiaries		*	*				*	*
Av. no. of vertically integrated EC subsidiaries		*	*				*	*
Av. no. of 100% owned daughter EC subsidiaries		*	*				*	*

Notes:
C = Characteristics of Co-ordination; LA = Characteristics of local adaptation
*   p < 0.050 – 0.07
°   Successful strategies

Table 4.12 summarizes the relevant characteristics of the two strategies.

Table 4.12   Significant relations between characteristics of direct investment and globalization strategies (success factors)

Direct investment	Globalization strategies 'transnational' and 'multinational'

Relevant determinants:
 	
• competitive and transaction cost advantages regarding
  –labour productivity
  –work climate
  –research and development
  –marketing
• location advantages regarding
  –assistance
  –labour costs
  –entrance to local markets
  –entrance to affiliated third markets
	Significant success conditions of co-ordination:
	
	• intersubsidiary exchange relations
	  –exchange of good
	  –exchange of finances
	  –exchange of know-how
	• centralization and socialization
	  –personnel assignment in EDM
	  –centralization

Relevant strategic characteristics of direct investment in the EDM: • No. of EC subsidiaries (production and sales) • degree of vertical integration in the EDM	Success characteristics of co-ordination and local adaptation • No. of EC countries with subsidiaries • importance of EC subsidiaries for total business • adaptation potential

As a corollary it can be stated that firms following 'transnational' and 'multinational' strategies are successful if (because) they are based on the following factors:

- superior labour productivity,
- capability to build up a good business climate in the parent company,
- capacity of superior Research and Development and well developed marketing,
- location advantages in the EC countries with respect to labour costs, which enables a supply of local as well as affiliated third markets,
- a relatively larger number of EC subsidiaries, and
- a substantial degree of vertical integration of the EC subsidiaries.

SUMMARY

1. Globalization must be seen in connection with foreign direct investment strategies. Although firms can be active abroad without direct investment, globalization and global competition strategies are only significant when some important elements of the value-added chain are transferred to a foreign country. So direct investment and globalization must also be theoretically looked at together.
2. The strategic planning model can be used as the integrating concept. On this basis it is possible to identify the influence and impact of direct investment on globalization.
3. The problem of globalization in the European Domestic Market is, therefore, not a question restricted to formulating competitive strategy, but rather a comprehensive problem of deciding on, establishing and managing foreign operations in the EC region.
4. The discussion regarding globalization in the European Domestic Market is thus especially relevant for small and medium sized enterprises (SMEs), since the larger companies have already been active for a long time with direct investment in most markets.
5. Considering the success factors of globalization, however, there are some constraints on the globalization of SMEs. In view of their limited resources, it can be hypothesized that SMEs will only insignificantly increase their present activity in the EC market.
6. In view of the limited resources, excessive expansion of the globalization of SMEs in the European Domestic Market would also not be recommended, because this would mean cutting short activity in other markets in the world. It is clear that Eurocentrism can lead to neglect of many important markets outside Europe.

There is an indication of non-European firms' strong motivation to invest in the European Domestic Market, in order to get into the 'fortress Europe'. So competition in the EC from these firms will grow. A sound counter-strategy on the part of European firms is to intensify competition in the respective home markets of the non-European firms, for example, with stronger presence in Asia. This would not be possible if EC firms tended toward Eurocentrism.

REFERENCES

Bartlett, C. and Ghoshal, S. (1989), *Managing Across Borders*, Boston, Mass: Harvard Business School Press.
Buckley, P. and Casson, M. (1976), *The Future of the Multinational Enterprise*, London: Macmillan.

Buckley, P., Pass, C. and Prescott, K. (1988), 'Measures of International Competitiveness: A Critical Survey', *Journal of Marketing Management*, **4** (2), pp. 175–200.

Buckley, P. (1988), 'The Limits of Explanation, Testing the Internationalization Theory of the MNE', *Journal of International Business Studies*, **19** (2), pp. 181–93

Caves, R. (1982), *Multinational Enterprise and Economic Analysis*, New York: Cambridge University Press.

Christensen, C. *et al.* (1982), *Business Policy*, 5th ed., Homewood, Ill: R.D. Irwin.

Doz, Y. and Prahalad, C.K. (1984), 'Patterns of Strategic Control within Multinational Enterprises, *Journal of International Business Studies*, **15**, Fall, pp. 55–72.

Dunning, J. (1988), 'The Eclectic Paradigm of International Production: A Restatement and some Possible Extensions', *Journal of International Business Studies*, **19** (1), pp. 1–32.

Goehle, D. (1980), *Decision Making in Multinational Corporations*, Ann Arbor: UMI Research Press.

Hinterhuber, H. (1992), *Strategische Unternehmensführung I*, 5th ed., Berlin: De Gruyter.

Hymer, S. (1960), *The International Operations of National Firms: A Chapter of Direct Investment*, Dissertation, MIT, Cambridge, Mass.

Knickerbocker, F. (1973), *Oligopolistic Reaction and Multinational Enterprise*, Boston: Harvard University.

Kobrin, S. (1991), 'An Empirical Analysis of the Determinants of Global Integration', *Strategic Management Journal*, **12**, Summer, pp. 17–32.

Kogut, B. (1983), 'Foreign Direct Investment as a Sequential Process', in: Kindleberger, C. and Audretsch, D. (eds.) *The Multinational Corporation in the 80s*, Cambridge Mass: MIT Press.

Kogut, B. (1989), 'A Note on Global Strategies', *Strategic Management Journal* **10** (4), pp. 383–90.

Kumar, B. (1987), *Deutsche Unternehmen in den USA*, Wiesbaden: Gabler.

Kumar, B. and Karlshaus, M. (1992), 'Auslandseinsatz und Personalentwicklung', *Zeitung für Personalführung*, **6** (1), pp. 59–74.

Levitt, T. (1984), 'Die Globalisierung der Märkte', *Harvard Manager*, **4**, pp. 19–31.

Magee, S. (1977), 'Information and the Multinational Corporation: An Appropriability Theory of Foreign Direct Investment', in: Bhagwati, T. (ed.), *The New International Economic Order*, Cambridge, Mass: Harvard University Press, pp. 317–40.

Maucher, H. and Brabeck-Lemathe, P. (1991), Auswirkungen des Gemeinsam Marktes auf die Möglichkeit regionaler Produkt- und Preisdifferenzierung – dargestellt am Beispiel der Nahrungsmittleindustrie, *Zeitschrift für betriebwirtschaftliche Forschung*, **12**, pp. 1108–128.

Meffert, H. (1989), 'Globalisierungsstrategien und ihre Durchsetzung im internationalen Wettbewerb', *Die Betriebswirtschaft*, **49**, pp. 445–58.

Meffert, H. (1990), 'Euro-Marketing in Spannungsfule zwischen nationalen Bedürfnissen und globalem Wettbewerb', in: Meffert, H. and Kirchgeorg, M. (eds), *Marktorientierte Unternehmensführung im Europäischen Binnemarkt*, Stuttgart, pp. 21–37.

Nohria, N. and Garcia-Pont, C. (1991), Global Strategic Linkages and Industry Structure, *Strategic Management Journal*, **12**, pp. 105–24.

Porter, M. (1989) (ed.), *Globaler Wettbewerb*, Wiesbaden.

Steinmann, H. and Schreyögg, G. (1997), *Management*, 3rd ed., Wiesbaden.

Vernon, R. (1966), 'International Investment and International Trade in the Product Cycle', *Quarterly Journal of Economics*, pp. 190–207.

Welge, M. and Böttcher, L.R. (1991), Globale Strategien und Probleme ihrer Implementation, *Die Betriebswirtschaft*, **51** (4), pp. 435–54.

Wiechmann, U. (1974), *Marketing Management in Marketing Intensive Multinational Firms*, Dissertation Harvard, Cambridge, Mass.

5. Regional headquarters in Europe: a new Japanese management initiative?

John B. Kidd

INTRODUCTION

Japanese firms have been represented in Europe since the mid 19th century, following the Meji revolution and the opening-up of Japan to external trade. However, the Japanese did not manufacture in Europe until 1966 when YKK and Pentel opened their factories in the UK and France respectively. Since then there has been a steady investment in productive capacity in Europe, slowing only as the global recession became an important factor in Japan. Currently there are close to 1000 Japanese production subsidiaries in Western Europe.

Through the 1970s to the present time we have seen the nature of many Japanese firms change as they move towards a more international form of operation rather than seeming to run a peripheral organization based solidly on the Japanese headquarters office. We note that there are now several offices in Europe which operate as Regional Headquarters (RHQs) of a particular firm, which will 'control' the operations of the subsidiaries, but their management style and operation is not clear cut.

In this chapter we present an interpretation of the role of the RHQs and conclude that in Europe national diversities and historical precedents play a major part in confounding organizational transitions. Yet the single factor – that of the general desire of the Japanese parent firms to operate in a coherent mode – may be a stronger catalyst for change than European legislation.

GROWTH IN JAPANESE FOREIGN DIRECT INVESTMENT (FDI)

Japanese Investment in Europe

In recent years, as the world recession has deepened, there has been a deceleration of investment by the Japanese in productive capacity in Europe, although

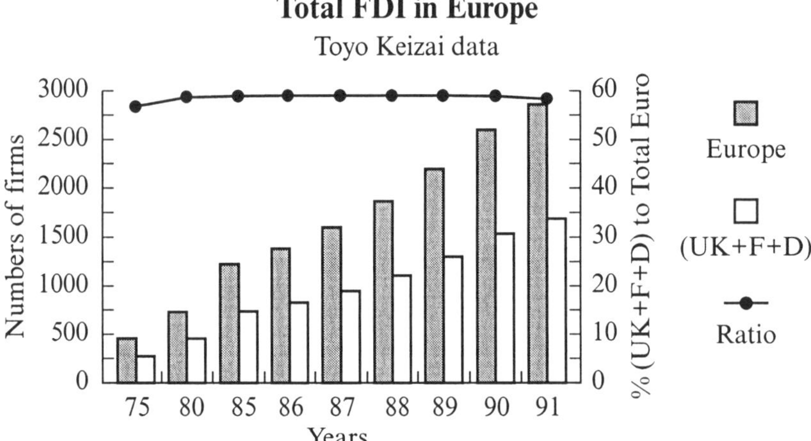

Source: Toyo Keizai Handbook of Overseas FDI (1993)

Note: UK + F + D = proportion of total FDI in Europe which is located in the UK, France and Germany

Figure 5.1   Comparisons of total Japanese foreign direct investment (FDI) by numbers of firms

investment in R&D centres continues unabated. To place the Japanese investment in perspective, we note that 62% of the planned investment in 1993–4 in Scotland came from the US and of this, 85% was reinvestment. In the same year, 22% of new investment came from continental EFTA countries, 11% from the UK, and only 4% from Japanese or Asian firms.

In Figure 5.1 we note the growth of Japanese FDI in Europe. The graph shows that three countries (the UK, Germany and France) tend to absorb about 55–60% of the overall European FDI from Japan in numerical terms (the same ratio holds if we consider only the numbers of firms engaged in production). Figure 5.2 indicates the distribution of the production enterprises (we should note that the term 'production' is defined by JETRO as 'a production firm in which there is at least 10% Japanese capital investment').

MANAGERIAL ISSUES IN RHQs

Since 1980, Teramoto and Kidd have elicited the concerns of Chief Executives (CEOs) of Japanese production firms: see Kidd and Teramoto (1991), Kidd

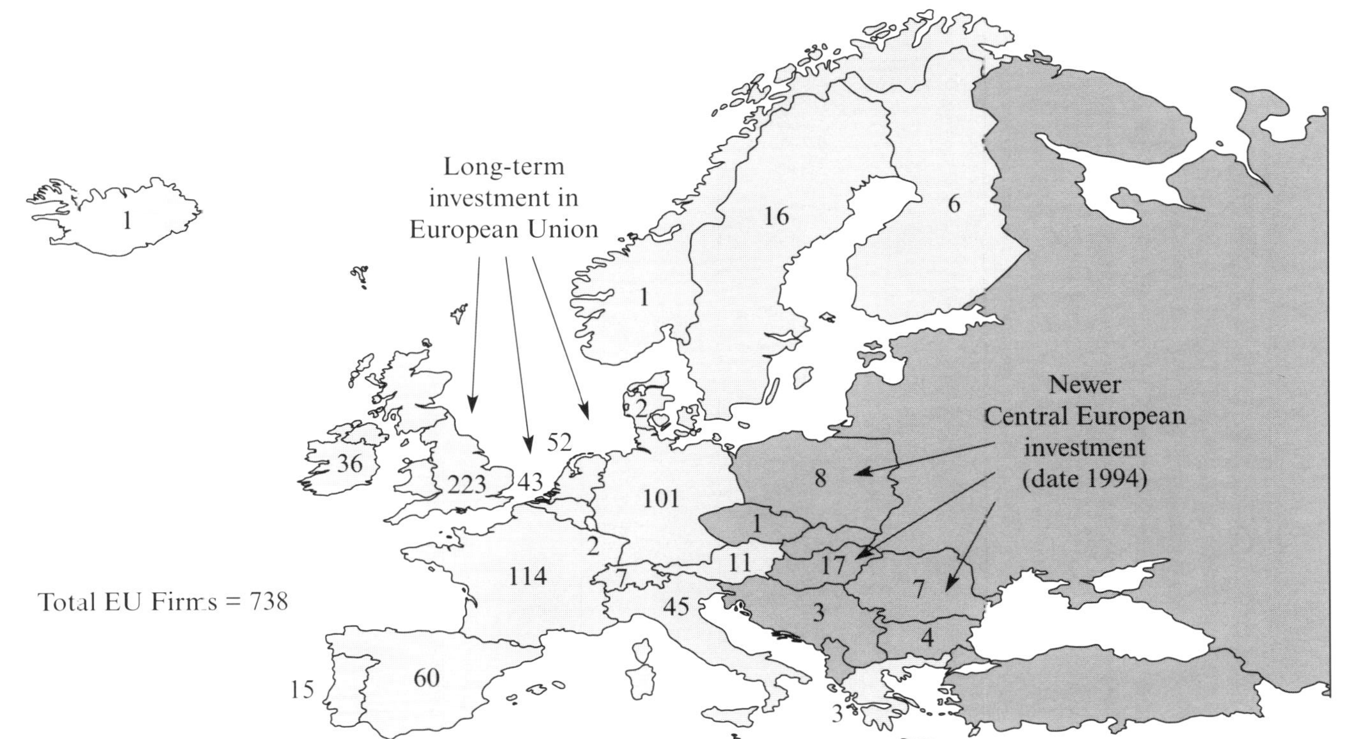

Source: 13th annual survey of production in Europe, JETRO, 1997 Central European data courtesy of Z. Bassa, Institute of World Economics, Budapest, 1994

Figure 5.2   FDI in production subsidiaries in Europe

(1991). We noted in general that production costs in the UK were generally lower than in Japan, but so were the production rates and the firms' efficiency. Two concerns mentioned in 1980, and repeated in 1990, were (a) the rules and regulations initiated by the commissioners of the European Union and (b) the difficulties of financing new ventures (other than through the parent firm). However, the most important issue concerned total quality management. This aspect was lax in the UK through the 1980s, and unfortunately is still behind the standards demanded by world class manufactures, in particular, Japanese car makers – Griffiths (1993) quotes several data, reproduced in Table 5.1.

Table 5.1   Characteristics of 'world class' plants versus 'other' plants

		World Class	Other
Productivity index (units per hour)	*	95.0	53.7
Quality (defects)	%	0.025	2.5
Space utilization index	*	89.4	64.4
Throughput time index	*	59.1	32.4
Operations automated	%	46.0	32.0
Rework and rectification	%	1.5	4.1
Stock turnover ratio (per year)	%	93.6	32.4
Employees in problem solving	%	80.0	54.0
Schedule variability	%	5.5	11.9

Note: *100 = best

Source: Lean Production Benchmarking Project: *Financial Times*, 8 January 1993

In interviews conducted through 1991 into 1994 Kidd and Teramoto concentrated more on the issues emanating from the CEOs of the European RHQs. These naturally focus on aspects of co-ordination (between the parent and between the local subsidiaries in several European countries and maybe also between themselves and other global RHQs). These CEOs have concerns which relate to the organizational design of the RHQ and its fitness in Europe. An associated issue is their concern about the many varying individual attitudes of their local European managers – which do not fit 'the Japanese way', nor even a 'European way' of management. Concepts relating to the latter may be found in Calori and de Woot (1994).

Operational Issues

The CEOs of the RHQs generally recognized the need for bureaucracy and formal meetings. They also recognized the need for cross-boundary meetings (socialization) where representatives from many countries could express themselves freely. Some CEOs said there were too many meetings, but in attempting to merge their many European offices into a new structure, they fell foul of old bureaucratic structures, and had to maintain too many meeting groups.

We recognize the potential for the RHQ to act as a catalyst for organizational learning, or indeed for the activity of learning to learn. Their supportive action would facilitate vertical and horizontal learning between and within divisions, and holistically between managers in the Japan HQ and in their overseas outposts. However, CEOs have to achieve a breakthrough in their ability to merge the local in-group discussions into pan-Europe discussions. These may be likened to *nemawashi*, but done in accord with local, national characteristics. The CEOs of RHQs have also to break down the strong traditional interlinks which have developed between the parent firm and the operating firms which tend to by-pass the managers in the RHQs. These interlinks are often based on a product or a divisional logic which may not be in accord with the regional needs of Europe (nor the US, nor south-east Asia if there are RHQs in those areas). If the RHQ managers are by-passed, their position and raison d'être will be brought into question by cost-cutting parent firms as they seek ways of alleviating the effects of the global recession. Figure 5.3 summarizes the difficulties of the RHQ, wherein one CEO described their operation as a 'roof-over-a-roof', implying that they were a potential failure as constituted at that time.

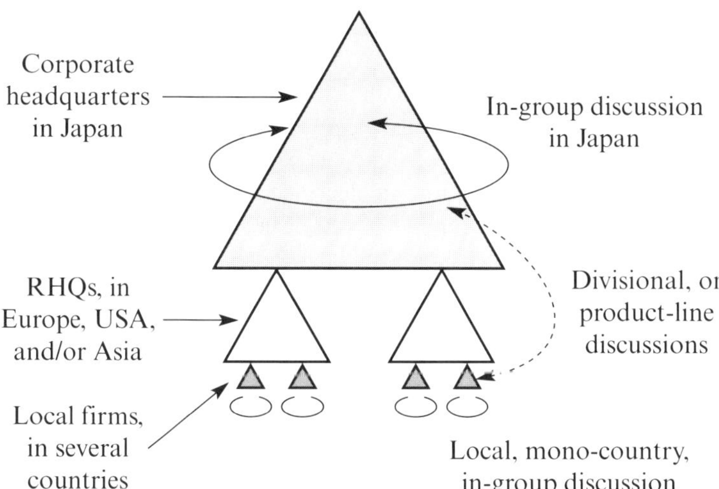

Figure 5.3   The roof over a roof issue

If the European RHQs are to be seen as a necessity, and not a roof-over-a-roof, they must be able to initiate useful policies of change and transformation relating to European managerial culture in general. Importantly, the RHQ CEOs will have to find ways to merge their parental corporate style with the styles present in local subsidiaries.

THE KEY ISSUES IN THE RHQS

We found several of the RHQ CEOs were senior managers in the overall global hierarchy of the parent firm. These persons may have had previous expatriate experience, often in the US, so they were familiar with the difficulties that indigenous managers have in aligning to the 'Japanese way'. Even with their background, many RHQ managers had learned new lessons from their recent European experience. Collectively they stated a wish for their office managers in the parent firm to recognize clearly the difficulties of working within the European cultural diversity. Individual homogeneity does not exist, nor does the product demand remain constant across each European country. These CEOs felt that their senior managers in Japan gave unduly greater support to their US equivalents, in part because the US RHQ was an older establishment, but also because of the greater homogeneity of the US market.

In general terms the Japanese organization faces the same pressures in the US, the UK, and continental Europe. It is unreasonable to suggest that their management strategy determines the structure of the firm, as Chandler (1962) would have had us believe. Nevertheless CEOs frequently mention their unease at the 'imposition' of a Japanese model organization upon their European operations. It does seem natural within the rapidly evolving and changing Japanese organizations in Europe, that the parent would wish to impose an office to act as a focus for their European regional operations. But are these RHQs an agent for change? Or are the RHQs simply a mechanism whereby the subsidiary managers, remote from the senior managers in Japan, may be controlled in the 'usual way'?

Individualism versus Organizational Learning

One of the learning aspects looked for by Japanese CEOs is that their staff should increase their learning about how their firm's culture operates. We had noted this clearly in 1992 following one long interview in which the CEO was at pains to discuss a mechanism, which reconciled the Japanese corporate culture with that of individualistic learning which is a characteristic of people from the United States and Europe. Whilst we have discussed the details in Kidd and Teramoto

(1991) we consider it important to reconsider its impact with respect to 'organizational learning'.

We had noted that newcomers to the firm tend to look for little information about the firm as a whole. They acquire only the data with which to survive in their daily task and complete their workload. Of course we would see this as a good initial personal strategy, but the CEO was concerned that these people maintained a too strong and continuing attachment to individualistic learning which precluded enquiry, and thus prevented broader learning about the firm as a whole. The CEO was striving to find a mechanism by which individualistic people could gain an holistic 'sense of the organization'.

It is clear that the achievement of organizational learning is difficult, even for Japanese staff. But they, under what was then a pervading regime of life-time employment for salaried staff, enjoy a long period of enculturation. However, for the non-Japanese staff who may have joined the firm relatively recently, there is little time to absorb the cultural values of the organization. Absorption is made more difficult for the Occidental in two ways – often they do not speak Japanese well, if at all, so will not understand the public addresses by the most senior staff as they expound the philosophy and the mission of the firm. Secondly, many expositions from senior staff are particularly oblique, and not easy to understand, even for long-term Japanese staff. We have noted a major cultural difference in so far as the Occidental, in particular people from the UK, wish to hear plain language, not broad generalities.

The 'Double-loop Learning' Firm

Argyris (1992) postulated the single versus double loop learning system to illustrate conflicts in organizational learning. His definition was taken up by others, such as McGill and Slocum (1992); the work of Hampden-Turner (1990) might be interpreted similarly.

Often managers will exhort staff to strive for better 'performance' or achieve better 'standards'. In Figure 5.4 we indicate that excessively strong pursuit of goals along either of the two 'performance' axes will be unwise; that is, adherence to standards without upholding good performance criteria, or vice versa. For instance, there is a global surge to gain the ISO 9000 series of quality accreditation (in the UK, formerly BS 5750). Initially this makes sense, yet the receipt of certification in no way guarantees the inherent quality of the goods or services – only that there are audit trails within the firm that will enable poor quality to be traced to its origin. Implicitly one expects that the provision of audit trails, and the necessary in-house research on the required paperwork, will raise quality awareness. It does not follow that 'awareness' is the same as the 'achievement' of high quality.

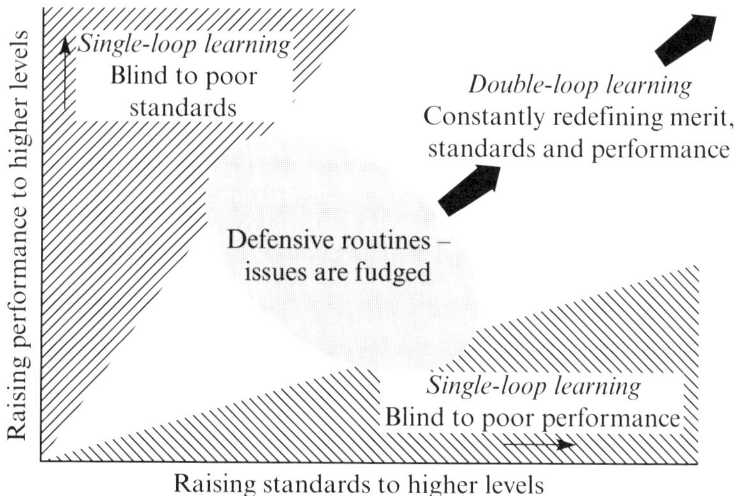

Figure 5.4   Single- and double-loop learning: following Hampden-Turner

We note that a bureaucratic environment is one that follows rules (thus lies on the 'standards' axis), and a political environment lies on the 'performance' axis, since it stresses, not the 'what' but the 'how'. We suggest that over emphasizing either of these (useful) activities in an organization may be damaging – as is a random mixture of the two. Good examples of the results of 'double loop learning' are seen in Garfield (1992).

Inertia – Continuity and Resistance to Change

We did not hear of many examples of 'double loop learning' in our RHQ interviews. Yet there were foundations in place in several firms for training courses: in one course, which was to be directed by the CEO, there was to be cross-functional divisional learning. Another example concerned the diffusion of Quality Assurance originating from the UK subsidiary (as BS 5750), into other European subsidiaries (as ISO 9000), and finally to the Japanese parent. In this case the CEO of the European RHQ acted as a catalyst, promoting and translating the message (about ISO 9000) from one subsidiary to another in Europe, and also 'upwards' to the parent firm. That Japanese parent managers are slow to press for certification under ISO 9000 is not a surprise: Kidd (1994) noted a similar reluctance in spring manufacturing firms in both Japan and South Korea. It was not that they have lax quality standards, but rather that the accreditation under ISO 9000 was perceived as irrelevant; with hindsight it is beginning to be seen as a necessity of commerce.

Some Japanese managers mentioned during our RHQ interviews that there were strong management pressures from their HQ in Japan, and that they were acceding to these, notwithstanding the local needs in each European country. Thus the needs of the local subsidiary are subsumed under a strong functional management from Japan. In this case the learning mechanisms are 'vertical', occurring only between members of the business division in the field and its members in the Japanese HQ. Although such learning might incline slightly towards the double-loop type, it is basically a complex form of single-loop learning. To transform this global organization to the transnational form requires sympathetic management – it needs a CEO to help establish the double-loop learning mechanisms.

We consider the rôle of the RHQ and its management to be the key to this transformation. In particular the RHQ CEOs must foster several changes in attitudes which may be difficult within the heterogeneity of European management. For instance there is the need to communicate more freely, but first individuals need to understand *why* and *with* whom they should communicate.

The Four Knows Training

Bartlett and Ghoshal (1989) state that the transnational firm has to indulge in 'socialization', and thus many people will be engaged in travel to distant outposts to diffuse the common gospel. We think some of this effect could be achieved by focused staff training, which we describe as the *Four-Knows* training. This may be stated as the four learning concepts that a person will have achieved through good in-house training (Kanda 1992).

These stages are applicable to all levels of the workforce from the CEO to the most junior operator:

- *Knowing how* – being trained in the best way to use the tools of one's trade, be it a machine on the shop floor, a telephone, or a personal computer for e-mail use.
- *Knowing what* – to understand the need to deliver on time, first time with the right quality, using the best tools, according to the needs of the customer.
- *Knowing why* – to understand broadly the reason for one's tasks and how they fit with the overall mission of the firm and its aspirations.
- *Knowing who* – to be able to communicate one's ideas or one's worries, or to enhance one's own skills and those of others through the exchange of data with a peer group, or even more widely, for the good of the firm.

The regular global movement of Japanese staff is well known and documented. Kidd (1983) noted the easy manner by which some Japanese staff enter conversations in their new employ through *Knowing who*. At the time Kidd called this 'potential nemawashi'. But the (nemawashi) of the expatriate manager is more than just being able to 'talk around the issue' with ones' colleagues; it relies on the Four-Knows being in place and operating. We consider that this ability is not restricted solely to Japanese staff – with suitable training schemes all staff can benefit.

We have to warn that while the *Four Knows* concept appears simple, its inception and practice is incredibly difficult. For instance, the programme demands that all people engage in the scheme (from CEO to lowest paid worker), and each should know what the other does, and why. It implies that the strategic vision is shared throughout the firm, that it can be clearly expressed and understood. It demands commitment management rather than a formal, scientific style of management – the former style is clearly stated by Mintzberg (1994) who seems currently to be reshaping his views on the strategy process. He states that better managers tend to engross their staff in a journey that encourages informal learning, which in turn creates new perspectives and new combinations.

Relationship with Time

There are considerable differences between cultures in their views of 'time' (see Trompenaars 1993). Some tend to support people who are essentially linear in their view and use of time – they would carry one planned activity to the next with little free time between activities. Other cultures are called synchronic (or polychronic), wherein its members tend to carry multiple threads of activity running in parallel, whilst not being strongly scheduled between tasks.

The 'time' aspect was noted by Kidd and Teramoto during the interview phase of their 1991 survey, but it was not reported. It illustrates one difference between the UK and the Japanese managers' attitudes in the Japanese subsidiaries in the UK. Although the story concerns a production subsidiary, we have found that the scenario is widespread, in sales, distribution, R&D and in the RHQs. The story unfolds as follows:

> Some managers were stating that their Japanese senior managers (usually their CEOs) were withholding information from them. In response to us, the researchers, the Japanese senior managers mentioned two things – first the UK managers generally did not speak Japanese, so were excluded from conversations with more senior managers from Japan about the long term future of their subsidiary. And, second, these conversations in Japanese usually concerned many potential future states – of growth, of mergers, of modifications to the status quo, and so on. In other words, the Japanese managers were considering and balancing multiple streams of data – being synchronic.

The Japanese managers recognised their own use of multiple potential futures, yet, in the past when pressed by their UK managers, they had proffered only a single, simple future scenario. Unfortunately, if this scenario was not realised, the UK managers were understandably anxious, and demanded of their Japanese seniors, 'what is going wrong? You told us one thing, and now something else is happening!'

Given that UK people tend to be linear in their time management, the synchronic Japanese had made a single (best) guess at the future – and because this scenario had not occurred, they, the Japanese, felt they had 'lost face'. Rather than letting this occur again, they became more reticent to offer forecasts. Thus the UK managers, wishing to grasp at a (linear time-based) straw, felt that they were being excluded from the process of management by being deprived of knowledge of the future by their Japanese seniors.

At the present time, there is no reason to believe the Japanese and the Europeans have altered their mechanisms of time use: the Japanese remain synchronic and the Europeans remain linear. This is a grave issue for the managers of the RHQs and their subsidiaries with respect to plans mooted by the parent in Japan. While the parent managers will talk in Japanese, be oblique, and present a fuzzy future many European managers, even if they understand Japanese, prefer to be offered clear alternatives of the future.

Cultural Dynamics

'Culture' is often a topic raised by the Japanese CEOs and by the non-Japanese managers in the RHQs. We feel that this is a very emotive topic which deserves care in its management. In conducting business, politics or pleasure in Europe we find there are many hidden nuances which baffle the Europeans themselves (see Mole 1992).

We have mapped in Figure 5.5 Hofstede's data of 1991 on two dimensions: the Power-Distance Index (PDI) and the Uncertainty-Avoidance Index (UAI). These dimensions refer to organizational attitudes in firms rather than to individualistic or personal aspects. Furthermore, the Power-Distance scale equates to the propensity to concentrate authority on fewer individuals (more concentration at higher PDI values). It is known that there is a greater structuring of activities at higher UAI values, which suggests a greater acceptance of bureaucracy for nations with high UAI scores. These findings come from the 'Aston' studies which commenced in 1961: see Pugh and Hickson (1976). The descriptions also concur with the work of Haiss (1990), who notes that the ability of an organization to learn is to some extent positively correlated with higher PDI values.

Hofstede (1991, pp 142ff) notes action-oriented research at INSEAD during the 1970s by Stevens, who found that managers and students performed a case analysis in differing ways according to their various cultural backgrounds. One culture group suggested that the solution was for the staff (in the case study)

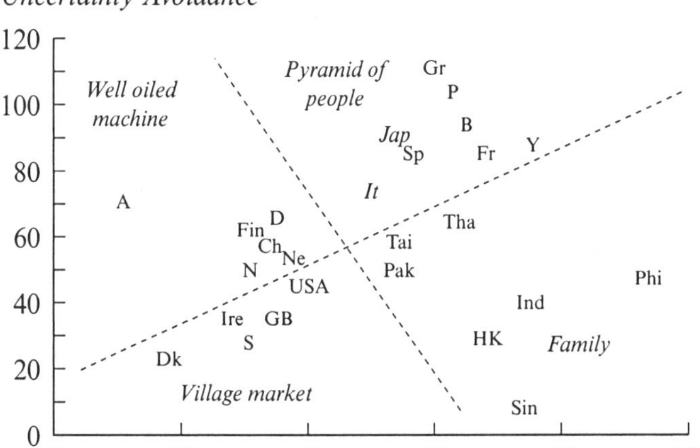

Notes: Country names generally follow International Transport Standards.

Source: Hofstede (1991)

Figure 5.5   National differences

to take their conflicts to their superiors for resolution; they described a very hierarchical system (the 'Pyramid of People'). Other culture groups described their solutions differently. One solution was the 'Well oiled machine', in which there is less hierarchy, but activities are so well codified that, in theory, there should be no circumstance in which the superior should be bothered by 'trivia', as all contingencies are covered by the rules. In the 'Village market' solution, there is no hierarchy and no rules, just a pragmatism that tends to treat each case afresh. This solution also tends to consider issues generally to be about human relations between people and their management.

We would suggest that these organizational aspects would indicate to the CEOs of the Japanese RHQs, once more, that there is ample opportunity for conflict between natural organizational styles and behaviours if, and when, Euro-Asian ventures are entered into. We have heard elsewhere that a senior European academic, who had advised a Japanese firm upon setting up a RHQ, was astounded when local subsidiary managers refused to talk to each other (in any meaningful way) at pan-Europe meetings. Thus the RHQ CEOs will have to be particularly sensitive to cultural nuances since they involve the (usually) Japanese CEO, and are enacted between national managers.

CONCLUSIONS

It is obviously a truism to say that defining the optimal structure for the Japanese RHQs in Europe is difficult. It is much more difficult than in the US (which is generally more homogeneous in attitudes, education and so on), and probably more so than in SE Asia (which in parts has a base of Confucian learning that stresses the value of loyalty and de-emphasises individuality).

Many difficulties in Europe are due to its cultural diversity, wherein there are centuries-old memories of long lost battles and of broken strategic alliances. Still farther back in time there were divergent developments in the origins of the peoples and their languages. These factors are supposedly subsumed under co-operative agreements within the European Union (EU).

The EU has a huge Gross Domestic Product, which acts as a trade target for all developed and developing nations. Thus it is not a surprise to find that (early in 1994) there are close to 800 Japanese production subsidiaries in the EU. To control many of these, the Japanese parents have inaugurated RHQs which could act as co-ordinators of their production, distribution, sales, marketing and sometimes their R&D operations within a global context. In every circumstance, the subsidiaries need to be advised, directed and controlled. It is the RHQ which may be able to do this – but only if the relevant firms accede to control. Subsidiaries operating in several countries will have been managed using local rules, regulations and culture, and above all, by local management. These aspects may not be easily merged into a coherent whole within Europe.

We suggest that haphazard development of the European subsidiaries of Japanese firms to become 'transnational' will not lead to success – nor will it lead to any clear competitive advantage. There are too many pressures to either 'become Japanised' or conversely to resist this pressure and say 'we incorporate the best global practices in our operations'. These statements both deny local identities, which will continue throughout the future decades, sometimes as espoused folklore, which may well form resistance to externally imposed change. While not wishing to be too gloomy, I have to note the final address by Hofstede (1993, pp. 18–19) wherein he notes '... the folly of expecting European countries to co-operate'.

We agree with Hofstede, but wonder if the Japanese, with their own form of pragmatism, may find a way of drawing together all the managers, subordinates and line workers in their subsidiaries who themselves would not naturally follow one target. We suggest that the RHQ may indeed be the agent of change, but only if the senior managers in Japan relinquish their demand for continuity and the perpetuation of the traditional Japanese way.

REFERENCES

Argyris, C. (1992) 'The Executive Mind and Double-Loop Learning' *Organizational Dynamics*, Autumn, pp. 5–22.

Bartlett, C.A. and Ghoshal, S. (1989) *Managing across Borders: the transnational solution*, London: Century Business.

Calori, R. and de Woot, P. (1994) *A European Management Model: beyond diversity*, New York: Prentice Hall.

Chandler, A.D. (1962) *Strategy and Structure*, Cambridge, MA: MIT Press.

Collins, P. (1994) *UK Quality Management – Policy Options*, London: SEPSU, Royal Society.

Coulson-Thomas, C. (1992) *Creating the Global Company: successful internationalisation*, Maidenhead: McGraw-Hill.

Emmott, W. (1992) *Japan's Global Reach: the influences, strategies and weaknesses of Japan's multinational companies*, London: Century.

Garfield, C. (1992) *Second to None: how our smartest companies put people first*, Business One, Irwin.

Gourley, R. (1994) 'Quality under Fire', *Financial Times*, 21 June, p. 14.

Grenier, R. and Metes, G. (1992) *Working Together – Apart*, Digital Press.

Griffiths, J. (1993) *'The Lean Enterprise Project'*, *Financial Times*, 8 January.

Haiss, P.R. (1990) *'Cultural Influences on Strategic Planning'*, Physica-Verlag, Heidelberg.

Hampden-Turner, C. (1990)*'Charting the Corporate Mind: from dilemma to strategy*, Blackwell.

Hofstede, G. (1991) *Cultures and Organisations: software of the mind*, Maidenhead: McGraw-Hill.

Hofstede, G. (1993) *Images of Europe*, Valedictory address, 1 October, University of Limberg, Maastricht.

JETRO (1997) *Thirteenth Annual Survey of Production in Europe*, Tokyo: JETRO.

Kagono, T. (1980) *Structural design of Headquarter-Division Relationships and Economic Performance: an analysis of Japanese firms*, School of Business Administration, Kobe University, Kobe, Japan.

Kanda, M. (1992) private discussion

Kidd, J.B. and Teramoto, Y. (1991) *Can the Japanese Localise?: a study of Japanese production subsidiaries in the UK*, presented to the 6th Triennial European Association for Japanese Studies Conference, Berlin, September.

Kidd, J.B. (1983) 'Potential Nemawashi: the benefit of long-term employment', *East Asia* **2**, pp. 84–105.

Kidd, J.B. (1991) *Globalisation through Localisation*. Presentation to 7th Euro-Asia Management Studies Association, INSEAD, Fontainebleau, Oct. 1991. In Schütte, H. (ed) (1994) *The Global Competitiveness of the Asian Firm*, New York: St Martin's Press, pp. 265–88.

Kidd, J.B. (1994) *Spring Manufacturing in Japan and South Korea ... Threat or Challenge*. Final report on the SRAMA 1993 fact-finding mission to Japan and South Korea, supported by the DTI (OSTEMS).

Kumar, B. (1992) *Global Competitive Strategies for Europe 1992*, presentation at EAMSA, Bradford, 27–29 November.

McGill, M.E. and Slocum, J.W. (1992) 'Management practices in Learning Organisations', *Organisational Dynamics*, Summer, pp. 5–18.

Mintzberg, H. (1979) *The Nature of Managerial Work*, New York: Harper & Row.

Mintzberg, H. (1983) *Structure in Fives: designing effective organisations*, London: Prentice Hall International.

Mintzberg, H. (1994) 'The Fall and Rise of Strategic Planning', *Harvard Business Review*, Jan–Feb., pp. 107–14. And more fully as *The Fall and Rise of Strategic Planning*, London: Prentice Hall International.

Mole, J. (1992) *Mind your Manners: managing culture clash in the single European Market*, London: Nicholas Brealey.

Norhina, N. and Eccles, R.G. (eds) (1992) *Networks and Organisations: structure, form, and action*, Harvard Business School Press.

Pugh, D.S. and Hickson, D.J. (1976) *Organisational Structure in its Context*, London: Saxon House.

Sony (1992) *30 years in Europe* (promotional literature).

Toyo Keizai (1993) *Handbook of Overseas FDI*, Tokyo: Toyo Keizai.

Trompenaars, F. (1993) *Riding the Waves of Culture: understanding cultural diversity in business*, London: The Economist Books.

ACKNOWLEDGEMENTS

I wish to thank Yoshiya Teramoto, who has offered much guidance over the years.

We wish to thank the CEOs of the following firms for agreeing to be interviewed and for the provision of data that was of aid in the preparation of this paper. Naturally their individual identity and any data used in the paper will remain confidential.

In 1992, in alphabetic order, Kidd and Teramoto interviewed CEOs of Fujitsu, Hitachi, Mitsubishi, NEC, NSK, Oki, Panasonic, Toray and Toshiba and in 1993 Canon, Epson, Konica, Omron, Ricoh, Sharp and Sony.

6. Japanese multinationals' strategies towards the process of European regionalization with special reference to former socialist countries: an empirical study (1990–1992) on Japanese multinationals' activities in Berlin and Eastern Germany

Sung-Jo Park, Heike H. Rudolph and Natascha Haehling von Lanzenauer

INTRODUCTION

The interest Japanese companies showed in the former German Democratic Republic (GDR) after the Berlin Wall fell seemed to suggest strategical plans for developing the East European markets from there. The aim of the summer 1990 survey 'Activities of Japanese Firms in the Berlin Area and the GDR' was to scrutinize this supposition. The results, already presented by us at the seventh EAMSA conference in Berlin, December 1990, confirmed the important role which the market potential of Eastern Germany and Eastern Europe had in Japanese companies' investment planning. It was likely that Japanese firms' activities would concentrate heavily on Eastern Germany; this was also indicated by the increasing number of newly established offices in Berlin.

Whereas German and Japanese hopes for future Japanese investments were high at the time of the economic, monetary and social union, until the end of 1992 these hopes had not been realized. Compared to other foreign investors in Eastern Germany, the involvement of Japanese companies is relatively modest. Up to then, merely three enterprise sales and one real estate sale to Japanese companies via the Treuhandanstalt are known of. Investment is rather low, however, since either parts of enterprises are taken over or centres for Research and Development and training are set up.[1] According to the Japanese Association of Trade and Industry in Berlin, there were about 70 Japanese companies in Berlin in 1992. These are mainly banks, financial houses, large general trading houses and building and construction companies. Since 1992 a continuous reduction of personnel in the branch offices can be observed. Employees were either transferred to newly opened bases in Eastern Europe or withdrawn to their main office in Japan, and the branch offices and agencies closed down.

The causes of this hesitant behaviour were investigated by a survey of Japanese offices in Berlin during the summer of 1992. In addition to the survey results, the latest trends concerning the conduct of Japanese investment activities in Berlin and the New Länder will be described.

SURVEY OF JAPANESE BUSINESS REPRESENTATIVES, SUMMER 1992

According to the results of a previous survey in summer 1990, Japanese companies judged the possibilities of investment in the Berlin area and the New Länder predominantly positively.[2] Roughly 70 percent of the enterprises surveyed were considering the expansion or the taking up of business activities at that time. Contrary to all expectations, though, there have not been – except for an increase in Japanese branches – any significant plans for investment in Eastern Germany in the past two years. Impediments affecting investors in general, however, are regarded as the reason for this. One can conclude that there must be specific reasons for the dilatory Japanese behaviour. Accordingly, the main question of this study is:

Why do Japanese companies – in contrast to general assumptions and other foreign investors' activities – hesitate to invest in Eastern Germany?

This leads to the following hypotheses:

1. There are specific reasons besides the general impediments.
2. Japanese overseas investment, within the long-term internationalization strategies, is currently concentrated on regions other than Eastern Germany.
3. As an economic and geographic centre in Central Europe, the Berlin area constitutes a particularly attractive location for Japanese enterprises.

During June and July 1992, seventeen Japanese firms in Berlin, representatives of the banking, finance, trade, construction, production and tourism businesses, were surveyed.[3]

RESULTS OF THE STUDY

This section presents the conclusions of the study in relation to each of the hypotheses.

Investment Impediments

Starting out with the hypothesis of specific and general causes for restrained Japanese investment in Eastern Germany, the following impediments were revealed as pertinent:

Investment impediments in general

Infrastructure   The poor condition of the infrastructure in the New Länder was considered to be the most important general impediment. The progress in setting up a highly developed communication network was positively valued; however, due to the high costs and the length of time needed until the infrastructure has been fully adapted to Western standards, activities of Japanese companies were not expected to increase soon. For example, the energy supply for hi-tech production was not sufficient by any means. The new international airport to be located in the south of Berlin and the extension of transportation routes to Eastern Europe, were mentioned as primary measures for the amelioration of the traffic infrastructure. The rapid development of this infrastructure would be a decisive factor in selecting an East German location rather than one in Eastern Europe.

Construction companies and general trading houses hope to take part in the development of the infrastructure. The tourism branch sees its priorities as the erection of the Berlin International Airport and the expansion of first-class hotel capacities for Japanese tourists.

Property questions   The unsettled questions of property were judged as one of the most significant impediments to Japanese investment. The so-called 'restitution-before-compensation' arrangement delayed investment planning and the economic upward trend. Solving this problem as quickly as possible was seen to be the responsibility of the Federal Government. Foreign investors especially felt disadvantaged by this regulation. One company interviewed mentioned a project in which the Japanese investor was rejected after objections by a former proprietor. Judicial uncertainties made it difficult, if not impossible, for foreign investors to purchase real estate. Judicial ignorance required engaging lawyers resident in Berlin as well as certified public accountants at great expense. Due to these problems and high real estate prices, Japanese investors were forced to wait and see, although they expected an easing of the situation before long. In order to handle the situation sensibly, the Berlin Senate or state governments of the New Länder were considering the provision of industrial sites.

Development of labour costs   After the Berlin Wall fell in 1989, many companies thought about transferring the production to Eastern Germany in view of low pay levels.[4] Today this locational advantage no longer exists, as East German wage levels were expected to reach West German standards by 1995, although they are still lagging behind. The quality of the infrastructure and qualification of the workforce are priorities in capital intensive investments. In view of this, Eastern Germany could be a favoured site of Japanese manufacturers. Therefore, because of wage intensive production, investment is likely to be carried out in Eastern Europe.

The short working hours, the amount of days off and sick leave of West German employees were criticized. The diligence and motivation of the East German employees were highly praised. However, extensive training measures are considered essential. Not all companies showed willingness to pay for the necessary costs. The still relatively slight influence of labour unions in Eastern Germany was assessed as an advantage.

Ecological burdens The problem of ecological burdens in Eastern Germany was rarely spoken of; probably not a single enterprise had been directly confronted by it until then. The extent of pollution was regarded as grave. In this respect, the Treuhandanstalt and the Federal Government were held responsible.

Specific impediments for Japanese investors

Bubble economy The effects of the Japanese finance and stock market crisis were always named as the most important cause for the decrease in, and more tentative behaviour of, Japanese investment. This does seem questionable, however, when applied as a general explanation. One can speak of a Japanese and global downward economic trend, but not all branches were affected to the same extent. Thus, this argument of 'bubble economy' seemed to be something of an excuse for Japanese investments which failed to materialize. Japanese investments are increasingly concentrated in the Asian region, a tendency also indicated by the fact of decreasing investment in Europe. The present investment climate in Eastern Germany was named as the reason for this. Also the Treuhandanstalt's short deadlines for invitation of tenders for its enterprises was criticized as a practice constituting disadvantages for long-term Japanese investment strategies.

Problems of co-operation with governmental authorities The following statements concern Berlin only. Co-operation with authorities is mainly dependent on the extent of planning and realization of projects. Disappointment with the Senate's policy was generally expressed. Administrative shortcomings were judged as grave. The bureaucracy of West Berlin was said to be complicated and not comparable to other German cities. The main complaint was the excessive amount of bureaucracy, which gives rise to the delaying of investment plans, for example, through the lack of clear distinction of responsibilities within the authorities. Insufficient co-ordination, such as between the authorities of building and transport, caused expensive delays for large scale projects. Or, as in the case of the work on the construction and traffic regulation of Potsdamer Platz, it required supplementary negotiations. Several representatives accused the municipal government of lacking any vision for the city's future development, especially concerning long-term city and traffic planning. Various representatives showed no sympathy for the decentralized division of authority between the Federal Government, the federal states and municipal districts, nor for the debates on the future architectural design of the city centre (for example Potsdamer Platz, and the Brandenburger Tor). In general, the Berlin Senate was criticized for not doing enough for the establishment of foreign enterprises. In their opinion, German companies had better chances to obtain the best sites using their informal contacts in the Senate. Japanese companies would have liked to see specific measures in Berlin and Eastern Germany, like those existing in Nordrhein-Westfalen, for attracting Japanese investors.

The lack of understanding on the part of the authorities for the establishment of a Japanese middle school was also regretted. Talks with representatives of the authorities, however, revealed that the allocation of sites is not decided by the Senate, but on a district level. Furthermore, the Japanese, expecting the same favourable terms as in Düsseldorf, were unwilling to pay the rent rate customary in Berlin. By autumn 1992 negotiations between Japanese companies in Berlin and the authorities were well advanced, and the school opened in 1993.

The representatives of several firms proposed special treatment of Japanese investors. This would send a positive signal and help to improve the badly damaged image of Eastern Germany among the Japanese public, and thus give rise to further investment. It was regarded as essential to employ experts in public administration who are familiar with the mentality and business practices of Japanese investors. Nearly all representatives stated disappointment with the Senate's way of attending to them and its maintenance of human relations, which in their opinion left much to be desired. This feeling was conveyed by the expression 'kimochi ga nai', meaning a lack of emotional content. As far as the Japanese desire for special treatment is concerned, it should be noted that other investors, despite considerable investment activities, do not claim special consideration.

Criticism of the Treuhandanstalt   The interviews with Japanese business representatives and the Treuhand staff clearly revealed opposing expectations between both sides from the beginning. The Japanese companies felt affronted by the fact that although they were called upon to invest, their specific needs, such as the supply of information or the deadlines for bidding invitations, were not appreciated accordingly. They felt excluded when the Treuhandanstalt sold selected automobile manufacturing sites to German companies, although Japanese investors were highly interested in them.

The Treuhand stated that merely setting up its office in Tokyo constituted special treatment. Due to the fact that there were three to four tenders for each of the 20 to 25 items for sale daily, consideration for the long-term decision-making process of Japanese companies could not be shown. 'First come, first served' was the acknowledged principle. Also, since other foreign competitors, such as the French and the British, automatically enjoy far better terms, for example geographical proximity, similar mentality, and more complex trade relations with the former GDR, the Japanese reproach of discrimination seems to be one-sided. The Treuhand made a tremendous effort to attract Japanese investors, despite high expenses and the hitherto poor levels of Japanese engagement. Hence, the Treuhand Office in Tokyo, the Federal Ministry of Economics, the Berlin and Brandenburg Economic Development Corporations and the German Chamber of Trade and Industry in Tokyo, worked together to promote the location of Japanese enterprises in Eastern Germany.[5]

Information deficiency   Access to general and specific economic information was stated as one of the main reasons for opening Japanese branch offices in Berlin. After the Wall fell, demand for information increased enormously. The collapse of the GDR government resulted in the loss of business connections for the trading houses which had been established in East Berlin for decades. They adapted to the new circumstances quickly, however. Since 1992, some of the trading houses have been reducing their staff as important information has become generally accessible. Offices are installed in Eastern Europe and above all, in the Commonwealth of Independent States in order to gather information there. In Berlin, Japanese companies receive most of their detailed information through Japanese banks, which have well-established links to political and financial institutions. Their respective head offices, Japanese trade organizations such as JETRO, the Japanese Chamber of Trade and Industry in Düsseldorf and the Japanese Association for Trade and Industry, Berlin, are additional suppliers.

Hostility to foreigners   The comments in the Japanese press on the growing hostility to foreigners, especially in the New Länder, are increasingly concerned. There were reports of Japanese individuals or tourist groups being robbed or assaulted. In order avoid becoming victims of racist violence, Japanese institutions and tourist organizations recommended, for example, not wearing jeans in Eastern Germany as this could result in being mistaken for a Vietnamese immigrant worker. Leading German business representatives considered these attacks, which are constantly increasing, as one of the most significant investment impediments. The representatives of Japanese firms, however, seemed more alarmed by the rise in crime than anti-foreigner violence. Nevertheless, the willingness to move eventually to Eastern Germany with one's family was assessed as extremely low.

Investment Strategies

EU domestic market
Investing in East Germany was deemed unimportant when considering the EU domestic market. The demand in Eastern Germany is covered by existing capacities in Western Europe, primarily in Western Germany and Great Britain. The unification has rendered investments for strategic purposes obsolete. The strategy phase regarding the EU single market was said to be concluded, as the most important industries had established themselves.

Eastern Europe strategies
The market potential of Eastern Europe was viewed positively by all branches. The speed of economic development in these countries had nevertheless been overestimated. The political and economic conditions for investment were not sufficiently given in 1992. Hungary and Czechoslovakia were most often named as attractive locations. Seen on a long-term basis, the East European markets, particularly in Russia, were considered as very promising by Japanese firms. Referring to the former Soviet Union, the following problems were mentioned:

- unclear political situation
- uncertainties on legal positions
- inefficient administrative structures
- financial difficulties
- unstable monetary policy
- poor purchasing power.

In the event of amelioration, Japanese investment can be counted on. A need for action was not perceived until these problems were resolved, and strategic thoughts were said to be secondary. While production in Eastern Germany for the East European market was taken into account in 1990, two years later direct investment in Eastern Europe would have been preferred. Moreover, this could avoid harsh competition with German companies. Nevertheless, on the grounds of cultural and ethnic attachments, Germans have an advantage here, too. For this reason Japanese companies favour the idea of developing the East European market in co-operation with German partners. In the field of mechanical engineering, for instance, German companies could provide the hardware and the Japanese the electronics. Small- and medium-sized companies would particularly benefit from this arrangement as deficits in overseas experience, language knowledge and management could be compensated for. Any stabilization of the political and economic situation in Eastern Europe was not expected for the next ten to fifteen years.

Southeast Asia strategy

Investments in Southeast Asia are easier and more lucrative for Japanese companies than in Eastern Germany or Eastern Europe. Consequently, there is a general tendency to transfer Japanese foreign direct investment to those regions. One of the representatives characterized this development as follows: 'Nine fingers in Asia, one finger here'.

The perceived advantages are:

- highest global profitability in investments
- geographic proximity
- traditional trade relationships with Japan
- great market potential
- rapid economic growth
- rarely any Western competition
- financial covering of projects in developing countries (ODA, now Department for International Development)
- Asian mentality and work ethic
- low wage levels.

However, preference for the Asian region for these reasons was not endorsed unilaterally. The preconditions, such as legal regulations relating to the establishment of production sites, locational factors such as human capital, the supply of raw materials and the provision of an adequate infrastructure differ greatly in the European and Asian markets. For this reason, there is no immediate competition between these economic regions.

Assessment of Berlin and Eastern Germany as Suitable Locations

Berlin area

Everybody unanimously stated that within one year the Berlin boom following the fall of the Wall gave way to disillusionment in respect of the various problems. Japanese companies had absolutely overestimated the rapidity of development. For the problems emerging from German unification to be settled, not just three to four years, as originally assumed, but eight to ten years were estimated as necessary. In the midst of the initial euphoria, it was mainly Japanese banks and developers who opened branch offices, but soon the companies were forced to wait and see. The representatives' assessments of various points regarding development in Berlin are presented below.

Berlin as seat of governments   All persons surveyed viewed the transfer of the seat of government to Berlin as a major factor for the city's economic development.[6] The Federal Government was generally criticized, though, for having no fixed schedule for moving. Whereas about 50 percent of the individuals questioned viewed the Government's move as a decisive factor in the establishment of Japanese companies, the other 50 per cent granted the city a great potential for growth even without this function; one frequent comment was: 'Berlin is a centre of the service industry, of culture and universities, and not a classic production site any longer as in prewar times'. For this reason the setting up of industrial concerns is more likely in such traditional locations as Saxony or the surroundings of Berlin. For representatives of banks, finance houses and tourism, one of the main motives for long-term investment in Berlin is the city's rising international attraction.

Transfer of head offices   Sony's decision to move its European headquarters to Berlin was judged favourably and followed closely by the interviewees. Yet this was not to have any significant effect on other Japanese companies, as assumed in the press, because Sony is not regarded as a typical Japanese firm. In the near future the transfer of the German head offices of Japanese companies to Berlin seemed to be less probable, as there had been vast investments in Düsseldorf shortly before the Berlin Wall came down. In addition, the representatives pointed out that a decentralized strategy is more appropriate in Germany, due to its federalist structure.

Locational factors of Berlin – a comparative survey   In the summer 1990 survey representatives of Japanese firms evaluated the status of various locational factors in the Berlin area. In the summer of 1992 the interviewees were given the same evaluation chart in order to detect changes in judgement. However, as the number and selection of interviewees differed, the results of both analyses are not directly comparable. Rather, emphasis is laid on the demonstration of general trends. Evaluation was carried out using a scale ranging from 1 (unimportant) to 6 (very important). The chart (Figure 6.1) shows the average index.

All of Berlin's locational factors were rated significantly higher in the second survey (summer 1992) – except for 'industrial site' which seems to have lost importance somewhat. 'Cultural centre' was the factor gaining most, followed by 'scientific centre' and 'centre of service industry'. The factors 'infrastructure', 'economic and geographic centre in Central Europe' and 'investment promotion'

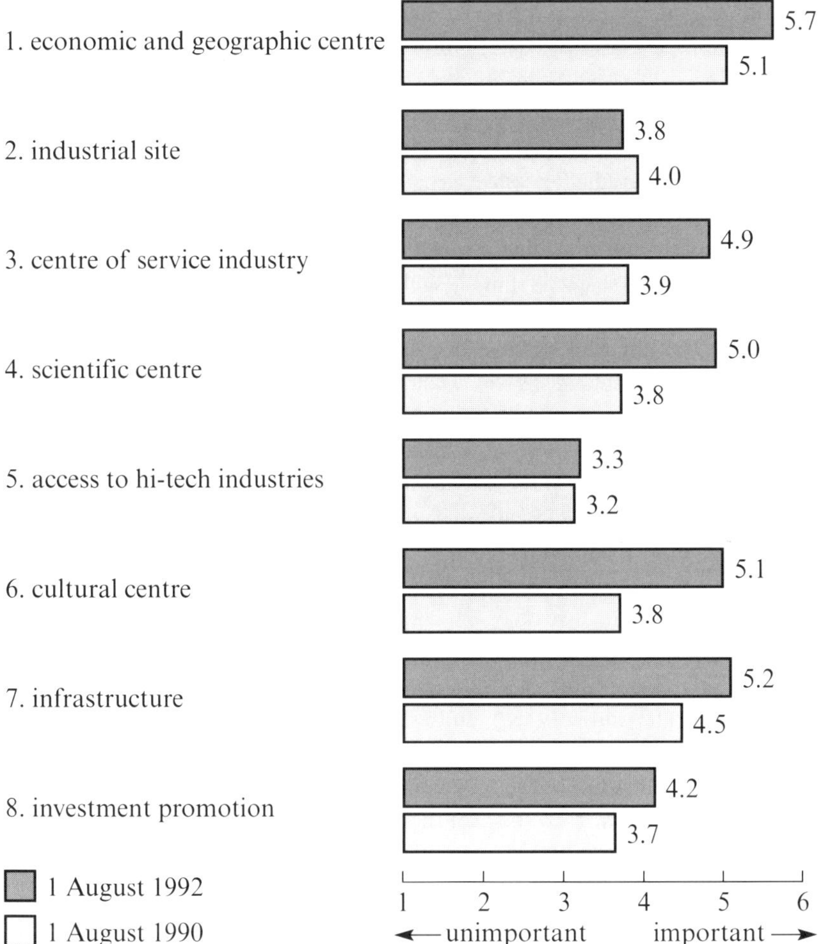

Figure 6.1   Location factors of Greater Berlin

were rated higher than in 1990 to approximately the same extent. Assessment of 'access to expanding hi-tech industries' remained the same.

Still ranking highest on the Japanese list of priorities were the factors of 'economic and geographic centre in Central Europe' and 'infrastructure', the latter having gained in importance considerably. Unlike the estimation in summer 1990, the factors 'cultural centre' and 'scientific centre' have come more intensely to the fore. This also reflects the statements made by Japanese business representatives on the large role Berlin will be playing in the future as a centre for services. These results confirm the confidence expressed in the interviews that in the long run the Berlin area – the current troubles notwithstanding – will develop into a very attractive location for Japanese investors.

Locational factors of Eastern Germany

The sudden rise in demand for consumer items following the turn of events in Germany decreased after one year. Among those capitalizing on the East Germans' pent-up demand were a considerable number of Japanese enterprises, the automobile and consumer electronics branches in particular. Meeting this rush for demand extremely quickly and flexibly, some firms set up service and distribution networks all over Eastern Germany.[7] Nonetheless, up to the end of 1994 not one major Japanese production site has been established. The companies' representatives saw the causes for this in the rapid rise in wage costs and the fact that the demand can be met by existing production capacities in Western Germany or Western Europe. As in the survey of 1990, all those asked rated highest the possibilities for the future of the Berlin-Brandenburg region and the free state Sachsen. Thüringen followed at a distance, whereas Sachsen-Anhalt and Mecklenburg-Vorpommern were hardly mentioned at all. Selecting the location is determined much more by strategic investments than geographical aspects. Investments by important German companies, for example Volkswagen near Zwickau (Sachsen), or Opel in Eisenach (Thüringen), are trendsetting for the respective regions' economic development. The decision of Mercedes-Benz in early November 1992 not to build the motor truck manufacturing plant in Ahrensdorf (30 km south of Berlin), planned for 1995/96, was received with great concern by both the Germans and the Japanese. Greater Berlin is particularly interesting for the building and construction industry. The area surrounding the planned international airport in the south was mentioned as a location well suited for industrial development.

SUMMARY

From the interviews with Japanese business representatives in Berlin and from various talks with institutions concerned with foreign direct investment, it is clear that the dilatory behaviour regarding Japanese investment in and around Berlin and Eastern Germany can be basically ascribed to the following causes:

1. The effects of the 'bubble economy' in Japan were much stronger than originally thought and thus hampered Japanese foreign direct investment considerably.

2. For Japanese firms, investing in the prospering Asian economic region is not only lucrative but also imperative, taking into respect the strong Korean and Taiwanese competition.
3. Japanese companies' strategies concerning the EU domestic market are already concluded. Moreover, the existing production capacities in Western Europe can sufficiently meet current demands.

This shows that in summer 1992 priorities were set in Japanese investment strategies which cannot be related directly to the situation in Eastern Germany. Should economic recovery in Japan and political and economic stabilization in Eastern Europe take place, Japanese investment activities can be expected. It is likely that Eastern Germany would be a favoured location, due to its geographical proximity and its highly developed standards in the fields of infrastructure and human capital. Greater Berlin constitutes an attractive base for Japanese companies from which activities in Eastern Europe and within the EU could be pursued. Furthermore, on the basis of Berlin's potential for economic development and its future function as the seat of government, an increase in the number of Japanese companies, especially from the service sector, seems to be very probable.

The German effort to attract Japanese investment in Eastern Germany clearly proves the significance of the 'difficult' Japanese trading partner. It also proves that economic survival cannot be attained by retreating to national markets, but by international co-operation only.

RECENT TRENDS

Since 1992, the situation of Japanese investment in Berlin and the New Länder has not significantly changed, though the sluggish recovery of the Japanese economy gives rise to the hope that investment activities will expand in areas other than the prospering Asian economies. Japanese representatives acknowledge the speed of development in the New Länder, for example concerning the modernization of infrastructure. Problems that had been regarded as major impediments, such as environmental problems or property rights, have been solved quicker than assumed. According to the study of the Japanese External Trade Organization (JETRO) (1993), decisive location factors for Japanese companies are a) closeness to sales markets, b) access to English-speaking staff, c) quality, productivity and labour costs, d) adequate infrastructure. Due to the continuous improvements in these areas, the New Länder are becoming more and more interesting for Japanese investors.

Germany is regarded as the core country within the European Union because of its geographical and economic importance. Berlin as the capital of Germany will become more attractive internationally, both politically and for business. One can say that the emotional approach of Japanese companies towards Berlin and the New Länder in 1990 has turned into a quite rational assessment of profitable future investment chances. They also seem to be much more optimistic about the future of this area than in 1992.

NOTES

1. According to the Treuhandanstalt (Sept. 1992) these four projects were: 1. Nippon Sanso – Thermos GmbH Langewiesen, Thuringia (1991); 2. Asahi Glass – Thüringer Spiegel- und Flachglas GmbH, Thüringen (1991); 3. Japan Motorholding – Auto Trans Berlin GmbH (1991); 4. Obayashi Gumi – property in Berlin-Pankow for the development of a business and housing complex (1992). Up to September 1994 there are at least two more projects, namely a joint venture of Asahi Glass and Schott Glas in Jena, Thuringia, and a small scale assembly of farming and construction machines by Kubota in Thuringia. Investment plans were announced for a Japanese subcontractor for BMW in Saxony as well as the acquisition of a chemical plant in Bitterfeld/Sachsen-Anhalt.
2. See Park, Rudolph and Haehling von Lanzenauer, (1992) p. 320.
3. Using a semi-standardized questionnaire, interviews were conducted in German, English and, partly, in Japanese for the length of 1 to 1.5 hours, along three blocks of subjects: (1) investment impediments, (2) choice of location, (3) investment strategies. The statements of all representatives interviewed were summarized and analysed taking into account the specific aspects of different branches of business.
4. See Park, Rudolph and Haehling von Lanzenauer (1992) p. 321.
5. Such measures were, for example, an invitation to Japanese financial journalists in September 1992, the visit of a Japanese economic delegation in December 1992, the journey of the Mayor of Berlin, Eberhard Diepgen, to Japan in November 1992, mailing campaigns by the Treuhand in Japanese, and so on.
6. According to the survey in 1990, the consideration that Berlin could become capital of united Germany played an important role in the companies' investment strategies. See Park, Rudolph and Haehling von Lanzenauer (1992) p. 322.
7. According to estimates of spring 1992, there were approximately 730 sales outlets in the automobile branch which employed about 5500 staff members. Exact numbers are not known, since there is no obligation to register.

REFERENCES

Japan Extended Trade Organization (JETRO) (1993), The 9th Survey of European Operations of Japanese Companies in a Manufacturing Sector, London: JETRO.
Park, Sung-Jo, Heike H. Rudolph and Natascha Haehling von Lanzenauer (1992) 'Economic Activities of Japanese Companies in the Former German Democratic Republic', in Sung-Jo Park (ed.) *Managerial Efficiency in Competition and Cooperation*, Frankfurt and New York: Campus/Westview.

7. Investment strategies of Japanese firms in the new Federal States

Dieter Beschorner and Christine Müller

INTRODUCTION

The opening of the eastern European countries with the subsequent unification of Germany (3 October 1990) exhibited new economic perspectives. Due to the political changes, access to undeveloped new markets was offered. We were interested in how Japanese companies reacted towards these changes and whether they showed a special interest in the new federal states. Among other things, we sought to elaborate the subject with the empirical tool of a questionnaire. Between August and September 1992 we sent questionnaires to 75 Japanese companies in Germany. From 14 returned questionnaires 50 per cent (7) had and 50 per cent (7) had not invested. The questionnaire was divided into three parts: *Part one* asked about general information on the companies such as the branch of industry, the number of employees and the products. *Part two* was for companies which had already invested in the new federal states, and it dealt with the place, the kind of investment, the reasons and the obstacles to the investor. Part two also tried to find out about the investors' experiences with the new federal states. *Part three* was for companies which had not invested in the new federal states, and sought to find out why.

JAPAN'S FOREIGN INVESTMENT IN THE PAST

Since 1985 Japan's total foreign direct investment (FDI) has increased by over 500 per cent (that is investment of $67 billion[1] in the year 1989). Traditionally Japan has invested in the United States, but since the mid-1980s, Europe has taken an increasing share of Japanese investment (see Figure 7.1 for the cumulative amount of Japanese FDI in Europe from 1951–1990). Japan's direct investment in Europe suddenly exploded from about $7 billion in 1987 to $9 billion in 1988, then up to over $14 billion in 1989. The big interest in Europe was a response to the need to establish a manufacturing and distribution

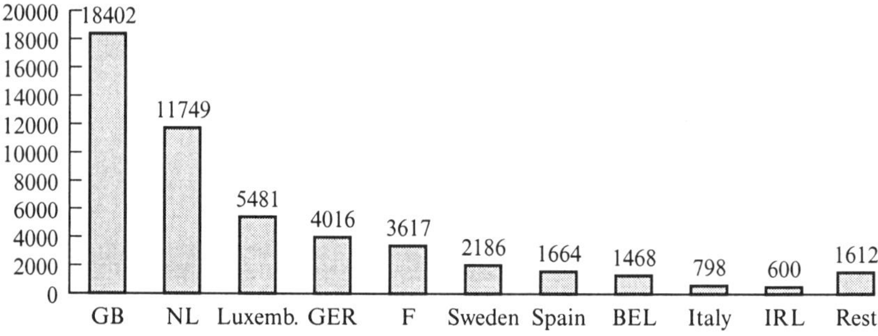

Source: Ministry of Finance, Japan

Figure 7.1   Japanese direct investment in Europe: regional distribution, cumulative from 1951–1990 in million US$

presence throughout Europe in order to benefit from planned economic integration in 1993. This rise in investment activity was caused not only by the desire to avoid trade barriers, but also by the overall globalization of enterprises and the urge to be close to local markets. With a few exceptions, the Japanese have not attempted to acquire large European companies whole. Instead, they have made small investments in big companies, such as Honda's 20 per cent interest in British Rover or C. Itoh's six per cent equity position in the German steelmaker Kloeckner. However, most of their takeover activity has focused on friendly acquisition of medium-sized European companies (for example, Sankyo Pharmaceutical purchased a majority interest in German drugmaker Luitpold-Werke for $129 million and Japan's Leyton House bought 54 per cent of Hugo Boss for $300 million). As a result there are numerous well-respected European brand names owned in full or in part by Japanese businesses: Laura Ashley, Aquascutum, Hugo Boss and Louis Royer cognac, just to mention a few.

The Japanese tried to be careful not to repeat the mistakes they made in the United States – purchasing Columbia Pictures and the Rockefeller Centre mainly aggravated *Japan bashing*.[2] One of the economic goals of the Japanese is to create a positive image about their business methods. The British legal structure, lifestyle, and especially the language, are similar to the USA, where Japanese companies had developed their foreign operational experiences, thus explaining why they choose to invest in the United Kingdom. At present, Japanese companies are well established in Europe, with strongholds in all major industries. The next stage in Japan's drive to be what Japanese managers call a 'good European corporate citizen' was to expand European-based research and development. The Japanese strategy of entering the EU began with information gathering. They then started with small investments in big companies, with a special interest in the United Kingdom. At the same time, they concentrated on medium-sized enterprises for friendly takeovers. Acquisition of European brand names and prestigious buildings, like the Frankfurter Messeturm, strengthened their presence. Their next step was to set up overseas operating plants to manufacture the goods in the European host country.

Traditionally, Japanese firms have placed emphasis on greenfield or start-up investments, which are normally less controversial than takeovers. But within the last few years a diversification of their direct investment activities has been observed. They have leaned more towards friendly merger and acquisition deals. However, all European firms acquired by Japanese companies since 1988 have been fully bought out.

In March 1991 JETRO[3] conducted a study of Japanese foreign direct investment. This showed that the decision about where to build a production or manufacturing site was mostly based on the proximity of the location to local markets, the ability to recruit English-speaking employees, the quality of the workforce, and the infrastructure. Financial incentives obviously did not have a significant influence on the decision about the location.

Japanese FDI in Europe seemed to be scattered at random. The results of opinion polls about motives for FDI varied between industries. Personal relationships are most important for business transactions with Japanese associates, so previous personal experience in certain European countries had an influence on the decision on where to invest.

WHY COULD THE NEW FEDERAL STATES BE INTERESTING FOR JAPANESE FIRMS?

Eastern Europe is virgin territory, and the people living there will generate demands for a whole range of goods. But the political and economic situation in these eastern European countries (CIS[4], former Czechoslovakia, former Yugoslavia, Rumania, Bulgaria, and so on) is very unstable and prevents foreign companies from taking the risk of investing heavily at present. Furthermore, the transition to a market economy will take time and money to develop in these countries.

The Former GDR[5]

The former GDR, certainly, is a special case. East Germany receives enormous support from West Germany. The political situation is stable and the efforts to switch to a social market economy are exceptional and already showing signs of success. Although it may look as though East Germany's buildings and real estate are of no value, they all have prime central locations in Europe and are therefore of intrinsic value. Investments in East Germany will be springboards for future expansion throughout eastern Europe. The business relations between Japan and the former GDR were very limited. The unified Germany, however, has not only an advantageous geographical position, but also feels a special commitment to eastern Europe due to its history. The previous trade links with the eastern countries enabled the former GDR to gain experience and knowledge which could provide an edge for new relations with the developing eastern European markets. Another advantage of East Germany is the ability to set up subsidiaries, representative offices or sales and services stations through already existing branches in West Germany. From doing business with West Germany, the Japanese are able to relate better to East German people, their mentality, culture, language, workforce, and laws, than to any other eastern European country. Thus, the new federal states can offer entrance into a new market without the disadvantages and risks normally associated with a completely new situation.

Our questionnaire, however, revealed that none of the above listed reasons stood behind Japanese investment in the years between 1990 and 1992. When asked the main reason for investment in the new federal states, five out of seven companies which had already invested named the new markets in eastern Germany as the main reason for investment. Only one stated the potential for entry into the markets of the eastern countries; one company added that its main reason was to provide adequate customer service.

The Japanese quickly detected the need and provided their products through newly established branch and representative offices. This explains why all seven companies from our survey named sales and services as their activity in the new federal states. It is known that the Japanese economy as well as the Japanese industry are planning in long-range terms. Accordingly, it is not very surprising that we did not find a great number of investments.

Japanese Investments in the New Federal States[6]

The mass media covered extensively all the investment activities in the new federal states, but Japanese companies were hardly mentioned. The newspapers continued to write about the same projects that is the acquisition of the Langewiesener Thermos[7] in Thüringen, by Nippon Sanso K.K.[8], and the purchase of the Fernmeldetechnik Nordhausen[9] by M.E.I. Japan Inc. (for example, Guardian, 12 April 1991; Frankfurter Allgemeine Zeitung, 5 July 1991 and 5 August 1991). Besides these fairly large projects, Japanese companies were hardly to be found as investors. More profound research confirmed this impression. Japanese companies were hesitant to invest in the new federal states. This does not mean that they are not present at all. Branch and representative offices have been set up by banks, trading firms, and construction firms, while the industry for automobiles and consumer electronics concentrated on developing sales and services networks throughout the new federal states. Other companies started joint ventures or other forms of co-operation. Only a few companies went beyond these activities and invested in larger scale projects. The previously mentioned purchase of Langewiesener Thermos by Nippon Sanso K.K. in the spring of 1991 is one of the few bigger investments. It was reported as the first Japanese acquisition in East Germany. Michio Kamei, the chief executive officer of the Nippon Sanso K.K., said in an interview (M&A Review, 1988) that his company intended to use the acquisition to gain a foothold in the European market for that industry and to benefit from the trademark 'Thermos'. The British Nippon Sanso subsidiary 'Thermos England' first negotiated directly with the parent company of the Langewiesener Thermos, the Glasring Thüringen. The Treuhandanstalt was informed in May 1990, about three months later. The Japanese side felt that financial difficulties have been the biggest problems they have encountered with this acquisition. Apart from a different understanding of terms like depreciation, sales control, and interest on capital, there was also confusion about the existing capital. Debts and conflicts due to unemployment and residual environmental contamination were not encountered, thanks to promises by the Treuhandanstalt.

Another large commitment of a Japanese firm in the new federal states was the 'acquisition' of Fernmeldetechnik Nordhausen by M.E.I. Japan Inc. It was reported by the press as an acquisition, but further research revealed that it was no more than a letter of intent to invest (Süddeutsche Zeitung, 16 June 1993).

The German Schott Glaswerke, Mainz and the Japanese Asahi Glass Co., Tokyo, were working on a joint research project in Jena, Thüringen. Schott owned the majority (51 per cent) of Jenaer Glaswerk, a glass production firm. For the end of 1993, Schott and Asahi planned to complete a new production unit in Jena making Borosilicatglass using the Float technique. Schott provided know-how in special glass while Asahi provided know-how in the Micro Float technique.

The majority of Japanese companies have opened representative offices in Berlin and Leipzig. The significance of representative offices in Berlin is obvious if it is noted that a Japanese company needs the approval of the Ministry of Finance in Japan (MOF) for every real estate purchase in a foreign country. One stipulation for approval is a representative office in the foreign country (see Baum, 1992). Thus, the Japanese have laid the groundwork for future investments in the new federal states, although their direct investment activities are rare. The strategic position of Berlin and Leipzig is an important aspect for the positioning of representative offices. Leipzig is one of the crucial industrial locations in the new federal states and Berlin is the developing and growing capital. According to an opinion poll of Nihon Keizai Shinbun in June 1990, 40.7 per cent of the Japanese questioned believed that Berlin would become

Germany's number one financial centre (Frankfurter Allgemeine Zeitung, 26 June 1990; Japan Economic Journal, 30 June 1990.)

The outcome of our questionnaire confirms these findings. All the seven companies which had already invested in the new federal states indicated sales and services as their activity. Of these, five invested in Sachsen, five in Berlin, four in Brandenburg, three in Sachsen-Anhalt, two in Thüringen and two in Mecklenburg.[10]

The investing companies in our survey were all in the field of consumer and industrial goods. So far, the main reason for investment has been to serve the consumer markets of the new federal states. The setting up of representative offices by banks indicates that there will be further investment.

Products of companies which had invested:[11]

Industrial goods:	14.3%
Consumer goods:	28.6%
Consumer goods and industrial goods:	57.1%

Although the seven investors from our survey encountered several difficulties, they rated their overall experiences positively: very good (14.3 per cent), good (71.4 per cent), and so-so (14.3 per cent). All seven recommended that Japanese companies invest now. They stated the time frame for their own future investment as follows:

short term: 14.2%   medium term: 28.6%   long term: 28.6%   none: 28.6%

Reviewing our results, the investment activities of Japanese firms in the new federal states were low. Above all, companies with consumer products got involved. But their goal was just to satisfy the East German consumer market. Japanese companies have evaluated and considered the new federal states for investment, but the indications have been against East Germany. In the competition for investment opportunities in manufacturing sites, the new federal states, with their increasing labour costs and their burdens from the former GDR existence, have lost against China and Asia. In the new federal states, the emphasis for Japanese investment – besides sales and services – will be on co-operation and joint ventures. A tendency towards co-operation and joint ventures with other European companies can be observed. Although the companies in our survey did not answer the question about preferred investment, other sources allow the presumption that co-operation and joint ventures are favoured by Japanese firms for investments in new markets. The few investments in the field of manufacturing and production were all co-operation or joint ventures.

REASONS FOR JAPANESE HESITATION TO INVEST IN THE NEW FEDERAL STATES

So far, the only two real investments of Japanese companies in the new federal states have been the acquisition of the Langewiesener Thermos GmbH, Thüringen, by Nippon Sanso K.K., and the involvement in the Fernmeldetechnik Nordhausen by M.E.I. Japan Inc. All other investments have concentrated on the sales and services sector and the opening of representative offices. What are the reasons for the reluctance of the Japanese to invest in the promising, albeit problematic, new market of the new federal states?

The reasons can be split in three groups:

1. Overall economic reasons
2. Reasons which are valid for the whole of Germany as an investment location
3. Reasons which solely concern the new federal states.

Overall Economic Reasons

In the questionnaire, six out of the seven companies which had not invested in the new federal states named the economic situation in Japan as a main reason for their reluctance to invest.

Japan's foreign direct investment of $41.6 billion in the fiscal year of 1991–1992 (4564 projects) was close to 27 per cent below the amount of the previous year. And 1990–1991 had failed to reach the high investments of 1989–1990 (Handelsblatt, 10 June 1992). The present economic situation in Japan was one reason for the change in the investment curve. The end of the 'bubble economy' – the long-lasting phase of low interest rates with consequential cheap capital and a high inflation of real assets – made it more difficult to get money for investment.

Reasons why Japanese companies have not invested in the new federal states

The weakness of the stock markets and the markets for real estate caused shortages in cash resources for many Japanese companies. As a result, several investment plans were put on hold. The big corporations will be facing enormous redemptions for the convertible and warrant bonds issued from 1987 to 1991, the years of sky-rocketing quotation of shares. In particular, the industries of electrical engineering, steel, automobiles, chemicals, and banks are threatened. These industries used to be business trend leaders. The entire Japanese business world has to economize and this leads to an overall reduction of investment. The press reported a planned reduction of direct foreign investment by over 40 per cent for the fiscal year 1992–1993. (Handelsblatt, 16 September 1992).

The extensive investment activities of Japanese firms in Europe in the second half of the 1980s were due to the fear of the economic unification of the European Community in 1993. They rushed to find a place within the boundaries of the future 'fortress Europe'. All major investments have been accomplished by now. The new federal states are no longer needed as a location to enter the EC.

Reasons Which are Valid for the Whole of Germany as an Investment Location

Manufacturing is extremely expensive because of high wage levels and low annual working hours in Germany. The intention to match the wage levels in East Germany to those in West Germany will take away a favourable location factor for the new federal states. The distance between Japan and Germany is another cause. This leads to higher costs for a production site, since the factory has to be completely equipped and cannot use facilities available in the mother company. Furthermore, important face to face discussions and meetings are very difficult to conduct. The president of the Japanese Chamber of Commerce in Germany, Shigenari Kito, sees another reason in the very high business taxation in Germany. A JETRO opinion poll supports Kito's point. Besides the high business taxation, companies also criticized the complicated German tax system[12] (Ernst and Hilpert, 1990).

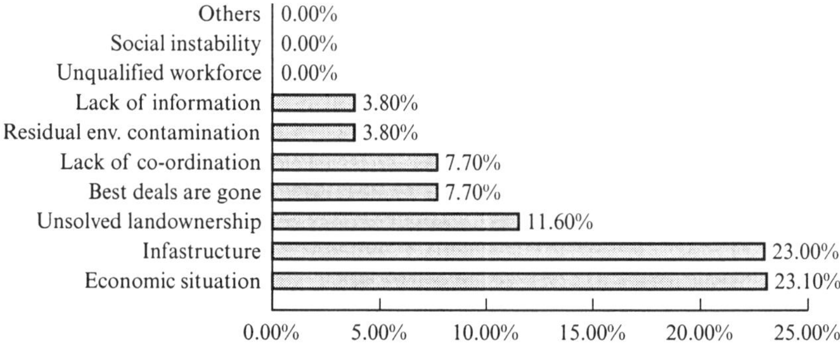

Source: Own survey Aug.–Sept. 1992

Figure 7.2   Reasons why Japanese companies have not invested in the new federal states

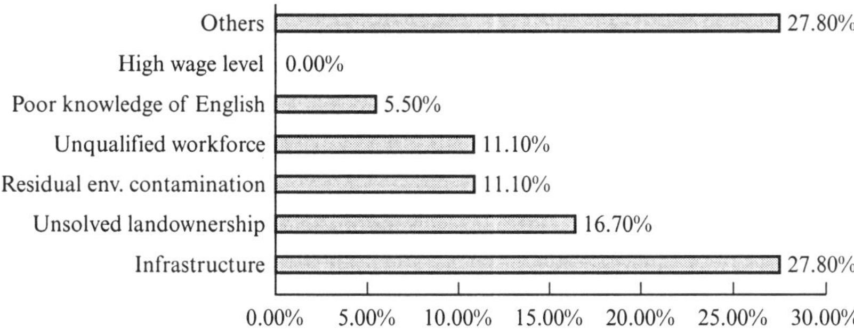

Source: Own survey Aug. Sept. 1992

Figure 7.3   Biggest problems for investors in the new federal states

Reasons Which Solely Concern the New Federal States

Our questionnaire detected as the biggest problems for investors in the new federal states the following points:

Infrastructure

In our survey, six out of the seven non-investing companies stated that the weak infrastructure was an important obstacle. The companies which had already invested graded the infrastructure good (14.2 per cent) so-so (42.9 per cent) and poor (42.9 per cent). And five of the seven named the infrastructure as one of the biggest problems they had experienced. Compared to many other countries which try to attract Japanese investors, the new federal states can only provide a limited communication and traffic network. Although every effort is being undertaken to upgrade and improve all the elements of the infrastructure as fast as possible, it will take time and energy before this problem is solved. Another point may be the desire of Japanese investors to find an environment suitable for Japanese needs, such as Japanese schools, restaurants, stores, and so on.

Former landownership

As soon as the wall came down, questions about former landownership arose. There was a lot of confusion about this issue. Investors were quickly confronted with the problem of claims from previous owners. The Treuhand[13] had to deal with many complaints and tried to solve this problem without scaring the desperately needed investors away. From the 1 660 800 private claims for compensation for buildings and real estate, only eight per cent had been decided by autumn 1992. Our survey listed former landownership as one of the biggest problems in three cases out of the seven investing companies. As a main reason not to invest, three out of seven non-investing companies named former landownership.

Residual environmental contamination

The environmental contamination within the former GDR was considered an invisible risk and therefore difficult to estimate. This factor caused investors to wait. A lack of environmental awareness in the former GDR caused heavy pollution of a considerable amount of land (15 500 former GDR companies and 700 sites from the defence industry are said to be contaminated). The Bundesumweltministerium[14] found about 60 000 suspected areas, 30 per cent of which have to be cleared. The sites of the large-scale chemical enterprises Leuna and Buna belong to the most severely polluted areas. An estimate of the total costs for the decontamination programme lies at 10.6 billion marks.[15] From the view of an investor, however, the statistics looked a bit better. The Treuhandanstalt was said to have 300 contaminated areas in its possession. Only two to three per cent of the industrially and commercially used territory represented an immediate danger. Heiner Bonnenberg, director of the Treuhand department for environmental protection, stated in June 1992: 'The contamination of industrially and commercially used areas is a problem that could be solved technically and financially.' (Oldag, 1992 p. 32) Dr. Charbonnier from the Treuhand even claimed that firms owned by the Treuhand originally were not more contaminated than American firms (Handelsblatt, 13 May 1992.).

Japanese companies obviously felt and experienced the same. Of the firms from our survey which had invested, only two out of seven named environmental contamination as one of the biggest problems encountered. And only one of the seven non-investor companies mentioned residual environmental contamination as a reason why they had not invested.

The loss of the eastern markets

With the new political independence of the former East Bloc, a confusing economic situation occurred. The traditional trade links within eastern Europe dissolved and the attempt to change to market economies brought initial economic instability which will last many more years. Markets which need to be served from a production site or an operation base in the new federal states will not develop for a while. With the recent rapid decline in business transactions with the ex-Soviet Union and East European countries, companies in eastern Germany had been compelled to search frantically for other export outlets. All efforts to promote investment will be in vain if East German companies cannot find markets for their products. An investor looks for a company with marketable products. This increasing change for the worse in the CIS did not favour the new federal states as a starting location for eastern European engagement.

Overcharged administration

In 1992 the Institut der Deutschen Wirtschaft[16] conducted a survey of 1500 East German enterprises (Handelsblatt, 2–3 October 1992). About 80 per cent of the companies surveyed found fault with the public authorities; the administration responsible for ownership questions was rated particularly poorly. The survey even showed that a third of intended investments in 1991 were not realised due to administrative obstacles. This is equivalent to an investment sum of 100 billion DM. The Investment Priority Law (see page 89), failed to speed up administrative processes. The local authorities were responsible for implementing the new law, but they had neither the qualified personnel nor the interest in accelerating the procedure. Note the emphasis on *qualified* personnel. A survey by Globus about bureaucracy in Germany revealed that the new federal states had the most civil servants per 1000 inhabitants.[17]

Unqualified workforce
Although the East German workforce was acknowledged as well educated, the Japanese doubted that people could have the right working ethic after living for over 40 years in a socialist planned economy. Retraining the workforce would be expensive and time consuming. Furthermore, personnel for the middle management positions did not exist. A colloquium to improve the knowledge of managers and students in problems of modern management, time-to-market, and lean production was held at the Bergakademie Freiberg (Sachsen) on 4–5 December 1991 (Sächsisches Wirtschaftskolloquium).[18] A lack of English was stated as being another impediment for investment. So Japanese companies were deterred when the Treuhandanstalt combined a guarantee of jobs with the sale of its enterprises. This guarantee of jobs collided with the idea of lean production; lean means only what is necessary, and requires team-oriented, flexible employees, who support and seek quality, and keep an eye on cost-effectiveness. Such aspects are not taught in a society which, in general, measures economic success in quantities of goods. Especially in the manufacturing technology, Japanese companies have a tendency towards a high percentage of automation. The productivity of the East German workforce had increased, but still did not meet the Japanese understanding of efficient use of working hours and reduction of slack time. Wage levels also increased disproportionately to productivity. While productivity only reached 35 per cent, wages climbed to 75 per cent of West Germany's level (Source: Plenary discussion in Leipzig, May 1992, see page 91). The two economic organizations, Deutsches Institut für Wirtschaftsforschung (DIW) and the Kieler Institut für Weltwirtschaft (IfW), emphasized that the wages policy will play an important role for the future competitiveness of East Germany, and demanded a change in it (Handelsblatt, 1 April 1993). The results from the questionnaire allow the conclusion that the workforce was not exactly what was needed, but that it did not impede investment. None of the seven non-investors saw in the workforce a reason not to invest in the new federal states. The seven investors found a workforce they rated poor (two), so-so (one), and good (four). The two companies which marked 'poor', listed an unqualified workforce as one of their biggest problems in the new federal states.

Lack of information

For Japanese, information about growth prospects for individual industries, demand for certain product groups, and other similar figures are of great relevance. But this data was not available for the new federal states. It was even difficult to estimate the need for investment after the acquisition of an East German company. This made cash-flow calculations nearly impossible. In the beginning, Japanese business people had to rely on information from the mass media, which spread a rather negative image about the new federal states. It was quite some time before substantial information was available to Japanese companies. According to our survey, a lack of information cannot be blamed for the reluctance of investment. Only one out of seven companies named a deficit of information as a main reason not to have invested.

Lack of co-ordination

Complaints about bad co-ordination between the Treuhand, the new federal states, and investors could be heard. The Treuhand sought to sell its holdings while the new federal states often favoured greenfield investment. Although investors received incoherent information, a lack of co-ordination did not seem to scare investors away. Only two out of seven companies mentioned this point as one of the reasons for not investing.

Social instability

Up to autumn 1992, social instability had played a minor role for investors. The existence of a certain fear of social unrest, in particular with the increasing unemployment, could be detected. As our survey showed, social instability was not a reason to hesitate with investment. However, news about confrontations with 'neo Nazis' caused firms to consider social instability as a decision factor for investment. An opinion poll by the Deutsche Presseagentur in Sachsen and Brandenburg (Handelsblatt, 5 October 1992, page 7) showed that a major concern for a foreign company is the level of hostility towards foreigners. The business world abroad monitored further developments closely.

ACTIVITIES TO PROMOTE INVESTMENT IN THE NEW FEDERAL STATES

Treuhand and Government Activities to Attract Investors

What has the Treuhand done to attract investors, in particular from Japan? Although it is an independent institution, the Treuhand relies on juridical support given to them by the government. In autumn 1992, about five per cent of East German businesses had been taken over by foreign investors. Promised foreign investment lay between 10 and 12 per cent. Japanese enterprises, however, were said to have bought only two out of 3500 privatized enterprises, and these purchases were done through affiliates in Europe. The foreign investors were mainly from France, Switzerland, and the United Kingdom.

The sales procedure

The sales procedure practised by the Treuhand was criticized as being confusing. Investors did not know how to apply for an enterprise. They felt that they did not have the same chances as German investors. That led the Treuhandanstalt to push a new policy: 'Die internationale Ausschreibung'.[19] Offers were sorted according to industries and presented publicly[20] with a deadline for bids. This procedure was supposed to be more transparent and attractive to foreign investors (Wirtschaftswoche Supplement, 10 February 1992).

The unsolved former landownership and the Investment Priority Law

An investor does not want to deal with the risk of a former owner surfacing and jeopardizing the investment, and he does not have the time to wait until the ownership question is resolved. The Investment Priority Law was established to solve this problem. Until the reform of the property law[21], the rule for assets was 'return the property before financial compensation'[22], as stated in the unification treaty[23]; this rule tended to scare investors away. Thus, the Investment Priority Law was put into effect in 1991. Paragraph 3a of the law allows the sale, lending, and leasing of former state owned land, buildings or companies to an investor, without worrying about a prior owner. By the end of April 1992, 481 requests for the use of the Investment Priority Law had been made to the Treuhand. By autumn 1992, 199 requests had been approved. Unfortunately, former owners still found ways to delay investment.[24] A second change in the property law allowed the Treuhand to decide independently about cases involving the Investment Priority Law. This faciliated the purchase of East German enterprises for foreign companies (Süddeutsche Zeitung, 6 June 1992).

Residual environmental contamination

Investors named residual environmental contamination as a problem on a par with former landownership. In the beginning, investors found it extremely difficult to obtain exact data on the degree of contamination. The fear of incalculable costs due to environmental burdens scared investors away. The Government saw the problem coming and had already incorporated possibilities for exemption in the unification treaty dated 31 August 1990. The buyer could be exempted from the public liability for environmental burdens. Within the framework of the Investment Priority Law and the Removal of Obstacles for Privatization[25] dated 22 March 1991, the opportunities for exemption from liability were extended. Exemption could be granted for damage caused by the acquired enterprise before 1 June 1990. This law only permitted exemption; it was not based on a statutory claim. It lay fully within the judgement of the authorities in the new federal states. Data from the Bundesumweltministerium[26] stated that 25 000–30 000 requests for exemption had been received by autumn 1992 and only 100–150 had been decided by then. The slow processing of applications by the new federal states was due to bureaucracy, lack of personnel, and the dread of financial risk.[27] The Treuhand itself had property equivalent to 50 per cent of the entire East German area.[28] With an agreement between the Federal Government and the new federal states, the Treuhand could offer to pay up to 90 per cent of the costs caused by residual environmental contamination to a potential investor (Oldag, 1992).

Activities of Other Organizations to Promote Investments in the New Federal States

The presence of Japanese enterprises in West Germany, along with the already developed business relations between Japan and West Germany, allowed the growth of several organizations such as DJW,[29] JETRO Germany,[30] the Ostasiatische Verein[31] and the Deutsche Ostasien Institut.[32] All of these organizations closely observed the events in East Germany. They offered services to acquaint Japanese companies with the new federal states, and tried to cater for the special needs of the Japanese business world.

In November 1990, an investment promotion seminar of all new federal states was held in Tokyo. The intention was to provide Japanese business people with first-hand information and to give them the opportunity to ask questions (see Bundesministerium für Wirtschaft, 1991b).

In the course of 1991, JETRO and the Treuhandanstalt under the control of DJW initiated the 'Triangle Project'. With regard to the individual situation of Japanese investors, the three organizations developed a special acquisition plan. JETRO discovered 21 Japanese companies with a basic interest in investment. In a survey, JETRO tried to find out the Japanese goals and their need for information. This knowledge allowed the Treuhand to point towards certain East German enterprises and to make specific information available.

Another interesting project was Keidanren's[33] Investment Promotion Mission to East Germany in October 1991. Members of Keidanren investigated the overall investment climate. They advertised East Germany as a country with a great deal of potential for development, but with a number of problems at the same time. The members strongly recommended that the new federal states should be considered for investment, in particular in regard to the economic integration of the EC, the reconstruction of East Germany, and the changes in the eastern European countries.

In May 1992, the DJW, in co-operation with the Chamber of Commerce in Leipzig, Sachsen, arranged a plenary discussion entitled: 'Improving competitiveness in the new federal states – Japan as a partner'. The three Japanese members of the panel emphasized that they saw the biggest obstacle for Japanese investors as being a lack of information. During the discussion, some of the participants blamed the absence of big Japanese corporations for the slow investment activity. Smaller Japanese companies wait for the big corporations to take action before they are willing to get involved. Mr Egawa from Sony Deutschland GmbH said: 'My company is mainly experimenting at this point'. They have emphasized sales and services because this does not require big investments. He pointed out that his company is interested in the new federal states, but he does not feel that they know enough about the conditions to risk investment in the production or research field. Plans do exist, but they will not be realized for a while. Lothar Späth from Jenoptik GmbH, Jena, Thüringen, saw an opportunity for Japanese and German companies to bring Japanese standardized products to East Germany, where they could be improved and further developed (Leipziger Volkszeitung, 13 May 1992; Handelsblatt, 13 May 1992; Die Welt, 13 May 1992; Handelsblatt 10 June 1992).

CONCLUSION

In the age of globalization and internationalization, the opening of the eastern European markets has represented new opportunities for Japanese firms. It was hoped that the unification of Germany would attract Japanese investors, but Japanese companies hardly participated in the investment boom of 1990. They are unwilling to enter the new market first. However, every large Japanese firm is watching closely the developments in East Germany and they are evaluating carefully their opportunities. Japanese companies have established sales and services networks and representative offices, mainly to serve the consumer market of East Germany. In the long run the investment structure will change. So far, Japanese companies are setting up the prerequisites for future investments. At this point it is too early to expect Japanese production and manufacturing sites in the new federal states. In summary, we assume that the Japanese investments to date will be sufficient to supply the EU market – even to serve the demands of the former eastern Bloc states.

NOTES

1. US billion = 1 000 000 000
2. The resentment towards the Japanese business people in North America.
3. (Ernst and Hilpert, 1990).
4. Commonwealth of Independent States.

5. German Democratic Republic.
6. Up to 1992
7. Flask maker
8. K.K. = Kabushiki Kaisha = stock co-operation.
9. Telecom equipment producer
10. multiple namings were possible.
11. Source: Own survey Aug.–Sept. 1992.
12. For more information about taxation in Japan, see Kuboi and Paufler (1988).
13. The public trust charged with privatizing the economic structure of former East Germany. It represented some 8000 East German firms. After unification, the Treuhandanstalt was formally linked to the Federal Ministry of Finance in Bonn but it enjoyed wide-ranging autonomy in its decisions. The headquarters are in East Berlin and there exist 15 regional offices responsible for small to medium-sized local firms (see Welfens, 1992, page 247).
14. Ministry of Environmental Affairs.
15. A study from the ifo-Institut München; not included are former Soviet military bases, nuclear contaminated ground, and the soil of forestry and agricultural industry.
16. Institute of the German Economy
17. Civil servants per 1000 inhabitants (1991): Berlin 126, Mecklenburg 120, Brandenburg 116, Hamburg 108, Bremen 104, Sachsen 95, Thüringen 87, Nordrhein Westfalen 63 see Süddeutsche Zeitung, 14–15 November 1992, page A8.
18. For information on qualifications, see Beschorner (1992).
19. The international bid procedure
20. öffentliche Ausschreibung
21. Vermögensgesetz
22. Rückgabe vor Entschädigung
23. Einigungsvertrag
24. An example: the ex-proprietor proposes his own investment plan which gives him priority. His plan cannot be carried out. Although he will be penalized for breaking the contract, he can still delay a decision for another investor by taking the penalty to court. This led to several unrealistic investment plans by ex-proprietors.
25. Beseitigung von Hemmnissen bei der Privatisierung von Unternehmen und zur Förderung von Investoren.
26. Ministry of Environmental Affairs
27. At the end of March 1992 the exemption rule ran out (Handelsblatt, 4 June 1992 and Handelsblatt, 2–3 October 1992).
28. The Treuhand is not responsible for real estate owned by the former Soviet Union or the past Nationale Volksarmee (national army of the former GDR). Areas of the former LPGs (Landwirtschaftliche Produktions Genossenschaft = agricultural co-operatives) and the uranium mining industry (DSAG = Deutsch-Sowjetische AG Wismut) are also not owned by the Treuhand.
29. Deutsch Japanischer Wirtschaftskreis, Düsseldorf (German-Japanese economical circle), founded 1986 (see Deutsch-Japanischer Wirtschaftskreis, 1992).
30. Japan External Trade Organization
31. East Asian Association
32. German East Asia Institute
33. Japan Federation of Economic Organization, the most influential economic organization in Japan. The chairman is unofficially known as 'zaikai prime minister' (zaikai stands for Japan's four major business organizations). Keidanren presents views on important economic issues, and submits recommendations to the government and the then ruling Liberal Democratic Party (see Keidanren, 1991).

REFERENCES

Baum, O. (1992), 'Zentren bleiben das Dorado für ausländische Investoren.' *Handelsblatt*, 179, 26–27 July.

Beschorner, Dieter (1992), 'Investieren in die Mitarbeiterqualifikation rechnet sich und wirkt doppelt', in R. Reichwald (ed.), *Marktnahe Produktion*, Wiesbaden, pp. 334–51.

Bundesministerium für Wirtschaft (1991a) *Ein internationaler Standort mit Zukunft: Die neuen deutschen Bundesländer*, BfW.

Bundesministerium für Wirtschaft (1991b) *Schrift des Bundesministeriums für Wirtschaft*, BfW.

Deutsch-Japanischer Wirtschaftskreis (1992) *Bericht des DJW-Sekretariats*, DJW. (Covers February 1991 to April 1992).

Ernst, A. and H.-G. Hilpert (1990) *Japans Direktinvestitionen in Europa – Europas Direktinvestitionen in Japan*, Munich: Ifo Institut für Wirtschaftsforschung.

Keidanren (1991) *Investment Promotion Mission to Eastern Germany and Denmark.* (Comments by the leader of Keidanren, 4–11 October).

Köhler, R. (1993) 'Treuhand gibt in Tokio auf', *Süddeutsche Zeitung*, 16 June p. 32.

Kuboi, T. and Pauflcr, A. (1988) *Unternehmung und Besteuerung in Japan*, Stuttgart.

Oldag, A. (1992) 'Altlasten behindern die Investitionen im Osten, *Süddeutsche Zeitung*, 3 June.

Welfens, P. (ed.) (1992) *Economic Aspects of German Unification;* Springer Verlag.

Unattributed Newpaper Articles*

Interview with Mr Michio Kamei, manager of Nippon Sanso AG, *M & A Review* 5 (7), 1988, pp. 8–11.

'Japan sieht Berlin als Finanzhauptstadt.', *Frankfurter Allgemeine Zeitung*, 26 June 1990.

'Financial Houses Eyeing Berlin', *The Japan Economic Journal*, 30 June 1990.

'Japan's top oxygen manufacturer', *Guardian*, 12 April 1991, p. 24.

'Japaner in Nordhausen', *Frankfurter Allgemeine Zeitung*, 5 July 1991, p. 18.

'Japaner engagieren sich in Nordhausen', *Frankfurter Allgemeine Zeitung*, 5 August 1991, p. 18.

Wirtschaftswoche, Supplement, 10 February 1992.

'Interesse der Japaner flaut ab', *Die Welt*, 13 May 1992.

'Japaner wollen investieren', *Leipziger Volkszeitung*, 13 May 1992.

'Nippons Investoren halten sich nach wie vor zurueck', *Handelsblatt*, 13 May 1992.

'Enthaftung zum Abbau von Entscheidungshemmungen', *Handelsblatt*, 107, 4 June 1992.

'Vorfahrtsspur wird verbreitert', *Süddeutsche Zeitung*, 6 June 1992.

'Kaum Hoffnung auf Investitionen in Ostdeutschland', *Handelsblatt*, June 1992.

'Nach dem Ertragseinbruch reduziert die Industrie ihre Investitionsbudgets', *Handelsblatt*, September 1992, p. 12.

'Schwerste Erblast ist das anhaltende Eigentumschaos', *Handelsblatt*, 2–3 October 1992.

'Investoren verunsichert', *Handelsblatt*, 5 October 1992, p. 7.

'Bürokratie in Deutschland', *Süddeutsche Zeitung*, 14–15 November 1992, p. A8.

'Institute: Die Lohnkosten sind die Achillesferse der Wirtschaft im Osten', *Handelsblatt*, 1 April 1993.

---

* In date order.

PART 3

Regionalism and North America

8. Regional economic agreements and multinational firms: the investment provisions of the NAFTA

Edward M. Graham and Christopher Wilkie

THE NAFTA INVESTMENT PROVISIONS AND INVESTMENT LIBERALIZATION

The formal investment provisions of the North American Free Trade Agreement (NAFTA), as articulated in Chapter 11 of Part V of the agreement and elsewhere, have instituted the most comprehensive rules on investment to date for multinational corporations and nation states. Although unquestionably an element of a regional agreement, the NAFTA investment provisions have considerable international ramifications, not only because many of the provisions extend to non-parties to the agreement, but also because of the precedent they set for other regional and indeed multilateral agreements. Although at first the goals of the negotiating parties seemed disparate – the NAFTA was the first comprehensive trade and investment agreement between developed and developing countries – converging attitudes on the part of the three signatories towards many of the investment issues under consideration enabled a jointly satisfactory outcome.

It is undeniable that substantial elements of the long standing US official agenda are embodied in the investment provisions. In particular, the US Government has long sought agreement on certain investment-related principles in fora such as the Organisation for Economic Co-operation and Development (OECD) and the General Agreement on Tariffs and Trade (GATT) that would enable business activities to operate relatively unencumbered across national boundaries. The policy goals which foster this include right of establishment, free transfer of funds, agreed standards for expropriation, national treatment for business entities under the control of foreign entities, restrictions on governmentally mandated performance requirements, and protection of intellectual property. Most of these goals were realized in Chapter 11 of the NAFTA agreement, which deals exclusively with investment issues, and in other chapters which have a bearing on international investment behaviour.

What is also true, however, is that as the 1990s dawned, acceptance of many of these same principles was sought by Canada and even Mexico, both of which had prospered from US investment, but which were traditionally wary of some of the implications of high levels of foreign investment in the domestic economy. Canada, for example, changed its approach to foreign direct investment (FDI) considerably during the 1980s. In 1985, Canada's Foreign Investment Review Agency (FIRA), which reviewed most foreign investment in Canada with a view to confirming 'substantial benefit' to Canada, had been replaced by Investment Canada, whose mandate was to emphasize investment promotion as well as a more streamlined and accommodating investment review procedure. Thus Canadian investment goals were largely embodied in the NAFTA as well. Like all countries, Canada of course had some sensitivities that it sought to accommodate because of domestic policy priorities, not least of which was a desire to nurture a small (in international terms) Canadian cultural presence – and this was protected in the NAFTA agreement as it had been in the US-Canada Free Trade Agreement (FTA) only a few years before. With respect to most of the investment issues mentioned in the preceding paragraph, though, Canada's policies largely coincided with those of the United States.

In addition, from Canada's perspective, NAFTA represented an opportunity to negotiate a regional trade and investment agreement which it might not normally have had. Canadian negotiating leverage with respect to Mexico was not great, underlined by the low stock of Canadian direct investment in Mexico (just under $US 580 million in 1992, versus $US 23.1 billion for the United States.)[1] Most importantly, however, it remained vitally important for Canada to consolidate the gains in both the trade and investment areas which were realized under the US-Canada FTA. From a Canadian perspective, it was important to trilateralize a US-Mexican agreement, if only to reduce the tendency towards a series of US bilateral agreements with her trading and investment partners, which arguably could compromise those gains.[2] This remains a primary raison d'être for multilateralizing investment provisions in other fora, and was underlined early on in the NAFTA process; some Canadian critics indeed believed that US bilateral arrangements could undermine the whole multilateral process. Great importance was attached to ensuring that the US did not become the

> ... hub of a rimless wheel [or that US bilateral agreements did not] become the ultimate abuse of the Article XXIV exemption to the GATT's most-favoured-nation principle. From the point of view of world welfare, preventing this development is arguably the most important reason for Canada to trilateralize the negotiations.[3]

The role of investment from the Mexican perspective was considerably different from that of either Canada or the United States. NAFTA may be seen as a major element in Mexico's recent unilateral opening (*apertura*) of her internal economy to one based on competitive private enterprise. One major goal of this liberalization was to attract foreign capital needed to modernize the Mexican economy, and NAFTA was seen by Mexican officials as an important means of attaining this goal.

The extent of the Mexican *apertura* before NAFTA must be qualified somewhat, given that Mexico was liberalizing one of the most restrictive investment regimes in the world. Articles 27 and 28 of the 1917 Mexican Constitution, for example, restricted to Mexican nationals vast swathes of the economy, including land, mineral resources and strategic sectors such as telecommunications and electricity. Under Article 27, Mexico earlier in this century nationalized railways and oil companies.[4] Although some elements of liberalization arguably began as early as 1965 (such as the creation of the *maquiladora* programme), Mexico's policies overall remained less than liberal until very recently. In particular, following the 1973 Law to Promote Mexican Investment and Regulate Foreign Investment, and the creation of the CNIE (*Comisión Nacional de Inversión Extranjera* or National Foreign Investment Commission) Mexico continued to pursue quite restrictive investment policies.

The current liberalization really began with steps taken by Mexico in preparation for joining the General Agreement on Tariffs and Trade (GATT) in 1986. In 1984 new investment regulations were published, the effect of which was to loosen the 1973 foreign investment restrictions in 'high-priority' industries such as heavy machinery, electronic equipment, high technology products, and tourism.[5] These same steps had as first priority the arresting of capital flight and declining inward direct investment. By 1988, then, this *apertura* was showing signs of success; in particular, incoming FDI reached US$3.1 billion, attaining the same level as 1981, the year preceding the debt moratorium.[6]

Further unilateral investment liberalization in Mexico occurred in 1989 with the passage of the Regulation of the Law for the Promotion of Mexican Investment and the Regulation of Foreign Investment.[7] While the 1973 Foreign Investment Law remained on the books, the 1989 Regulations were intended 'to increase the flow of foreign investment by providing legal certainty and by simplifying the administrative rules and procedures to which it is subject'.[8] The details of this foreign investment liberalization may be found elsewhere.[9] The main point here is that NAFTA essentially codified this earlier liberalization and helped to propel further momentum in this regard. Indeed, during and after the NAFTA negotiations, Mexico continued to liberalize unilaterally, one example being the passage of the 28 June 1991 Law for the Promotion and Protection of Intellectual Property. And in June 1993 it was announced that Mexico would incorporate into domestic law all of the reforms undertaken under NAFTA, and extend these to investors of all nations (that is, they were to be extended under unconditional 'most favoured nation' terms), even if NAFTA were to fail to come into effect. The new legislation formalizing this was introduced in late 1993 (the 1993 Foreign Investment Law of Mexico, or Ley de Inversión Extranjera 1993).[10] The benefits of this liberalization have thus been well recognized by the Mexican government.[11]

Indeed the investment liberalization which has recently taken place, and which has been codified in the NAFTA, could be argued to be amongst the most important aspects of the agreement from the Mexican perspective. Certainly its importance within the NAFTA cannot be underestimated – as the Conference Board of Canada simply stated: '... for Mexico, the main rationale of the NAFTA lies in the investment dimension [–] perhaps more than on trade liberalization'.[12] While Mexican restrictions sanctified by the NAFTA are still greater in scope than US or Canadian restrictions, the precedent of NAFTA for developed and less developed country investment agreements should not be underestimated.

Thus, despite the asymmetries in investment relations and economic development among the NAFTA signatories, a closer look at prevailing trends in all three countries indicates that Canada, the US, and Mexico were able to further their investment policy priorities. It should also be noted that a growing congruence of views on investment was due in some degree to relatively new US sensitivities to foreign direct investment; through the 1980s the US had become a host as well as home to FDI[13], which could also be argued to have sensitized the US to some of the same concerns witnessed by many of her trading partners in the 1960s and 1970s.[14]

NATIONAL TREATMENT AND RELATED PROVISIONS OF THE NAFTA (CHAPTER 11, SECTION A)

The core provision of contemporary international investment agreements is 'national treatment', whereby foreign companies or investors are essentially treated the same as domestic (or national) companies. Ideally, this is true of companies seeking to invest for the first time (pre-establishment) as it is of companies seeking to change existing operations (post-establishment). The NAFTA national treatment obligation is comprehensive in this regard: it embodies the right of establishment and an obligation of each signing party to accord to investors (and investments of investors) of other signing parties treatment 'no less favourable than that it accords, in like circumstances, to its own investors with respect to the establishment, acquisition, expansion, management, conduct, operation, and sale or other disposition of investments' (Article 1102.1). This provision goes beyond those of other international agreements. The recently negotiated Asia-Pacific Economic Cooperation

(APEC) investment code also contains a national treatment obligation; unlike the NAFTA, however it is non-binding.[15] In contrast to the OECD National Treatment Instrument as well, Article 1102 of the NAFTA is binding and thereby requires signatories to grant national treatment to investors and investments of investors of the other signing parties.[16]

National treatment is also often complemented and strengthened by most-favoured-nation (mfn, also termed non-discrimination) provisions in investment agreements, and this is true of the NAFTA. In the mfn (Articles 1103 and 1104) and minimum standard of treatment (Article 1105) provisions of the NAFTA, signing parties must grant investors and investments of other signing parties treatment no less favourable than that granted to investors and investments of non-signing countries and that provided for under international law. In addition the national treatment provisions of the NAFTA generally apply to 'third party' investors and their investments. (For example, if a Canadian subsidiary of a European corporation holds an investment in Mexico, the Canadian subsidiary would be a 'third party investor' and its Mexican subsidiary a 'third party investment'.) However, under Article 1113, there are exceptional circumstances where these obligations could be denied.

Finally, the NAFTA national treatment obligations apply to state and provincial governments, as they do in principle to regional and municipal governments and to subnational state agencies (Article 1108.1). As all three signatories are *de jure* federal states, constitutional considerations were a factor in the resolution of this conundrum, but in each case subnational entities, like their federal counterparts, were initially required to list their non-conforming measures within a two year time frame.[17] In practice, however, existing subnational non-conforming measures were eventually simply 'grandfathered', in effect freezing non-conformity to existing measures only. Thus most reservations and exceptions applying to the federal level of government were detailed in annexes to the agreement, discussed later in this article.

Another important feature of recently negotiated investment agreements has been a prohibition or limitation on performance requirements. Again, the NAFTA contains a rather strong provision to limit these limits on the behaviour of investors or investments in the territory of the signatory governments (Article 1106); notably, this provision goes further than similar provisions negotiated in other international fora. In particular, the Uruguay Round's Trade Related Investment Measures (TRIMs) agreement to restrict certain types of performance requirements, is a weaker instrument than is NAFTA Article 1106. While there is a prohibition on several types of performance requirements in the TRIMs agreement, the sample list is narrower than that specified in the NAFTA, and, as the TRIMs agreement itself states, it essentially codifies existing practices by prohibiting TRIMs that are 'inconsistent with the provisions of Article III or Article XI of the GATT'.[18]

From an economic perspective, restrictions on performance requirements are logical because these requirements often result in much the same distortions as traditional trade restrictive devices.[19] Thus Article 1106 of the NAFTA may be judged a success in that it is arguably stronger than the equivalent provision of the US-Canada FTA, itself quite a strong measure to ban most new performance requirements and to phase out most old ones. The NAFTA provisions go still further in that the ban on new performance requirements (and phasing out of old ones) covers some additional categories that continued to be permitted under the FTA. In particular, technology transfer and 'exclusive supplier' requirements have been added to the list of FTA prohibitions, covering export requirements, minimum domestic content, and domestic sourcing requirements (Article 1106.1).[20] Furthermore, under Article 1106.3, the linking of subsidies with certain performance requirements such as domestic content, domestic sourcing, or trade balancing is also prohibited, as is the linking of sales to export requirements and the earning of foreign exchange. There are mitigating circumstances however. Performance requirements to promulgate environmental standards are permitted (Article 1106.2; see also Article 1114), as are requirements for employee training (Article 1106.4). Also, there is no ban on requirements for the performance of research and development (Article 1106.4), a provision which may have increasing national treatment repercussions in the future in high-tech industrial sectors.[21] And finally, the NAFTA phases out Mexican performance requirements, which were placed on automotive manufacturers at a slower rate for incumbent firms than for new entrants, and thus were biased in favour of the latter. (This arrangement apparently was introduced in order to offset biases claimed to exist by incumbent producers, resulting from the fact that their operations were historically subject to Mexican performance requirements.) Most importantly, however, Article 1106 of the NAFTA applies to performance requirements placed on any investment, not only investments of a country that is party to the NAFTA; the importance and possible ramifications of this has been relatively ignored in the literature thus far.

Article 1110 of the NAFTA pertains to expropriation and compensation for expropriated properties. Provisions relating to these issues have long roots in international investment agreements, in that most bilateral FIPAs (Foreign Investment Protection Agreements) or BITs (Bilateral Investment Agreements) between developed and developing countries have sought to create conditions to ensure that, if stability for investors could not be secured, then as a second best alternative some form of compensation would be forthcoming.[22] Just as important in the North American context, these have been contentious issues, particularly between the US and Mexico (and, in recent times, between Canada and certain Caribbean and South American countries). Article 1110 basically forbids expropriation except for a public purpose, and then it must be done without discrimination, and with due process. The remainder of NAFTA Article 1110 is designed to consolidate this provision by, for example, declaring that compensation payments should reflect market value (Article 1110.2) and that payments must be prompt and in a G7 (or fully G7-convertible) currency (Article 1110.2–1110.6), thereby avoiding undue investor exchange risk.[23]

Article 1110 may be viewed as an achievement in the context of investment relations with Latin American countries, which have been traditionally wary of investment agreements. It should be recalled, however, that attitudes towards FDI have been changing in Latin America, not least because of a growing realization that in order to attract scarce foreign capital, a liberal policy on expropriation and compensation was necessary. Likewise, on transfers of capital, a matter that has historically also been a sore issue between the US and Mexico, a liberal position again largely prevailed, doubtlessly because Mexican negotiators believed that in order to attract foreign capital, Mexico should guarantee normal transfers of earnings and other capital items. Thus, NAFTA allows no restrictions on such transfers except for those required for balance of payments reasons or where issues pertaining to bankruptcy and creditors' rights, criminality, or other exceptional circumstances are extant (Article 1109).[24]

DISPUTE SETTLEMENT IN THE NAFTA INVESTMENT CHAPTER (CHAPTER 11, SECTION B)

Section B of Chapter 11 of the NAFTA (Articles 1115 through 1138), establishing a set of procedures for resolving investment disputes, is one of the most innovative features of the whole NAFTA agreement. These procedures in fact go beyond those proposed in any other international agreement on investment thus far, and may be argued to have set an important precedent for any future multilateral agreement. Under these procedures in the NAFTA, most investors (but not investments) may seek arbitration of a dispute against a signing party to the NAFTA. In other international dispute settlement mechanisms, including those of the FTA and the GATT, only governments have 'standing', and hence an investor must be represented by a government (usually its home government) in seeking resolution of any claim it might have against another government. Under NAFTA, however, an investor can pursue a claim on its own behalf (or on behalf of its investment) against a signing party, if it can claim monetary loss or damages involving alleged breaches of obligations under Section A of Chapter 11 (the provisions discussed above) or certain other articles of the NAFTA.[25]

An effort must be made to solve the dispute first by means of consultation and negotiation (Article 1118). If this fails, the dispute can then be submitted to binding arbitration under the rules of the World Bank (International Centre for Settlement of Investment Disputes (ICSID) Convention) or the United Nations (United Nations Commission on International Trade Law (UNCITRAL)). Under either set of rules, a Tribunal (arbitration panel) is established that is empowered to order interim measures to protect the rights of the disputing investor. Although the Tribunal cannot order a government to revoke a measure alleged to constitute a breach of the NAFTA, it can order that an award be made to the investor, including monetary (but not punitive) damages and/or restitution of property, plus applicable interest (Article 1135.1). If the claim is made by an investor on behalf of an investment, any award granted by the Tribunal is without prejudice to any right that the investment might have to relief under domestic law.

Apart from their innovative aspects and the precedent that they set for other international negotiations, these provisions resolve a long standing dispute over the 'Calvo Doctrine', under which Mexico and other Latin American nations have held that the sole means for resolving a dispute between a sovereign state and an investment within its territory must be judicial proceedings in local courts. Exactly why Mexico agreed to allow the NAFTA dispute settlement procedure effectively to supersede the Calvo doctrine is not entirely clear.[26] Nonetheless it may be observed that the Calvo doctrine in practice has acted historically as a deterrent to foreign direct investment in Mexico, as a result of foreign investors' perception of Mexican judicial proceedings as being other than fair and impartial. Furthermore, from the Mexican perspective, the NAFTA provision could serve to deflect the sometimes heavy-handed diplomatic pressures from Washington which have often characterized disputes between US investors and the Mexican Government. And finally, Mexican agreement to the dispute settlement mechanism also may be perceived as a welcome reform which will have domestic ramifications as well:

> [T]he option for the investor to resort to investor-state binding arbitration or the country's domestic courts in order to obtain monetary damages ... is ... a substantial improvement, as it can save investors the complex network of Mexican litigation which is often extremely lengthy and costly. Rather than a concession to the U.S., this is an improvement on the present legal regime, where investors (both foreign and national) lack guarantees of appropriate arbitration, since the Mexican Judicial Power is not sufficiently independent from the Executive. An example of bad arbitration is the land expropriation carried out by President Echeverría in north-west Mexico in November 1976, compensation for which was still being paid in 1991.[27]

While the investment dispute procedures are an important stabilizing influence with respect to investor confidence in the Mexican investment environment, there do remain a few minor troublesome points. These mostly reflect problems with ICSID and UNCITRAL, rather than with the concept as a whole. For example, unlike the traditional dispute settlement mechanisms embodied in

Chapters 19 (antidumping and countervailing duties) and Chapter 20 (state-state disputes) of the NAFTA, none of the arbitration mechanisms mentioned in Chapter 11 (ICSID, ICSID's Additional Facility, or UNCITRAL) contain any time limits on actual arbitration, although Articles 1116–1120 and 1126–1127 do impose strict time limits on what the parties to a dispute must do to initiate and/or respond to proceedings.[28]

The NAFTA investment dispute settlement mechanism also embodies important departures from traditional investor-state dispute settlement. Under the latter, both parties must customarily agree to dispute settlement, while Article 1120 of the NAFTA allows the investor unilaterally to initiate proceedings.[29] Furthermore Article 1136.5 goes on to say that in the event of a signatory refusing to abide with a final award, a Chapter 20 panel may be instituted, with a request that the Party ultimately comply with the award.[30] Both of these provisions have the potential to have far-reaching consequences, and while it is much too early for analysis, future developments warrant close attention. Finally, there are a number of exceptions where NAFTA investment dispute settlement provisions cannot be used. These are discussed in the section following.

Early on in the negotiations, the World Bank (that is, ICSID) and the International Chamber of Commerce (ICC) were both suggested as institutions for commercial arbitration.[31] However, it was only ICSID which resurfaced as part of the agreement, and the inclusion of ICSID but not the ICC seems odd given the comparative records of the two institutions in dispute settlement.[32] ICSID has been used relatively infrequently, for instance. Since its inception in 1966 ICSID has ruled on only 26 cases and in 11 of these, over three years has elapsed before an initial decision.[33] In contrast to ICSID, the ICC receives over 300 requests for its facilities every year, and approximately one-third of cases involves a state entity.[34] Finally, the ICC has had a much better record of settling disputes on a timely basis than has ICSID.[35] Perhaps, however, one reason for a reluctance to stipulate the ICC's procedures is a hesitancy to involve itself too heavily in arbitration of disputes not strictly commercial in nature.[36] However, one should note that there is nothing to stop signatories from suggesting other institutions for the resolution of commercial dispute settlement – indeed this is stipulated under Article 2022 and, with respect to conciliation procedures rather than more formal arbitration, Article 1118 of the investment chapter.

Despite these last points, there is little doubt that the investment dispute settlement mechanism of the NAFTA is a major accomplishment, and has been recognized to be so to varying degrees by many.[37] In addition, mechanisms for the improvement of the already innovative investment dispute settlement mechanism are embodied in the NAFTA agreement itself. Chapter 20 establishes the more traditional sovereign state dispute settlement procedures for disputes similar to those of Chapter 18 of the FTA, and these can be invoked as an alternate means for settlement of investment disputes if both parties to a dispute agree that it is necessary (and Chapter 20 procedures can also be used, of course, for disputes other than investment disputes).

NAFTA also includes an article on alternative dispute resolution (Article 2022). Subject to the will of the signatories, this article could have implications for investment dispute settlement as well. Article 2022.1, for example, stipulates that signatories 'shall, to the maximum extent possible, encourage and facilitate the use of arbitration and other means of alternative dispute resolution for the settlement of international commercial disputes between private parties'. As we have seen, this notion was also given impetus within the investment dispute chapter under Article 1118. Thus other more informal and presumably less costly venues and vehicles for dispute settlement may be encouraged – these could include the ICC, or any number of new centres from British Columbia to Cairo that have recently been established to help in dispute settlement. Notably, provision for this has also been accommodated in the NAFTA, in that Article 2022.4 states that an Advisory Committee on Private Commercial Disputes shall be established, again with the intention of furthering the resolution of these disputes.

Indeed, for this last category of less formal disputes, Article 2022 procedures might prove to be more frequently utilized than those of Chapter 11 or the traditional state-state dispute resolution mechanisms of Chapter 20. Under Article 2022, the emphasis would be on conciliation rather than arbitration. Without formal state involvement, the opportunity would be present for quick, low profile, low cost resolution of commercial disputes. This conjectural opinion should not, however, detract from what we have said at the outset: that the investor-state dispute settlement mechanism of the investment chapter is one of the most innovative features of the NAFTA agreement, and that any future binding international investment agreements, whether at the regional or multilateral level, will have to take into account these procedures.

RESERVATIONS AND EXCEPTIONS TO CHAPTER 11 (INCLUDING SECTORS RESERVED FOR THE STATE)

Under the NAFTA both Canada and Mexico are allowed to continue with the review of certain investments, and to all intents and purposes this also may be said of the US with respect to national security provisions. For example, decisions taken pursuant to Annex 1138.2, under which decisions taken by Canada under the Investment Canada Act and by Mexico by the National Commission on Foreign Investment with respect to whether an acquisition should be allowed to proceed, are not subject to the investment dispute mechanism.[38] Under Article 1138, this exclusion also extends to actions 'taken by a Party pursuant to Article 2102'. Article 2102 is a national security 'carve-out' that also allows the signing parties to take actions 'deemed necessary for the protection of its essential security interests', relating to traffic in military goods, materials, and technology, or taken in time of war or other international emergency, or relating to nuclear proliferation. Thus Article 1138 also renders decisions taken by the United States to block Canadian or Mexican acquisitions of US firms under the Exon-Florio provision of the Trade Act of 1988 as not subject to the investment dispute settlement mechanism, or at least not if such blockage is consistent with Article 2102.

There are other domains where Chapter 11 investment dispute settlement provisions do not apply or apply with qualifications. For example, Article 1307 makes the status of the telecommunications sector with respect to the Chapter 11 investment dispute mechanism ambiguous. Under Article 1415 pertaining to financial services, the investment Tribunal must refer to the Financial Services Committee (Article 1412; Annex 1412.1) to rule whether disputes in this sector are to be subject to the investment dispute mechanism. This would seem to at least discourage the use of the mechanism in this sector.[39] Finally, reflecting the greater relative importance of state enterprises in the Mexican economy, state enterprises are treated in a separate Chapter 15 of the NAFTA, whereas under the FTA they were dealt with under a national treatment exception clause of the investment Chapter (FTA Article 1602.5–7). Although state enterprises are subject to investment dispute settlement (Article 1503.2), anti-competitive practices, for instance, are not (Article 1501).

The NAFTA contains many other reservations and exceptions to the provisions of Chapter 11, most of which are spelled out in the annexes to the agreement. Mexico continues to exclude the petroleum sector from foreign direct investment. With respect to the US the whole of the maritime sector is excluded, and, with respect to Canada, continuing cultural exemptions remain a thorn in the US side.[40] The reason for the Mexican exclusion is the Mexican Constitution, under which the petroleum sector is to remain state-owned. In practice, PEMEX has been a classic example of an inefficient state-run monopoly, although PEMEX reduced its employment level by almost half (to 120 000) between 1988 and 1993.[41] Importantly, foreign investment restrictions have also recently been weakened with respect to some of the outer-reaches of the vertically and horizontally integrated PEMEX empire, such as secondary petrochemicals, and PEMEX recently announced that foreign firms would receive national treatment with respect to its petrochemical privatization programme.[42] Nevertheless, Mexico has still retained several constitutionally-mandated foreign investment restrictions in other sectors, listed in Annex III (indeed Mexico is the only signatory with Annex III exceptions). These exceptions were based more on political factors than economic ones, and it seems that US and Canadian negotiators believed that to have pushed hard on the issue of Mexican constitutional change to eliminate these restrictions could have derailed the whole negotiation.

What must not be lost sight of here is that in the investment domain (as well as other areas) Mexico has liberalized much more than either the US or Canada. Admittedly, she was starting from much further back, but the Government at least partially opened two sectors that were formerly closed to investment: electricity generation and distribution, and secondary petrochemicals. The US by contrast has not opened sectors that have for historical reasons not been open to foreign ownership (such as the maritime sector). This is in spite of the fact that, whatever the reasons for the closure historically might have been, many of these reasons have lost much of their potency with the passage of time. Thus, for example, Canada and the US refuse to allow the other's citizens or those of Mexico to own air transport services in their territories. Mexico has a similar exception. Canada has retained the cultural carve-outs of the FTA (in Article and Annex 2106 of the NAFTA), but has otherwise continued to liberalize: it was announced in 1992, for example, that the Investment Canada Act would be further liberalized to allow US investors access to the oil and gas sectors at the same US$150 million threshold as in other sectors; at the same time a new policy framework for book publishing, and other cultural policy changes, were also announced.[43]

The full lists of reservations, exceptions, and sectors reserved for the state are contained in Annexes I–IV of the NAFTA – these have been summarized elsewhere.[44] It should be pointed out here, though, that Annex I restrictions cover investment restrictions in industries that are 'frozen', that is, cannot be made more restrictive than they already are. Annex II restrictions, by contrast, are subject to increasing restrictions. These include US investment restrictions in the maritime industry, something that must be viewed as a success for the US maritime lobby but a disappointment for overall liberalization. Annex III restrictions, as already noted, are limited to those mandated by the Mexican constitution. These annexes do not include complex rules of origin definitions which can have the effect of restricting or deterring investment; these are addressed below.

Other irritants still exist, of course: in addition to those mentioned above, issues relating to extraterritoriality, technological consortia, subsidies, and especially Exon-Florio, are examples of US irritants that remain from a Canadian and international perspective. Nevertheless, in spite of the blemishes created by reservations, exceptions, and sectors reserved for the state, the NAFTA formal investment provisions in Chapter 11 constitute a triumph for investment agreements. The reservations are real, but they are outweighed by the positive features of the investment provisions, whether judged against all three governments' goals or against economic criteria.[45]

PROVISIONS RELATING TO DIRECT INVESTMENT WHICH ARE NOT IN NAFTA CHAPTER 11 OR ITS ANNEXES

There are provisions in the NAFTA that bear upon investment but which are not found in the investment Chapter (Chapter 11). Among these are the intellectual property provisions. Part VI of the NAFTA, containing just Chapter 17 (intellectual property), is aimed largely towards bringing developing country law and practice with respect to intellectual property roughly into line with developed country law and practice.

As with other provisions of the NAFTA, much of Chapter 17 is in fact designed to lock in reforms that Mexico had already taken unilaterally with the 1991 passage of a new law on intellectual property, with some steps taken to extend this law.[46] Mexico's major objective in passing this law was parallel with its goal to attract more inward foreign investment; notably it wanted this investment to bring with it the technology transfer needed to modernize the Mexican economy. Even so, US and Canadian concerns remain over Mexican enforcement standards post-ratification.

Chapter 17 also provides for national treatment with respect to intellectual property, but with some exceptions. 'National treatment' in this instance implies that nationals of signing parties operating within the jurisdiction of another signing party, and enterprises under the control of such nationals, are accorded the same rights and privileges pertaining to intellectual property as are nationals of that signing party. In the case of Mexico, the main exception pertains to who holds the copyright in a live performance (under Mexican law it is automatically the performer or performers, but not necessarily so under Canadian or US law), and hence this category is subject to reciprocity. In the case of Canada, it is still maintained by US firms operating in the affected industries that Canada's 'cultural industries' exemption is tantamount to denial of national treatment (but see footnote 40). The exceptions and qualifications notwithstanding, Chapter 17 of the NAFTA reinforces the investment provisions of Chapter 11, in so far as investment and intellectual property policies should be complementary. Relative to what has been negotiated in the domain of intellectual property in the GATT Uruguay round, namely the Trade Related Investment Procedures (TRIPS) agreement, Chapter 17 is highly satisfactory from the perspective of the negotiating parties.

A necessary element of any free trade agreement is a set of rules of origin, because they determine whether a product claimed to be produced in the territory of a party to the agreement does in fact qualify for preferential treatment when sold in the territory of another party. This, in turn, can have important ramifications on investment. Economists are prone to worry about such rules because they tend to create welfare-reducing 'trade diversion' (as indeed will the NAFTA, at least initially).[47] In fact the NAFTA rules of origin in this regard are probably more worrisome than they could have been. These rules, laid out in Chapter 4, are complex. In particular, the simplifying 'roll-up' provisions of the FTA are eliminated. The NAFTA rules were clearly crafted to protect the interests of certain incumbent firms, especially those in the textile and auto sectors where, to qualify as 'North American', a very high regional content must be demonstrated.

With respect to the activities of multinational firms, these rules can be pro-incumbent because newly established operations (that is, investments) of such firms tend to source significantly more inputs from home nations than do long-established firms. The evidence would suggest that over time, the local content of the output of such operations tends to rise. Thus, operations of multinational firms from non-party home nations would tend to be at a disadvantage relative to incumbent firms if they cannot initially meet rules of origin requirements. The same may not, however, apply to newly-established operations of a firm based in another party, whose inputs would most likely come from a nation within the NAFTA.

In consequence, the NAFTA rules of origin implicitly discriminate against new investments of firms not domiciled within the region. The exact amount of this discrimination is dependent upon how valuable the preferential measures are. This in turn depends upon how much trade liberalization is achieved upon the Uruguay Round's implementation.[48] In the textile and apparel industries, for example, all quotas from 1994 onwards are to be removed within ten years. But the exact amount of trade liberalization will depend upon the tariffs on textile and apparel products that will replace the quotas, and for most products under quota these would appear to be high. Thus the NAFTA rules of origin could have the effect of discrimination against new investment in these industries.

Another effect of this rules of origin bias could be to create an incentive for non-North American multinational firms to locate their operations inside the territory of their largest North American national market. To the extent that this is true, the rules of origin would thus induce such firms to locate in the United States in preference to Canada or Mexico. Restrictive rules of origin can also implicitly discriminate against some North American producers as well. Suppose, for example, a Mexican firm is a potential competitor to a US firm, and that the United States accounts for most of the demand for the product of these two firms. Suppose further that both firms source an important component from outside North America whose value is high enough that the final product does not meet rules of origin. Finally, suppose that no North American suppliers of this component exist. Under these circumstances, the Mexican firm might find that its failure to qualify for preferential treatment under the NAFTA renders it uncompetitive relative to the US firm in the US market.

Thus, the rules of origin are among the least free trade oriented of any of the NAFTA Chapters, even if they doubtlessly do meet the goal of protecting certain incumbent (usually US) interests. The purpose of a free trade agreement is, after all, to stimulate commerce and to make firms more competitive. But the pro-incumbency biases of the NAFTA rules of origin work against this. In a broader context, rules of origin will probably not be subject to agreement in any prospective investment accord. But it is important to realize that trade rules can have important investment ramifications, and vice versa.

One more provision in the NAFTA that affects direct investment is the very short Chapter on competition policy, monopolies, and state enterprises (Chapter 15). Article 1501 of this Chapter indicates that each signatory to the NAFTA 'shall adopt or maintain measures to proscribe anti-competitive business conduct and take appropriate action with respect thereto, recognizing that such measures will enhance the fulfilment of the objectives of the Agreement'. This worthy language did enable fulfilment of one important goal, the creation in 1992 by Mexico of a competition (antitrust) law and enforcement agency. This law was doubtlessly enacted to meet the NAFTA requirement and, although it is too early to assess its impact, it, like the intellectual property law, may further Mexican interests in any case.

Nonetheless competition policy as addressed in Article 1501 of the NAFTA remains relatively weak, at least when compared with the other main regional agreement, the EU. In contrast to the rather tentative language of the NAFTA, the Treaty of Rome establishing the European Common Market contains strong language to prohibit monopolies, cartels, and abuse of dominant firm position. This Treaty also provides for rather stringent limitations on state aid to industry, including to state-owned enterprises. And, most importantly, the Treaty of Rome grants to the European Commission significant powers to enforce these provisions. The NAFTA, by contrast, goes little beyond exhortation.[49]

Chapter 15 also sanctions state monopolies (Article 1502) and state-owned enterprises (Article 1503). In addition, it calls for the creation of a working group on trade and competition (Article 1504) to be charged with making recommendations on 'further work as appropriate' within five years of the date of entry into force of the NAFTA.[50] Problems in the competition area are an example of certain investment provisions of the agreement that are not fully resolved. However, many of them have been flagged for further attention by the negotiators. The committees and working groups listed in Annex 2001.2 will be considering many of these issues in the future, and there is, of course, nothing to prevent such issues from being addressed in future agreements in other fora.

CONCLUSION

In sum, the investment provisions of the NAFTA must be judged as highly positive. These provisions lay a groundwork for a more stable environment for investment activity in North America. This positive accomplishment is especially remarkable given the differences in goals and policy priorities of the three signatories, although the fact that these were resolved indicated that they were more apparent than real. Although the conclusion of an investment treaty between a less developed country and two highly developed ones at first seemed highly unlikely, the successful conclusion of the NAFTA rested upon a degree of convergence concerning attitudes towards FDI, not least accompanied by policy reforms that Mexico was prepared to take unilaterally.

The investor-state dispute settlement mechanisms of the investment Chapter must be singled out as a most innovative element of the accord, and a key precedent for other regional and multilateral investment agreements. The negotiation of this section of the investment Chapter should be seen as one of the most remarkable achievements of the whole NAFTA agreement because it provides new standing for multinational firms in disputes with governments. This should provide a more secure investment environment, particularly in Mexico. There are, however, areas for improvement in the dispute settlement mechanism which have been discussed above and to which Articles 1118 and 2022 already accommodate themselves.

Another 'new issue' in the investment arena which may emerge in future investment negotiations is that of subsidies. The control of subsidies to new international investments and other investment incentives is not broached in the NAFTA, even though investment incentives have potentially distortive economic effects. An additional and sensitive concern in this regard is that subsidies are often granted by subnational entities. Other priority areas for improvement in the NAFTA investment provisions include rules of origin and competition policy. Competition policy in particular might some day replace less-than-fair-value provisions of trade law (that is, antidumping, and countervailing measures against subsidies) as a means of regulating potentially anticompetitive trade practices, as is now the case within the European Union.

Although it is premature to ask what influence NAFTA will have on other investment negotiations, it is apparent that there will be further international work on investment issues. Such work continues as part of a prospective Organisation for Economic Co-operation and Development Multilateral Investment Agreement, for example. The OECD has expanded this in its terms of reference beyond its existing instruments, to include new investment issues (on performance requirements, for example) and to explore dispute settlement provisions.[51] While NAFTA did not have much impact on the now completed Uruguay Round of the GATT, the inclusion of trade-related investment measures together with a commitment to discuss investment questions more broadly in the future, has put investment clearly on the World Trade Organization (WTO) agenda. And finally, within one week of US Congressional endorsement of the NAFTA agreement in late 1993, the heads of state of the APEC countries endorsed in principle the idea of a voluntary Asia-Pacific investment agreement. This bore fruit in the successful negotiation of a non-binding investment code in Jakarta in November 1994.[52]

Thus, the investment provisions of the NAFTA agreement point to new directions for fora which have found investment negotiations particularly prickly. In addition, they represent a further step towards a new *lex mercatoria* and international legal standing that nation states and increasingly globalized firms are seeking.[53] More broadly the NAFTA investment provisions have further endorsed a rules-based international system in which the complementarity of trade and investment issues is implicitly recognized. This is significant if only because it mirrors the continued importance of international investment flows to economic growth, which has become particularly evident during the past twenty years. Although the next steps are not entirely clear, investment issues cannot help but figure prominently whatever the future of the world trading system. Furthermore, given the transposition in relative importance of global trade and investment flows since 1950, it could be argued that ultimately a comprehensive multilateral investment accord will be as important for the global economy of the next fifty years as international trade agreements have been for the past fifty years.

NOTES

1. This asymmetry is echoed in trade data: according to the Bank of Mexico, in 1992 the US was the destination for 81% of Mexican exports and 71% of her imports; the comparable figures for Canada were 2.2% and 1.7% respectively. See Banco de Mexico (1993), table 53 p. 312, and table 58 p. 317. See also Husband *et al.* (1991) and Hufbauer and Schott (1992).
2. Hill and Wonnacott (1991) and Wonnacott (1991). In the private sector, fears of a dilution of the gains established under the FTA were also recognized: see for example, Royal Bank of Canada (1990), p. 8.
3. Wonnacott (1990), p. 4.
4. Carillo (1991), pp. 649–50
5. United Nations Centre on Transnational Corporations (1992), p. 14.
6. Carillo (1991), pp. 658–9.
7. *Reglamento de la Ley para Promover la Inversión Mexicana y Regular la Inversión Extranjera,* 16 May 1989.
8. Banco de Mexico (1993), p. 216.
9. For example, see Carillo (1991); Banco de Mexico (1993). See also Ortiz, 'NAFTA and Foreign Investments in Mexico: Sectoral Impacts and the Financial Sector', in Rugman (1993), United Nations Centre on Transnational Corporations (1992), pp. 13–20; also various business handbooks, such as Price Waterhouse (1991) and Ernst & Young (1992).
10. See *Diario Oficial* 27 December 1993. For an English summary of the legislation, see Valdez (1994).

11. For example Mexican Trade Minister Jaime Serra also announced in late 1992 a 'Program to Boost Competitiveness', which led to a law on economic competitiveness (*Ley Federal de Competencia Economica*, see *Diario Oficial*, 24 December 1992 creating a new Federal Commission on Competitiveness) and which tends to further liberalization. Also the Mexican Government has recognized the importance of continued liberalization in its investment promotion activities abroad. For example, SECOFI (*la Secretaría de Comercio y Fomento Industrial*) notes in conjunction with two Canadian firms: 'Foreign investment has been attracted to Mexico by the dismantling of investment restrictions [which had preceded NAFTA] and the country's economic recovery. It is important to note that it is not only NAFTA that has attracted the new investment ...' ('Mexico/Canada – Forging A New Relationship', p. 26, column 1 (published by the Mexican Embassy and SECOFI's representative office in Canada).
12. Loizides and Rhéaume (1993), p. 17.
13. See Graham and Krugman (1995).
14. See Ahmad *et al.* (1994) pp. 193–5.
15. See 'APEC Officials Agree on Code for Investors', *Financial Times*, 11 November 1994.
16. However, in its recent preliminary discussions of a prospective Multilateral Investment Agreement, the OECD is also considering a binding national treatment provision. See Smith (1994), and UNCTAD-DTCI (1994), p. 280.
17. Local governments are not required actually to list their exceptions. Thus, the case could be argued that *de facto* the obligations will be difficult to enforce at this level. One consequence is that preferential purchasing by these entities (for example, under various state-level 'buy American' laws in the United States) might not be held in violation of the national treatment provisions. Concerning a related issue, government procurement is governed by rules spelled out in Chapter 10 of the NAFTA agreement. This chapter calls for, *inter alia*, further negotiation on state, provincial, and local government procurement prior to 1999.
18. The illustrative list of TRIMs includes domestic content requirements, trade balancing requirements, or restrictions on imports of products used in or related to the local production of a foreign-owned enterprise. It applies to goods only.
19. An examination of the economic effects of performance requirements and a bibliography of the relevant literature is contained in Graham and Krugman (1991).
20. On this, see Rugman and Gestrin (1993).
21. See Warner and Rugman (1994), pp. 945–82.
22. UNCTAD's Division on Transnational Corporations and Investments estimated that 570 bilateral treaties for the promotion and protection of FDI had been negotiated by January 1994. See UNCTAD-DTCI (1994), pp. 277, 279.
23. As a technical matter, it should be noted that the relevant provisions of the NAFTA pertaining to expropriation of investor property and compensation thereof (Article 1110) do not pertain to intellectual property; intellectual property rights are, however, spelled out in Chapter 17 of the NAFTA (see also page 109, below).
24. The relevant article (1109) does not apply, however, to transfers associated with issuing, trading, or dealing in securities.
25. The investor can clearly press claims against the governments of Canada, Mexico, or the United States and apparently also state and provincial governments of these signatories.
26. However, *in extremis*, Articles 1115 and 1138 allow some latitude concerning investment disputes with respect to both traditional state-state dispute settlement under Chapter 20 and national security provisions in Article 2102.
27. Rogelio Ramirez De la O, (1993), pp. 78–9.
28. Horlick and DeBusk (1993), p. 53.
29. Wisner (1993).
30. Horlick and DeBusk (1993), p. 56.
31. *Inside US Trade*, **10** (5), 31 January 1992, p. 10.
32. This is particularly true given the flexibility of ICC Rules, which have been used for traditional commercial dispute settlement as well as investor-state and even some narrowly defined state-state conflicts. See Toope (1990), pp. 204–15; see also Lange and Born (1987).
33. Horlick and DeBusk (1993), pp. 53–4

34. Toope (1990), p. 205. Precedents also already exist for ICC arbitration to be stipulated in investor-state contracts. See *ibid.*, p. 213, also Reisman (1989), p. 757. Indeed an international lawyer affiliated with the ICC in the 1960s pointed out that the involvement of the ICC in investor-state dispute settlement was common, and had been so since 1922. Furthermore, an example was noted of an ICC arbitration clause in a contract between the Nigerian Government and a Canadian oil company in the 1960s. See Böckstiegel (1965), p. 581.
35. A. Redfern and M. Hunter (1986), *Law and Practice of International Commercial Arbitration*, as quoted in Toope (1990), p. 203.
36. See Part IV 'Resolving Extraterritoriality Problems' in Lange and Born (1987), pp. 44–57.
37. For the United States, see Hufbauer and Schott (1993). For Canada, see Gestrin and Rugman (1993). Concerning Mexico, see Ortiz, 'NAFTA and Foreign Investment in Mexico', in Rugman (1993). See also Horlick and DeBusk (1993), and Fasken Campbell Godfrey (1993). In Mexico, it is also quite apparent that the Mexican Government attaches prime importance to the passage of NAFTA. See, for example, 'Into the Spotlight', *The Economist* Survey of Mexico, 13 February 1993, pp. 6–8; also *Financial Times* special survey on North American Free Trade, 12 May 1993, 'Impact on Mexico – Overwhelming Importance Attached to Pact', p. 28. See also page 102 above.
38. Under Annex 1607.3 of the FTA, Canada agreed to increase the threshold of reviewable direct acquisitions by US investors from $CDN 5 million to $CDN 150 million in four years, and to eliminate the review of indirect acquisitions by US investors over the same period. In the NAFTA, Mexican and Canadian thresholds will probably converge over time, but there was also a change to the method of calculation of the annual adjustment for the review thresholds. The effect of this was to adjust the thresholds for economic growth as well as inflation.
39. Importantly, both the telecom and financial services sectors have been traditionally among a few qualitatively different industries, partly due to their status as services rather than goods industries. But with the GATS (General Agreement on Trade in Services) agreement in the Uruguay Round, there is more than a hint that international trade in services, too, will be subject to further international agreement that will also have an impact on international investment.
40. There remains some controversy over whether the Canadian cultural exemption may have been widened in the NAFTA compared to the FTA, due to the inclusion of copyrights in the NAFTA. In practice, however, as Hufbauer and Schott (1993) point out, the cultural industry exemptions are rarely invoked. Furthermore Article 1112.1 notes that in the event of inconsistencies between the investment chapter and another chapter, the other chapter shall take precedence. Thus Article 2106 (and Annex 2106), which codify the Canadian cultural industries exemption as it appears in the FTA, would seem to take precedence in this case.
41 Fredell (1993), p. 6.
42. *ibid.* pp. 4–5, 8.
43. 'Amendment to the Investment Canada Act', Investment Canada Press Release, 18 June 1992. The bill formalizing these provisions was enacted in June 1993.
44. There are seven annexes. Annexes I–III are covered in Gestrin and Rugman (1993), pp. 12–19; see also Hufbauer and Schott (1993). Annexes IV–VII cover mostly historical carve-outs in all three countries, such as broadcasting, aviation, fisheries, postal services, and so on.
45. See especially Hufbauer and Schott (1993), chapter 4. Hufbauer and Schott grade the investment provisions of the NAFTA as 'A–' on a scale of A to F, where A is outstanding and F is failing. Canadian reaction has also been largely positive, although Gestrin and Rugman (1993) also draw attention to specious US national security arguments in the US which serve to restrict FDI.
46. Specific extensions are discussed in Hufbauer and Schott (1993), p. 85.
47. 'GATT Mexico Review Praises Reforms, Flags NAFTA, Dumping Concerns', *Inside U.S. Trade*, 23 April 1993, p. 1.
48. At the time of writing, the US Congress had not ratified the Uruguay Round and hence, whether it would in fact be implemented was still subject to uncertainty.
49. Some ideas for improvement of the NAFTA in this area are contained in Graham and Warner (1994).
50. This is only one of a series of committees and working groups summarized in Annex 2001.2, which have been instituted to address some of the more problematic areas which remain in

the agreement. These include financial services and private commercial disputes (committees), and rules of origin and trade, and competition issues (working groups).
51. See Smith (1994); UNCTAD-DTCI (1994), p. 280; and Organization for Economic Cooperation and Development (1994), p. 26.
52. See 'APEC Officials Agree on Code for Investors', *Financial Times*, 11 November 1994.
53. See, for example, 'Multinationals Seek Investment Treaty', *Financial Times*, 9 May 1994, p. 2.

BIBLIOGRAPHY

Ahmad, Ash, *et al.* (1994) '*Formal and Informal Investment Barriers in the G-7 Countries: the Country Chapters*' (Occasional Paper **1** (1), Ottawa: Industry Canada.
Banco de Mexico (1993) *The Mexican Economy 1993*, Banco de Mexico.
Böckstiegel, K.H. (1965) 'Arbitration of Disputes Between States and Private Enterprises in the International Chamber of Commerce', *American Journal of International Law*, **59**.
Carillo, Arturo (1991) 'The New Mexican Revolution: Economic Reform and the 1989 Regulations of the Law for the Promotion of Mexican Investment and the Regulation of Foreign Investment', *George Washington Journal of International Law and Economics*, **24** (3).
Eden, Lorraine (ed.) (1994) *Multinationals in North America*, The University of Calgary Press for Industry Canada.
Ernst & Young (1992) *Doing Business in Mexico*, Ernst & Young.
Fasken Campbell Godfrey (1993) '*The North American Free Trade Agreement: A Guide for Business*' (law firm report), Toronto: Fasken Campbell Godfrey.
Fredell, Eric (1993) *Opportunities in the Mexican Energy Sector: NAFTA and Beyond*, SRI International: Business Intelligence Program.
Gestrin, Michael and Alan M. Rugman (1993) 'The NAFTA's Impact on the North American Investment Regime', *C.D. Howe Institute Commentary*, no. 42.
Globerman, Steven (ed.) (1991) *Continental Accord: North American Economic Integration*, Vancouver: The Fraser Institute
Globerman, Steven and Michael Walker (eds) (1993) *Assessing NAFTA: A Trinational Analysis*, Vancouver: The Fraser Institute.
Graham, Edward M. and Paul R. Krugman (1991) 'Trade Related Investment Measures', in Schott (1991).
Graham, Edward M. and Paul R. Krugman (1995) *Foreign Direct Investment in the United States*, 3rd ed., Washington: Institute for International Economics.
Graham, Edward M. and Warner, Mark A. (1994) 'Competition Policy and North American Direct Investment and Trade, in Eden (1994).
Hill, Roderick, and Ronald J. Wonnacott (eds) (1991) 'Free Trade with Mexico: What Form Should It Take?', *C.D. Howe Institute Commentary*, no. 28.
Horlick, Gary N. and F. Amanda DeBusk (1993) 'Dispute Resolution under NAFTA: Building on the U.S.-Canada FTA, GATT and ICSID', *Journal of International Arbitration*, **10**, no. 1.
Hufbauer, Gary Clyde, and Jeffrey J. Schott (1992) *North American Free Trade: Issues and Recommendations*, Washington: Institute for International Economics.
Hufbauer, Gary Clyde, and Jeffrey J. Schott (1993) *NAFTA: An Assessment*, Washington: Institute for International Economics.
Husband, David, *et al.* (1991) 'The Opportunities and Challenges of North American Free Trade: A Canadian Perspective', Ottawa: Investment Canada Working Paper No. 7.

Lange, Dieter and Gary Born (eds) (1987) *The Extraterritorial Application of National Laws: The International Chamber of Commerce*, Deventer, The Netherlands: ICC/Kluwer Law and Taxation Publishers.

Loizides, Stelios and Gilles Rhéaume (1993) '*The North American Free Trade Agreement: Implications for Canada*', *Conference Board of Canada*, report 99-93.

Nymark, Alan and Emmy Verdun (1994) 'Canadian Investment and NAFTA', in Alan M. Rugman, *Foreign Investment and NAFTA*, Columbia, South Carolina: University of South Carolina Press.

Organisation for Economic Co-operation and Development (1994), *Annual Report 1993*, Paris: OECD.

Price Waterhouse (1991) *Doing Business in Mexico*, Price Waterhouse.

Reisman, W. Michael (1989) 'The Breakdown of the Control Mechanism in ICSID Arbitration', *Duke Law Journal*, **4**, September.

Rogelio, Ramirez de la O. (1993) 'The North American Free Trade Agreement from a Mexican Perspective', in Globerman and Walker (1993).

Royal Bank of Canada (1990) 'Mexico-U.S. Free Trade Talks: Why Canada Should Get Involved', *Econoscope* special edition, September.

Rugman, Alan (1994) *Multinationals and NAFTA*, Columbia, South Carolina: University of South Carolina Press.

Rugman, Alan and Michael Gestrin (1993) 'The Investment Provisions of the NAFTA', in Globerman and Walker (1993).

Safarian, A.E. (1993) 'Investment Aspects of the Canada-U.S. Free Trade Agreement', in Murray G. Smith and Frank Stone (eds) *Assessing the Canada-U.S. Free Trade Agreement*, Halifax: Institute for Research on Public Policy.

Schott, Jeffrey J. (ed.) (1991) *Completing the Uruguay Round: A Results-Oriented Approach to the GATT Trade Negotiations*, Washington, DC: Institute for International Economics.

Schott, Jeffrey J. and Murray G. Smith (eds) (1988) *The Canada-United States Free Trade Agreement: The Global Impact*, Washington: Institute for International Economics and Halifax: The Institute for Research on Public Policy.

Shaiken, Harley (1990) *Mexico in the Global Economy: High Technology and Work Organization in Export Industries*, San Diego: Center for U.S.-Mexican Studies, University of California, Monograph Series 33.

Smith, Alister (1994) '*The Development of a Multilateral Investment Agreement at the OECD: A Preview*', November, Georgetown University Law Center Conference on An APEC Investment Regime (mimeo).

Steger, Debra P. (1988) *A Concise Guide to the Canada-United States Free Trade Agreement*, Toronto: Carswell.

Toope, Stephen J. (1990) *Mixed International Arbitration: Studies in Arbitration Between States and Private Persons*, Cambridge, England: Grotius Publications, Ltd. for the Research Centre for International Law.

UNCTAD Division on Transnational Corporations and Investment (1994) *World Investment Report 1994: Transnational Corporations, Employment, and the Workplace*, Geneva and New York: United Nations.

United Nations Centre on Transnational Corporations (1992) 'Foreign Direct Investment and Industrial Restructuring in Mexico: Government Policy, Corporate Strategies and Regional Integration', *Current Studies* Series A, no. 18, (ST/CTC/SER.A/18), New York: United Nations

Valdez, Abelardo L. (1994) 'The New Mexican Foreign Investment Law', *Direct Investment in North America*, March, Special Report.

Warner, Mark A.A. and Alan M. Rugman (1994) 'Competitiveness: An Emerging Strategy of Discrimination in U.S. Antitrust and R&D Policy?', *Law and Policy in International Business*, **25**, 3.

Wisner, Robert (1993) *Investment Policy and Dispute Resolution Under NAFTA*, University of Toronto Law School (mimeo).

Wonnacott, Ronald J. (1990) 'Canada and the U.S.-Mexico Free Trade Negotiations', *C. D. Howe Institute Commentary*, no. 21.

Wonnacott, Ronald J. (1991) *The Economics of Overlapping Free Trade Areas and the Mexican Challenge*, Washington and Toronto: Canadian-American Committee

9. Canada, the Free Trade Agreement and US trade actions: the implications for business

Mary-Anne Stevens

INTRODUCTION

This chapter discusses American trade actions as they were applied to Canadian companies pursuant to the Free Trade Agreement (FTA). One of Canada's goals in entering into the Free Trade Agreement was to control the number of trade actions that American firms were initiating against their Canadian competitors. The chapter explores what Canada was hoping to achieve through a negotiated agreement, the actual dispute mechanisms that were negotiated as part of the Agreement, trade action activity from January 1989 until 1992 and the implications for business. The chapter also discusses the North American Free Trade Agreement (NAFTA) and the dispute settlement mechanisms negotiated as part of that Agreement.

WHAT CANADA HOPED TO ACHIEVE

The Canadian Government was clearly worried about increased American protectionism and the use of trade remedy laws when the free trade negotiations were initiated. The Government felt that if the American deficit was not reduced, if domestic demand remained low and if the American dollar remained weak, then the stage was set for increased American protectionism. In the light of this scenario the Government felt that the Free Trade Agreement (FTA) would be very important in securing the American market and ensuring that it remained open to Canadian goods. The Government's position was that increased American protectionism would have a negative impact on both export based industries and domestically-focused industries. This contention was based on the fact that the US is Canada's largest trading partner. To lose this market would have a serious effect on the economy of Canada (Department of Finance Canada, 1988; Doern and Tomlin, 1991).

The Canadian Government was concerned with the number of trade actions being brought against Canadian products. Between 1980 and 1986 the US had filed fifty countervailing and anti-dumping cases against Canada (Rugman and Anderson, 1989). The actions were brought by companies and industries that felt they were being injured by Canadian imports. The Canadian Government did not want the trend towards trade actions to escalate.

Trade actions can be brought in the US where a company can show that it is being materially injured by imports. A company can ask the International Trade Commission (ITC) to impose tariffs to correct the unfair situation. In the case of countervail actions, when the US Department of Commerce and the US International Trade Commission receive a complaint, they undertake a preliminary investigation to determine if the import received a subsidy, if the reduction in price and the volume of goods could cause significant damage to the complainant, and if the subsidy was the cause of the injury. If the complaint is found to be valid, then a preliminary finding is issued and the importers must post a cash deposit or a bond equal to the estimated subsidy. A further investigation is then carried out to determine the full extent of the injury and a countervailing duty may then be calculated. Negotiations may be undertaken before the final determination in order to come to some sort of settlement. Until the FTA the final determination could only be appealed in the domestic courts. Court actions could take years, during which time the exporters had to pay the duties (Lipsey and York, 1988).

In a survey done by Rugman and Anderson (1989) it was found that the ITC voted in 70 per cent of the cases that the American complainant had suffered material injury. This meant that the finding would have to be appealed by the Canadians. Only 30 per cent of the ITC's findings were upheld, but the investigation and appeal was an expensive process which Canadians had to undertake in the American court system.

There were and are four main types of actions being brought by American firms and industries. Actions can be taken to safeguard industries from imports even though the imports are being brought in fairly. Antidumping measures are taken where imported goods are being offered below cost. Countervail actions can be taken where unfair government policies give imports an advantage. There are also import restrictions which can be placed on countries that are involved in unfair trade practices. Safeguard actions, antidumping actions and countervail actions are primarily used against Canadian imports. The apparent trend towards an increase in trade actions during the 1980s was worrisome to the Canadian Government and exporters (Doern and Tomlin, 1991).

Developing some sort of dispute settlement mechanism was of great importance to the Canadian negotiators. The Canadians had suggested that a set of joint rules be established to govern trade disputes between the two countries. A subsidies code would be developed that would outline prohibited and permissible practices. This proposal was not accepted, and existing trade law was left intact. What was agreed to was an appellate procedure that allowed a review of domestic trade remedy law in a more bipartisan manner. It was felt that the Chapter Nineteen dispute settlement mechanisms would secure access for Canadian exporters by making countervail and antidumping actions less politically motivated, and by shortening the appeal process to less than a year (Lipsey and York, 1988).

Under the North American Free Trade Agreement (NAFTA) between Canada, the United States and Mexico, a dispute mechanism similar to the existing mechanisms in the FTA was developed. Mexico had similar concerns to Canada regarding trade actions brought by the US against Mexican goods. They too hoped that the dispute mechanisms would quell any trends towards protectionism (Meehan, 1992).

CHAPTER 18 AND 19 DISPUTE SETTLEMENT MECHANISMS

Chapters 18 and 19 were the negotiated response to Canada's desire to deal with American trade remedy law. The two sections set up appellate mechanisms in the form of binational panels which can review decisions based on national trade remedy laws. Chapter 18 provided for general dispute settlement provisions and Chapter 19 dealt specifically with antidumping and countervailing duty applications.

Chapter 18 started by suggesting that any matter which affected the operation of the Agreement should be dealt with through a consultative process (Article 1804), but if consultation failed then the matter would be referred to the Canada-United States Trade Commission (Article 1805). The Commission was composed of equal numbers of representatives from both countries and it was the Commission that chose the arbitrators. The Commission referred disputes to an arbitration panel when consultation failed (Article 1806). The panel was made up of five members. There were two Canadians and two Americans, with a fifth member chosen jointly (Article 1807).

Matters reached the Commission through a notification procedure. Upon notification there were 30 days in which to pursue consultations. If settlement had not been reached in 30 days then the Commission referred the matter to the arbitration panel. The panel had three months after a chairman was appointed to issue a preliminary report containing findings of fact, which was a determination as to whether the matter was inconsistent with the FTA and the recommendations of the panel. The parties had 14 days to respond to the report.

The panel had to issue a final report within 30 days of the issuance of the initial report (Article 1807).

Relatively few binational panel actions were brought under the Chapter 18 provisions, the Chapter 19 provisions were utilized far more. Chapter 19 was the answer to Canada's request for a subsidies code, and dealt specifically with appeals from antidumping and countervailing duty cases. The dispute mechanism was meant to increase predictability and security for Canadian exporters. Chapter 19 settlement mechanisms replaced judicial review by domestic courts of countervailing and antidumping orders with a binational trade panel (Article 1904).

Under Chapter 19, either government could seek the review of an antidumping or countervailing duty order. Existing trade remedy law remained the same in each country. However, relief that was granted by the national authority (the Department of Commerce or International Trade Commission in the US and the Department of National Revenue or the Canadian Import Tribunal in Canada) could be subject to challenge and review by the binational panel. The findings of the panels were binding on both governments. The panel had the ability to determine whether the law was properly applied by the administering authority. If the law was improperly applied then the issue was sent back to the administering authority to correct the matter and make a new determination (Article 1904). The Chapter 19 binational panel was made up of five members, who were chosen in a similar fashion to the Chapter 18 panel.

Either party could request a panel review within 30 days of notification of a determination by the national authority, and the authority which issued the order had the right to appear before the panel. The panel applied the legal principles that the courts of the importing party would apply. The panel could uphold the determination or send it back to the determining authority for action which was consistent with the panel's decision. Once the panel had received all materials and heard all arguments, they had 90 days to issue a written decision. The rules for filing were developed so that a final decision would be rendered within 315 days from the date on which a request for a panel was made (Article 1904).

Under Chapters 19 and 20 of NAFTA, the existing mechanisms that were developed under the FTA have been retained and redrafted to include a third party, Mexico. Consultation is to be used where possible, and where consultation is ineffective a dispute settlement panel will be used to resolve matters.

The general dispute settlement mechanism requires that the two parties involved, each choose two panel members (each country will maintain a roster of qualified individuals) and the fifth member will be chosen by consensus of the parties involved. The panel applies the law of the importing country when reviewing the complaint and will either uphold the determination or remit it back to the appropriate administrative body for the appropriate remedial action.

Countervailing duty actions and antidumping actions will also be dealt with by a panel using similar mechanisms to those set out in the FTA. NAFTA goes further than the FTA and creates an extraordinary challenge procedure which may be used to appeal the decision of a panel. It has been stated that the Chapter 19 provisions have been further strengthened by a clause which prohibits the use of local laws to frustrate the binational panel's decisions. A special committee can be established to determine if a country's domestic law frustrates the decisions of a panel, and actions can be taken to ensure that corrective measures are taken by the offending country (Government of Canada 1992).

Nothing in NAFTA affects the ability of any of the countries to bring trade actions. Mexico, like Canada, wanted an agreement in order to deal with what they viewed as American protectionism and establish some ground rules for Mexico. Mexican exporters felt that when they made successful inroads into the American market, the Americans were quick to invoke antidumping procedures in order to frustrate trade (Meehan, 1992). The Canadian experience under the FTA has shown that the provisions of a free trade agreement may not stop trade actions, but they can be used so that trade actions are dealt with more quickly.

CONTINUING TRADE ACTIONS AND THE IMPLICATIONS FOR BUSINESS

Canada's desire in negotiating Chapters 18 and 19 of the FTA and Chapters 19 and 20 of NAFTA was to curtail trade remedy actions against Canadian exporters. The Government wanted predictability and secure access for Canadian industries. The process may be more predictable under the dispute mechanism provisions, but many industries would argue that their access to the American market is no more secure then it was prior to either the FTA or NAFTA. Trade remedy actions have been brought against a diverse number of industries ranging from agricultural products to stretch limousines. Businesses and industries in the US have continued to request investigations, and the ITC and the Commerce Department have continued to make findings against Canadian products. Investigations have been undertaken against such products as beer, limousines, pork products, automobiles, lumber, engine parts, portable seismographs, iron construction castings and brass sheets and strips.

American businesses have not reduced the number of trade remedy actions or the lobbying for trade protection. For example, between the inception of the FTA and 1992, Canadians had to launch two disputes requiring Chapter 18 panels and 16 disputes requiring Chapter 19 panels. The United States had filed five Chapter 19 disputes (Dearden and Palmeter, 1992). The Chapter 19 disputes focused on raspberries, pork, steel rail, and replacement parts for paving equipment exports. A number of decisions upheld the American authority's orders and a number of decisions remitted issues back to the US to be reconsidered. For example, in the case of red raspberries the duties were ultimately rescinded. There were five applications relating to pork exports, which covered the export of live swine, fresh killed and frozen pork. The duties on live swine were rescinded. The issues in the fresh killed and frozen pork had to do with provincial and federal subsidies. The panel affirmed some of the duties and sent other determinations back to the Commerce Department. The first pork dispute was brought in 1989, and disputes have continued under NAFTA. The actions brought regarding new steel rail all went in favour of the American complainants. Actions were also brought concerning beer and softwood lumber, and disputes involving these products have continued under NAFTA. Disputes involving products ranging from carpeting and apples to steel products have been brought pursuant to NAFTA.

The two Chapter 18 disputes dealt with fish landing requirements in Canada and automobile parts. The fish landing rights were found to be protectionist as opposed to conservation oriented. Based on the panel's ruling, the matter was settled. One of the matters dealing with automobiles was decided in Canada's favour.

Most of the actions were brought under the Chapter 19 provisions to deal with dumping and what Americans perceived as unfair government subsidies. The Chapter 19 provisions meant that Canadians did not have to deal with the American court system in order to launch an appeal. The strict timetable for appeals outlined in Chapter 19 also benefited Canadians who might otherwise have had to fund proceedings that might last for years in the national court system. The government became the instituting party and not the individual, which meant that the individual no longer had to shoulder the cost of bringing an appeal in the American court system alone. However, businesses still had the burden of paying duties in the interim when there was a finding against a business or an industry. They also had the burden of supplying data to the Government. Canadian businesses and government do not have the supportive tradition that exists between American businesses and their government.

Nothing in Chapter 19 of the FTA or Chapter 19 of NAFTA stops the use of American trade remedy law, but the provisions have helped to streamline the appeal procedure.

Whether the FTA dispute mechanisms worked or not depended on who was doing the talking. The fact that trade disputes did not stop disappointed some (Herman, 1990). The fact that disputes were dealt with in a more streamlined manner was cited as a benefit by others (Horlick and Debusk, 1991). Both observations are true. For the exporter the reality was and is that with or without the FTA or NAFTA, Americans would and have continued to bring trade actions against Canadian goods. Under both agreements the cost factor of impeded trade still exists, but the costs are reduced because the Government brings the redressing actions and the time period for a decision is reduced. The FTA and NAFTA have also allowed greater access to trade actions by Canadians against US goods, because the actions are brought by the Government and not the individual.

Some suggested that the US was not abiding by the spirit of the FTA by continuing their adversarial approach to trade (Crawford, 1992). This adversarial approach has continued under NAFTA. Therefore, Canadian businesses will have to continue to fight for a piece of the American pie.

Besides the trade barriers created by ITC investigations, the Americans have also been utilizing GATT to protect home markets. The US has brought a number of trade disputes against products such as ice cream and sugar to GATT panels. The FTA and NAFTA do not preclude the use of GATT tribunals, which essentially means that the parties can choose whatever forum they feel is most appropriate.

The Americans have also been using various border measures which impede exports. For example, potato carriers have been forced to unload entire loads at US borders under the guise of a quality assurance programme. Meat exporters had experienced similar treatment (Free Trade Observer, issues 4 and 6, 1990). Eddy Match had a truckload of matches sent back because the country of origin was not stamped on the packages. This requirement had never been enforced before, although it had been part of the US regulations (Freeman, 1991).

The US Government has also utilized Section 301 of the US Trade Act to bring actions against Canadian companies. Several American breweries filed petitions pursuant to Section 301 claiming that Canadian pricing, distribution and listing practices were an unfair trade barrier.

For Canadian exporters, the current approach of American businesses and the US Government means that in order to penetrate the US market, they will have to be prepared to fight appeals and export under the shadow of possible investigations and duties. This means that they continue to deal with uncertainty. Canadian exporters will have to monitor developments and develop relationships with government agencies in order to combat the current situation. Companies are already taking proactive steps such as lodging complaints against American imports. For example, the Canadian Government was asked to investigate carpet imports, which led to a countervailing duty of 11.97 per cent being imposed on American-made carpets (Free Trade Observer, issue 31, 1992).

The Canadian governments, both Federal and Provincial, have had subsidy programmes called into question, and will continue to have their subsidy programmes scrutinized by the US. The Americans have used the FTA to attack the subsidy programmes which they feel are unfair.

Canadian governments have on occasion altered trade policies because of American trade actions. For example, when US Customs set up border meat inspections, the Canadian decided to alter their policy of destination inspections and they too started border inspections. These slowed the importing process because goods had to be unloaded and reloaded at the border and then unloaded at the final destination (Motherwell, 1991).

Canadian businesses have a number of strategic options. They may choose to avoid the trade issue altogether by choosing a domestic focus. The Ontario wine industry is a good example of this. The industry as a whole has purposely focused on domestic consumption in order to build market share. The danger of this choice is that they may face American competition on their own turf. Businesses may choose to export to the US and prepare themselves for possible trade barriers by developing industry associations and relationships with the various government agencies. For example, the pork industry has fought a number of trade actions and so has the lumber industry. Some businesses may decide to set up operations in the US, especially if this is the target market, and export back into Canada. With NAFTA, businesses now have the option of setting up operations in Mexico, although geographic distances may deter some businesses. Firms which have a specific expertise that can be marketed globally may choose a global strategy as opposed to focusing on the North American market. Industry characteristics and firm size will obviously affect the choices that a business makes.

The strategic implications for foreign firms faced with trade actions are similar to many of the issues faced by domestic firms, but, the problems are compounded because they are not party to the FTA or NAFTA.

Continuing trade disputes suggest several implications for Europe and Asia. First, the use of Canada as a gateway into the US may be a questionable strategy. Secondly, exporters are faced with the possibility of increased trade actions, and thirdly the protectionist implications of the North American trading bloc could affect the choices of exporters.

Firstly, the idea of using Canada as a gateway to the US may not hold as much appeal in the light of continuing trade actions brought by the US against products originating in Canada. Foreign companies looking to set up plants in North America may decide it is easier to set up in the US, which is the target market, rather than face the potential of trade restrictions on Canadian goods exported to the US. The Honda case is a good example of this dilemma. The US contended that Honda did not meet the component requirements set out in the FTA, which would allow it to be treated as a Canadian good. The dispute dealt partly with the inclusion of interest costs in the calculation of territorial content, and partly with the inclusion of intermediate materials from third countries. The US contended that only interest from mortgaged land could be included, while Canada asserted that all interest costs relating to land, buildings and equipment are eligible. The US contended that engines which include third party elements are not originating parts and therefore could not be considered when determining territorial content. Under the FTA 50 per cent of the cost of the automobile had to be incurred in either Canada or the US.

After a two year audit, US Customs claimed that Honda fell below the 50% level (Free Trade Observer, issue 30, 1992). Three other automobile plants were also targeted for audits. This sort of activity has some obvious implications. For example, foreign companies may decide that if they are going to face trade actions anyway, they might as well set up in some third country where they can enjoy less expensive production facilities and fight their trade battles through GATT.

The second implication is that direct exporters to the US may receive similar attention from US industry as Canadian exporters when it comes to trade actions. This sort of attention has been evidenced in the auto market, where Japanese sales have been hurt by the lobbying of US automakers. Canada is not the only country to face the trade barriers used by the US. Europe and Asia may have to cope with a regional trading bloc that is not user friendly. The US is worried about the economy, and is worried about past liberal trading policies which some perceive as hurting their competitive position.

The US appears to have moved into an era of government intervention and managed trade. The 1992 trip by President George Bush and auto industry leaders to Japan and the subsequent trade missions by President Clinton are an indication of this trend towards managed trade as opposed to free trade. The use of Section 301 of the Omnibus Trade and Competitiveness Act 1988 to accuse countries of unfair trade practices is another indication of the Government's willingness to manage trade (Phillips, 1992; Economist, 22 September 1990). If this trend accelerates to a more protectionist level, it will obviously affect trade relations with Canada, Europe and Asia.

Further evidence of perceived US protectionism can be found in criticisms by a GATT tribunal which was reviewing American trade practices. The GATT tribunal accused the US of using protectionist measures to curb imports, and criticized the US for its growing use of antidumping procedures (Globe and Mail, 13 March 1992).

The third implication is that NAFTA compounds the fear that America is becoming more of a trading bloc and more protectionist. The Agreement could mean that Europeans and Asian companies will be faced by even more managed trade. Several of the provisions in the agreement could be seen as strengthening trade within the trading bloc to the exclusion of outsiders. For example, the rules regarding foreign textiles and yarns in apparel have been strengthened. To qualify for preferential treatment, more textiles and yarns from North America will have to be used.

The automobile industry is another area where local content is required. The requirement for cars and light trucks has been increased from 50 per cent to 62.5 per cent. This would appear to be a move to bolster the domestic industry at the expense of foreign producers.

The preamble to the Agreement could also be seen as the trading bloc overtaking multilateral trade. It speaks of stronger ties between the three countries and the creation of greater co-operation between the parties. This might suggest that the parties will be focused on one another at the expense of foreign entities. NAFTA could end up diverting trade from traditional third party suppliers to suppliers within the trading bloc (Economist, 27 June 1992). European and Asian firms may be viewed as second class citizens in the light of the energy that is being put into trilateral co-operation. These fears were expressed by Japan and Malaysia when they voiced their opposition to the Agreement on the basis that it split the world into trading blocs (Cooke, 1992).

Between 1987 and 1991, the US increased its trade with Mexico to $33 billion dollars. Mexico is now the third biggest trading partner of the US. Mexican trade with the US was $31 billion in 1991 (Mexican/Canadian trade is $2.2 billion with Canada having a trade deficit of approximately $1 billion in 1990) (Dearden and Palmeter, 1992). For the Agreement to be effective, Mexico needs to increase its standard of living and move into the world of industrialized nations, so that it can consume exports from Canada and the US. Given these two facts, increased trade and the desire to move Mexico into the 'first world', America's energy could be focused within the trading bloc, where they envision the biggest gains for the economies of the partners (Economist, 15 August 1992). This could mean that non-member exporters will find it more difficult to access the American market.

It has also been suggested that NAFTA is viewed as an alternative to GATT and not a companion document. If this is true, then it could undermine the enthusiasm and energy that is put into the GATT negotiations. Multilateral trade would quite obviously be hurt if the GATT negotiations fail, and the fear of trading blocs and protectionism within the trading blocs will become more real. Trading blocs in the Pacific, Europe and North America could potentially develop. The EC and the FTA exist as functioning entities that are linked by GATT. If GATT fails, the NAFTA and the EC will continue to exist with the possibility of an increased regional focus (Economist, 27 June 1992 and 15 August 1992; Yoshihide, 1992). The optimistic side suggests that NAFTA could be expanded to include many nations and thus accomplish what GATT negotiations have been unable to accomplish (Economist, 27 June 1992; Magnusson, 1992). Latin American nations are looking to join in the agreement (Magnusson, 1992) and it has been suggested that the agreement could be expanded to include Eastern Europe and New Zealand (Chicago Tribune, 24 September 1992). If GATT fails, then Asia would need to align itself in its own trading bloc or with one of the existing agreements. If NAFTA expands to encompass other countries, then again Asia needs to decide what alliances to develop. The development of regional accords could also stimulate renewed energy at GATT negotiations by those parties who do not want to see GATT dissolve.

The adversarial approach to trade and the development of free trade arrangements poses a number of questions. Where should a firm's market focus be, and if the firm is a multinational, where should it set up production in order to deal best with the possibility of trade actions? Should firms set up production facilities within regional trading blocs or should they export and deal with trade disputes through mechanisms such as GATT? Should governments be developing trade policies that will allow them to develop their own trading blocs so that the various regions can negotiate on the same power plain? These are just a few of the issues that could develop given the current state of affairs.

The FTA and NAFTA raise a number of questions for European and Asian exporters. The first set of issues focuses on how to deal with NAFTA and trade actions, while the second set of issues revolves around the larger question of regionalism versus multilateral trade. It is interesting to note that many of the issues that NAFTA raises are similar to the issues raised in Asia and North America about the EC and 'Fortress Europe'.

CONCLUSION

The FTA and NAFTA did not create an open border or a more secure market place for Canadian exporters. The parties to the Agreement continue to bring trade actions in an increasingly adversarial trade arena. The appeal procedure, while creating a more streamlined system on paper, may not actually add any certainty to the situation. Although determinations are made fairly promptly, the national authority does not always act as expected. A number of actions that have been remitted back to the national authority for correcting have had to go back a number of times because the national authority did not act according to the conclusions brought by the binational tribunal. This foot dragging caused the Canadian exporters continuing losses. This situation highlights a dilemma in international trade. Negotiations towards more open global markets go on at one level while the dogfights continue in the streets.

NAFTA has not necessarily meant that the borders are any more open than under the FTA. The spirit of the agreement will continue to be put to the test. Therefore, member countries will have to be aggressive in order to obtain a share of the North American market.

The implications for Europe and Asia are based more in the spirit of the times than in the written agreements. The agreements in themselves do not create regionalism, protectionism or managed trade. The way the agreements are interpreted and implemented and the Government policies that set the tone for trade relations are the determining forces that can set the stage for protectionism.

REFERENCES

Cooke, Kieran (1992) 'Canada Counters E. Asia's NAFTA Fears', *Financial Times*, 8 September, p. 8.

Crawford, Michael (1992) 'Who's Abusing Whom?' *Canadian Business*, August, pp. 32–8.

Dearden, Richard G. and David Palmeter (eds) (1992) *Free Trade Law Reporter*, Toronto: CCH Canadian Ltd.

Department of Finance, Canada (1988) *The Canada-U.S. Free Trade Agreement, An Economic Assessment*, Ottawa: Federal Government.

Doern, G. Bruce and Brian W. Tomlin (1991) *Faith and Fear: The Free Trade Story*, Toronto: Stoddart.

Freeman, Alan (1991) 'Eddy Match feels heat from U.S.', *Globe and Mail*, 9 January, p. B1.

Government of Canada (1992) *North American Free Trade Agreement: An Overview and Description*, Ottawa: Government of Canada Publication.

Herman, Lawrence (1990) 'FTA Panels Not Living Up To Advance Billing', *Globe and Mail*, 3 November, p. B4.

Horlick, Gary and Amanda DeBusk (1991) 'Dispute Panels Worth Their Salt – Or Pork', *Globe and Mail*, 12 January, p. B4.

Lipsey, Richard G. and Robert C. York (1988) *Evaluating the Free Trade Deal*, Toronto: C.D. Howe Institute.

Magnusson, Paul (1992) 'Building Free Trade Bloc By Bloc', *Business Week*, 25 May, pp. 16–17.

Meehan, Sheila (1992) *Conference Explores Issues, Obstacles, and Support for NAFTA Agreement*, IMF Survey, pp. 242–5.

Motherwell, Cathryn (1991) 'Canada Beefs up meat inspection', *Globe and Mail*, 21 June, p. B11.

Phillips, Kevin P. (1992) 'US Industrial Policy: Inevitable and Ineffective', *Harvard Business Review*, Jul.–Aug. pp. 104–12.

Rugman, Alan and Andrew Anderson (1989) 'Business Concerns about Implementing the Free Trade Agreement', *Business Quarterly*, Spring, pp. 23–6.

Yoshihide, Ishiyama (1992) 'Regional Routes to a New World Order, *Japan Echo*, **XIX** (1), Spring, pp.16–22.

Newspaper Articles[*]

Free Trade Observer, **4**, 1990, p. 42.
Free Trade Observer, **6**, 1990, p. 79.
'World Trade: Jousting for Advantage', *Economist*, 22 September 1990, pp. 7–40.
Free Trade Observer, **30**, 1992, pp. 473–6.
Free Trade Observer, **31**, 1992, p. 492.
'GATT Slams U.S. for Trading Practices', *Globe and Mail*, 13 March 1992, p. A1.
'The Trouble with Regionalism', *Economist*, 27 June 1992, p. 91.
'America Builds A Trade Block', *Economist*, 15 August 1992, pp. 55–6.
'Just the Beginning', *Chicago Tribune*, 24 September 1992, Section 3, p. 1.

---

[*]   In date order

10. The NAFTA and the Single European Market: an empirical study of Canadian and UK companies' trade and investment strategies

Christopher L. Pass, Kate Prescott and Peter J. Buckley

INTRODUCTION

Historically, Europe and North America have forged strong trade and investment linkages. With the increasing 'regionalization' of these areas, ensuing from the Single European Act 1986 (the so-called '1992' initiative) and the establishment of the North American Free Trade Agreement 1989 (NAFTA), the future of these cross-Atlantic flows has been called into question. The dominance of regional concerns and issues in both governmental and corporate decision making has raised the spectre of 'inwardness', protectionism and the sidelining of GATT. This paper looks at Canadian companies' views and responses to the Single European Market (SEM) initiative and likewise UK companies' views on the NAFTA. Unlike *national governments*, which tend to view trade and investment issues in a somewhat parochial manner, *multinational companies* (MNCs) typically formulate their foreign market servicing strategies on a broader scale, using cross-border exporting, strategic alliances and overseas investment to reduce costs and enhance their marketing effectiveness. From their perspective, the formation of regional blocs may cause some temporary 'inconveniences', such as the need to adjust to revised product specifications, technical standards, environmental protection measures and overt discrimination against 'outsiders' in the form, for example, of local content rules. However, they also create greater opportunities for business expansion through their trade creation effects. Moreover, the flexibility accorded to multinational companies through their ability to select a marketing servicing mode most appropriate to the new circumstances, can be used to minimize or remove strategic disadvantages. For example, in the face of discrimination against imports, MNCs may replace exporting by investing in a local manufacturing plant.

SURVEY OF CANADIAN AND UK COMPANIES

This section presents details of the foreign market servicing strategies of a sample of Canadian companies with business interests in the European Community (now the European Union), and UK companies with trading and investment interests in North America. In-depth interviews were conducted with 10 Canadian companies and 15 UK companies operating in eight industrial sectors, broadly defined (see Table 10.1). These sectors were selected on the basis of their importance in Canadian and UK trade and investment flows, respectively. The sampled firms vary greatly in size (including associated *resources* available for international expansion) and *experience* of international markets. They range from smaller-sized firms (overseas turnover under £50 million) with only a limited international involvement, to larger-sized firms (overseas turnover £200 million plus), which are mainly established multinational companies with extensive international operations.

Table 10.1   Classification of sample companies

Industry Sector	Firm Code UK	Firm Code Canada
Pharmaceuticals	1.1	
	1.2	
Wood, paper and pulp		2.1
Food and drink	3.1	3.4
	3.2	3.5
	3.3	
Transport equipment and systems	4.1	4.3
	4.2	
Financial services	5.1	5.4
	5.2	5.5
	5.3	5.6
Communications	6.1	6.2
		6.3
		6.4
General industrial equipment and systems	7.1	
	7.2	
Power supply and equipment	8.1	
	8.2	

UK Companies and the NAFTA

The general consensus of UK firms regarding NAFTA is one of greater opportunity (see Table 10.2). Many firms feel that the long-term potential is greater freedom to offer goods across the whole of North America, which broadens market scope and size. Nevertheless, in strategic terms, there are several firms who maintain that a 'presence' in both markets will continue to be important in the future despite these changes, and it is therefore not the existence of operations in themselves, but more likely the form of these representations which will change. Therefore, for firms operating through intermediaries, while some opportunities exist for securing distributors who will service the whole of North America, the preferred approach is securing new intermediaries to further develop business potential in other areas. For firms with established subsidiaries in both markets, replacing subsidiaries with representative offices in the wake of more harmonized legislation is more likely than attempts at cross-border business. For firms with manufacturing facilities in both markets, a certain degree of rationalization may be possible, although the continuation of local representation through sales/marketing offices retains priority. Most firms within the sample which see possible future potential in cross-border business are those contemplating the replacement of indirect means of exporting with a company sales office. For these firms, most of whom are relatively small and lacking in resources for investment, the ability to establish single sales marketing facilities in one market (particularly the USA) appears advantageous. Nevertheless there is evidence of companies outside of our sample who are not directly represented in Canada, but instead use their US subsidiaries' distributors to sell into Canada. A number of UK food groups are a case in point. RHM's subsidiaries, Red Wing and Carriage House Foods, sell a range of their sauces, preservatives and peanut butter in Canada through distributors. Likewise, Dalgety uses its USA catering distribution subsidiary, Martin-Bower, to service fast food restaurant customers such as McDonalds in both the USA and Canada.

Thus, while strategies are likely to be adapted in the wake of the greater freedoms, there remains evidence of firms maintaining separate organizational arrangements in both markets. While some UK firms are establishing new business operations in Canada and others are consolidating existing positions, there is little evidence to suggest that these businesses will form the only focus of their North American business. While for certain firms it provides a 'platform' for expanding into the USA, in most cases this expansion is likely to take the form of establishing separate operations (be they new distributorships, further acquisitions, establishment of sales/marketing facilities and so on). This may be partly attributable to the size of the North American market (and with Mexico also included, this is extended further), which make it difficult to regard the market as a single entity. Equally, however, there remain certain

Table 10.2   UK firms: foreign market servicing modes in the Canadian and USA markets

Company	Current Foreign Market Servicing Mode in Canada and USA	Likely Impact of NAFTA on Servicing Strategy
1.1	• Established Canadian sales office in 1950 • Acquisition of Canadian producer (1958) giving it a 'secondary' manufacturing facility • Established USA sales office in 1950 • Co-marketing agreement with Swiss company (1963) to sell key new drug in USA • Established major greenfield manufacturing/sales/R&D operation in USA in 1964	• Product line rationalization involving greater intra-plant specialization and cross exporting to enhance both 'presence' advantages (e.g. local product customization) and plant operating economies
1.2	• Began exporting to Canada in 1989 using distributor (one product only)	• Initial involvement has proved promising and may lead on to selling more products through distributorships or a company sales office NAFTA has alerted the company to the opportunities for selling its products in the USA. Distributors being sought
3.1	• Acquisition of a major Canadian flour miller and food products company in 1987 • Acquisition of Canada's largest food processing company in 1990 • Joint-venture company formed with USA flour milling group (1992) • The company has a number of subsidiaries in the USA but market penetration remains small	• Strategic alliances with major USA producers would help the company make a bigger impact with major US food store groups NAFTA is expected to create added opportunities for selling the company's leading brands on a pan-American basis
3.2	• Exports to Canada through a long-established distributorship • Exported to USA using (initially) regional distributors • 3.2 was acquired in 1984 by a UK food company who then sold it to another UK food company in 1989. This latter company has a sales/marketing subsidiary in the USA which now handles 3.2's products in the USA	• NAFTA has led to a review of the company's overall North American operation and it is possible that the USA sales subsidiary will take over responsibility for handling 3.2's brands in Canada
3.3	• Initially exported to Canada via a distributorship established in 1985 (Distributor approached the company) • Currently a number of 3.3's products are produced locally under a licensing agreement organized by the distributor, who continues to handle sales and marketing. • No USA business.	• The Canadian and the USA soft drinks markets (the latter dominated by Coca Cola and Pepsico) are seen by the company as 'separate' markets. 3.3 has been approached by a USA company with a view to establishing a joint-venture operation

Com- pany	Current Foreign Market Servicing Mode in Canada and USA	Likely Impact of NAFTA on Servicing Strategy

4.1	• Originally exported to Canada via a distributorship established in the early 1960s
	  • In 1983 a dispute between 4.1 and its distributor led to the termination of the agreement and the withdrawal of the company's products from the Canadian market
	The distributor then set up a manufacturing facility producing a '4.1 style product'
	  • The company subsequently attempted to re-enter the market under a new distributor, but this ended in dispute
	  • A USA distributorship was established in the 1970s
	In 1980 the company acquired its distributor, taking the view that a company-owned network would provide a more dedicated basis for expansion
	  • In 1984 the USA operation was closed down as a cost cutting measure (the UK business was seriously affected by the recession of the early 1980s)
	  • The company's products are now handled by an independent distributor in the USA
		• NAFTA is seen as offering opportunities for expansion. A dedicated sales/ marketing subsidiary covering North America would be the 'preferred' mode of servicing, but since the company's finances are in poor shape, this possibility is ruled out for the present

4.2	• Established sales/distribution subsidiaries in Canada and USA in 1948 to supply the 'aftermarket' in car parts (i.e. 'replacement' equipment). Exports from the UK
	  • In 1959 the company established a greenfield plant in the USA to obtain 'original' equipment business. The company currently has six manufacturing plants in the USA
	  • The Canadian market is now mainly serviced from the USA plants
		• The 1965 'Auto Pact' between Canada and the USA partially liberalized trade in cars and car parts, leading to a substantial increase in cross-frontier trade
		• NAFTA further liberalizes this sector and extends the new freedoms to Mexico. A substantial amount of car investment has been undertaken in Mexico. 4.2 is well placed in this respect, having established a 'source' company in Mexico, which services components from the USA plants and the company's joint-venture company in Brazil

5.1	• Only recent involvement in N. American insurance market. UK-based personnel are sent out to Canada and the USA to establish client contacts	• May establish a N. American sales/marketing office. Operationally, the Canadian and USA markets are seen as 'separate' entities, given current legislative differences

5.2	• Acquired a Canadian bank in the 1950s
	  • In the 1970s the company changed direction and established a separate subsidiary in Canada specializing in servicing the needs of corporate clients
	  • Established USA corporate banking operations in the 1950s, based in New York
	  • Currently the Canadian business is managed (in strategic terms) out of New York
		• Harmonization of banking laws and the fact that many of their larger corporate clients already operate on a pan-American basis will probably lead to a more integrated approach under the direction of the USA subsidiary

Table 10.2　continued

Com- pany	Current Foreign Market Servicing Mode in Canada and USA	Likely Impact of NAFTA on Servicing Strategy
5.3	• Currently operate an 'export-type' approach. UK-based personnel are sent out to the Canadian and USA markets to establish client contacts for their investment management business	• Greater harmonization of Canadian and USA investment management rules and regulations will provide opportunities. 5.3 may establish a sales subsidiary in the USA to put its operations on a more dedicated basis
6.1	• Acquired 51% stake in Canadian telecom manufacturer (1986). This has been sold as 6.1 has decided to focus on the provision of value-added telecom services • Various acquisitions in the USA from 1986 onwards, taking the company into voice messaging, cellular and data communication services • Canada now serviced as part of a broader based Pan-American operation centred in the USA.	• The company's N. American strategy is to provide telecom services to local and international companies. Deregulation of the telecoms market and NAFTA will help the company's position insofar as greater integration of client companies' North American activities will favour companies who are able to provide cross-border and global telecom services
7.1	• The company which supplies fluid power systems established a greenfield operation in Canada in 1975 • It has since consolidated its position through acquisitions, including a USA-based subsidiary in 1987 and a further Canadian subsidiary in 1988 • The company has an extensive network of sales offices and a number of assembly plants in Canada and the USA, which produce customized fluid process systems for clients	• NAFTA is not expected to change things much. Sales offices provide a key customer linkage and the company is already well-represented across North America, as in this respect 'on the ground representation is crucial'. In theory, assembly operations are more 'footloose' and some rationalization may be undertaken
7.2	• Exports its products (precision measuring equipment) via distributors. A Canadian distributorship was established in 1978 • The company appointed a USA distributor in 1968. A second distributor was appointed in 1991 after the original distributor got into financial difficulties	• The NAFTA is expected to increase competitive pressures and to break down regional 'spheres of influence', giving the company's products access to, and a higher profile in, areas where it has been hitherto underrepresented. Long term, sales offices may be established
8.1	• Acquired a 51% stake in a Canadian gas exploration and production company in 1988 • Acquired an 85% stake in Canada's largest gas distribution company in 1990 • The company has acquired a number of oil and gas exploration concerns in the USA	• Tight regulatory control of public utility operations and little likely relaxation under NAFTA has resulted in the company selling its gas distribution interests in Canada (1993)

Com-pany	Current Foreign Market Servicing Mode in Canada and USA	Likely Impact of NAFTA on Servicing Strategy
8.2	• The company is a joint-venture concern set up in 1989 to create a stronger international power systems business • Both parent companies operated sales offices in Canada prior to the formation of the joint venture, and these were consolidated into a sales/marketing subsidiary • The company has a subsidiary in the USA which is mainly concerned with obtaining sales, although it also undertakes limited production	• NAFTA has led the company to consider establishing a major manufacturing presence in North America. At the present time, however, the company has a highly successful technical collaboration agreement with the leading USA power systems supplier, and this could be seen as a factor in inhibiting 'aggressive' expansion in its partner's traditional territory

Note: The numbers in col. 1 refer to the classifications in Table 10.1

barriers between the two markets which makes a singular approach difficult: legislative differences arising out of historical developments in the case of financial service firms, local content rules in the case of car manufacturing, product testing and registration for pharmaceutical companies, barriers to establishing brands in the case of food and drink companies; different levels of deregulation and liberalization in telecommunications and gas supply; different levels of indigenous competition between the USA and Canada; and the continued demands of customer proximity in many sectors. It is, therefore, the promise of greater freedoms, along with the growing power of the region brought about by the NAFTA, which is catalysing consolidation of effort, rather than 'real' economic benefits from the establishment of a single market. Most firms recognize that the market is not homogeneous, and although there are movements which are suggesting a coming together of legislation and practices, these will not be felt for some time. Continued discretion and a willingness to be adaptable and flexible appears prudent.

Canadian Companies and the Single European Market (SEM)

Table 10.3 reports the likely response of Canadian companies to the establishment of the SEM. For Canadian companies, while changes are expected to come about as a result of the Single European Market initiative, the extent of these changes centres more on business consolidation than on major strategic change. To this end, firms are more concerned about taking greater advantage of the internal freedoms promised by the Single Market, and are thus keen to secure their strategic positions to take advantage of liberalization. However, firms expressed a degree of caution about regarding the Single European Market as a homogeneous business centre, and parallel developments between markets are likely to continue into the future.

Table 10.3   Canadian firms: foreign market servicing modes in the UK and the EU

Company	Current Foreign Market Servicing Mode in UK and EU	Likely Impact of Single European Market on Servicing Strategy
2.1	• Established UK sales subsidiary (1967) (timber/wood pulp) • Acquisition of UK manufacturer of wood products (1989) • Strategic alliances (joint ventures) in Netherlands and Germany (sourced by exports of timber and wood pulp from Canada)	• Further joint ventures in mainland Europe. Deeper direct investment, including local sourcing to counter the EU's 'protectionist' stance on imports of timber and wood pulp
3.4	• Licensing deals with several UK brewers to gain access to 'tied' public house chains. Local brewing of company's 'standard' draught lager brand, incorporating a yeast ingredient exported from Canada • Wider distribution of 'premium' packaged brand through the licencee's public houses • Strategic alliance (joint venture) to build up a public house chain • Acquisition of two brewers in Italy	• Further European investments when opportunities present themselves. Wide diversity of demand across the market requires acquisition of, and strategic alliances with, local brewers with strong established brands. The company's own brands can be slotted into local product portfolios as appropriate
3.5	• Established UK manufacturing subsidiary (1968) • Established and acquired manufacturing plants in Holland, Spain, Belgium and France and sales offices/subsidiaries in EC markets • Cross-border exporting of some products to expand local product portfolios.	• Will establish or acquire businesses to increase market penetration as appropriate • Development of pan-European brands in certain product lines
4.3	• Established UK sales office (1986) • European port calls to collect/deliver cargo, but no mainland offices	• Possibly sales offices in main European ports. Integration will benefit transportation companies in general but the company is concerned that the EU might impose a 'flag' preference system, giving EU-owned vessels priority over foreign fleets
5.4	• Long-established UK sales subsidiary (1893) which runs an extensive network of branch offices • Established sales office in the Republic of Ireland, but no other European business	• The company has adopted a 'wait and see' posture for the present, unlike many UK insurers who have entered into strategic alliances with other European insurers and broad-based financial services groups

Com-pany	Current Foreign Market Servicing Mode in UK and EU	Likely Impact of Single European Market on Servicing Strategy
5.5	• Long-established treasury office in the UK (1870) • Acquired UK broking business to give the company European legal status – important in obtaining freedom of access under the 2nd Banking Directive. However, as yet, the company has no business outside the UK	• May establish offices in other European financial centres (Paris, Brussels) if treasury business moves away from London. As with Company 5.4 the company has adopted a 'wait and see stance. The issue of 'reciprocity' is being looked at by the EU and NAFTA authorities.
5.6	• Established UK sales subsidiary (1987) • Established sales/branch office in Brussels (1989) to develop European business contacts and 'monitor' new legislation	• No immediate plans to set up further local offices
6.2	• Established UK sales subsidiary (1978) sourcing products from overseas plants • Established various manufacturing operations in England, Wales and Northern Ireland (1980s) • Acquisition of major UK-based equipment manufacturer (1991) with European plants and sales networks • Strategic alliances (joint ventures) to provide further expansion into Europe – Germany (1991), Poland (1992), Spain (1992) and France (1992)	• Further strategic alliances to widen and deepen access to 'big ticket' procurement contracts. Some concerns at moves to harmonize technical standards around local firms systems (under CEN/CENELEC) and 'local fiefdoms' in perpetuating procurement bias
6.3	• Established UK sales office (1970) sourcing computers and periphals from USA-based parent and Canadian subsidiary • Exports to mainland Europe via distributors, sourcing from overseas plants and Ireland (see below) • Established greenfield manufacturing plant in Republic of Ireland (1988) as an 'export platform' into the UK and mainland Europe	• Local content issues are very much to the fore as the company's Irish plant sources some components from its overseas plants. The company is currently 'negotiating' with the European Commission to clarify local content status, the likelihood being that more items will need to be sourced locally for its products to qualify as 'authentic' European products, thus avoiding import restrictions
6.4	• Exports of 'know-how' and space/satellite equipment through UK and European strategic alliances (co-production and installation consortiums) • Acquired USA company (1989) producing related products, which brought in a UK manufacturing subsidiary. Subsidiary used to 'co-ordinate' the company's participation in European strategic alliances	• Continuance of the strategic alliance format. Like Company 6.2 the company is concerned at the implications of CEN/CENELEC arrangements for 'foreign' companies – the 'reciprocity' is between the EU and NAFTA

Note: The numbers in the first column refer to the classification in Table 10.1.

The findings here differ from those regarding UK firms entering Canada in the greater attention to specific elements of new legislation. Whereas the NAFTA concerns free trade and a general move towards liberalization, the extent of these moves and the scope of the new legislation is far less than in the European Union, where as one interviewee put it, the changing legislation is 'all-embracing'. It is therefore the specifics of the new programme which firms are addressing in their strategic developments. For example, the critical facets of change are provided by issues such as mutual recognition and home country control in financial services, harmonisation of technical standards for communication firms, and the longer-term issues of Nordic and Eastern European country integration for the producers of wood, paper and pulp. Consequently, although the future of the European Union is still shrouded in much uncertainty in some areas (for example, which countries will initially join the common currency block in 1999) the clarity of the SEM's overall objectives has given firms a clearer idea of the specific nature of future strategies for Europe. Rather than simple expressions of 'greater opportunities', firms' comments were articulated how the key elements of the new legislation were going to impact on their business. Another issue which deserves comment is the concern over Europe being protectionist. Various concerns were voiced including:

Reciprocity   Company 5.5 (treasury services) expressed concern at the reciprocity sanctions incorporated in the second EC Banking Directive. Specifically, this requires foreign countries to allow open access to their financial markets in return for open access to the EU. Because Canadian banking regulations limit foreign access via ownership some Canadian banks have established 'European Status' by setting up or acquiring *locally incorporated* banks and securities firms. Company 5.5 acquired a UK broking business in the late 1980s and thus qualifies as a bona fida European bank.

Technical Standards   These are under debate at the present time, particularly the matter of standardisation in key technological areas (The European Committee for Standardization (CEN) and the European Electrotechnical Standardization Committee (CENELEC), for instance). Company 6.2 (telecommunications) intimated that it was concerned that leading indigenous suppliers (Alcatel and Siemens) were exerting 'pressure' on the European Commission to adopt formats which excluded North American standards.

Procurement Bias   The SEM initiative is aimed at creating a 'level playing field' in the area of public procurement. However, Company 6.2 and Company 6.4 (satellites) both expressed concern at the persistence of 'local fiefdoms' limiting market access. A direct investment presence in the market is seen as important in this context as it provides a local 'persona'.

Local Content Complications Company 6.3 (computers) is currently involved in a dispute with the European Commission over its sourcing policies. The company has a manufacturing plant in the Republic of Ireland which exports through local sales subsidiaries to the rest of the EU. The potential of the European operation has been hampered by a local content issue. Certain components used in the production of computers at the Irish plant are imported from Japan and the USA. The European Commission has challenged the 'authenticity' of the final product as a truly European product and hence fully tradeable across EU markets without impediment.

CONCLUSION

This paper has attempted to identify the impact of economic integration on the sample of firms by addressing the specific challenges posed by the North American Free Trade Agreement and the Single European Market. By looking at Canadian firms' impressions of the Single European Market, UK firms' attitudes towards NAFTA, and responses to changes in the operating environment within each economic group, it is possible to establish some understanding of the trade creation and trade diversion effects of economic integration. What quite clearly emerges from the analysis is a generally positive attitude towards economic integration. There appeared to be little indication of trade (and investment) diversion away from established international markets. Canadian firms are keen to expand and consolidate in Europe, and UK firms continue to view the North American market as critical to the future of their business. From this perspective, it is apparent that the growing trend towards international trading blocs is fostering both inter- and intra-regional trade and investment.

One major difference between Canadian and UK firms did, however, emerge. While many Canadian firms view the UK as a 'gateway' to the European Union, allowing them to build on existing business to expand across Europe, this view was not reciprocated by UK managers. Indeed, there was evidence to suggest that UK firms are more likely to establish businesses in the USA from which they may serve the Canadian market. At present, however, continued differences between the Canadian and US markets mean that many companies are continuing to treat the markets as two separate entities. Whether this thinking will be sustained in the future, however, in the wake of increased liberalization, is open to question.

The effects of economic integration are, however, more pervasive than just changing the strategic focus of firms on a bilateral basis. With the growing dominance of the global triad, it is clear that managers cannot remove from their considerations the impact of integration on the world economic order as a whole. Integration must therefore be seen as posing new challenges for business consolidation and rationalization within 'domestic' trading blocs as well as impacting on bilateral relations between trading blocs. Relating to the first point, Canadian firms voiced a great deal of concern over the impact of NAFTA on the Canadian economy and the long-term effects for Canadian competitiveness. The removal of US branch plants from Canada, and the potential for Canadian firms to relocate activities in Mexico, is adding to the already severe recessionary pressures besetting the economy. This is shaping an outward-looking view for Canadian firms which see growth opportunities outside of Canada and the US as offering sustainable potential. This growth can only be achieved with improved competitiveness, with emphasis being placed on research and development, innovation and greater company efficiency. A more liberal stance on inward investment has also emerged in Canada, and while there remain concerns in 'sensitive' areas, where 'net benefit to Canada' considerations remain important (such as the resources/energy sector), and a 'preference' for maintaining some local ownership interests, the new mood is one of openness. Nevertheless, these concerns were balanced against more positive responses which see NAFTA as stimulating efficiency and comparable wage and tax levels. The idea of free trade and its impact on the economy was not, therefore, regarded adversely; it was rather seen as a stimulus to improving competitiveness and taking a more proactive stance in developing business in the USA.

11. Overseas production activities of Toyota Motor Corporation

Hiroshi Kumon

INTRODUCTION

The main objective of this paper is to explain specific features of the overseas production activities of Toyota Motor Corporation (hereafter Toyota), based on our field research[1].

Toyota was very reluctant in making decisions concerning overseas ventures, compared with the other major Japanese automobile firms[2]. Toyota lagged behind them in making inroads into developed countries, by choosing to export finished cars instead of becoming involved in risky local production. What stimulated a change of the strategy was a restriction of export volume to the US due to the voluntary exports restriction. In spite of reluctance to go abroad, the Toyota production system is applied most successfully at local plants compared to other Japanese firms.

TOYOTA'S OVERSEAS EXPANSION PROCESS

Toyota was reluctant to set about local production in developed countries, compared with Nissan and Honda. Because Toyota had stuck to the home market and avoided such a risky business as production in developed nations, it was behind not only in local production but also in setting up regional headquarters. The process by which Japanese automobile companies took on overseas operations developed from the export of finished cars to local production in developing countries then local production in developed countries. After that it began to establish regional headquarters.

Toyota produced automobiles in developing countries for about 20 years before starting production in developed countries. Though a production activity, it was conducted through a form of knockdown assembly, which was somewhere between export and production. Automobile companies adopted this sort of system as an alternative to the export of finished cars, when countries resorted to embargos or restrictions on car imports, or raised tariff barriers against foreign cars.

Although automobile companies must accept the limitations in an independent operation due to governments' support of local industry, and there are problems in achieving advantages of scale due to small scale markets, there is some merit for knockdown assembly in those countries. Because governments protect the home market against foreign competition, companies producing there can get a kind of monopolistic profit.

According to Table 11.1, Toyota started its first overseas production in Brazil in 1959; Nissan began in Taiwan in the same year. However, Honda started its overseas automobile production in Taiwan in 1969, being behind Toyota and Nissan. Honda started business as a manufacturer of motor cycles, so it was late in entering into automobile production. Honda was notable for making inroads into both developing and developed countries at the same time in the 1980s.

Nissan and Honda are distinguished in the advancement of overseas production in developed countries. Honda was the front runner among companies which embarked on local production in the US. It started producing motor cycles in 1979, and automobiles in 1982. After this, Honda expanded its operation very smoothly and began to produce automobiles in Canada in 1986. Honda stands first in production volume among Japanese-affiliated companies in North America. Nissan began to internationalize production activities rapidly in the 1980s, especially in advanced nations. It started independent operations in the US in 1983 and then expanded its capacity.

In contrast to these, Toyota was very reluctant to go to the US. At first, it chose to enter into a joint venture with General Motors that did not include independent operation. This choice seemed typical of Toyota's prudence. Eventually it started its independent operations in the US and Canada in 1988. It now has three plants in North America. Because of the potential ability to produce, it is recovering from its backwardness there.

Reluctance in making inroads into Europe is also distinctive of Toyota. Each auto company tried to find a way of starting local production in Europe in the latter half of the 1980s, because of the probable continuation of import restrictions after 1992. Nissan was the first to start independent operations there. It took an active attitude towards making an inroad into Europe and set up an automobile plant in the UK, after making a licensing agreement in Greece and a joint venture in Spain. In the UK, it started operation in 1986 and then expanded its capacity. Honda has promoted a licensing agreement, co-operative research, and the development of a new automobile with Rover Group since 1979, but it needed much time to build a manufacturing plant there due to the focus of its efforts on plant operations in the US. In 1989, Honda agreed a joint venture with Rover, and the plant began operation in October 1992. The joint venture was cancelled in 1994, because the German company BMW bought whole stocks of the Rover. Honda now operates the plant independently.

Table 11.1   Start up of overseas production plants of three Japanese automobile firms by country

| | Toyota | | | Nissan | | | Honda | | |
	Year	Entry Form	Product	Year	Entry Form	Product	Year	Entry Form	Product
USA	1984	JV	C&T	1983	WO	C&T	1982	WO	C
	1988	WO	C						
Canada	1988	WO	C				1986	WO	C
UK	1992	WO	C	1986	WO	C	1992	WO	C
Germany	1989	L	T						
Spain				1983	JV	T			
Portugal	1968	JV	T	1968	L	T			
Greece				1980	L	C&T			
Mexico				1966	WO	C&T			
Brazil	1959	JV	T						
Venezuela	1981	JV	C&T						
Peru	1967	JV	C&T	1966	JV	C&T			
Uruguay	1985	L	C&T						
Ecuador	1986	L	T	1987	L	T			
T.& Tobago	1971	L	C&T	1970	L	C&T			
Kenya	1977	L	C&T	1978	L	C&T	1986	L	C
Zambia	1983	L	T						
S. Africa	1962	L	C&T	1963	L	C&T	1981	L	C
Zimbabwe	1981	L	C&T	1981	L	C&T			
Iran				1984	L	T			
Australia	1963	JV	C						
New Zealand	1967	WO	C&T	1976	WO	C&T	1988	WO	C
Taiwan	1988	JV	C&T	1959	JV	C&T	1969	JV	C
Korea				1987	L	T			
Malaysia	1968	L	C&T	1976	L	C&T	1983	JV	C
Philippines	1989	JV	C&T	1971	JV	C&T	1992	JV	C
Indonesia	1970	JV	C&T	1982	L	C	1984	L	C
Thailand	1964	JV	C&T	1962	JV	C&T	1984	JV	C
India	1985	JV	T	1985	JV	T			
Bangladesh	1985	L	T						

Notes: 1. 'WO' means Wholly-Owned.
'JV' meas Joint Venture, which includes equity joint venture and excludes contractual joint venture.
'L' means Licensing.
'C' means Passenger Car and 'T' means Truck.
2. The table shows plants which produce automobiles and trucks.

Source: Toyota Motor Corp. (ed.) (1990) General View of Automobile Industry, Tokyo.
Nissan Motor Co. Ltd. (ed.) (1990) Globalization of Nissan Motor Co, Tokyo.
Sangyo Journal (ed.) (1990) Real Situation of Toyota Motor Group. IRC, Tokyo.
Sangyo Journal (ed.) (1990) Real Situation of Nissan Motor Group. IRC, Tokyo.
Sangyo Journal (ed.) (1991) Real Situation of Honda-Giken, Honda-Gijyutsu -Kenkyusho Group. IRC, Tokyo.

Toyota first agreed to a joint truck production with Volkswagen and started production in Germany in 1989. Truck production is also carried out through licensing in Portugal. In 1989, Toyota formally announced an independent operation in the UK. The capacity for engine production was intended from the beginning, and an assembly and engine plants began production in 1992.

Nissan and Honda established regional headquarters in the US and Europe recently, but Toyota has not yet taken any steps in this direction. In Toyota, overseas activities are controlled by several departments, including the Overseas Operations Department at the headquarters in Japan. In fact, the regional headquarters of Nissan and Honda are responsible for managerial matters among the local companies, rather than functioning as real regional headquarters. Even though the Japanese headquarters of the two companies seem still to play decisive roles in managing overseas activities, they have taken a step to prepare for further globalization. Toyota should come to grips with organizational measures for globalization in the near future, and establish regional headquarters.

Toyota had a prudent strategy, avoiding probable risky business in developed countries and attached great importance to the domestic market. But once it decided to enter into developed countries, it applied its unique system successfully. It is possible to infer that this reluctance is consistent with the positive application of its unique production system. Because of the uniqueness of the system, based on its cultural and historical background, Toyota hesitated to go abroad, but having done so, applied the system positively in order to retain competitive advantage after starting local production.

I should explain the Toyota production system here. Fordism realized mass production by introducing conveyor belt systems and specialized tools, as well as deploying semi-skilled workers. This system completely divides functional work into the engineering of process technology, quality control, and direct work on the shop floor. In addition, each production process pursues economies of scale. Accordingly, lots of parts inventories are necessary in each process. In contrast to this scheme, the main concept of the Toyota production system is to eliminate every form of waste. Having followed the conveyor belt system of Fordism, Toyota developed a unique system, which has two main pillars, the Just-In-Time system and 'Jidoka'. The Just-In-Time concept refers to efficiency, which provides parts as they are needed for the final assembly process. 'Jidoka' refers to the quality of the product, signifying the self-regulation of the entire process. Machines stop automatically when a manufactured product with a defect is detected and workers have a right to stop the line when they detect a defect. This system reqires flexible work organization. Workers are required not only to do their job, but also to be multi-skilled, taking on other jobs as needed and being responsible for some maintenance and quality control.

FOUR OF TOYOTA'S OVERSEAS MANUFACTURING PLANTS: APPLICATION OF THE TOYOTA PRODUCTION SYSTEM

Toyota produces automobiles, trucks and parts at 35 plants in 26 countries; this includes licensing agreements, joint ventures, and independent operations as well as plants under construction like those in the UK. Of those, I had a chance to visit four plants, which are in the US, Canada, and Taiwan, and started operation in the 1980s (see Table 11.2).

The Japanese Multinational Enterprise Study Group has done research on Japanese-affiliated plants in North America. The central theme of the study was how the Japanese production system can be effectively transferred to American society, where the socio-cultural environment is different. We focused our concern on the application of the system in relation to local environments. We set 23 elements in order to quantify and illustrate major findings from our field observation, and created a five-point grading technique for each element. Within this ranking, a five-point score indicates the highest possible degree of application of the Japanese system and a one-point ranking indicates the highest possible degree of adaptation to local environments. By this ranking, we can easily estimate application-adaptation levels, though not exactly. In addition, we arranged the 23 elements into two different groups. One is 'Six group evaluation', in which we classify the 23 elements into 6 related groups. The other is 'Four aspects evaluation', in which we classify 19 elements out of the 23 into 4 groups[3].

One purpose of this paper is to show positive applications of the system, so I use both the average points of the 23 elements, and the 'Four aspects evaluation' here. 'Four aspects evaluation' covers 'Human methods', 'Material methods', 'Human Results, and 'Material Results'. This needs further clarification. The concept 'Methods' covers the transfer of Japanese systems, such as job classification, wage systems and quality control. The concept 'Results' represents the transfer of technology and people, for example, production equipment constructed in Japan, and Japanese expatriates. See Table 11.3 and the accompanying note.

Nine Japanese-affiliated automobile plants in North America were considered, and the three Toyota plants were compared with overall performance. When looking at 'Methods', the three Toyota plants consistently outperformed the average. The average 'Methods' rating was 3.5; all the Toyota plants exceeded it. New United Motor Manufacturing Inc. (NUMMI) had 3.6 points, Toyota Motor Manufacturing USA Inc. (TMM) had 3.7 points, and Toyota Motor Manufacturing Canada Inc. (TMMC) had 3.6 points. Under 'Human Methods', the three plants exceeded the average (3.6) by 0.1 or 0.2. This was their strong

Table 11.2 Profile of Toyota's four automobile plants in North America and Taiwan

Plant	Location	Start of Operation	Owenership (Japanese ratio)	No. of Employees	No. of Japanese expt. (%)	Capacity (annual)	Volume of Production	Product Models	Structure of Plant
NUMMI	USA, CA	1984	Joint-Venture (50%)	2,800	34 (1.2%)	200 000	204,285	Pass. Car2	Stamping, Welding, Painting, Assembly
TMM	USA, KY	1988	Wholly-owned	2,950	72 (2.4%)	200 000	211,131	Pass. Car1	Stamping, Welding, Painting, Assembly, Engine, Plastics
TMMC	Canada	1988	Wholly-owned	1,000	31 (3.1%)	50 000	60,793	Pass.Car1	Stamping, Welding, Painting, Assembly
Kouzui	Taiwan	1988	Joint-Venture (49%)	1,441	34 (2.4%)	40 000	18,167	Pass.Car1 Truck4	Stamping, Welding, Painting, Assembly

Notes 1. "Pass. Car" means Passenger Car. 'No. of Japanese expt.' means Number of Japanese Expatriates.
2. Volume of Production indicates production in 1990 except for the Taiwanese plant, which is 1989.
3. NUMMI added a truck line with 100,000 capacity in 1991. TMM added another 200,000 capacity for passenger car production in 1994. TMMC expanded its capacity to 100,000 in 1992.
4. Kouzui had started truck production through licensing in 1984.

Source: Interviews in 1989 and 1990. Japan Automobile Manufacturers Association, Inc., *The Motor Industry of Japan*, 1991

Table 11.3   Four aspects evaluation of the hybrid model for Japanese-affiliated plants in North America

	Average (4 Ind.)	Home Elect.	I.C.	Auto. Parts	Auto Assem.	NUMMI	TMM	TMMC
Human Methods	3.1	2.4	2.9	3.4	3.6	3.7	3.8	3.7
Material Methods	2.8	2.4	2.4	3.1	3.3	3.3	3.3	3.3
Human Results	3.6	2.9	3.9	4.3	3.6	2.5	3.5	4.5
Material Results	3.6	3.2	4.2	3.8	3.3	3.0	3.7	3.7
Methods	3.0	2.4	2.8	3.4	3.5	3.6	3.7	3.6
Results	3.6	3.1	4.1	4.0	3.4	2.8	3.6	4.0
Average (23 Elem.)	3.3	2.7	3.2	3.6	3.5	3.4	3.7	3.8

Notes:
1. Average was calculated for 34 Japanese-affiliated plants of 4 industries: Home Electronics (9 Plants), Integrated Circuit (7 Plants), Automobile Parts (9 Plants), and Automobile Assembly (9 Plants) in North America.
2. 23 Elements include (1) Job Classification, (2) Wage System, (3) Job Rotation, (4) Education & Training, (5) Promotion, (6) Role of Supervisor, (7) Production Equipment, (8) Quality Control, (9) maintenance, (10) Plant Operation, (11) Local Content, (12) Suppliers, (13) Procurement System, (14) Small Group Activities (15) Information Sharing, (16) Unity, (17) Employment Policy, (18) Employment Security, (19) Union,(20) Grievance System, (21) Ratio of Japanese Expatriates, (22) Delegation of Power, (23) Managerial Status of Local Managers.
3. Human Methods include (1), (2), (3), (4), (5), (6), (14), (15), (16), (18), and (20).
4. Material Methods include (8), (9), and (13).
5. Human Results include (21) and (23).
6. Material Results include (7), (11), and (12).
7. Methods include Human Methods and Material Methods.
8. Results include Human Results and Material Results.

Source: Calculation by the Japanese Multinational Enterprise Study Group.

point – under 'Material methods', they all had an average score (3.3). In the 'Results' category, two plants achieved higher results than the 3.4 average. TMM achieved 3.6, and TMMC 4.0; both are newly-constructed on greenfield sites.

Looking at the assessment of the 23 elements mentioned above, the two wholly-owned plants (TMM and TMMC) exceed the average under both 'Methods' and 'Results'. Compared to the average 3.5 scored by the nine plants, TMM achieved 3.7 and TMMC 3.8. NUMMI underperformed slightly, scoring 3.4.

How about in Taiwan? It is very interesting that Toyota's Taiwanese plant (Kouzui) has almost the same type of application as TMM. The average for the 23 elements for five Japanese-affiliated plants was 3.3, which is less than the average in North America. This is because all Taiwanese plants are joint ventures, localization of management goes forward more than in North America, and there are difficulties in adoption of the Japanese type procurement system due to a lack of reliable parts makers. Nevertheless, the average in 'Methods' is 3.5, which is the same as in North America (Table 11.4). The applications relating to human methods were accepted easily in Taiwan, contrary to expectations. Kouzui is at the 3.9 point mark in 'Methods', which exceeds the average by 0.4. 'Human methods' gets an unusually high 4.0, which surpasses not only the Taiwanese average but also that of North America. In addition, the 'Results' category rated high at 3.4, which goes far beyond the average of 2.7. As a result, the average (23 elements) of Kouzui is 3.7, which exceeds the average of the five plants by 0.4.

Table 11.4 Four aspects evaluation of the hybrid model for Japanese-affiliated automobile plants in Taiwan

	Average	Kouzui
Human Methods	3.7	4.0
Material Methods	3.0	3.3
Human Results	2.0	3.0
Material Results	3.1	3.7
Methods	3.5	3.9
Results	2.7	3.4
Average (23 Elements)	3.3	3.7

Notes: 1. The average was calculated for five Japanese-affiliated Automobile plants in Taiwan
2. Other remarks are the same as in the Table 11.3.

Source: Calculation by author.

In summing up the situation for the four plants in North America and Taiwan, firstly, they show high average scores and 'Methods' scores. They are particularly strong in 'Human methods'. This means that Toyota applies its unique production system successfully in order to retain a competitive advantage in foreign countries. Secondly, three plants (all except NUMMI) also show high scores in the 'Results' category. High scores in both aspects imply that the two categories are suppporting each other. Thirdly, TMM and Kouzui have similar scores. This suggests that when Toyota puts a great deal of effort into applying its unique production system in local plants, this type of organization appears.

NUMMI

NUMMI, which is a joint venture with General Motors, has recently become a model for other local plants constructed by Toyota. It applies the unique production system successfully. It changed the traditional work organization, and adopted a flexible system, so that workers perform multiple jobs and shift positions in order to implement the production system. Simplification of job classification was a necessary condition for achieving this.

The new job classifications consist of only one production category and two maintenance categories, which were traditionally named 'skilled trades'. Based on this reform, Toyota introduced a team system modelled on the Japanese group work system. Leaders are given the right to control ordinary work and manage workers. Thus a unique work organization was adopted which entrusts rights relating to manufacturing automobiles to workers and leaders on the shop floor. Accordingly, workers on the shop floor not only perform direct work, but also have some responsibility for the quality and maintenance of machines. Of course, there are special divisions of quality control and maintenance. The new system makes it possible to broaden one's responsibilities by crossing traditional job boundaries. Workers are required to do job rotation within a team in order to become multi-skilled and to avoid monotony. Leaders check workers' progress in skill. Together with this reform of the traditional job classification system, Toyota put a limit on the operation of seniority. Promotion, shift preference, and transfer are determined primarily by ability, and if this is equal among applicants, then seniority becomes effective.

Regarding grievance procedures, there is a policy of resolving problems at the shop floor level through talks between workers and leaders, without going through the formal grievance route. Rare cases go to the final fourth step of outside arbitration. In addition, arbitration is restricted. Wages, production standards, and health and safety cannot be arbitrated. In such cases, unions in the 'Big Three' have kept the right to resort to strikes even during the terms of contract, because after the establishment of Fordism, managers had decided to change workloads by changing line speed unilaterally. Apart from such general agreements, the local union sanctioned abandonment of the right to strike on these matters.

Last, I should mention Japanese expatriates. Even though there are clear parallels regarding work organization, production control, procurement of parts, group consciousness, and labour relations among Japanese-affiliated plants in North America, the number and role of Japanese expatriates are different for each company. Honda sends a lot of Japanese, reaching 4 or 5% of all employees; and they are posted at formal higher managements levels as well as in advisory positions. Nissan sends an extremely small number of Japanese, who constitute less than 1% of all employees, and they are stationed as advisers to local managers. In contrast, Toyota sends a relatively moderate number of Japanese, constituting about 1 or 2% of all employees, and they are posted in both formal management positions and advisory positions. Almost all Japanese-affiliated plants belong to this type. Looking at NUMMI, there are 34

Japanese expatriates, comprising 1.2% of all employees. They fill positions such as president, some vice presidents, senior managers and advisors.

It is not clear whether Toyota had planned to build a new plant independently, after they got an agreement for a joint venture with GM. It could be that the less risky choice of joint venture included a possibility of independent operation through gaining experience in plant management in the US. In fact, Toyota decided to build plants both in the US and Canada.

TTM

Regarding TMM, there are 72 Japanese expatriates comprising 2.4% of the total employees. The number and percentage are in the intermediate range for such plants, between Nissan and Honda. Concerning administrative organization, Japanese expatriates hold positions as president, one vice president, and some senior managers, but other responsible positions are given to local managers. Even in the latter case, Japanese expatriates take positions as partners with them, and teach them Japanese style management.

TMM follows NUMMI's management system basically regarding work organization and group consciousness, but there are some revisions in terms of application. First, it established a prudent policy in hiring. Employees were appointed through careful selection procedures composed of five steps, and most hourly workers came from the local area, Kentucky. Great importance was placed on potential and understanding rather than experience or skill as selective factors. As a result, not a small number of hourly workers had college degrees. It seems that TMM expected hourly workers to be multi-skilled and take part in Kaizen activities (continuous improvement). In addition, positive selection of minorities and women was implemented, and they were placed not only in production jobs but also maintenance job.

TMM has an interesting training and education project. It hired rather larger numbers of maintenance workers than the other plants in order to implement the unique production system, and provide a systematic training plan. The training scheme was written in Japan at first, where workers master a knack and the art of efficient ways of work through On-the-Job-Training. This was later revised in the US. It subdivides tasks of maintenance into 27 000 elements and regroups them into seven steps systematically, so that workers can master the tasks through training at the training centre within the plant during three years.

Finally, a great importance was placed on production control by providing larger staff than in Japan for the development of logistics. Due to a lack of continuous delivery of good quality parts, the mother plant in Japan was prepared to send parts unremittingly. Though the unique production system was applied within plant operations, they could not easily ask parts makers for the

Just-In-Time delivery. So multi-deliveries from Japanese-affiliated parts makers were introduced. TMMC followed NUMMI's management policy.

Kouzui

There are ten car makers and excessive competition amongst them in Taiwan. The sales volume of cars is about 500 000 units, including passenger cars and trucks, and of that, imports have a 40% share. No plants have sufficient capacity to enjoy economies of scale. Kouzui is the ninth entry, having a 40 000 unit annual capacity. It is a typical small volume, multi-product production plant.

Unlike the US, there is no established system like Taylorism and Fordism in Taiwan. Also, parts makers have not developed, due to the short period of automobile manufacturing history. Therefore, there are two different aspects to the application of the Japanese production system: an easy aspect and a difficult one. In the US, Japanese managers had to change the systems formed under Taylorism and Fordism in order to apply Japanese style work organization, labour relations, and so on. But they did not need to change such an established system in Taiwan. Taiwanese management environments are very agreeable for the Japanese system. This may come from the late industrialization of the Taiwanese economy, and the common character in culture between Japan and Taiwan. Thus the application of Japanese-style work organization and labour relations was relatively easy. On the other hand, there were some adverse conditions: a high rate of staff turnover, a lack of skilled workers, and insufficient quality of parts. Because this was such a different environment from the US, the method of application was also different in Taiwan.

There were no difficulties in introducing Japanese-style work organization institutionally in Taiwan. Kouzui adopted a typical Japanese-style wage system, and promotion was determined by the recommendation of a candidate by the direct supervisor and by performance evaluation. In addition, a team system was introduced naturally. But problems have occurred in the system. Firstly, Kouzui has still not implemented job rotation because of a high rate of turnover. Theirs is more like a Japanese wage system in which seniority is functional as a determinant. In this system, the wage level at hiring remains relatively low, so it does not suit needs well, given the high rate of worker turnover. Though they had introduced the Japanese wage system to create a productive work organization, Japanese managers have had to decide whether their decision was right or not. The problem is how to decrease the turnover. In addition, workers have not been accustomed to teaching each other, so they must bring such a new corporate culture into the plant through training and education. They have the same system of group consciousness and labour relations as in Japan.

There are also problems with the quality of local parts, and careful attention must be paid to this. Toyota required Japanese parts makers to work with them in North America. They have a special room to display parts, listing makers' products within the plant. Also they have a policy of encouraging local parts makers through long-term trade, including guidance for quality comparable to Japan.

Concerning Japanese expatriates, the situation is almost the same as in the North American plants. As already stated, all Japanese-affiliated plants are joint ventures with Taiwanese capitalists. Of five plants visited, three local partners have leadership in management, and Japanese partners have managing rights at the other two plants which have started recently. In the case of Kouzui, Toyota has leadership in management. Japanese expatriates number 34 persons, including those Japanese sent by other Japanese companies joining it. The rate of expatriates has reached 2.4 % of all employees, which is the same as in TMM. The chairman of the board is Taiwanese and the president is Japanese. The main posts are shared by both partners.

CONCLUDING REMARKS

The major features of Toyota's multinationalization should be characterized as reluctance, prudence in decision making concerning overseas expansion, and successful application of the Japanese production system. It lagged behind Nissan and Honda in making inroads into developed countries, because of the policy of choosing to export finished products as a means of obtaining a foothold in developed countries instead of risky local production. What stimulated the move from exports to local production was a limitation of export volume to the US due to voluntary exports restriction and an extension of market share through local production by Nissan and Honda, especially Honda.

Upon initiating local production, the company was very prudent. In the US, at first, it selected a joint venture with one of the Big Three. They used a closed plant belonging to the American partner, supplying products for both companies. After achieving organizational restructuring for overseas activities, Toyota launched into local production in North America. Then it decided to build two plants in the US and Canada. It also lagged behind Nissan in local production in Europe. A plant in the UK is under construction now. Three plants in North America are extending capacity or have announced a plan to construct another plant. Though it is developing local production, Toyota is still reluctant to have a regional headquarters. Nissan and Honda built regional headquarters in the US and Europe and have begun to delegate powers from Japan to them. Toyota controls overseas activities through the Overseas Operations Department at home, still showing reluctance in this aspect.

Toyota applied the Japanese production system successfully in North America and Taiwan. According to our evaluation points, four plants recorded high scores, especially in 'Methods'. At the same time, TMM, TMMC, and Kouzui showed high scores in the 'Results' (ready-made) category. This implies that a high score in 'Methods' accompanies a high score in 'Material Results' and 'Human Results', which means bringing 'ready-made' from Japan into local plants; or that 'Results' supports a high score in 'Methods'. It is possible to infer that a high rate of application of the Japanese system and a high rate of application of both 'Methods' and 'Results' stemmed from the management policy of Toyota, because it put a great importance on building those three plants, after having prepared for positive overseas activities. The percentage of Japanese expatriates ranges from 1.2% to 3.1% of all employees, which is intermediate between Nissan and Honda. Nissan sent the smallest number of Japanese overseas, at less than 1%. Contrary to this, Honda sent lots of Japanese, reaching 4 or 5% of its total employees.

NOTES

1. The Japanese Multinational Enterprise Study Group, to which I belong, conducted field research on Japanese-affiliated plants in the US in 1989. The result of the research was published in Abo (1994). I also had a chance to do research on the Japanese-affiliated automobile and electronics firms in Taiwan in 1990. I evaluated the hybrid ratio for the plants using the same criteria for the US plants shown in the above publication.
2. Dr M. Trevor defined Japanese multinationals as 'reluctant multinationals' (Trevor, 1983). Toyota could be called as a typical 'reluctant multinational'. However, Toyota changed its overseas production strategy in 1995. It announced a Global Business Plan, containing an expansion plan for its overseas production capacity and for setting up new ventures. One of the new ventures is the construction of an automobile assembly plant in France.
3. See the evaluation model in our book (Abo, 1994, pp. 30–35).

BIBLIOGRAPHY

Abernathy, William J., Kim B. Clark and Alan M. Kantrow (1983) *Industrial Renaissance: Producing a Competitive Future for America*, NY: Basic Books.
Abo, Tetsuo (1992) 'Overseas Production Activities of Nissan Motor Company: The Five Large Plants Abroad', in Sung-Jo Park (ed.), *Managerial Efficiency in Competitive and Cooperation*, Frankfurt: Campus.
Abo, Tetsuo (ed.) (1994) *Hybrid Factory: The Japanese Production System in the United States*, N.Y.: Oxford.
Beale, Dave (1994) *Driven by Nissan?: A Critical Guide to New Management Techniques*, London: Lawrence & Wishart.
Bratton, John (1992) *Japanization at Work*, London: Macmillan.
Cusumano, Michael A. (1985) *The Japanese Automobile Industry*, Cambridge, MA: Harvard University Press.
Dohse, Knuth, Ulrich Jurgens and Thomas Malsh (1985) 'From "Fordism" to "Toyotism"? The Social Organization of the Labor Process in the Japanese Automobile Industry', *Politics and Society*, **14** (2), pp. 115–46.

Florida, Richard and Martin Kenney (1991) 'Transplant Organizations: The Transfer of Japanese Industrial Organization to the U.S.', *American Sociological Review*, **56** (June), pp. 381–98.

Garrahan, Philip and Stewart Paul (1992) *The Nissan Enigma: Flexibility at Work in a Local Economy*, London: Mansell.

Institute of Social Science (1990) *Local Production of Japanese Automobile and Electronics Firms in the United States*, Research Report No 23, University of Tokyo.

Jones, Stephanie (1991) *Working for the Japanese*, London: Macmillan.

Katz, Harry C. and Charles F. Sabel (1985) 'Industrial Relations and Industrial Adjustment in the Car Industry', *Industrial Relations*, **24** (3), pp. 295–315.

Kenney, Martin and Richard Florida (1993) *Beyond Mass Production: The Japanese System and Its Transfer to the U.S.*, NY: Oxford.

Kumon, Hiroshi (1992) 'Multinationalization of Toyota Motor Corporation', *Journal of International Economic Studies*, **6**, pp. 80–99.

Kumon, Hiroshi (1993) 'Japanese-affiliated Auto Plants in the United Kingdom', *Journal of International Economic Studies*, **7**, pp. 67–88.

Kumon, Hiroshi (1994) Japanese-affiliated Automobile Plants in the United States and Taiwan, in H. Schutte (ed.) *The Global Competitiveness of the Asian Firm*, London: Macmillan.

Law, Christopher M. (1991) *Restructuring the Global Automobile Industry*, London: Routledge.

Morales, Rebecca (1994) *Flexible Production: Restructuring of the International Automobile Industry*, Cambridge: Polity Press.

Oliver, Nick and Barry Wilkinson (1988), *The Japanization of British Industry*, Oxford: Blackwell.

Parker, Mike and Jane Slaughter (1988) *Choosing Sides: Unions and the team Concept*, Boston: South End Press.

Tolliday, Steven (1991) *The power to Manage? Employers and Industrial Relations in Comparative-Historical Perspective*, London: Routledge.

Tolliday, Steven and Jonathan Zeitlin (1987) *The Automobile Industry and its Workers*, NY: St. Martin's Press.

Toyota Motor Corporation (1988) *Toyota: A History of the First 50 Years*, Toyota Motor Corporation.

Trevor, Malcom (1983) *Japan's Reluctant Multinationals*, NY: St. Martins's Press.

Wells, Peter and Michael Rawlinson (1994) *The New European Automobile Industry*, NY: St. Martin's Press.

Wickens, Peter (1987) *The Road to Nissan: Flexibility, Quality, Teamwork*, London: Macmillan.

Wickens, Peter (1995) *The Ascendant Organization*, London: Macmillan.

Wilkinson, Barry, Jonathan Morris and Nick Oliver (1989) *Japanizing the World: The Case of Toyota*, Paper presented to the APROS Conference on Organizations, Technologies and Culture in Comparative Perspective, Australian National University, Canberra, 13–15 December.

Womack, James P., Daniel T. Jones and Daniel Roos (1990) *The Machine that Changed the World*, NY: Rawson Associates.

12. Toshiba's overseas production activities: seven large plants in the USA, Mexico, the UK, Germany and France

Tetsuo Abo

INTRODUCTION

Toshiba Corporation is, along with Hitachi and Mitsubishi, one of the big three 'integrated' electronics companies in Japan. With its suitable domestic market position supported by a long history since 1875 (since 1939 as Tokyo Shibaura Electric Co. and since 1978 Toshiba Corporation), developing from a heavy electric company to a 'one set' electronics maker, it has been among the typical Japanese 'conservative' multinational enterprises (MNEs), in comparison with the active MNE-type consumer electric and electronics companies such as Matsushita, Sanyo and Sony. However, in terms of foreign investment size, Toshiba is grouped into the most active MNEs.

I previously have considered Sony, Nissan and Sanyo[1] as case studies of Japanese manufacturing MNEs, and here I am going to add the Toshiba case in order to illuminate some important aspects of Japanese MNEs. The theoretical and analytical frameworks and the data for the case studies were principally based on the research of the Japanese Multinational Enterprise Study Group (JMNESG) and on plant visits by the JMNESG members and myself.

The main points are as follows:

1. How different is Toshiba's case from that of a few more active Japanese MNEs in the electronics industry such as Matsushita, Sanyo and Sony and in the automobile industry such as Nissan and Honda; on the other hand, how similar is it to that of a large number of 'conservative'-type MNEs (called 'reluctant multinationals' by M. Trevor)[2] such as Mitsubishi and Hitachi in the electronics industry and Toyota and many other makers in the auto industry.
2. What similarities and differences are there among Toshiba's seven plants taken up in this paper?

3. What similarities and differences are there between Toshiba's plants and western MNEs, especially electronics firms such as GE, Philips, and Thomson, or IBM and Motorola?
4. The reasons for these characteristics of Toshiba's activities as an MNE and where they stem from.

My primary concern in this research is the causal relationship between the Japanese-style production system and Toshiba's particular behaviour as a Japanese MNE. The JMNESG members and I have developed, based on large-scale joint field research and theoretical analysis, an 'International Transfer Model'(or 'Application-Adaptation Dilemma Model') of the Japanese-style production systems which reveals the essential elements and their systematic composition, with special emphasis on the international transfer of each element[3]. According to this model, it would be natural for many Japanese manufacturing firms to be reluctant to produce abroad. They would rather export their finished goods produced in domestic plants because the comparative advantages of their production system are closely related to human factors in the workplace, and these factors must be viewed against their unique social and historical background in Japan. Assuming that this model is consistent, I will show how Toshiba's case can help to clarify the characteristic features and various aspects of Japanese manufacturing MNEs, the reasons for that, and its implication for the development of Japanese MNEs in the future.

Of course, recently there have been some significant changes in the typical behaviour of Japanese MNEs toward a more global orientation, due to various changes in the economic and social environment in and out of Japan: the appreciation of the yen, the pressure and need of 'internal internationalization', which stems from criticism of Japanese firms and society, the shortage and ageing of human resources, the burst and collapse of the 'bubble' economy, and so on. We should take into account these changes. But I think it is also important to recognize that the Japanese production system is a function of historical contingencies and developments, and so, as a system, it is likely to take several decades before undergoing a paradigm change. (As a nation, on the other hand, industrial Japan may suffer much earlier from the 'ruleless' yen appreciation).

OVERALL OVERSEAS PRODUCTION STRATEGY AND ACTIVITIES OF TOSHIBA

One of the distinctive characteristics of Toshiba in the electronics industry is a contrast between the higher level of overseas investment and loan outstanding

(second group) and the almost lowest level of overseas production ratio (10%).
Compare the overseas sales ratio: 34% in 1991 (see Table 12.1).

Table 12.1　Overseas production activities of Japanese consumer electronics companies

	Overseas Production Ratio (%)*	No. of Expatriates	No. of overseas Manufacturing Plants	Overseas Investments & Loans Outstanding (billion Yen)
Sanyo	27.0	625	58	151.1
Matsushita	14.0	1000	80	136.7
Toshiba	10.5	540	23	157.9
Sony	20.0		19	774.6
Hitachi		450	26	60.0
Mitsubishi	7.0	390	20	28.0
Sharp	25.0	345	11	91.6
JVC		10		
NEC[†]	7.0	692	25	118.0

Notes:

*　　*Amount of overseas production (sometimes sales amount)*
　　　Overseas production & Domestic production

[†]　This is not the consumer electrics company

Source:　Toyo Keizai, Kaishabetsu Kaigai Shinshutsu Kigyo, 1991–2

The primary strategy for its overseas activities has been 'export-led→trade
friction→local production', a typical Japanese 'reluctant'-style. Until the first
half of the 1980s, exports produced at the home plants were more profitable for
Toshiba than local production. Therefore its overseas plants have been organized
as the 'branch factories' of home plants in terms of delegation of power, though
most of them are legally subsidiaries.

The main stream in Toshiba's history of overseas production activities is
summarized below (Table 12.2).

1. Until mid-1970s: licensing and assistance of technologies for import
   substitution-type economic development in the developing countries, mostly
   in South-East Asia.
2. From mid-1970s to mid-1980s: trade friction adaptation-type local production
   in the US and the UK; colour television (CTV) plants in the US and UK and
   chassis assembly plant for these CTV plants in Singapore; a semiconductor
   plant in the US. The strategic change was necessitated by the sharp

Table 12.2 A comparison of Toshiba's seven large plants abroad (1989–1991)

	TACP (US)	TDD (US)	TAEC (US)
1. Location	Lebanon, Tennessee	Horsheads, NY	Sunnyvale, Ca
2. Start-up	1979	1986 (I), 1989 (II)	1980 (Acquisi.)
3. Space (000m²)	L 506, F 206	L 128	
4. Capital (m. US$)	23	I: 40 (50%), II: 100 (100%)	20
5. Investment (cum. m.)		I: 70, II: 110	
6. Production (1000s p.a.)	CTV (all sizes, 1000 MO (3 sizes) 450	CPT (19", 20") 1600 units (30", 32") 360 units	IC (Memory: 1 MEGA, ASIC) 12000KP
7. Export	10% (Can., Mid-Ame., JPN)	Plan (Europe)	
8. Employees			
Total	700	1242	209
White	100		79
Blue	600 (Main 10, QC 20)	828 (Main 233)	115
Japanese	12	8	26
Female/Total (%)	70	30	(Minority 80%)
9. Turnover Rate (% p.a.)	2	36	2
10. Absenteeism (%)	4–5	4–5	5.4
Visitor (Date)	JMNESG (9, 1989)	JMNESG (9, 1989)	JMNESG (8, 1989)

Notes: MO: Micro oven; Main: Maintenance; CTV: Colour television;
VTR: Video tape recorder; QC: Quality control.

appreciation of the yen in the later half of the 1970s and serious trade frictions during the great fluctuation of the world economy after the second oil shock.

3. Since the mid-1980s: more earnest and world-wide logistics-type local production under the second round appreciation of the yen after the Plaza agreement by G5 and the strong movement towards an integrated Europe since the Agreement for an Integrated Europe in 1986. This resulted in the Maquiladoras chassis assembly plant (for the US CTV plant) in Mexico; the colour picture tube plant in the US; the semiconductor assembly plants in Malaysia; the portable personal computer plant and the video tape recorder (VTR) plant in (West) Germany (shifted from the UK plant); the paper copier assembly plant in France; and plants for the productions of various consumer electric appliances and parts in Asian countries such as Thailand and North China.

ANALYTICAL METHODS

The next section covers the composition and features of the JMNESG's working model, which was designed to represent the characteristics of the Japanese

TE (Mex)	TCPE (Germany)	TCP (UK)	TS (Fr)
Tijuana (Maquiladoras)	Mönchengladback, NRWF	Plymouth, Devon	Dieppe, Seine Maritime
1987	1987–1995 (closed)	1981	
L 64, F 10	L 58, F 8		
3.9	45DM (Govt subsid. 20%)	L17	
3.9	45DM		
Chassis 800 units	VTR: 550 large var.-small vol.	CTV (14" – 28": 6 sizes) 580	Paper copier
All products to TAC	Share: 5% – EC, 2.5 – Germ.	Ex. rate: 53% (Europe)	
706	241	1091 (Temporary 11)	310
45	48	211	60
645	193	734	250
9		7	
65	68	60	
128	0	24	
3.8	5	3.7	15.4?
JMNESG (9, 1989)	ABO & D.S. CHO (8, 1991)	ABO & CHO (8, 1991)	

production system, paying particular attention to its internationalization aspects.[3] A major distinctive feature of the Japanese production system has been its ability to achieve high product quality and business efficiency over a wide range of operations, through a strong sense of employee identification with the company, and through flexibility resulting from its 'work-oriented operations'. Here, human factors related to workers at the shop floor level are quite important, with human-oriented methods deeply rooted in the particular customs and institutional background of Japanese society.

Our working model is in the left column of the table composed of six major groups with 23 element items ('6-G 23-I', sometimes '7-G 24-I') to assess the level and degree of international transfer of the Japanese-style management and production system (see Appendix). For each element here, I have picked out the significant points regarding the seven Toshiba plants, derived from my own and our group's plant visits; these are among the key factors for evaluating the degree of transfer of the practices of the parent plants to each of the local plants.

Considering the salient features of Japanese-type, culture-embodied production technologies formulated in Table 12.3, it is easy to understand why Japanese firms, when applying their technology advantages to foreign countries, would

Table 12.3   'Hybrid ratios' of Toshiba's seven overseas plants

Oper. & Manage.		TACP (US)	TDD (US)	TAEC (US)	TE (Mex)	TCPE (Germany)	TCP (UK)	TS (Fr)
I	**Work Org./Adm. av.**	**1.5**	**3.0**	**3.5**	**1.8**	**2.3**	**3.3**	**3.7**
(1)	Job Classifi.	2	2	4	2	2	4	5
(2)	Job Rotation	1	3	4	1	2	2	4
(3)	Training	1	3	3	2	3	3	3
(4)	Supervisor	2	3	3	2	3	3	3
(5)	Wage	1	2	3	2	1	4	3
(6)	Promotion	2	3	4	2	3	4	3
II	**Produ. Control av.**	**3.3**	**4.0**	**3.3**	**3.9**	**3.3**	**2.8**	**3.8**
(7)	Equipment	4	5	5	5	4	4	4
(8)	Quality Control	4	4	2	4	3	2	4
(9)	Maintenance	1	3	3	3	2	3	3
(10)	Oper. Control	4	4	3	3	4	2	4
III	**Parts Procure. av.**	**2.3**	**2.7**	**3.7**	**3.3**	**2.7**	**3.0**	**3.7**
(11)	Local Content	2	2	4	4	3	3	3
(12)	Suppliers	3	4	5	4	3	3	4
(13)	Methods	2	2	2	2	2	3	4
(IV)	**Team Sense av.**	**1.7**	**2.3**	**3.7**	**3.3**	**3.0**	**2.7**	**3.0**
(14)	Small Group	1	2	4	1	2	1	2
(15)	Information	2	3	4	4	3	3	3
(16)	Unity	2	2	3	5	4	4	4
(V)	**Labor Relat. av.**	**1.8**	**2.5**	**3.0**	**4.0**	**2.5**	**3.0**	**3.3**
(17)	Employ. Policy	3	3	2	3	3	3	4
(18)	Employ. Securi.	1	2	2	4	4	3	3
(19)	Union	1	3	5	5	1	4	3
(20)	Grievance	2	2	3	4	2	2	3
(VI)	**Parent/Subsi. av.**	**2.7**	**2.3**	**4.3**	**3.3**	**2.7**	**1.7**	**2.7**
(21)	JPN Ratio	2	1	5	2	2	1	(2)
(22)	Power Delega.	3	3	4	4	3	2	3
(23)	Local Managers	3	3	4	4	3	2	3
Total average		**2.1**	**2.9**	**3.5**	**3.1**	**2.7**	**2.8**	**3.4**
VII	Local Community			3	4	3		

Notes:
'Hybrid ratios' are evaluated by a 5-point grading system: 5 = the highest degree of 'application' (the lowest 'adaptation'), 1 = the lowest 'application' (the highest 'adaptation'). The scores were evaluated by JMNESG members for the US and Mexico plants, and by myself for the plants of Germany, UK, Spain and China. (For visitors, see Table 12.2.)

have to face problems in adapting local environments. We, therefore, call our working model 'application-adaptation dilemma model', which indicates the difficult or even trade-off relationship between both aspects. We also developed a 'Hybrid ratio' (HR) to test the correlation between the degree of 'application' of Japanese management techniques at the plants abroad and of 'adaptation' to the local climates. 'Application' represents aspects of an MNE's activities which retain competitive advantages by introducing its methods to local production facilities. In MNE theory it is referred to as 'firm-specific factors'. 'Adaptation' represents other aspects of the MNE's activities, which involve modifying or adjusting parent practices to various kinds of local environment. In MNE theory it is described as the main aspects of 'location-specific factors'.[4] What interests us most here is the degree of mixture or 'Hybrid ratio', in other words, the extent to which the system of Japanese manufacturers is either applied or adapted to the local climates.

In order to quantify and illustrate major findings from our field observations, we then adopted a five point grading technique for each category. Within this ranking a 5-point score indicates the highest possible degree of application (and, consequently, the lowest level of adaptation – this would be given to a Japanese plant operating in Japan). A 1-point ranking indicates the highest possible degree of adaptation (and, would be given to a local plant operating in a foreign country). Although these rankings are by no means exact, we can nevertheless easily estimate application-adaptation levels.

One more important evaluation method that we developed is 'Four-Perspectives Evaluation'(4PE). This is to analyse which aspects of '6-G 23-I' elements were transplanted, in order to distinguish more clearly those elements that make a substantial and vital contribution to the transfer of the Japanese system to the local environment. The Four-Perspectives (in Table 12.5) derive from rearranging '6-G 23-I' elements, and distinguishing in particular 'Method' transfer aspects from 'Result' transfer aspects. 'Result' means to introduce from Japan 'ready-made' elements such as equipment, parts ('Materials') and Japanese people ('Human'); 'Method' is to transplant the 'logic' or know-how of the system to local people. 'Result' may guarantee immediate better performance at the local plant, but 'Method', in the long run (not necessarily in the short run), must promise a substantial technology transfer to the local soil (and 'Result' may not).

SEVEN LARGE OVERSEAS MANUFACTURING PLANTS

Toshiba's seven plants studied for the research are outlined in Table 12.2. Three plants are located in the United States, one in Mexico and three in the European developed countries – Germany, the UK, and France. The main data for these plants and Toshiba's international activities were principally collected by plant visits and interviews at the Japanese headquarters by the JMNESG members and myself. But if we want to have a recent overview of Toshiba's production activities abroad we miss here a couple of important assembly plants in the south Asian countries mentioned on pages 160 and 170. Some additional material on these plants can be found in the Conclusion.

Three US Plants

These three plants in the US are considerably different in their products, and accordingly in their nature, that is, their 'Hybrid ratios'('HR') and performances, but they also have some similarities.

Toshiba America Consumer Products, Inc., Manufacturing Division (1979–)[5]

This is one of the representative Japanese colour television (CTV) plants set up late to cope with the US-Japan trade friction and appreciation of the yen. The transfer of the CTV assembly line here is limited to the final processes, composed of the relatively simple manual work of assembling and testing. The overall average of HR for this plant [2.1] (see Table 12.3) represents very low application (high adaptation) as the systems of work organization and their operations have largely followed ways similar to that of most American firms (application scores for GI (Work Organization and Administration) [1.5], GIV (Team Sense) [1.7] and GV (Labour Relations) [1.8] are extremely low). The competitive advantage of this plant, on the other hand, is primarily derived from bringing in hardware technologies such as equipment and key components, and their Toshiba-style sophisticated operation techniques (application scores for GII (Production Control) [3.3], GIII (Parts Procurement) [2.3] and GVI (Parent-Subsidiary Relations) [2.7] are relatively high).

According to our 'Four-Perspective Evaluation' in Table 12.4, while the application scores of 'Method' transfer-related elements, such as all the items in GI [1–2], G2, (9) Maintenance [1] and almost all the items in GIV and GV [1–2] are very low, those scores of 'Result' (Ready-made) transfer elements such as (7) Equipment [4], (12) Suppliers [3], (23) Local Managers [3] are much higher.

The above must mean that this plant has been operated smartly with a convenient combination ('HR') of American and Japanese elements. However, it also suggests two questions: first, problems of flexibility in plant operations might occur because the systems and their administration at this plant are largely organized on American-type 'demarcation' principles; second, there is an issue of the extent to which the 'Result'-oriented application of Japanese system can contribute to the real transfer of Japanese production technologies to American society.

Table 12.4   Four perspectives evaluation of the 'hybrid ratios' of Toshiba's overseas plants

		TACP (US)	TDD (US)	TAEC (US)	TE (Mex)	TCPE (Germany)	TCP (UK)	TS (Fr)
	Human	1.6	2.5	3.4	2.8	2.5	3.1	3.4
Method	Material	2.5	3.5	2.5	3.5	2.5	2.5	3.5
	Average	2.1	3.0	3.0	3.2	2.5	2.8	3.5
Result	Human	2.5	2.0	4.5	3.0	2.5	1.5	(2.5)
('Ready-	Material	3.0	3.7	4.7	4.3	3.3	3.3	3.7
Made')	Average	2.8	2.9	4.6	3.7	2.9	2.4	3.1
Method (av) % Result (av)		75.0	103.4	65.3	86.5	86.2	116.7	112.9

Toshiba Display Devices, Inc. (1986–)

This is a colour picture tube (CPT) plant with a unique hybrid created as a combination of several factors different from TACP. It is a Japanese-led, greenfield, CTV assembly plant; a plant that is led by the 'Japanese-style' understanding of an American human resources director. It changed from a joint venture with Westinghouse to Toshiba 100% owned, and relies on equipment such as a semiconductor plant.

The overall average application score [2.9] of TDD in Table 12.3 is distinctly high in the consumer electronics industry and rather closer to TAEC (semiconductor). There is a sharp contrast between two different directions of application and adaptation: higher application scores for GI (Work Organization) [3.0] and GII (Production Control) [4.0], and lower application (higher adaptation) scores for GIV (Team Sense) [2.3] and GV (Labor Relations) [2.5]. This means that the higher application of the core parts of Japanese system at this plant has been attained without gaining much support from their sub-system and environmental conditions, which are deeply influenced by socio-cultural factors.

The exceptionally simple job description ((1) Job Classification [4]) and the corresponding (job-centered) wage system ((5) Wage [2]) in the consumer electronics industry partly reflect length of service and individual performance evaluation systems (IPES). An American human resources director practised the above 'Japanese-style' at the former non-union plant of Westinghouse and introduced it to this plant.

The most crucial elements for high efficiency and quality at this plant, however, must be the high application of (7) Equipment [5], (8). Quality

Control [4] (which is a computer aided system) and (12) Suppliers [4]. According to 4PE, therefore, we can also see a unique mixture: a higher transfer of 'Material' and a lower transfer of 'Human' in 'Result' perspective; and in 'Method' perspective a higher 'Material' and, contrastingly, higher 'Human' (GI) and lower 'Human' (GIV and GV) (compare Table 12.4). This means that this is quite a different case from the usual Japanese transplants, not only in consumer electronics but also in other industries.

The implications from this case may be significant for the transferability of the Japanese system, in that local managers can operate Japanese plants by introducing a suitable hybrid of both 'Human' and 'Material' core parts, in 'Result' and 'Method', without much support from socio-cultural conditions. However, with the relatively low team sense and long-term commitment of employees suggested by the very high turnover ratio (36% per annum, Table 12.2), it would not be easy to sustain the present performance for a long time.

Toshiba America Electronic Components, Inc., Microelectronic Center (1980–)

This is a different type of semiconductor plant organized and operated with high application orientation in both 'Result' and 'Method', but in the process of reducing the size of local production. From the beginning when Toshiba acquired the small Integrated Circuits (IC) plant from a Japanese company in the US, this was not a very serious plan for the large-scale production of memory IC in the US (local production rate to total sales = 10%).

On the other hand, it was Toshiba alone that was manufacturing 1 MEGA DRAM IC (256 K DRAM at the other five plants) as of 1989, and planning 4 MEGA and Gate Array in 1990 or the near future. Along with ASIC manufacturing, this was still an important plant to enable Toshiba to sustain a production basis in the US.

In this plant the overall application score [3.5] is not only higher than other Toshiba plants but also than the average of the whole semiconductor industry ([3.2] in Abo (1994), T. 3–3). This is partly because the 'Result' transfer of (7) Equipment [5], (12) Suppliers [5] and (21) Japanese expatriates [5] is very strong, which is one of the common features of semiconductor plants abroad. But partly because the 'Method' scores such as GI (Work Organization) [3.5] and GIV (Team Sense) [3.7] are particularly high, this is a semiconductor plant that is operated with exceptional flexibility. The reasons for the interesting 'Japanese-style' are as follows: 1) This is not a mass-production plant but a customer-oriented 'large variety in small volume' plant, which has been a new direction in local production of ICs by Japanese firms, and was created through 'down-sizing'; 2) Although the Japanese ratio is extremely high, it is led by an American manager who understands Toshiba style very well and has been contributing to the unique 'Method' transfer.

Toshiba Electromex, S.A. de C.V. (1987–) in Mexico

This is a cost centre that assembles and supplies chassis to the CTV plant in the US (TACP) by utilizing low wage costs in a free trade zone (FTZ). Maquiladoras is located just at the national border between the United States and Mexico[6].

There is hardly any notable application of Japanese 'Methods', except for some surrounding elements related to GIV (Team Sense) and GV (Labor Relations) such as (15) Information [4], (16) Unity [5], and (18) Employment Security [4] (so far these practices are not playing an important role).

Each element of GI [1.8], the core part of 'Human-Method', gained very low application scores because of an extremely high turnover ratio (128% in 1989) and an academic career-oriented society. Under these conditions, needless to say, it is difficult to set up more simple job descriptions and to train employees on the On The Job rotation system on a long-term basis (compare the role of some supervisors trained in Japan). 'Material-Result' (equipment and parts) is the key factor for this plant to retain cost advantage. The maintenance of the introduced machine and equipment (9) Maintenance [3] is mainly implemented by Japanese expatriates (21) Japanese Ratio [2] and Japanese machine-tool makers near the plant (see Appendix).

Three European Plants

Toshiba Consumer Products Europe GmbH (1987–1995) in Germany

This is an interesting case showing how Japanese production systems can be applied to the German industry, where Japanese makers have to challenge the established 'qualification system' against the traditional Meister system, AZUBI (Auszubildende = German apprenticeship), and also the high wage level (much shorter work time) and the rigid work rule backed by the strong union, IG Metal.

The most signficant factor at this video tape recorder (VTR) plant, whose VTR production was transferred from TCP (UK), described below, is that a kind of Japanese style flexible operation for 'large variety in small volume' (LVSV) production has been implemented; such an LVSV is essential in the European situation, where TCPE has to supply a wide range of models and sizes of VTRs to European countries which have quite different TV broadcasting systems, such as PAL, SECAM, and so on. (This is a quite different situation from the TACP in the US).

The Japanese president, who had much experience in parts manufacturing in Japan, has adeptly led the LVSV, including the U-shape line, with the co-operation of German production managers who have more or less understood the Japanese style (see the application scores for (10) Operation Control [4] and (23) Local Manager [3] in Table 12.3).

The supervisors and multi-skill-oriented workers, who are trained and promoted internally through On The Job training, contribute to flexible operations, which are needed not only for the LVSV but also for the complicated mechanism of VTR, with a large number of parts and components ((3) Training, (4) Supervisor and (6) Promotion are all [3]). However, the more basic organizational systems at the shop floor do not necessarily correspond to the above practices, as the job description is firmly decided in the agreement with IG Metal ((1) Job classification [2] – there are nine categories – and (5) Wage [1]). It was interesting to hear from the president that the problem of demarcation due to the rigid job classification was considerably cleared here by paying extra wages.

Fair and flexible operations are enabled by an emphasis on the 'Method' aspect of 'Material' ((10) Operational control, in particular) supported by some elements of the 'Method' aspect of 'Human' ((3) Training, (4) Supervisor and (6) Promotion in GI). However, allowance has to be made for the rigid German framework, with lower applications for the core parts of the 'Method' aspect of 'Human' ((1) Job classification, (5)Wage, and so on in GI). To what extent can we generalize this case to other Japanese plants in Germany? Or is this a special case just for such a medium-sized plant with 240 employees? Finally, however, it should be noted that this plant had not yet attained positive earnings by 1990, taking depreciation into account; it was finally closed and its VTR production was again transferred to TCP(UK) in 1995, partly because of the high appreciation of the German Mark.

Toshiba Consumer Products (UK) Ltd. (1981–)[7]

This is an important colour television (CTV) plant that has been successfully managed as a 'British-led Japanese company'. Although this plant moved from a joint venture to a 100 per cent-owned and from a British president to Japanese one, the 'British-led' feature does not seem to have undergone any basic change. For this the exceptionally low application scores for GVI (Parent/Subsidiary) [1.7] and (21) Japanese Ratio [1] in GVI are symbolical.

The overall average HRs of both TCPE (Germany) [2.7] and TCP (UK) [2.8] are almost equal (interestingly this level may be a 'European level' of consumer electronics plant, because the HRs of Sanyo's two plants in Germany and the UK are also comparable, at [3.0] and [2.9]),[8] but the locational combinations of HRs of the 6 groups or 23 elements are contrastingly different. At the German and UK plants respectively, in Table 12.3, the HRs are as follows: GI [2.3], [3.3]; GII [3.3], [2.8]; G III [2.7], [3.0]; GIV [3.0], [2.7]; GV [2.5], [3.0]; GVI [2.7], [1.7].

In particular, the combination of a higher application score for GI (Work Organization) [3.3] and a lower score for GII (Production Control) [2.8] at the UK plant are notable, compared with other consumer electronics plants. In terms of the core part of 'Human-Method', the application-orientation of this plant is strong as, in GI, the wage and promotion systems, based on individual performance evaluation system and length of service ((5) Wage [4] and (2) Promotion [4]), correspond to the Japanese-style flexible Job grades ((1) Job classification [4]). By contrast, in terms of 'Material-Method', the application-orientation is rather weak, as the operations techniques of Toshiba, including Quality control ((10) Operational Control [2], (8) Quality control [2]) have not been introduced so much. This would mean that at this plant, the British-led management has created a Japanese-style human related organizational basis, but has not sufficiently built up the engineering and production techniques. However, since the spring of 1991, three Japanese engineers have been dispatched to this plant in order to assist the new plant expansion and to reassess production skills.

This plant was a pioneer of the 'single union agreement', along with Sony (UK)[9]. Toshiba set up this system by introducing a Company Advisory Board to liaise between the company and the union, EEPTU. Traditionally, a British company usually has several agreements with different unions. The role of the single union and its influence on nationwide industrial relations has, needless to say, been great. This is because, where Japanese systems are introduced, the 'homogeneous' human resource condition, including union activities, is vital for their 'demarcation-free' flexible systems; also, such a single union type activity would encourage British unions to go toward 'company unions', which are more or less 'classless unions'.

Toshiba Systems (France) S.A. (1986–)

This is a unique assembly plant amongst Japanese electronics factories abroad, which emphasizes the application of 'Methods' in both the 'Human' and 'Material' elements.

From one point of view, the HR situation of this paper copier assembly plant is quite similar to that of TAEC (US), a semiconductor assembly plant: 1) the total average scores of TS and TAEC – [3.4] and [3.5]; 2) the score of each group – comparable for GI, GII, GIII, and GV; 3) the score of each element – comparable for many. These similarities probably come from the following reasons: 1) both are manufacturing more or less high technology and non consumer products, for which performance and quality of the products is more important than the cost; 2) the scales of the plants are not very large, so that it is easier and more necessary to implement Japanese style methods and techniques carefully.

There are, however, some significant differences between these two plants: 1) GIV–[3.0] and [3.7]; 2) GVI–[2.7] and [4.3]; 3) (8) Quality control [4] and [2]; 4) (10) Operational Control [4] and [3]; 5) (13) Procurement Methods [4] and [2]; 6) (17) Employment Policy [4] and [2]. The big difference regarding GVI is interesting in that at the French plant, the management team has much more local staff, with relatively fewer, but carefully selected Japanese expatriates (lower Human-Result). They have conducted the more Japanese-style, 'Method'-oriented practices. The higher application scores for Quality control, Operation control, and Procurement method show the active transfer of the 'Methods' aspect of 'Material'. As for procurement, attempts have been made to build up long-term reciprocal relations with local suppliers by painstaking persuasion and teaching the importance of quality.

The exceptionally high application score for GI [3.7] and its composite elements at an electronics plant (in Table 12.3) are also noticeable. These reflect the positive practices for multi-functional and flexible operations at the shop floor, such as very simplified job grades, in-house training for multi-skilling using an individual personal evaluation system (IPES), score boards, and training in Japan (for all the workers within five years?) (see Appendix).

It goes without saying that the above high density practices must be costly in terms of both money and time. In fact, here also, the earning performance of this plant was still negative as of 1991. Therefore, we should take into account the long-term cost and benefit performance at this plant.

CONCLUSION AND PROSPECTS

Similarities and Differences among Toshiba's Seven Plants

1. Of all the seven Toshiba plants discussed in this paper, the application-oriented plants are more dominant over the adaptation-type; in my overall judgement (not only on the average application score), four are application-types (TDD, TAEC, TCPE and TS), one is fifty-fifty (TCP), and two are adaptation-types (TACP and TE).

2. Though all the plants have a higher application level in the 'Material-Result' perspective (equipment and parts is the minimum core for the competitive edge), both aspects of application and adaptation have been combined in various ways: American-type organizational management plus Japanese production control (TACP), Japanese-type flexible methods for both 'Material' and 'Human' by American managers (TDD) or by Japanese managers (TCPE), Japanese-type 'Human-Methods' (lower 'Material-Methods') by British managers (TCP), and so on.

3. The general impression of Toshiba's overseas plant management, as we have observed above, is that it is one of the very strongly application-oriented companies among Japanese electronics MNEs, but not consistently organized by its Japanese headquarters. In other words, plant-site level managers have substantial discretionary powers in their operations at the local plants,

just as in Japan. This is the main reason why the ways of applying the principles of the parent factories to their local subsidiaries are so different.

Comparison with Other Japanese Electronics Multinationals

1. Toshiba is a typical 'conservative' Japanese electronics MNE. As one of the big three 'integrated' electronics companies in Japan, enjoying a more profitable domestic market, its primary overseas strategy has been 'export-led' and its overseas production ratio is among the lowest in Japanese consumer electronics companies. It is true that until very recently the manufacturing activities of Toshiba at the parent plants in Japan have remained most efficient, as suggested particularly by its semiconductor production. But this situation is decisively changing, as seen in the last Section, under the 'ruleless' appreciation of the yen since the early spring of 1995.

2. Then, once it decides on local production, Toshiba seems to be relatively eager to apply its own manufacturing methods to the transplants. To give an example, although not a strict comparison, the average application scores for the seven plants of Toshiba and Sanyo are 2.9 and 2.6[10].

3. A Merger and Acquisition (M&A) basis to the start of its foreign operation is one of the distinct features of Toshiba relative to other Japanese MNEs, which have not traditionally adopted an alliance strategy so often. Of all the seven cases, three are joint venture or acquisition-oriented, though all three were finally changed to wholly-owned subsidiaries. This may reflect Toshiba's historical experience, especially the long relationship beween Toshiba (and its antecedents) and General Electric (GE) through licensing and joint venture agreements since the late 1880s[11]. One of the main reasons for the above three must have been the company's 'conservative' decision making approach, showing a step by step approach. However, as mentioned below, this may have been a more active weapon in the recent strategic alliances in its global business activities.

Comparison with Western Electronics Multinationals

1. The most important difference between Toshiba's overseas production activities and those of western electronics firms would be its emphasis on the application-oriented plant-level management, which is one of the major comparative advantages of Japanese manufacturing firms, especially of Toshiba.

    The representative western electronics firms, such as GE, IBM, Motorola and Philips,[12] usually seem to be emphasizing the competitive advantages of product and/or marketing technologies, and leaving plant management largely to local engineers who are only requested to follow the basic manuals brought in from parent companies. In contrast, Toshiba in particular, and other Japanese MNEs in general, do not have any definite manuals for plant operations both at home and abroad, although preparation of some kind of manuals has been tried recently for their local plants.

2. Thus, the degree of integration of Toshiba's global production activities looks weaker than that of western MNEs which have established formal control systems by using various manuals, especially for financial reports. By contrast, Toshiba, like many other Japanese firms, has relied on a 'human information network', implemented through the dispatch of Japanese expatriates. As a result it is my impression, as drawn from my own interviews[11], that the headquarters of Japanese MNEs have more organized information about their local operation situations, except for financial reports such as balance sheets and earning/loss accounts.

3. The noticeable similarity of Toshiba to western MNEs is, as mentioned above, its M&A related strategy in international business. This may largely change the image of Toshiba's global activities in the near future.

Future Prospects[13]

Ever since the early 1990s, when the second stage of drastic yen appreciation after the Plaza Agreement of 1985 began, the overseas production strategy of Toshiba has been changing remarkably from a typical 'conservative' MNE to a more aggressive stance. The establishment of a VTR joint venture production base with French Thomson in 1988 in Singapore (International Video Products), was an epoch-making decision for Toshiba in the sense that, for the first time, it set up its large-scale overseas plant in Asia through the formation of a joint-venture contract, one of the company's forte, with a European electronics giant. At the plant, three million VTR sets were produced in 1994 and four million in 1995. Of these, 1.2 million were received by Toshiba and sold in North America, South-east Asia and China.

In the summer of 1994, the reshuffle of the world CTV production organization of Toshiba was decided in response to NAFTA. The Singapore CTV plant, which was set up in 1979 as a chassis production base for the assembly plant in the US (TCP), was upgraded to the position of the Asian CTV production centre (1.3 million in 1995) as a third regional centre, together with North American and European centres. A CTV production for export from the Japanese parent plant was shifted to small volume products such as high-added value and special type CTVs. As a result, the chassis production in Singapore was shifted to the Mexican plant (TE).

Also, Toshiba has been involved in various East Asian countries such as China, the Philippines, and Korea. Now, we can say that the company has become seriously committed to the dynamic process of creating the world growth centre of the electronics industry in Asia[14]. In 1995, its overseas production ratio will reach 90% for VTR and 70% for CTV.

Another significant case, where Toshiba recently has taken advantage of its M&A strategy in the developed countries, is the joint-venture semiconductor production contract with IBM in 1995, under the third 'ruleless' yen appreciation. At this latest large scale plant in the US, Toshiba will at last be able to overcome the limits of scale at US-TAEC, described above, and produce 64 MEGA-DRAM from 1997. It is interesting to add that Toshiba has also had a joint-venture production contract of 16 MEGA-DRAM with Motorola in Japan and a close joint research and development contract of 256 MEGA-DRAM with Siemens and IBM. How can Toshiba manage this kind of complicated international relations?

Our next concern is the effects of these aggressive multi-dimensional global strategies on Toshiba's production technology. Toshiba headquarters must have been playing a remarkable role in its new stage of worldwide production activities. If we take the Bartlett and Ghoshal model, it is changing from 'Multinational' to 'Global' or 'International' MNE[15]. However, how can production and engineering sections follow up this kind of complicated internationalization of production activities? The case studies show that the key factor in retaining the company's competitive advantage is the distinctly high level of Toshiba's material and personal engineering technologies at the plant sites.

Last, but not least, the question needs to be considered, not only for Toshiba but for almost all the Japanese MNEs, whether it can continue from now on to develop R&D activities at home, closely related with factory-level practices, without having appropriate domestic plants. Of course, so far, the majority of Japanese manufacturers have been able to upgrade, more or less, their products and production technologies, corresponding to the phased shifts to overseas production.

NOTES

1. See, Abo T. (1987) 'A Report of On-the-Spot Observation of Sony's Four Major Color TV Plants in the US, UK, West Germany and Japan', *Annals of Institute of Social Science, University of Tokyo*, **29**, (also in J. Stam (ed.) *Industrial Cooperation Between Europe and Japan*, Rotterdam: Erasmus University, 1989); Abo, T. (1992) 'Overseas Production Activities of Nissan Motor Co.: The Five Large Plants Abroad,' in S.J. Park (ed.) *Managerial Efficiency in Competition and Cooperation*, Campus Verlag and West View; Abo, T. (1994) 'Sanyo's Overseas Production Activities: Seven Large Plants in the US, Mexico, the UK, Germany, Spain and China', in H. Schutte (ed.) *The Global Competitiveness of the Asian Firms*, London: Macmillan; Abo, T. (1997) 'Electronics Assembly Industry' in H. Itagaki (ed.) *The Japanese Production System: Hybrid Factories in East Asia*, London: Macmillan.

2. Trevor, M. (1983) *Japan's Reluctant Multinationals*, New York: St. Martin's Press.
3. For our 'Application-Adaptation Model', see, Abo, T. (ed.) (1994) *Hybrid Factory: The Japanese Production System in the United States*, Oxford University Press, Chs. 1 and 2.
4. Dunning, J.H. (1981) *International Production and Multinational Enterprise*, Part I, Allen & Unwin.
5. For TACP (US), see Abo, T. (1985) *US Subsidiaries of Japanese Electronics Companies Enter a New Phase of Activities*, Occasional Paper No. 47, Social and Economic Research on Modern Japan, Berlin: Ute Schiller (also in *Annals of the Institute of Social Science*, **26**, 1984).
6. For the situation in the Mexican Maquiladoras, see research conducted by M. Kenney and R. Florida, for example, 'Japanese Maquiladoras: Production Organization and Global Commodity Chain', *World Development* **22** (1) 1994.
7. For reliable information and an excellent analysis of TCP (UK), see Trevor, M. (1988) *Toshiba's New British Company: Competitiveness through Innovation in Industry*, Policy Studies Institute.
8. Abo, T. (1994) *op.cit.* (note 1) Table 12.4, pp. 188–89. However, I should add that this 'European level' must have more-or-less changed recently. According to our research in the UK in the spring of 1997, the average HRs of TCP and Sanyo were much higher ([3.3] and [3.6]), and the direction of the Four perspectives evaluation scores were towards higher 'Methods' and lower 'Results'.
9. See, Abo, T. (1987) *op. cit.* (note 1).
10. Calculated from Table 12.3 in this article and Table 12.4 from Abo, T. (1994) *op.cit.* (note 1).
11. According to the data collected from the corporate materials of, and interviews at, both Toshiba and GE.
12. For some examples of western electronics firms, Wilkins, M. (1974) *The Maturing of Multinational Enterprise*, Harvard University Press; Abo, T. (1985) 'The International Business Activities of General Electric Company, 1920–1940', *Annals of the Institute of Social Science*, **27**; Slater, R. (1993) *The New GE: How Jack Welch Revised an American Institution*, Business One Irwin; Sobel, R. (1981) *IBM: Colossus in Transition*, Times Books Co. Inc.; Fisher, R.M. *et al.* (1983) *IBM and the US Data Processing Industry*, Praeger Publishers; Bartlett, C.A. and Ghoshal, S. (1989) *Managing Across Borders*, HBS Press, (looks at Philips Electronics).
13. The data for the following were mostly collected from the newspapers such as Nippon Keizai Shinbun and other publications.
14. See, Abo, T. (1997) *op. cit.* (note 1)
15. Bartlett and Ghoshal, (1989) *op. cit.* (note 12) Ch. 4.

ACKNOWLEDGEMENTS

I am greatly indebted to many Toshiba people for kindly taking the trouble to receive my colleagues and myself at their plants and headquarters abroad and in Japan, and for arranging our visits and providing various data related to this paper. First of all, I wish to express my sincere thanks to Mr. T. Isono (Deputy Managing Director) at General Planning Division of the Japanese Headquarters, who, for more than ten years, has not only very kindly arranged visits to various Toshiba plants for us, but has also been so co-operative in receiving our interviews, sometimes by himself, and in supporting a research project on the foreign investment frictions by Japanese firms. In particular, I would like to thank Messrs T. Yokoyama (Manager) at General Planning Division; K. Hiyama (General Manager) and K. Komada (Executive Engineering Manager) at Fukaya Plant in Japan; H. Ikeda (President), S. Ogi (Vice-President), T. Hashimura (Vice-President) and Y. Kokyo (Manager) at TACP (US); Y. Aono (President) and J.J. Perrotta at TDD (US); T. Nakagawa (Executive Vice-President), M. Hitosugi (Vice-President), J.E. White (Director), H. Matsumoto (Senior Manager) and K. Katoh (Director) at

TAEC (US); H. Sano (General Manager), M.A. Castillo (Manager), H. Nagashima (Manager), M.L. Garcia (Manager), S. Inagaki (Manager), K. Ogashiwa (Manager) and O. Ueno (Assistant Manager) at TE (Mexico); Y. Kawada (President) at TCPE (Germany); G. Harris (Director), F. Woodcock (Manager), K. Ishikawa (Manager), Y. Tamagoshi (Manager), R. Pemkerton (Senior Shop Steward, EETPU) and Ms. C. Penny (Officer) at TCP (UK); S. Nakajima (Vice-President), P. Delahaye (General Manager), T. Sato (Senior Manager) and J.F. Costa (Manager) at TS (France). Each person's title was such at the time of our interview.

Finally, I wish to thank the team members of JMNESG, especially those who have contributed towards this paper: Professors K. Kamiyama (Josei University), H. Itagaki (Saitama University), T. Kawamura (Teikyo University) and D.S. Cho (Nagoya University).

APPENDIX

This appendix describes the main data for evaluating the 'hybrid ratio' at Toshiba's seven large overseas plants; the information given is for 1989–91. The numbers relate to the 23 categories of assessment.

For the variables involved in making these assessments, see Table 12.2.

TACP (US)

Operations and management

Work organization and administration:
  1. Job classifications: seven items, including four related to maintenance and inspection.
  2. Job rotation: jobs are assigned rigidly.
  3. Training: on-the-job training.
  4. Supervisors: internal promotion; narrow opportunities.
  5. Wages: rigidly related to job classifications.
  6. Promotion: by seniority.

Product control:

  7. Equipment: from Japan, and local Japanese vendors.
  8. Quality control: manufacturers take the lead; barcoding is used.
  9. Maintenance: outside specialists are used.
 10. Operational control: Smart hybrid.

Parts procurement:

 11. Local content: 70–80% (exclusively chassis).

12. Suppliers: parts from TDD and RCA; chassis from TE.
13. Methods: rely on Maquiladora, and TDD, which has a big depot.

Team sense:

14. Small groups: none.
15. Information: open style.
16. Unity: /

Labour relations:

17. Employment policy: a homogeneous rural environment.
18. Employment security: there are sometimes lay-offs.
19. Trades Unions: IBEW; there have been strikes.
20. Grievance procedures: foremen are responsible for arbitration.

Parent/subsidiary relationships:

21. Ratio of Japanese staff: 1:7 – the Director, technicians, and production control are Japanese.
22. Power delegation: Japanese staff take the lead.
23. Local managers: in quality control of manufacturing, finance, human resources, and purchasing.

Local community: degree of 'unity' exhibited.

Performance

Productivity: 98% of Japanese (including indirect).
Market share: not known

TDD (US)

Operations and management

Work organization and administration:

1. Job classifications: four items, including three related to maintenance and inspection.
2. Job rotation: within the same job grade; narrow opportunities.
3. Training: all supervisors and many team leaders are trained in Japan.

4. Supervisors: internal promotion; for 50% of posts, as in Japan.
5. Wages: related to job classifications, with ranges.
6. Promotion: by seniority, but also includes an individual performance evaluation system.

Product control:

7. Equipment: Japanese-based. Local purchases comprise 20%.
8. Quality control: manufacturers lead, as in Japan.
9. Maintenance: mostly from outside, but includes a trainer from the Board of Co-operative Education Services.
10. Operational control: the lead is taken by industrial engineering, and includes the use of a microcomputer.

Parts procurement:

11. Local content: parts, less than 50%; materials, 60%.
12. Suppliers: key parts are from Japan and local Japanese suppliers.
13. Methods: short-term technical assistance.

Team sense:

14. Small groups: 12% of the workforce are allowed off during worktime; this is subsidized.
15. Information: various meetings, presided over by workers.
16. Unity: semi-open offices; special events.

Labour relations:

17. Employment policy: a relatively homogeneous environment.
18. Employment security: attempts a 'no lay-off' policy.
19. Trades Unions: IBEW – this was formerly a US plant.
20. Grievance procedures: the team leader is the first resource, then the unions, then the manager of the manufacturing process.

Parent/subsidiary relationships:

21. Ratio of Japanese staff: 2:3 (on management committee only).
22. Power delegation: management is relatively localized.
23. Local managers: there are five American directors.

Local community: donations of 1% of total sales ($2m).

Performance

Productivity: 80% of Japanese (direct sales only).
Market share: /

TAEC (US)

Operations and management

Work organization and administration:

1. Job classifications: three items including assembly testing and water fabrication.
2. Job rotation: active; staff are multi-skilled.
3. Training: quality control meetings in Japan.
4. Supervisors: mostly internal promotion, including some management posts.
5. Wages: not job-related; some have an individual performance evaluation system.
6. Promotion: mostly internal promotion; some use of individual performance evaluation systems.

Product control:

7. Equipment: Japanese.
8. Quality control: /
9. Maintenance: internal promotion for specialists.
10. Operational control: less flexible than in Japan.

Parts procurement:

11. Local content: 25%.
12. Suppliers: materials 5% (95% from Japan).
13. Methods: /

Team sense:

14. Small groups: 100% Total Productivity Movement; meetings are in work time.
15. Information: various meetings, led by managers.
16. Unity: semi-open offices.

Labour relations:

17. Employment policy: 80% from minority ethnic communities (Asian and Mexican).
18. Employment security: there are sometimes lay-offs.
19. Trades Unions: non-unionized.
20. Grievance procedures: /

Parent/subsidiary relationships:

21. Ratio of Japanese staff: 12:4. Of the President and Directors, five out of nine are Japanese.
22. Power delegation: /
23. Local managers: of the directors of human resources, quality assurance, manufacturing and maintenance, four out of nine are local.

Local community: degree of unity exhibited.

Performance

Productivity: 25% of Japanese (the size is very different).
Market share: 10% of Toshiba's US sales.

TE (Mexico)

Operations and management

Work organization and administration:

1. Job classification: there are many items, which are rigid and job-related.
2. Job rotation: none.
3. Training: supervisors and staff at a similar level are trained in Japan for one month.
4. Supervisors: work standard time, and have no career prospects.
5. Wages: not job-related; includes an individual performance evaluation system.
6. Promotion: similar for supervisors and staff

Product control:

7. Equipment: Japanese; some local adjustment.
8. Quality control: of manufacturing; more inspectors than the norm (in Japan).

9. Maintenance: by specialists in the Japanese manufacturers.
10. Operational control: 15% less flexible than in Japan.

Parts procurement:

11. Local content: 33%.
12. Suppliers: materials, 25% (Japan, 75%).
13. Methods: delivery is much longer.

Team sense:

14. Small groups: not yet.
15. Information: manager leads meetings.
16. Unity: a uniform is supplied; various special events.

Labour relations:

17. Employment policy: high turnover (128% per annum)
18. Employment security: no lay-offs.
19. Trades Unions: non-unionized.
20. Grievance procedures: human relations department communicates to supervisors.

Parent/subsidiary relationships:

21. Ratio of Japanese staff: 1:3.
22. Power delegation: management is Japanese-led.
23. Local managers: two of the five managers are Mexican.

Local community: various donations.

Performance

Productivity: lower costs than Singapore.
Market share: /

TCPE (Germany)

Operations and management

Work organization and administration:

1. Job classifications: ten items (there is an agreement with IG Metall).

2. Job rotation: none, except for those being prepared for promotion to supervisor.
3. Training: 85% on-the-job training; some use of external institutions and visits to Japan.
4. Supervisors: internal promotion; much job rotation.
5. Wages: a minimum wage; rigidly related to job classifications.
6. Promotion: only internal promotion to supervisor.

Product control:

7. Equipment: Japanese; some local adjustment.
8. Quality control: manufacturing quality control only; wage incentives.
9. Maintenance: by specialists in the Japanese manufacturers.
10. Operational control: staff work standard time, with local adjustments. The Large Variety in Small Volume system is used.

Parts procurement:

11. Local content: 54% (the EC standard is 45%).
12. Suppliers: 38% Japanese; 19% Asian; 43% European.
13. Methods: delivery time is much longer.

Team sense:

14. Small groups: Total Productivity Movement; groups are led by supervisors.
15. Information: managers lead meetings.
16. Unity: open offices; cafeteria; uniform.

Labour relations:

17. Employment policy: homogeneous rural environment.
18. Employment security: lay-offs are difficult.
19. Trades Unions: IG Metall.
20. Grievance procedures: union-led.

Parent/subsidiary relationships:

21. Ratio of Japanese staff: 1.6%.
22. Power delegation: management of manufacturing is relatively localized.
23. Local managers: Vice-President and General Manager (Industrial Engineering) are local.

Local community: supports the disabled, and so on.

Performance

Productivity: 80% of Japanese.
Market share: 5% of the EC; 5% of Germany; 10% of France.

TCP (UK)

Operations and management

Work organization and administration:

1. Job classifications: Japanese style; seven job grades.
2. Job rotation: /
3. Training: an in-house programme, and college courses.
4. Supervisors: internal promotion.
5. Wages: individual performance evaluation system, plus length of service.
6. Promotion: internal promotion by job grade.

Product control:

7. Equipment: older machines from Japan.
8. Quality control: quality control panels at the end of each production line.
9. Maintenance: internal promotion; staff are multi-skilled.
10. Operational control: no work standard time; realignment of production control.

Parts procurement:

11. Local content: 59%.
12. Suppliers: Japan, Asia and Europe.
13. Methods: delivery times are set for local vendors.

Team sense:

14. Small groups: no quality control circle.
15. Information: manager leads meetings.
16. Unity: open office; cafeteria; uniform.

Labour relations:

17. Employment policy: re-employment from joint-venture partner's personnel.
18. Employment security: /

19. Trades Unions: EEPTU (single union). Company Advisory Board.
20. Grievance procedures: first supervisors, then shop stewards, then the local office.

Parent/subsidiary relationships:

21. Ratio of Japanese staff: 0.6%.
22. Power delegation: local managers lead the management.
23. Local managers: seven local directors out of eleven.

Local community: /

Performance

Productivity: 90% of Japanese.
Market share: 9.8% in Europe.

TS (France)

Operations and management

Work organization and administration:

1. Job classifications: two job grades: operator and materials handler.
2. Job rotation: often; the aim is multi-skilled staff.
3. Training: on-the-job and in-house.
4. Supervisors: internal promotion for two out of four posts.
5. Wages: individual performance evaluation system – step by step.
6. Promotion: most promotions are internal.

Product control:

7. Equipment: Japanese; some local R&D.
8. Quality control: in process and specialist.
9. Maintenance: internal promotion and specialists.
10. Operational control: some use of work standard time; 10% work less.

Parts procurement:

11. Local content: 50%.
12. Suppliers: 50% Japanese.
13. Methods: long-term close co-operation.

Team sense:

14.   Small groups: Total Productivity Movement in worktime.
15.   Information: /
16.   Unity: nice cafeteria; uniform.

Labour relations:

17.   Employment policy: rural young women.
18.   Employment security: attempted 'no lay-off'.
19.   Trades Unions: possibly active.
20.   Grievance procedures: /

Parent/subsidiary relationships:

21.   Ratio of Japanese staff: /
22.   Power delegation: local management, but Japanese control of marketing.
23.   Local managers: relatively active.

Local community: /

Performance

Productivity: 90% of Japanese.
Market share: 70% of Toshiba European sales.

PART 4

Regionalism and Asia

13. Growth triangles: a new approach to Asian economic co-operation

Min Tang*

INTRODUCTION

Asia used to be the least regionalized area in the world. However, since the late 1980s, this trend has changed dramatically, as many innovative regional initiatives have been established. One such initiative is the formation of *growth triangles*. A *growth triangle* is a transnational economic zone spread over well-defined, geographically proximate areas that usually covers parts of at least three countries. Factor endowment differences and economic complementarities are exploited by the subregion to promote natural and human resource development, domestic and foreign investment, external trade, tourism, and infrastructure development. This paper aims to compare the *growth triangle* approach with other forms of regional co-operation and subsequently to explain why the former is popular in Asia.

This chapter is divided into four sections. These describe recent developments in the Asian *growth triangle*; the distinguishing characteristics of the *growth triangle*; and prospects and challenges for *growth triangles* in Asia. Finally, there is a summary of the main findings of the paper.

RECENT DEVELOPMENT OF GROWTH TRIANGLES IN ASIA

During the 1950s and 1960s, while the wave of regionalism spread throughout the world,[1] the pace of the development of regional co-operation was rather slow in Asia. The Association of Southeast Asian Nations (ASEAN) was probably an exception. However, the success of ASEAN was more in political aspects than in economic co-operation. Tang (1995) lists several reasons for the slow

* The author wishes to thank Loretta C. Jovellanos and Elizabeth E. Elizan for their invaluable assistance. The views expressed in this paper are those of the author and do not necessarily reflect the views and policies of the Asian Development Bank.

pace of regionalism in Asia. First, there had been the lack of incentives for Asia to form its own trading bloc, since the majority of its trade had been with countries outside the region. Second, the diversity of economic systems and the strong protectionist sentiment in Asia in those days had made it difficult for Asian countries to harmonize their trade and investment policies. Finally, during the period of the Viet Nam war, political conflict among the Asian countries had made it impossible to form a trading bloc in the region.

In recent years, however, the attitude towards regional co-operation has changed dramatically in Asia. Regional co-operation has become one of the most outstanding developments in the Asian economy. In 1992, for example, the six ASEAN countries decided to form the ASEAN Free Trade Area (AFTA). Within a few years, substantial progress will be achieved in lowering tariffs and reducing other trade barriers in intra-ASEAN trade. It was agreed that tariffs on manufactured goods would be reduced to below 5 per cent by the year 2003.

The Asia–Pacific Economic Co-operation (APEC) was established in 1989 in response to the growing interdependence among Asian Pacific countries. The eighteen major economies comprising APEC have a combined aggregate output almost equal to half of the world's GDP, and supply 40 per cent of total world exports. At the 1994 Summit in Bogor, Indonesia, APEC member countries decided that by the year 2010, APEC's developed member countries shall remove all trade barriers, and by the year 2020, the whole APEC region will enjoy free trade. The APEC meeting in Osaka, Japan in November 1995 came up with a detailed action agenda for trade liberalization and economic and technical co-operation. It included tariff reductions, gradual liberalization of farm trades and multi-fibre arrangements, harmonization of product standards, customs and testing procedures, and dispute mediation services, as well as deregulation of domestic rules.

The South Asian Association for Regional Co-operation (SAARC),[2] which was inactive for years, has also recently agreed to implement the South Asian Preferential Trading Agreement (SAPTA) by the end of 1995. This agreement involves lower tariffs on imports among member countries. Commodities imported from one another will have 10 per cent lower tariffs than those imported from non-SAARC countries. It was also agreed that joint efforts will be made to eradicate poverty in the region.

Aside from these large-scale regional integration arrangements, there are other innovative types of subregional economic co-operation arrangements in Asia (see Figure 13.1). The formation of a *growth triangle* is one such kind of subregional co-operation. Usually consisting of parts of at least three countries, a *growth triangle* is a transnational economic zone of well-defined, geographically proximate areas, where factor endowments and economic complementarity among triangle members are explored to promote socioeconomic development

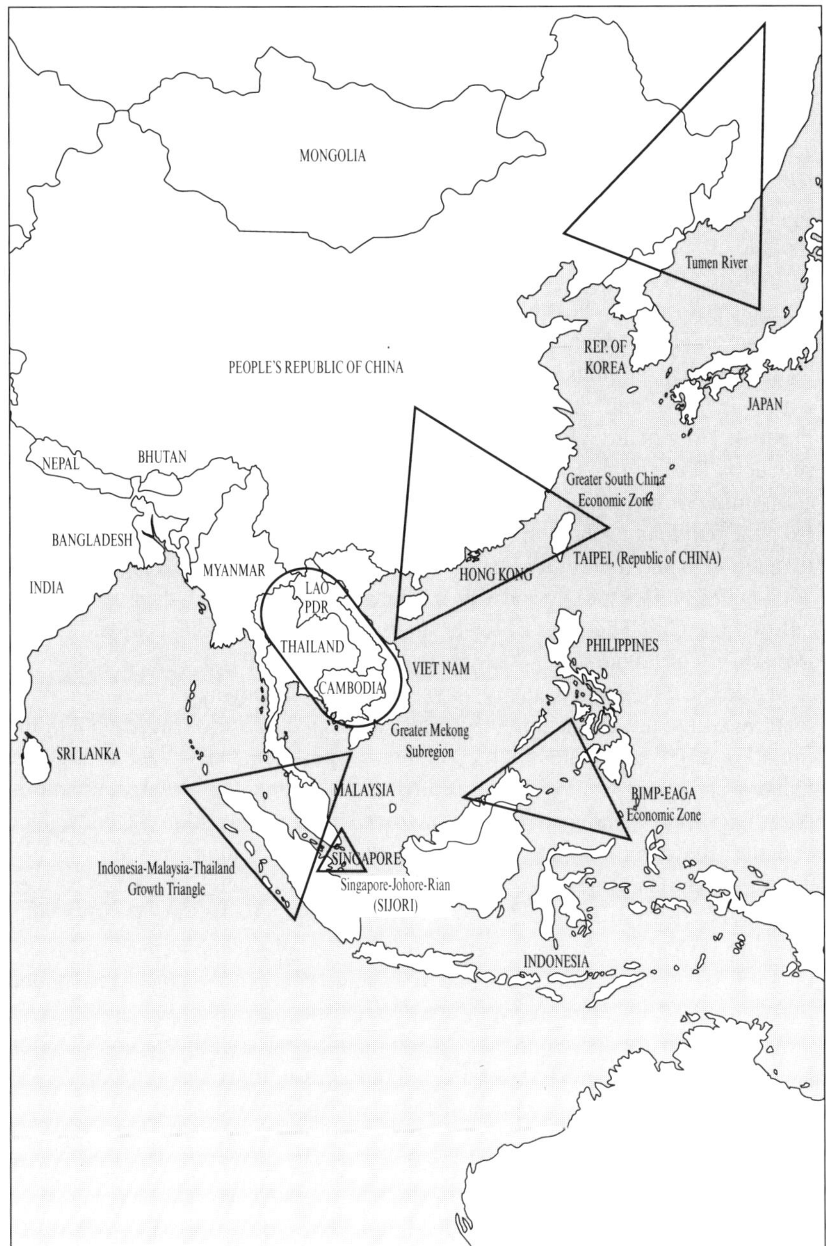

Figure 13.1   Growth triangles in Asia

Southern China Growth Triangle (SC–GT)

The economic co-operation between Hong Kong, Taipei (Republic of China) and the southern part of the People's Republic of China (mainly parts of Guangdong and Fujian provinces) is called the Southern China Growth Triangle (see Table 13.1). The opening up of China to the rest of the world and the establishment of the Special Economic Zones in Southern China has provided enormous opportunities for domestic and foreign investments. Preferential policies, which include tax concessions, reduction in land use fees, and flexible procedures and formalities for project approval, have also helped to attract investments to Southern China. On the other hand, rising labour and land costs have changed the comparative advantage of the manufacturing sector in Hong Kong and Taipei. Both economies are undergoing a transformation from the first stage of export-led development, which relies heavily on the export of labour-intensive products, to a stage which focuses on technology- and knowledge-intensive products. These mutually complementary economies form a solid foundation for economic co-operation. Within SC-GT, Southern China has benefited much from the building up of an export-oriented economy using the capital, technology, management and marketing skills available in Hong Kong and Taipei.

Conversely, Hong Kong and Taipei have gained greatly from their investments in Southern China because of lower production and labour costs as well as the availability of labour.

While the SC-GT is in many ways similar to the others, it also has unique features. First, unlike the other triangles, which were formed mostly out of the initiative of governments involved in the co-operation, the SC-GT is largely a market- and private sector-driven arrangement. There is no formal co-operation plan or agreement among the officials involved in the co-operation. Second, ethnic and linguistic affinities play an important role in the development of the triangle. The use of the Cantonese language in both Guangdong and Hong Kong, as well as Fujianese in Fujian and Taipei increases business trust and interpersonal bonding. Finally, there has been a clear tendency for the expansion of co-operation in this triangle. During the early stage, co-operation had been limited mainly to the Special Economic Zones. Later, the entire Pear River Delta area was involved in the development of the co-operation. Presently, the co-operation and business operations are extended to almost the entire Guangdong and Fujian provinces, and are gradually moving to the internal province of China (Wang, 1994)

Singapore-Johor-Riau Growth Triangle (SJR-GT)

The SJR-GT encompasses the three contiguous areas of Singapore, Johor state in Malaysia and the Riau Islands in Indonesia. The basic premise of this triangle is that, as production costs in Singapore increase, manufacturing plants will move

Table 13.1   Regional co-operation in Asian and Pacific developing countries

Name	Date of Inception	Current Participating Countries or Area	Population Involved	Focus
Southern China Growth Triangle	Early 1980s	Southern China, Hong Kong and Taipei (Republic of China)	120 million	Relocation of manufactured production and export of labour-intensive goods
Singapore-Johor-Riau Growth Triangle	1989	Indonesia, Malaysia and Singapore	6 million	Production relocation from Singapore to Johor and Riau Islands, and exploitation of economic complementarity among the three subregions
Tumen River Area Development	1991	North Korea, People's Republic of China and Russia	–	Joint natural resource development, infrastructure and free trade zone development
Indonesia-Malaysia-Thailand Growth Triangle	1993	Southern Thailand, Northern Malaysia, DI Aceh and North Sumatra of Indonesia	21 million	To exploit economic complementarities and enhance subregional competitiveness for trade and investment, and reduce production and distribution costs through the improvement of infrastructure linkage
Brunei Darussalam-Indonesia-Malaysia-Philippines East ASEAN Growth Area	1994	Brunei Darussalam, Indonesia, Malaysia and the Philippines	24 million	To improve the economic and transportation linkage of the region, and sector co-operation in mineral, forest and marine resources
Greater Mekong Subregion	1991	Cambodia, Lao PDR, Myanmar, Thailand, Viet Nam and Yunan Province of People's Republic of China	220 million	Joint development of natural and human resources, and strengthening the intraregional economy linkages by improving the infrastructure

from Singapore to Johor and the Riau Islands, while the designing, marketing and distributing functions remain in Singapore to take advantage of the city-state's excellent service industries and infrastructure. Political factors played an important role in the launching of SJR-GT. While there was no formal trilateral agreement, there were a few bilateral co-operation agreements. Those arrangements focused more on resource pooling and investment co-operation than on market integration and trade liberalization. From 1990 to 1993, Singapore had invested more than US$600 million in Johor and nearly US$350 million in the Riau Islands. Eight industrial estates have been established. These include the Batam Industrial Park, which employs 32 000 workers and generates US$600 million worth of exports.

Tumen Delta Development Area (TDDA)

The third *growth triangle* in Asia is located at the Tumen River Delta area in Northeast Asia, bordering the Jilin province of China, and includes Siberia (Russia) and the Democratic People's Republic of Korea (DPRK). Other countries like Japan, the Republic of Korea, and Mongolia are also involved in the development of the TDDA by providing capital, natural and human resources. The Tumen River Area Development Plan, financed by the United Nations Development Programme (UNDP), involves a massive development of infrastructure and transportation networks. The rationale for the establishment of the TDDA is to use low-cost labour from China and DPRK to exploit and process natural resources from Siberia and Mongolia. These finished products would then be shipped to markets in Japan, the Republic of Korea and Europe. The Tumen Delta will also become one pole of the Trans-Siberia Land Bridge between Europe and Asia. According to UNDP's estimates, the development of specialized ports, roads, airports and an international city for the Tumen River Economic Zone will cost US$30 billion over a period of 20 years.

Indonesia-Malaysia-Thailand Growth Triangle (IMT-GT)

The IMT-GT comprises the states of Northern Sumatra and DI Aceh in Indonesia, the four states of Perak, Penang, Kedah and Perlis in Northern Malaysia, and the five provinces of Songlehla, Satun, Yala, Narathiwat and Pattani in Southern Thailand. The IMT-GT covers a wide range of natural resources and has a large potential for complementarity in trade and investment. The overall objectives of this co-operation arrangement are to promote private sector-led growth to enhance investments, generate exports and reduce production and distribution costs. Co-operation in the infrastructure and agriculture sectors could also generate substantial development potential. The recently completed study financed by the Asian Development Bank draws up a master plan for IMT-GT identifying the set of policy, programme, project and institutional actions that will facilitate the development of the area. The study also outlines nearly 100 project proposals costing US$15 billion over the next 10 years.

Brunei-Indonesia-Malaysia-Philippines East ASEAN Growth Area (BIMP-EAGA)

The BIMP-EAGA is a recently established subregional co-operation in Asia which includes Brunei Darussalam, West and East Kalimantan and North Sulawesi in Indonesia, Sabah and Sarawak in Malaysia and Mindanao and Palawan in the Philippines. BIMP-EAGA covers a land mass of about 700 000 sq. kms with a population of more than 24 million. There is a great potential for co-operation because of the area's rich resources, which include forestry and timber products, marine products, oil, gas, gold, diamond and crystal sand. The main constraint for the development of the BIMP-EAGA area is the lack of economic linkages within the region particularly the inadequate infrastructure. Moreover, BIMP-EAGA is considered as the least developed area, because all the areas are far from their respective national capitals. As requested by the governments involved, the Asian Development Bank has recently embarked on a study to identify opportunities and areas for economic co-operation, and has recommended policies and projects for the subregion. The study is organized in four key areas: human resource development, agriculture and fishing, transport and communication, and energy and power.

Greater Mekong Subregional Co-operation (GMSC)

While many scholars do not classify the GMSC as a *growth triangle*, because of its subregional co-operation nature, it is nevertheless reviewed in this chapter. The GMSC includes Cambodia, Lao PDR, Myanmar, Thailand, Viet Nam and the Yunnan province of China. Recent improvements in the political situation have led to renewed interest in jointly exploiting economic complementarity in the Mekong area. There is an urgent need to improve the transportation linkages among the countries in the subregion. Energy is also a major sector that has substantial possibilities for co-operation. Since 1991, six countries in the Greater Mekong Area have set up a subregional working committee to study the potential for development of the region. Assisted by the Asian Development Bank, many initiatives have already been proposed and feasibility studies of some of the projects have been completed (Tan, Pante and Abonyi, 1995).

DISTINGUISHING CHARACTERISTICS OF GROWTH TRIANGLES IN ASIA

Compared with other forms of regional co-operation, like the European Union (EU) and the North American Free Trade Agreement (NAFTA), the *growth triangle* approach has its unique features.

First, unlike the EU and NAFTA, which involve the entirety of each member country and require changes in administrative and institutional arrangements nationwide, a *growth triangle* usually involves limited areas in the countries and needs only localized policy arrangements. Therefore, the establishment of a *growth triangle* requires less time and entails lower economic costs. Consequently, the political and economic risks associated with this type of economic co-operation are much smaller. If a triangle succeeds, its benefits can easily be extended to other parts of its member countries. On the other hand, if anything goes wrong, adverse consequences are felt only by the areas concerned. This feature is particularly attractive to countries in transition from a closed and centrally planned to an open and market-oriented economic system.

Second, the *growth triangle* approach is non-discriminatory to the non-members. For a long time, many economists have been sceptical about regional arrangements in the world economy, since they may discriminate against free trade and global integration. They believe that regionalism could lead the world economy away from the path towards global free trade (de Melo and Panagariya, 1993). They argue that Asia's current economic boom came about without the formation of a trading bloc or any other arrangements which grant special economic benefits to members and discriminate against non-members. Contrary to all these, the *growth triangle* approach does not discriminate against non-member countries. In fact, its export-oriented structure makes it particularly favourable to free trade policy. It is capable of extending economic benefits even to non-member countries by providing trade and investment opportunities.

Third, a *growth triangle* arrangement is not a mechanism solely to promote free trade. In many cases, its primary goal does not involve tariff reduction at all. Instead, it is more of a scheme to promote and rationalize direct investment as well as strengthen economic co-operation by improving infrastructure linkages within the area. Operation scope in a *growth triangle* is usually very comprehensive, encompassing developments in trade, investment, infrastructure, agriculture and industry, human and natural resources and environmental protection.

Finally, *growth triangles* can be classified into two: the metropolitan spillover type and the infrastructure development type (Chia, 1995). Models of the first type are the Singapore-based SJR-GT and the Hong Kong-based SC-GT. In this type of *growth triangle*, the relatively less developed peripheral areas benefit from the higher investments and better services provided by the metropolitan core. On the other hand, the metropolitan area benefits from the relocation of its industries to the less developed areas, to take advantage of cheap factor prices and large markets. These allow domestic industries to engage in higher value added manufacturing and service activities.

The second type of *growth triangle* is best typified by the Greater Mekong Co-operation Area and the Tumen Delta Development Area. The IMT-GT and BIMP-EAGA also belong to this category. This type of *growth triangle* does not usually have a metropolitan core, hence the less important role played by spillover effects. Potential economic benefits are more in joint resource exploration, regional market promotion, human capital development, cross trade and technological co-operation. Countries belonging to this type of *growth triangle* are usually at the early stage of their development, where market forces and private sector initiatives are rather weak. Because of this, government initiatives and strong political commitment play a key role in developing this type of triangle. In the IMT-GT, for example, the three governments played a crucial role in initiating and bringing the co-operation towards success.

Eliminating infrastructure bottlenecks is usually the single most important factor in the creation of this type of triangle. It is well recognized that in the absence of good infrastructure linkages, the potential for co-operation would not be realized. Therefore, infrastructure projects like roads, railways, waterways, communication, power generation and transmission, and water supply often formed a main part of the co-operation plan. For example, in the IMT-GT development plan, a number of infrastructure projects to integrate these three subregions physically have been proposed. In the Tumen River Area Development Programme, the Greater Mekong Subregional Co-operation Plan and BIMP-EAGA, infrastructure development has also been the focus of the development plan. Since this type of *growth triangle* arrangement often involves the distribution of huge costs and benefits among its members, due to their non-partisan position, international organizations could play an important, and sometimes unique, role in supporting co-operation arrangements. For example, UNDP supported and co-ordinated a comprehensive development programme for the Tumen River Area. The Asian Development Bank has also been actively involved in designing a number of master plans for subregional co-operation in Asia, which include: a comprehensive study of economic co-operation in the Great Mekong areas, a master plan for the Indonesia-Malaysia-Thailand *growth triangle*, and a master plan for the Brunei Darussalam-Indonesia-Malaysia-Philippines East ASEAN Growth Area.

PROSPECTS AND CHALLENGES FOR GROWTH TRIANGLES IN ASIA

The past experience of Asia suggests that *growth triangles* are the appropriate form for many Asian countries which are looking for effective ways of attaining regional co-operation. Firstly, the *growth triangle* approach is particularly appropriate for countries in the process of transition from a centrally-planned to a market-oriented economy. Because economies in transition face considerable economic and political risks, a gradual opening up of the economy and transformation of economic systems are extremely important for the success of the transition. The *growth triangle* approach provides a good means for this transition.

Secondly, for countries which have only recently discarded serious biases against market economies and exports, such as some South Asian countries, the *growth triangle* approach could be an effective means of pursuing outward-oriented and export-led growth strategies.

Thirdly, the *growth triangle* could be complementary to other forms of regional co-operation in Asia such as ASEAN, AFTA and APEC. In recent years, a number of regional initiatives have been proposed and endorsed in Asian countries. The *growth triangle* approach is compatible with this large-scale co-operation, as its focus is also on co-operation in trade and investment. In fact, IMT-GT and BIMP-EAGA were proposed by the ASEAN Summit and were well accepted as part of the ASEAN co-operation arrangement.

While the *growth triangle* approach seems to be a good solution to the problem of regional co-operation among the Asian countries at different stages of economic development, several conditions need to be met to ensure its success. A fundamental requirement is the existence of economic complementarity between the different members of the triangle. Geographical proximity is also an important factor in forming a *growth triangle*, in order to reduce transportation costs and to take advantage of cultural and linguistic affinities. Furthermore, participating countries must be politically committed and willing to provide policy and fiscal support (Tang and Thant, 1995).

It should also be realized that the formation of the *growth triangle* poses a number of challenges to the region. First, the primary challenge is the enormous investment requirement. Every triangle has a huge investment plan, particularly for infrastructure development. For example, the total investment for the Tumen River Area Development Programme alone needs as much as US$30 billion. Many governments expect to obtain foreign capital to fill the financial gap. However, given the size of the total resource requirement and the increasing competitiveness in the world capital market, such an amount of capital may not be automatically available.

Second, while disparities in the level of income and stages of development could generate substantial complementarities in Asian countries, it could also cause many difficulties for co-operation. In particular, benefits from trade liberalization and market integration may not be equally distributed among the member countries. Considerable efforts should be put into designing a well-balanced arrangement which could provide equitable sharing of costs and benefits as much as possible.

Lastly, since the *growth triangle* involves only parts of countries, it could generate some conflicts between the central and local governments, and local governments within and surrounding the triangles. Some groups of people will lose (or gain) more than others. Also the ability of the government to provide an adequate social infrastructure, such as education and a legal framework, will also be crucial to the success of the triangle.

CONCLUSION

As a new form of regional co-operation, *growth triangles* have developed rapidly in Asia. The *growth triangle* approach is a good solution to the problem of regional co-operation among the Asian countries at different stages of economic development. *Growth triangles* could also be complementary to the other forms of regional co-operation.

Compared with the other forms of regional co-operation, the *growth triangle* approach has its unique features. Since it involves only limited areas in countries, it can be established at relatively low cost within a short period of time. If conditions permit, it can even be expanded incrementally. The *growth triangle* is non-discriminatory against other countries because of its export-oriented nature. Therefore, it is less likely to provoke any retaliation from non-members.

The experience in Asia shows that a few conditions need to be met to ensure the success of *growth triangles*. Economic complementarity, geographical proximity, infrastructure development and political commitment, as well as policy co-ordination, are the most significant requirements for the success of the *growth triangle*. The future of *growth triangles* in Asia also depends upon how the participating countries will be able to solve the problem of insufficient financial resources, fair distribution of benefits and costs among the members, and balance of central and local governments.

NOTES

1. In Europe, the European Common Market, European Free Trade Area and Council for Mutual Economic Assistance were established in the 1950s and 1960s. In Latin America, there were the Latin American Free Trade Association, Caribbean Free Trade Area, Central American Common Market, and so on. Even in Africa, several regional co-operations were developed, such as the Central African Customs and Economic Union, West African Customs Union, East African Community, and so on.
2. The SAARC was formally launched in 1985 during the first summit of seven South Asian countries – Bangladesh, Bhutan, India, the Maldives, Nepal, Pakistan and Sri Lanka.

REFERENCES

Chia, Siow Yue (1995) *Investment and Trade Facilitation in the Asia-Pacific: The Role of Subregional Economic Zones*, Paper presented at the Second APEC Roundtable organized by the Institute of Southeast Asian Studies, 23–24 June, Singapore.

De Melo. J.D. and A. Panagariya (1993) (eds) *New Dimensions in Regional Integration*, Cambridge: Cambridge University Press, Introduction.

Tan, Ricardo, Filologo Pante, Jr. and George Abonyi (1995) 'Economic Cooperation in the Greater Mekong Subregion', in Kiichiro Fukasaku (ed.) *Regional Co-operation and Integration in Asia*, Paris: Organization for Economic Co-operation and Development.

Tang, Min (1995) 'Asian Economic Co-operation: Opportunities and Challenges', in Kiichiro Fukasaku (ed.) *Regional Co-operation and Integration in Asia*, Paris: Organization for Economic Co-operation and Development.

Tang, Min and Myo Thant (1995) *Recent Developments of Growth Triangles and the Implications for Labor Mobility in Asia*, Paper presented at the Meeting on Regionalization and Labor Market Interdependence in East and Southeast Asia, 23–26 January, Bangkok, Thailand.

Wang, Jun (1994) 'Expansion of the Southern China Growth Triangle', in M. Thant, M. Tang and H. Kakazu (eds) *Growth Triangles in Asia: A New Approach to Regional Economic Cooperation*, Hong Kong: Oxford University Press.

14. The ASEAN Free Trade Area: attractive for international business?

Jacques Pelkmans and Annette Balaoing

This chapter is a provisional attempt to understand the initiative to construct an ASEAN Free Trade Area (AFTA) and its significance for international business. Launched in January 1992 through the Singapore Declaration, the AFTA is envisioned as a liberalising force that will increase intra-ASEAN trade and enhance the region's attractiveness as a production base geared to the world market. The AFTA target is to remove tariffs and non-tariff barriers initially over a 15-year period starting 1 January 1993; this was later shortened to a period of 10 years.

The chapter begins by discussing the potential economic advantages of regional integration in ASEAN. In that light, AFTA can be studied more profitably. The next section provides a highly provisional briefing on some of the winners and (short-run) losers and the dangers of such a view. The concluding section answers the question whether AFTA may serve as an additional incentive to invest in ASEAN.

THE BASIC ECONOMIC EFFECTS OF AFTA

There are two complementary approaches to understanding the economic effects of AFTA. The traditional economic perspective of free trade areas can generate empirical estimates of the effects on trade flows and Gross Domestic Product (GDP). However, the underlying assumptions of the models, as well as inevitable data constraints, amount to such serious drawbacks that the nature of the conclusions as well as the range of magnitudes may well be misleading rather than helpful. The more informal approach is based on the dynamic effect attributed to regional integration: economies of scale; increased opportunities for regional sourcing and subcontracting; and enhanced efficiency and productivity. Jointly, they largely overcome these drawbacks and hence provide a more sophisticated view of the AFTA potential, but at the expense of formal simulations. In assessing the AFTA potential, both approaches assume AFTA to be completed by definition. Questions such as an incomplete AFTA or the intermediate impact during the transmission period are not addressed. Particularly for the second, more informal approach, this implies that some heroic assumptions about the adjustment and development strategies of ASEAN Member Sates are critical.

The Traditional Perspective

As a variant of the theory of customs union, the theory of free trade areas emphasizes the excess of trade creation over trade diversion as a measure of welfare improvement.[1] The analytical framework is one of comparative statics: the underlying production functions are given and the initial trade pattern will only respond to the tariff costs envisaged. By ignoring scale and dynamic effects, as well as public and private strategies in response to AFTA, it would be surprising if the empirical estimates based on the traditional approach would be sizeable. It is known from well-established literature on the effects of the EC customs union and other cases that these static effects will always be relatively small.[2]

The reliance on the initial trade pattern is particularly inappropriate in the case of ASEAN. The main reason for that is that intra-ASEAN trade was small to begin with, while ASEAN exports to, and imports from, the rest of the world are much higher, and grow rapidly. Thus, intra-ASEAN trade is generated by Singapore and Malaysia; significantly the bulk of that trade is bilateral, with a good deal of entrepôt trade through Singapore included. If AFTA were to have any economic impact, the focus should be on the three large Member States. Not only did those three generate little more than a quarter of 1992 intra-ASEAN trade *together*,[3] but the structure of that trade does not suggest a great regional attachment. First, 1992 intra-ASEAN trade is only 11.9% of all Indonesian trade; bilateral exports to Singapore dominate all of its other bilateral intra-ASEAN exports together. For Thailand, the intra-ASEAN trade share is 12.7% and again exports to Singapore dominate all other bilateral flows together. For the Philippines, the intra-ASEAN trade share is 8% and the exports to Singapore just exceed all other bilateral flows.

This is not merely due to protection, but also to underdevelopment, as will be discussed on page 202. The implication is that the empirical simulations, based on trade structures having remained so underdeveloped, should be studied with extreme caution. As a very long-run benchmark, the great potential for intra-ASEAN trade would seem to be undeniable, and this is not at all borne out by empirical studies based on a traditional, static approach.

The studies presently available, unfortunately, rely on data based from the mid- or late-1980s. Therefore, they inherently limit the potential (that is, calculated) impact of AFTA even more.

The main studies give the following results:

- Imada, Montes and Naya (1991), in their general equilibrium approach, simulate a 50% tariff reduction; intra-ASEAN trade increases by 11.4%, the increases being largest in the big three (19.8% for Indonesian intra-ASEAN exports; 30.3% for the Philippines; 24.2% for Thailand), but all from a low base. The growth effects are minuscule, the highest two being in Malaysia (0.7% of GDP) and the Philippines (0.54%). Interesting also is that the EC would suffer an export decline of 1.9% (to ASEAN), whereas the US and Japan would increase exports by 0.6%.
- Toh and Low (1992), a simulation at a very high aggregate level, find that AFTA would lead to a 14.7% increase in intra-ASEAN trade. ASEAN GDP would increase by 3.1%, with the lowest growth in the Philippines (25%); the Philippines, Thailand and Indonesia score the highest import growth rates (intra-ASEAN), all 25–27%. Toh and Low add the interesting exercise of simulating the intra-ASEAN trade growth arising purely from GDP growth in the Member States (that is, without AFTA but with a sound economic policy); they took growth forecasts for 1992. They find that it needs no more than three years of (below-record) ASEAN growth to generate the same or higher intra-ASEAN trade as would be expected from AFTA after 15 years.
- Toh and Low also report studies by Westcott and Philip (1992) and Yap (1992). The former finds modest export increases (highest for Singapore) and import increases of up to 20%. The welfare effect is positive but minimal. The data reported refer to the increases of overall trade (not just ASEAN): for exports they hover between 0.2% (Indonesia) and 0.53% (Singapore); for imports, between 0.25% (Singapore) and 5.08% (Philippines). Growth effects range from a negative 0.3% for Thailand to 1.5% for Malaysia.

These simulations, based on the traditional perspective confirm that AFTA would have positive but unimpressive effects on trade and growth. And they would take 10 years to materialize. Being worthwhile gains in themselves, they would add little to current incentives to invest in ASEAN.

Scale and Dynamic Arguments for AFTA

Scale and sufficient demand

The merits of the market size argument are much debated, also in Europe since the Cecchini report (on EC-92 effects). The gains to be reaped if there is no demand constraint[4] critically depend on two factors:

- the technical nature of the production process, in other words, the downward slope of the scale curve and at what output minimum costs are realized.
- the initial position, that is, what additional gains can be had when potential demand expands from constrained to unconstrained.

On the first point, Pratten's (1988) survey for the Cecchini report has shown that scale economies vary considerably from sector to sector. In many sectors the gains from scale are below 10%. In the light of the managerial problems in actually realizing[5] the scale effects, as indicated by engineering estimates, this margin will not often be decisive. Its relevance, moreover, hinges on the second factor, the initial position. The Pratten study is based on the traditional assumption of moving from 50% of minimum efficient scale (MES) output to full MES. The gains from scale would be smaller still, if extra output only amounted to, say, 10% or 20% of MES. For ASEAN, these points are fundamental. During the 1980s, five[6] ASEAN countries were or became major industrial exporters to OECD markets. Frequently this export drive was fostered by links with international business; in some sectors (such as electronic components; sporting shoes and telecom equipment) direct investors from Japan, the EC and the US, some EFTA countries and Canada were the source of these exports. As these suppliers were not locked into protected domestic markets, there is little reason to assume that these export-related plants are often sub-scale.

The *relevant question* therefore, is whether regional integration would reduce any demand constraints to such an extent that substantial additional scale economies could be achieved. This would be an argument to expand local sales, to rationalize and hence exploit scale better or to convince potential investors that a critical overall demand threshold is overcome by the addition of regional demand, so that establishment will pay off. It may well be that the question is more pertinent to ASEAN-owned companies and to those multinational corporations (MNCs) having invested purely for local supply or consumption, rather than for export-oriented plants.

Indeed, before the AFTA initiative of January 1992, scale (or its obverse, underutilization of capacity) was the critical reason for ASEAN to promote ASEAN Industrial Joint Ventures (AIJV) in full, with a minimum of 40% ASEAN equity (see below).

The scale arguments are complicated, however, by the significance of unbundling the production of components and final assembly. When industries develop, cost reduction, flexibility and sometimes innovation may be achieved by unbundling (at least, if market structures allow for that). It might mean that scale effects in some components can be exploited to the full, while the crucial aspects in assembly become flexible manufacturing, quick response to market trends and tailor-made deliveries for major purchasers, rather than mere scale.

An obvious point making scale more relevant to AFTA (other things being equal) is that market size and growth are not independent in the long run. ASEAN national growth rates have been so high over the last decade, that market size has more than doubled.

Regional sourcing and subcontracting

The point on 'unbundling' ties in with the ASEAN potential for regional sourcing. There is little doubt that ASEAN-wide sourcing and subcontracting was almost impossible a decade ago. The main reasons included:

- high protection in Indonesia, Thailand and the Philippines, and selective protection in Malaysia;
- severe customs problems;
- competing sectoral industrialization objectives in ASEAN countries (thus, five ASEAN countries attach value to 'national' car components, if not a national car industry; similar preferences may play a role in steel, petrochemicals, consumer electronics and cement);
- lingering problems of constancy and level of quality as well as insufficient industrial and technological infrastructure.

All four problems have reduced in importance. Protection has been reduced unilaterally in all four countries, customs problems in, for example, Indonesia have been drastically curtailed by the partial privatization of control and surveillance (by SGS)[7]; selected ways around 'competitive' industrialization have been found; and the industrial fabric of ASEAN countries has greatly improved, especially as a result of successful export-led growth and its trickle-down effects.

Probably the greatest obstacle consists in the national industrialization strategies. Three public policy approaches to ASEAN-wide industrialization have been pursued in the past. The record is not a good one. *First*, emerging from planning and import substitution philosophies, the ASEAN Industrial Projects (AIP) were tried. They amounted to large government-owned instruments (joint targeting). It proved almost impossible to align national, heavy-handed industrialization policies so as to achieve joint targeting; not unlike the ASEAN Pact, there was no willingness to have AIP override national developmental interests.

Second, rather than a planned *inter*-industry specialization in the AIP, the ASEAN Industrial Complementation (AIC) pursued an *intra*-industry division of labour. Such a vertical specialization was to be organized between the public and the private sector. As Langhammer (1991) and others have pointed out, AIC is a typical second-best approach: first best would be to dismantle barriers within ASEAN and let the private sector (including international business) determine the scope for vertical ASEAN-wide specialization. Again, the AICs have not been successful. However, the car industry has negotiated a so-called brand-to-brand variety of AICs which has received official endorsement. Under this construction the companies can conduct intra-ASEAN trade in car parts of their own making in a production and trade network of three or four countries. The official blessing was given in October 1988[8]. Tariff preferences are at least 50%, but in fact higher, and local content accreditation is automatic for own-brand products or 'brand-related' original equipment manufacturers.

The *third* approach consists in the ASEAN industrial joint ventures (AIJVs). This is clearly an activity from the private sector (with a maximum equity participation from outside ASEAN of 60%), based on the exploitation of economies of scale and hence a competitive marketing edge in the world market. Though less heavy-handed than AIP and AIC, it took half a decade before, in the Manila summit of 1987, the AIJV was made more attractive to business. Further adjustments in 1990 were marginal. The margin of preference is now 90%, and that is often an incentive. A drawback is that ASEAN Member States typically use the granting of the preference (which is not automatic but goes through a high level group[9] for obtaining AIJV product status) as a leverage for the negotiation of special demands. There are also complaints about complexities in the bureaucratic implementation. AIJVs are not a failure, but neither are they a success. Mid-1991 COIME listed 18 products or groups of (related) products having AIJV status; in at least six cases European business is involved[10].

The rules do not, however, tell the full story. The notion behind AIJVs is still a concept of co-operation which avoids direct competition in the region. In a recently published AIJV guide[11], business recommendations for what is conducive for AIJVs include:

* products 'preferably with high locally available material content'
* 'the product should not compete with locally produced products i.e. an import substitution product'.

It is therefore possible, but still far from easy, to pursue regional sourcing and subcontracting or to start ASEAN joint ventures exploiting differential advantages through the region. It is here that AFTA might come in. Regional market integration could greatly facilitate regional sourcing and put it on a less distortive basis. What this means for future intra-AFTA trade would seem to be unpredictable. Numerous opportunities for regional sourcing and subcontracting still have to be explored. Moreover, as ASEAN is enmeshed in Pacific Asia, regional free trade will merely be one element in a range of factors determining the location and spread of sourcing and subcontracting networks in a wider economic area than ASEAN.

Exposure to regional competition

There is little doubt that the four ASEAN countries having an active trade policy[12] liberalized in the 1980s on an 'most favoured nation' (MFN)-basis.

Officially there was also an extension of the ASEAN Preferential Trading Agreement (PTA) in terms of the numbers of products covered and the higher margins of preference accorded. However, unilateral liberalization, and especially the PTA, have been carefully designed to limit the intra-ASEAN competitive exposure.

The upshot is that the four ASEAN countries still have tariff peaks and non-tariff barriers which perpetuate elements of the 'high cost economy' and otherwise limit competition. Malaysia is farthest down the road towards liberalization. Tariff peaks are mainly a problem in Thailand today; Indonesian tariffs now hover around 21% on average, with much reduced peaks, but there are important non-tariff barriers, often of an opaque nature such as the (import of distribution monopolies). The Philippines embarked on a rationalization scheme of tariffs in the early 1980s, which was broken off halfway. In 1995, the Ramos government implemented a new series of tariff reductions with the goal of a uniform tariff of 5% by 2004. This has given proof of the government's intent on finally increasing the competitive exposure to Filipino business, while reducing the high costs of imported inputs.

One surmises that, besides protection, there are other reasons for the lack of market penetration, such as a high degree of overlap in agri-food and other primary products, semi-processed goods based on minerals, and simple, labour-intensive manufactures. This refers to an old debate in ASEAN about the complementarity versus competitivity of Member States' economies. Many ASEAN policy makers were (and probably still are) convinced that economies should have a complementary product structure in order to make regional exchange profitable. To put it simply, what gains can be had if ASEAN countries trade their mangoes, tropical hardwood, minerals, rice, fish products and palm oil? Given industrialization strategies and the inclination to protect agriculture, this reaction is understandable, but not necessarily sound economically. Once development takes off, the relevant distinction is between homogeneous and differentiated products. This is really a spectrum ranging from perfectly homogeneous to extremely refined differentiation. Only in perfectly homogeneous goods will pure *inter*-industry trade arise; the impact will be stronger still if scale economies are significant and initial cost levels differ (such as cement). But these industrial goods no longer dominate ASEAN countries' exports. Given the rapid industrialization of ASEAN over the last few years, the opportunities for *intra*-industry trade are bound to multiply rapidly. Of course, such an increase in intra-ASEAN intra-industry trade represents a healthy form of competitive exposure, as it would force import competing industries to become price-competitive or to develop niche specializations for intra-ASEAN exports. Economists in

ASEAN rightly begin to turn their attention to actual and potential intra-industry trade.

Another reason for intra-ASEAN trade being so minuscule is probably that multinational production of components, purchases by trading companies and specific forms of subcontracting are geared towards the OECD market. Indeed, a good deal may consist of intra-firm trade, and the issue of the ASEAN market either does not arise or stands in sharp contrast to intra-EC or intra-NAFTA commerce. Trade within the latter two regional markets is greatly facilitated by a very refined, diversified and fairly competitive supply of transport services, using a highly developed surface transport infrastructure. Nothing like this exists in ASEAN, and the underdevelopment of intra-ASEAN trade fails to provide much incentive to overcome this severe obstacle. AFTA trade tends to be conducted via maritime shipping, and freight costs are bound to be a relatively high share of the value of the merchandise (as against North/South) trade where the absolute shipping rates are only marginally lower but the value of goods is much higher). In intra-ASEAN trade therefore, transport costs may act like a tariff. Moreover, given low incentives, there are problems of frequency and length of transit times. Road haulage is underdeveloped and only works (but far from smoothly) between Singapore and Malaysia. All this tends to discourage the gradual development of direct bilateral intra-ASEAN connections, facilitating trade. This is further pre-empted by Singapore's permanent efforts to offer superb transit services and hub connections. Fourth, and remarkable to Europeans used to intense cross-border contracts, is that ASEAN business is often much more familiar with marketing in the US, Japan and Europe than with their neighbouring markets. All these factors are to some degree a product of history and hence can be overcome.

On the other hand, export successes have reduced fears in such countries as Thailand, Malaysia and Indonesia about engaging in ASEAN competition as well.

One should therefore expect regional market integration to heighten competitive exposure but its effects will tend to be slow and undramatic, except for certain sectors which have had excessive protection.

AFTA SCENARIOS

Basic Rules, Scope of Play

The short-term threats and opportunities in AFTA largely depend on the pattern of tariff concessions exchanged by Members so far. Under the Common Effective Preferential Tariff (CEPT) Scheme, the main implementing mechanism for AFTA, countries may categorize products according to the following:

- *fast track tariff reductions*: for products with tariff rates above 20%, AFTA tariff targets (0–5%) must be reached by 2000; products with tariffs at or below 20% must reach the targets by 1 January 1998;
- *normal track*: tariffs above 20% must fall to 20% by 1 January 1998 (and to 0–5% by 1 January 2003), while tariff rates at or below 20% must be reduced to 0–5% by 1 January 2000.
- *temporary exclusions*: tariff reductions for products deemed 'sensitive' may be postponed till 1 January 2000. However, all these products will be phased in to the inclusion list in equal instalments beginning 1 January 1996 to 1 January 2000.
- *general exceptions & sensitive agricultural products*: products excluded for the protection of national security, public morals, health and environment; while agricultural products are covered by the CEPT Scheme, some products may be classified as 'sensitive' and excluded from tariff reductions.

Apart from tariff reduction, quantitative restrictions must likewise be eliminated and non-tariff barriers must be removed on a gradual basis within a period of five years from 1992. Rules of origin, on the other hand, have been made especially liberal to encourage joint ventures and further enhance the region's attractiveness to foreign investment. The local content requirement, which refers to both single country and cumulative ASEAN content, is 40%.

It may come as a surprise to some AFTA sceptics, that out of a total of 48 993 combined tariff lines in ASEAN, 91% are subject to tariff reductions under the CEPT Scheme (see Table 14.1). The product coverage is significant also in terms of trade values. The coverage is expected to broaden even more as the temporarily excluded products are gradually included in the reduction programme. For instance, in the case of the Philippines (said to be the most restrictive in its offer, second to Indonesia), the scope of inclusion is 79% of total tariff lines, having a corresponding worth of 65% of total trade to ASEAN. The coverage is expected to broaden as the pace of AFTA is accelerated; more agricultural products will be included, and a clear mechanism for including temporarily excluded products might be set.

Winners and Losers in Business?

Exporting industries whose products are included in CEPT and whose major ASEAN trading partners include the same product lines, are undoubtedly the big winners in AFTA[15]. So are those whose inputs are likewise included in the CEPT. In the short-run, one may even list import-substituting industries whose products have been excluded as among the gainers. It is important to remember however, that these potential winners and losers are not clear cut. Long-run effects

*Table 14.1   Summary of lists of product inclusions and exclusions**

Country	Inclusion List	Temporary Exclusion List	General Exception
Brunei	6 112		209
Indonesia	7 910	1,317	47
Malaysia	10 494	470	83
Philippines	4 694	562	28
Singapore	5 708		123
Thailand	8 867	147	30
Vietnam	857	1,189	146
Total	44 642	3,685	666

Note: *In terms of tariff lines

Source: AFTA Reader, Vol. IV, 1996.

such as more investments, competitive exposure and technological learning could transform short-run losers into winners. Indeed, if the threat of trade liberalization spurs productivity and modernization, the long-run gains of AFTA would be far larger.

Tables 14.2 and 14.3 specify winners and losers in the 15 'fast track' sectors; however, it should be stressed that the empirical basis of these tables has not been verified due to insufficient access to data. Moreover, as previously mentioned, the term 'loser' is highly subjective and reveals a short-run business horizon. The tables are based on current (1992) levels of trade protection, which may be misleading (for instance, because there may be 'water', that is, redundancy, in the tariffs).

First, protection may have become redundant over time and is no longer a proper indicator of vulnerability – one imperfect way to verify that is whether the relevant companies are active exporters. Thus, Thai ceramics show healthy exports (with 8% even going to ASEAN), yet ceramics are heavily protected with tariffs of 20%–80%. There is also empirical economic literature showing that, in ASEAN, there is a considerable degree of tariff redundancy (see for example, Langhammer, 1988).

Second, protection may be related to input tariffs/quotas for firms which do not enjoy 'drawbacks'[16]. In other words, a 'domestic' sector consisting of MNCs importing heavily, adding relatively little value and re-exporting to OECD markets, may have high formal protection but virtually no actual trade protection. An example can be found in Thai electronics, which is heavily dependent on imported components, with tariffs averaging 20%. MNCs typically

Table 14.2   Winners and losers in the 'fast track' sectors

Sector	Likely to gain	Likely to lose
Cement	Indocement (I) Siam Cement (T)	Cement Ind (M) Boonotan Cons Ind (P)
Ceramic & glass products	MCB Holdings (M)	Thai Glass Ind (T) Indonesian and Philippine glass companies
Chemicals	Salim Group * (I) Chemical Co (M)	
Copper cathodes	Atlas Cons. Mining (P) Indonesian mining companies	Malaysian and Thai mining companies
Electronics	Matsushita Electric (M) Precision Electronics (P)	Sanyo Universal (T) Indonesian electronics firms
Fertiliser	Pacific Chem (M) Altas Fertiliser (P) Charoen Pkphand Feedmill (T)	Indonesian fertiliser companies
Gems & jewellery	Pranda Jewelry (T)	Malaysian and Indonesian jewellery makers
Leather goods	Indonesian and Thai leather	
Pharmaceuticals	Kalbe Farma (I) Metro Drug (P)	
Plastics	Bimantra Group * (I) Malaysian Pacific Ind (M)	Thai Plastic & Chem (T)
Pulp	Sinar Mas * (I) Chapter Ind Corp (P) Malaysian chapter companies	Siam Pulp & Chapter (T)
Rubber products	Gadjah Tunggal (I) Kumpulan Guthrie (M) Philtread Tire & Rubber (P) Bangkok Rubber (T)	
Textiles	Argo Pantes (I) Saha Union (T)	MWE Holdings (M) Filsyn Corp (P)
Vegetable oil	Salim Group * (I) Sime Darby (M)	NDC-Guthrie Plantations (P) Thai plantation firms
Wood & rattan furniture	Indonesian and Malaysian furniture makers	Philippine furniture makers

Notes:

1   Advantage and disadvantage are determined by the extent to which companies in the sector are currently protected within their domestic market, and an estimate of the company's current export capability.

2.   Brunei and Singapore companies are not included as they are all likely to gain from the fast track CEPT sectors.

3.   In countries where there is little domestic activity in a sector, the country is likely to benefit from lower tariffs as a consumer. In such cases there is neither a company or country notation on the chart.

*   Unlisted group, although some individual companies within the group may be listed.

Source: Asian Business Research

Table 14.3   Winners and losers by country

	Problem Areas	Areas of probable comparative advantage
Indonesia		Wood/rattan furniture
		Chemicals
		Plastics
		Cement
Malaysia	Cement	Fertilizer
	Textiles	Pulp
	Gems/jewellery	Wood products
		Rubber products
Philippines	Cement	Fertilizer
	Textiles	Pulp
	Vegetable oil	
	Rubber Products	
	Wood/Rattan	
Thailand	Pulp	Textiles
	Plastic resins	Gems/jewellery
	Vegetable oil	Plastics
	Glass, mirrors	Cement
	Electrical	Chemical products
	Rubber	ceramics
	Leather	

Source: adapted from Toh and Law, 1992.

enjoy full drawbacks. Local assembly for local sales is, however, discouraged as no drawbacks are available. Once local supply capacity began to grow, in the early 1990s, a unilateral tariff cut from 20% to 5% was decided for computers and parts (and a special tax was reduced).

Third, a prospective loser may successfully adjust, diversify, or create joint ventures with 'winners' in other ASEAN countries. As noted, this highly beneficial effect of AFTA would be misconceived by calling it a 'loser'.

How careful one needs to be utilising the information in the 'winners and losers' table is demonstrated in the following example. The 'losers' column shows Thai Glass Industry. This is probably based on the observations of substantial glass imports into Thailand from other ASEAN countries and a tariff of 30%. However, in all likelihood these are inadequate indicators because half of all Thai glass bulbs, presumably with a major part enjoying drawbacks as TV sets, are exported worldwide. The competitiveness issue is whether Thai Glass Industry makes other glass products and operates in different market segments.

Table 14.3, taken from a chapter by Toh and Low (1992), only shows partial overlap with the first table, which can be taken as evidence that simple extrapolations get rather different results. Also, Indonesia has no 'problem areas', a curious assessment with which Indonesian trade negotiators do not agree.

As noted earlier, intra-ASEAN trade is so underdeveloped that future intra-AFTA trade is largely unpredictable. It will depend strongly on corporate strategies in import competition and exporting sectors as well as on structural factors such as infrastructure and transport. Seen in this perspective, foreign direct investors will not merely study business opportunities and the trading environment as a given, they will be instrumental in shaping and transforming it, once AFTA has established credibility.

CONCLUSIONS

Will AFTA make ASEAN more attractive for international business? A number of tentative answers can be given based on this preliminary assessment:

1. based on comparative statics economic simulations, the additional intra-ASEAN export demand is not impressive;
2. the addition to growth in ASEAN attributable to AFTA (again, in these static simulations) is less than 1%, often less than 0.5%;
3. however, even without a technical discussion about the models used, the utility of these estimates is greatly reduced by their reliance on the initial trade structure (which is not merely distorted, but reflects the severe underdevelopment of trade, transport and distribution connections among ASEAN countries); the lack of scale economies in the models and the impossibility of forecasting how MNCs and ASEAN businesses will create new trade as a result of corporate strategies, networking and direct investments. The underestimation of the AFTA gains is likely to be very large.
4. exposure to ASEAN competition has been revealed to be a sensitive issue, even in the 15 fast track sectors; again, if the AFTA cold shower works (that is, if 'exit' problems remain limited and instead, an efficiency and diversification drive improves performance), economic growth and competitiveness will further increase.

What is obvious from the back-of-the-envelope calculations, but very hard to verify analytically is the enormous potential for intra-ASEAN trade in the long run, that is over a time span comparable to the AFTA build-up period (up to 2003 and beyond).

A short-run (comparative static) perspective would be mistaken therefore. Strategies need to be long-run. A long-run strategic perspective does not depend on the details of AFTA. The four key variables to look at would seem to be:

- economic growth averages for the next decade, which will remain high (even for the Philippines, if the Ramos government can sustain current policies);
- the underlying shifts to greater market orientation and trade liberalization at Member States' level, which provide a robust foundation for AFTA to develop (critical, here, are the big three).
- the costs of a realistic ASEAN-wide entry strategy, be it for production networks and world-wide final sales or for regional sales (this would include a realistic assessment of the evolution of the underdeveloped intra-ASEAN trade, transport and distribution infrastructure).
- the way ASEAN is and will be enmeshed into Pacific Asia, especially at the business level (Japan; overseas Chinese networks; Pacific strategies of MNCs).

In the light of these strategic variables, direct investments in ASEAN are often attractive. The critical contribution of AFTA consists of taking away, over time, a set of trade constraints, while also exposing local business to more vigorous competition. It would also heighten competition in the region, sharpen the national strategies for promoting competitiveness by improving the business environment and cutting the costs of non-specific inputs (like banking, insurance, energy, information, and so on) and hence, add to the motives to be present there.

NOTES

1. The two theories only differ with respect to the possibilities of (1) indirect trade deflection and (2) a non-uniform price level in free trade areas. This need not concern us here, except that indirect trade deflection is an additional factor for intra-area trade increase. However, it is unlikely that these subtleties play a role in any of the models discussed below.
2. See, for example, the surveys in Balassa (1975) and Pelkmans (1984), Chapter 1.
3. This compares, for instance, with a share of roughly 65% for the four largest EC Member States in 1990 intra-EC trade. Of course the three largest ASEAN Member States are also the three poorest ones. Ignoring this for a moment, it is striking that the big three comprise 91% of ASEAN population; the big EC four 'only' 71% in 1990. In the long run, this suggests a tremendous potential for intra-ASEAN trade.
4. So that the minimum efficient scale (MES) output, that is the lowest possible average cost point on the scale curve, can be reached.
5. Several studies have failed to find empirical evidence of scale advantages arising from mergers, as they were either not realized or compensated by diseconomies.
6. Brunei's attempt to diversify industrially has not yet yielded significant results.
7. The Philippines currently involves SGS as well.

8. Memorandum of Understanding, Brand-to-brand complementation on the automotive industry, under the Basic Agreement on AIC. The companies which have been approved by ASEAN are: Mitsubishi, Toyota, Volvo, Mercedes Benz, Nissan and Daf Trucks. Renault obtained approval in 1991 for a two countries' scheme. In October 1991 this approach was broadened to non-automotive products.
9. COIME, which is the ASEAN committee on industry and mining.
10. Grunfors pumps (1 case), DAF Trucks parts (1 case) and Nestlé (4 cases).
11. ASEAN-CCI (1991). The quotations are on p. 15.
12. Singapore and Brunei are virtually tariff-free and quota free. Singapore levies heavy taxes on car imports and uses an auctioning system to restrict the annual growth of the local car population. No industrial protection is behind this (the aim is anti-congestion).
13. During the Fourth ASEAN Summit of January 1992, 15 product groups were identified to accelerate the implementation of AFTA: vegetable oils; chemicals; fertilizer; rubber products; pulp and paper; wooden and rattan furniture; gems and jewellery products; cement; pharmaceuticals; plastics; leather products; textiles; ceramics and glass products; copper cathodes; electronics.
14. As part of the Acceleration programme of AFTA decided in 1994, it was agreed that countries will now have the option to include agricultural raw materials.
15. Based on the Reciprocity Principle, a country enjoys concessions only on products it has itself included in the CEPT Scheme for tariff reduction
16. Drawbacks amount to waivers or restitutions of MFN tariffs for inputs into products which are exported.

REFERENCES

AFTA Reader, ASEAN Secretariat, September 1996.

ASEAN-CCI (1991), *Guide to AIJVs*, Kuala Lumpur: Federation of Malaysian Manufactures.

Balassa, B. (ed.) (1975), *European economic integration*, Amsterdam/Oxford (North Holland).

Felipe, J. and R. Westcott (1992), 'The welfare effects of an ASEAN free trade area: a simulation analysis', paper presented in Kita Kyuchu City.

Imada, P., M. Montes and S. Naya (1991), *A free trade area: implications for ASEAN*, Singapore: ISEAS.

Langhammer, R. (1988), 'Tariff reductions and tariff redundancy in ASEAN countries', *ASEAN Economic Bulletin*, **4** (3).

Langhammer, R. (1991), 'ASEAN economic cooperation: a stock-taking from a political economy point of view', *ASEAN Economic Bulletin*, **8** (2).

Pelkmans, J. (1984), *Market integration in the EC*, The Hague/Boston (M. Nijhoff).

Pelkmans, J. (1993), 'Institutional requirements of ASEAN with special references to AFTA', in Imada, P. and S. Naya (eds), *AFTA, the way ahead*, Singapore: ISEAS.

Pratten, C. (1988), 'A Survey of economies-of-scale, background study for the Cecchini report', published in *Economic Papers*, EC Commission (DG 11), Brussels.

Toh, M.H. and L. Low (1993), 'Is the ASEAN free trade area a second best option?', *Asian Economic Journal*, **7** (3).

Yap, J. and R. Edillan (1992), 'Stimulating the effects of an ASEAN free trade area using a multi-country model', paper presented at Kita Kyuchu City.

15. Japanese international investment in the regions of East Asia and the Pacific: a horizontal division of labour?

Shigeki Tejima

INTRODUCTION

Japanese Foreign Direct Investment (FDI) in Asia since the late 1980s is distinguished by its mixture of four types, of FDI motivations. These four FDI motivations have decided Japanese companies' international division of work in the Asian region, that is, either a horizontal division of labour or a vertical division of labour.

The first type of motivation is typical of FDI between a developed country and a developing country based on the factor price equalization theorem. The second type is the establishment of export bases serving the markets of the USA/Canada and the EU, utilizing the abundant human resources of Asian countries, as a response to trade frictions with North American and Western European countries under the dramatically appreciated Japanese yen. The third type is the construction of supply bases, serving the Japanese market, which has accelerated strongly because of the appreciation of the Japanese yen recently. The fourth type is new establishment or reinforcement of supply bases mainly serving the growing Asian markets.

Naturally, the first category of FDI has been the basic motivation of Japanese companies' FDI in Asian countries. However, it should be noted that Japanese FDI in Asia has increased significantly only since the intensification of trade frictions with the USA/Canada and the EU, and the dramatic appreciation of the Japanese Yen. The third type of FDI has increased particularly, since the yen appreciation of 1993 onwards. The fourth has become prevalent in ASEAN countries and China, and will be the mainstream Japanese FDI in Asia in the long term.

In this chapter, these four categories of Japanese FDI will be explained briefly in relation to a historical review of the recent trends of Japanese FDI in Asia. Then, the advantages of Japanese production systems are discussed relative to Japanese FDI in Asia.

Before the appearance of serious trade frictions and yen appreciation, Japanese companies had relied more on the effectiveness of domestic production systems combined with export, than on overseas production. However, since 1985, when the 'Plaza Accord' was settled, Japanese companies have started to rely more on overseas production than before. In that sense, J. Dunning's concept of Internationalization, Ownership and Location advantages seems to have begun to work better to stimulate Japanese FDI recently (Dunning, 1993). They are now eager to reconstruct or reinforce their effective international production and sales networks between assemblers and parts suppliers throughout all the Asian region. In other words, they prefer international open networks, including new Japanese and foreign suppliers, to conventional domestic networks in Japan.

The next section discusses present and future Asian networks relative to the Japanese economy. Japanese production networks in Asia are of two types: vertical and horizontal divisions of labour.

As a trend, horizontal division of labour will become more important between Japan and Asian countries where per capita incomes reach a relatively high level, and capital and human resources are accumulated substantially. On the other hand, vertical division of labour will still prevail in countries like China, where large-scale pooling of labour supply exists and, therefore, the comparative advantages of labour intensive industries can be maintained even when they have high economic growth.

I should like here to define horizontal division of labour more precisely. Japanese companies have a general policy of transferring matured goods produced with established technology to production bases in Asian countries, because Asian-made products have better price competitiveness than products made in Japan. However, we cannot call it genuine horizontal division of labour unless Asian production bases or Asian countries have the innovative capability to develop and produce sophisticated higher value-added goods.

Finally, Japanese companies' Asian production networks will be discussed relative to structural change in the Japanese economy, specially referring to so-called 'hollowing out', and its effects on the development of the Asian economy. I shall conclude that Japanese FDI will contribute to the accelerated development of the Asian economy and to the enforcement of the international competitiveness of the Japanese economy.

First, then, I shall discuss the recent trends of Japanese FDI, using the basic categories and motivations of FDI, as described above.

RECENT TRENDS OF JAPANESE FDI AND ITS FOUR CATEGORIES

Japanese companies' foreign direct investment (FDI) increased dramatically in the late 1980s, but in the early 1990s, it has tended to decline. However, it rebounded to an upward trend in the financial year (FY) 1993 (April 1993–March 1994) (see Table 15.1). It seems that Japanese FDI is now at the turning point toward a new era of 'Globalization', as defined in this section.

Table 15.1 indicates the recent trends of Japanese FDI, where FDI in the USA/Canada and the EU has fluctuated from a dramatic increase (in the late 1980s) to a sudden decrease (in the early 1990s) and a gradual recovery (since 1993). On the other hand, FDI in Asian countries has steadily increased, while popular destinations have shifted from Asian NIEs to ASEAN countries and to China. The differences in FDI trends by region originate in the differences in FDI motivations, and in business performance as a result of FDI in each region.

The basic motivation of FDI in Asia, the first category of Japanese FDI, is seeking production sites which offer lower production costs, especially lower labour cost, according to the factor price equalization theorem. Japanese companies have the rational intention of transferring labour intensive industries (or products) from Japan to Asian countries, because Japan has relatively abundant (or cheap) capital and relatively scarce labour (or relatively expensive wages) while Asian countries have relatively abundant labour (or relatively cheap wages) and relatively scarce (or expensive) capital. Japanese companies have the rational motivation of utilizing labour – abundant Asian countries' comparative advantages by transferring their production bases to Asian countries. The more production facilities of labour-intensive goods are shifted to Asian countries, the more demand for labour is created there and the less demand for labour in Japan. As a result, wage rates are increased in Asian countries and decreased in Japan, thus narrowing the gap in wage rates. In reality, Japanese companies seek new destinations in other Asian countries offering lower wage rates, before wage rates are truly equalized between Japan and the first host country in Asia.

Table 15.2 shows that this type of FDI, looking for low labour costs, has been very popular, especially in Asian countries, in comparison with the USA/Canada and the EU. The information comes from a survey for the Export-Import Bank of Japan, conducted by myself for FYs 1991, 1992, 1993 and 1994 (hereafter, respectively, Tejima 1991 survey, Tejima 1992 survey, Tejima 1993 survey and Tejima 1994 survey),[1] and further surveys in 1995 and 1996. In Table 15.2 the motivation of seeking for low production costs is most strong in China and noticeably weakened in Asian NIEs. The motivation in ASEAN countries is in between China and the Asian NIEs, because ASEAN includes Malaysia and Thailand, whose labour markets are relatively satiated, and Indonesia and the Philippines, which are still labour abundant. No doubt, Japanese companies intend to diminish the effects of the comparative disadvantages of their home country through FDI and overseas production in Asian countries. It can be regarded as one part of the 'Globalization' of Japanese companies.

Table 15.1   Recent trends of Japanese FDI (units: %)

FY	Total FDI (Million US$)	% change over previous year	North America	USA	Latin America	Asia	NIEs	ASEAN	China	Middle East	Europe	Africa	Oceania	Exchange Rate(¥/US$)
1968	557	102.6	33.2	26.0	7.2	14.0	3.1	10.6	0.0	5.0	27.5	7.7	5.6	
1969	665	19.4	19.4	17.9	15.0	29.6	6.0	10.7	0.0	5.7	14.0	2.7	13.4	
1970	904	35.9	21.2	10.3	5.1	18.5	6.6	11.6	0.0	3.1	37.1	1.6	13.6	
1971	858	−5.1	26.8	25.2	16.3	27.6	11.2	16.1	0.0	4.2	9.8	2.5	12.8	
1972	2338	172.5	17.4	15.2	12.1	17.2	9.7	7.4	0.0	10.1	40.0	1.5	1.8	
1973	3494	49.4	26.1	22.9	23.5	28.6	12.9	15.6	0.0	3.2	9.7	3.0	6.0	273.26
1974	2395	−31.5	23.0	20.8	29.2	30.5	8.9	21.4	0.0	2.7	7.9	2.3	4.5	292.70
1975	3280	37.0	27.6	25.8	11.3	33.5	8.5	24.4	0.0	6.0	10.2	5.9	5.6	299.01
1976	3462	5.6	21.6	19.2	12.1	36.0	6.5	29.4	0.0	8.0	9.7	7.9	4.7	292.37
1977	2806	−19.0	26.2	24.5	16.3	30.8	10.3	20.3	0.0	8.0	7.8	5.0	5.9	256.55
1978	4598	63.9	29.7	27.9	13.4	29 1	12.9	16.2	0.0	10.7	7.0	4.9	5.2	201.38
1979	4995	8.6	28.8	26.9	24.2	19.5	12.3	6.8	0.3	2.6	9.9	3.4	11.7	229.38
1980	4693	−6.1	34.0	31.6	12.5	25.3	8.1	16.8	0.3	3.4	12.3	3.0	9.6	217.43
1981	8932	90.3	28.2	26.4	13.2	37.4	8.1	28.8	0.3	1.1	8.9	6.4	4.8	227.58
1982	7703	−13.8	37.7	35.5	19.5	18.0	9.6	8.1	0.2	1.6	11.4	6.4	5.5	249.68
1983	8145	5.7	33.2	31.5	23.1	22.7	13.7	8.0	0.0	2.2	12.2	4.5	2.3	236.41
1984	10155	24.7	34.9	33.1	22.6	16.0	8.0	6.7	1.1	2.7	19.1	3.2	1.6	243.93
1985	12217	20.3	45.0	44.2	21.4	11.8	5.9	4.9	0.8	0.4	15.8	1.4	4.3	221.68
1986	22320	82.7	46.8	45.5	21.2	10.4	6.9	2.5	1.0	0.2	15.5	1.4	4.4	159.87
1987	33364	49.5	46.0	44.1	14.4	14.6	7.7	3.1	3.7	0.2	19.7	0.8	4.2	138.45
1988	47022	40.9	47.5	46.2	13.7	11.8	6.9	4.2	0.6	0.6	19.4	1.4	5.7	128.34
1989	67540	43.6	50.2	48.2	7.8	12.2	7.3	4.1	0.6	0.1	21.9	1.0	6.8	142.82
1990	56911	−15.7	47.8	45.9	6.4	12.4	5.9	5.7	0.6	0.1	25.1	1.0	7.3	141.52
1991	41584	−26.9	45.3	43.4	8.0	14.3	5.3	7.4	1.4	0.2	22.5	1.8	7.9	133.31
1992	34138	−17.9	42.7	40.5	8.0	18.8	5.6	9.4	3.1	2.1	20.7	0.7	7.0	124.73
1993	36025	5.5	42.4	40.9	9.4	18.4	6.7	6.7	4.7	0.6	22.0	1.5	5.6	107.79
1994	41051	14.0	43.4	42.2	12.7	23.6	7.0	9.5	6.2	0.7	15.2	0.8	3.5	99.33
1995	50694	23.5	44.9	43.8	7.6	24.2	6.3	8.1	8.8	0.3	16.7	0.7	5.5	96.30
1996	49172	−3.0	48.0	45.8	9.2	24.2	7.4	10.3	5.3	0.5	15.4	0.9	1.9	112.46

Source: Produced by EXIM Bank of Japan with Ministry of Finance statistics

217

Table 15.2   Changes in motivation for medium term FDI (FY 1990 and 1996 survey) (all industries) (%)

Region	Asian NIEs							ASEAN							China					
Year of the survey undertaken	90	91	92	93	94	95	96	90	91	92	93	94	95	96	91	92	93	94	95	96
Motivation for foreign direct investment																				
Preservation and/or expansion of market share	55.6	59.1	50.0	60.0	55.3	69.7	75.4	39.8	47.8	46.4	50.5	54.8	64.7	63.6	22.9	39.0	33.6	34.3	48.1	62.4
Development of a new market	18.5	13.6	19.4	17.5	17.5	23.5	32.3	19.5	12.2	15.5	20.0	13.5	31.5	32.7	28.6	37.3	44.9	54.2	54.1	53.9
Reverse exports to Japan	16.7	10.2	6.5	11.3	16.5	22.7	12.3	17.7	8.7	10.3	21.0	23.2	36.0	25.3	8.6	8.5	19.6	22.3	36.6	35.5
Exports to a third country	5.6	11.4	8.1	26.3	26.2	31.8	32.3	13.3	16.5	12.4	32.4	23.9	42.6	38.3	8.6	6.8	15.9	15.7	32.2	34.8
Response to voluntary export restraints, dumping tariffs and other trade regulations by the host country	0.0	1.1	0.0	0.0	2.9	1.5	1.5	0.9	2.6	3.1	1.0	1.3	1.5	1.2	2.9	3.4	0.9	0.0	1.1	0.7
Promotion of specialization with the firm	11.1	12.5	16.1	2.5	2.9	4.5	3.1	9.7	12.2	16.5	7.6	7.1	5.6	4.9	2.9	5.1	3.7	1.8	4.4	3.5
Shifting existing domestic production bases overseas	18.5	18.2	11.3	8.8	13.6	22.0	27.7	31.9	23.5	18.6	20.0	22.6	31.0	37.0	14.3	6.8	15.0	17.5	31.1	33.3
Securing inexpensive labour forces	11.1	6.8	3.2	2.5	8.7	11.4	9.2	38.1	27.8	27.8	20.0	20.6	40.1	36.4	40.0	11.9	30.8	31.3	59.0	46.1
Supplying parts to an assembly manufacturer (including Japanese overseas affiliate)	7.4.	2.3	0.0	3.8	10.7	23.5	13.8	4.4	6.1	8.2	17.1	17.4	32.5	24.1	0.0	3.4	12.2	10.2	21.3	12.8
Securing stable supply of raw materials	5.6	10.2	8.1	2.5	1.9	6.1	3.1	6.2	12.2	9.3	1.0	4.5	5.1	3.7	5.7	11.9	1.9	1.2	4.4	1.4
Request from the host country	5.6	4.5	0.0	1.3	1.9	2.3	3.1	0.9	4.3	5.2	1.9	1.3	3.0	3.1	14.3	16.9	6.5	5.4	8.2	4.3
Avoiding foreign exchange risk	3.7	1.1	1.6	3.8	8.7	20.5	10.8	2.7	0.9	4.1	10.5	9.7	21.8	8.6	0.0	5.1	6.5	4.8	13.7	5.7
Development of products adapted to the local market	3.7	2.3	1.6	1.3	2.9	6.1	9.2	2.7	3.5	2.1	2.9	3.9	6.6	8.6	2.9	3.4	1.9	1.2	6.0	12.8
Number of responses	54	88	62	80	103	132	65	113	115	97	105	155	197	162	35	59	107	166	183	141

218

Region	US/Canada							EU							Latin America						
Year of the survey undertaken Motivation for foreign direct investment	90	91	92	93	94	95	96	90	91	92	93	94	95	96	90	91	92	93	94	95	96
Preservation and/or expansion of market share	53.4	57.7	54.9	55.6	55.9	77.3	82.1	55.8	52.3	55.7	51.9	51.9	78.4	76.1	66.7	60.9	36.7	55.2	42.5	60.0	47.6
Development of a new market	22.7	25.2	18.7	12.2	9.8	25.0	29.5	31.7	27.1	29.1	13.0	17.3	29.4	34.3	8.3	17.4	16.7	20.7	32.5	44.4	45.2
Reverse exports to Japan	5.7	2.4	4.4	5.6	6.9	16.7	10.5	0.8	0.9	1.3	1.3	1.2	7.8	5.0	0.0	0.0	3.3	3.5	2.5	8.9	4.8
Exports to a third country	0.0	2.4	0.0	1.1	5.9	13.6	11.6	3.3	1.9	1.3	3.9	11.1	25.5	16.4	8.3	8.7	13.3	17.2	7.5	28.9	23.8
Response to voluntary export restraints, dumping tariffs and other trade regulations by the host country	20.5	9.8	16.5	6.7	12.7	11.4	10.5	20.8	18.7	13.9	15.6	11.1	7.8	6.0	16.7	0.0	3.3	6.9	5.0	8.9	7.1
Promotion of specialization with the firm	10.2	10.6	8.8	2.2	2.0	1.5	4.2	11.7	9.3	11.4	1.3	2.5	2.9	3.0	8.3	8.7	3.3	3.5	2.5	2.2	2.4
Shifting existing domestic production bases overseas	25.0	18.7	12.1	20.0	30.4	23.5	30.5	22.5	16.8	10.1	16.9	18.5	25.5	16.4	41.7	21.7	6.7	10.3	5.0	24.4	26.2
Securing inexpensive labour forces	1.1	0.0	2.2	0.0	2.0	2.3	2.1	0.0	0.9	2.5	1.3	0.0	7.8	0.0	41.7	4.3	10.0	13.8	12.5	20.0	14.3
Supplying parts to an assembly manufacturer (including Japanese overseas affiliate)	9.1	5.7	4.4	3.3	11.8	21.2	16.8	5.8	5.6	6.3	14.3	12.3	11.8	10.4	8.3	8.7	3.3	3.5	12.5	20.0	21.4
Securing stable supply of raw materials	2.3	1.6	5.5	3.3	2.0	1.5	3.2	0.8	1.9	1.3	0.0	2.5	2.0	0.0	8.3	0.0	13.3	3.5	5.0	2.2	7.1
Request from the host country	1.1	1.6	1.1	0.0	1.0	0.8	3.2	1.7	0.0	0.0	0.0	0.0	0.0	1.5	0.0	4.3	3.3	0.0	0.0	0.0	0.0
Avoiding foreign exchange risk	2.3	0.8	1.1	8.9	17.6	24.2	21.1	1.7	2.8	3.8	3.9	6.2	24.5	9.0	0.0	4.3	0.0	0.0	7.5	13.3	7.1
Development of products adapted to the local market	18.2	10.6	8.8	13.3	9.8	15.2	13.7	15.0	15.9	13.9	3.9	7.4	11.8	11.9	8.3	4.3	0.0	0.0	2.5	4.4	11.9
Number of responses	88	123	91	89	102	132	95	120	107	79	77	81	102	67	12	23	30	31	40	45	42

In this chapter the 'Globalization' of Japanese companies is defined as Japanese companies' global strategies to do businesses in the best places in the world. This involves seeking for the most appropriate places to produce and sell goods, procure spare parts and raw materials, finance FDI costs in foreign capital markets and implement research and development, considering each country's competitive advantages. These, as shown in Porter (1990), are local demand, production factors, supporting industries and the degree of competition of local markets.

We now turn to the second category of FDI. We should note that Japanese FDI in Asia has not increased consistently. Instead, it was prompted, especially, in the period after the yen appreciations of 1985 and 1993. Japanese firms seem to have been eager to establish production bases outside Japan to avoid the exchange risk of the yen, and to decrease Japan's trade surplus with America and Europe by shifting export from Japanese companies to Asian companies.

They had the same motivation to invest in the USA, Canada and the EU but the performance of their FDI there was relatively unsatisfactory compared to FDI in Asia because of higher investment cost, higher labour costs and the slowdown of the European and American economies at the beginning of the 1990s. The differences in profitability made Japanese firms more positive in Asia and more prudent in the USA, Canada and EU at the beginning of the 1990s.[2]

Interestingly, at the beginning of the 1980s, many Japanese firms believed that to produce electric/electronic products and automobiles in Japan and to export those goods, was the most effective way to supply world markets, because they could utilize flexible production systems supported by excellent parts industries and qualified human resources. Close communication networks between assemblers and parts suppliers were stimulating continuous improvement of products and production processes. Certainly, Asian countries had advantages in labour costs but, considering the difficulty of accessing qualified local supporting industries and human resources in Asia, they were rather reluctant to transfer production bases to foreign countries until they suffered high pressures from yen appreciation and trade frictions.

Therefore, the first FDI category was not enough to expand Japanese FDI in Asia and the second FDI category was an important trigger of the high growth of Japanese FDI there. Recently, yen appreciations have again stimulated Japanese FDI in Asia. Table 15.2 shows the FDI motivations to export to third countries have been strengthened since 1993; the motivation to decrease exchange risk was empowered during 1994–6 in the Asian NIEs, and during 1993–6 in the ASEAN countries.

Table 15.3 suggests that Japanese companies' production subsidiaries in Asia have played an important role as export bases. Some of them are intended to export to the USA, Canada, and the EU. Table 15.3 (based on the TEJIMA 1991 survey) indicates that in the case of 300 production companies in Asian NIEs, 11.7% are mainly oriented toward the USA, Canada and the EU and 8.3% are mainly oriented toward Japan. In the case of 322 production companies in ASEAN countries, 12.8% are aimed at the USA, Canada and the EU and 14.9% are aimed at the Japanese market.

Table 15.3   The most important customers for existing production bases (FY 1991 survey) (unit: %)

** \ *	Japan	NIEs	ASEAN	Other Asian Countries	USA/ Canada	EU	Latin America	Total number of firms
NIEs	8.3	73.8	5.7	1.0	10.0	1.7	–	300
ASEAN	14.9	9.9	61.8	0.6	8.1	4.7	–	322
Other Asian Countries	22.0	10.0	2.0	58.0	6.0	2.0	–	50
USA/Canada	4.1	3.6	0.0	0.0	92.1	0.3	–	365
EU	0.9	2.2	0.0	0.0	2.2	94.8	–	232

Notes:
*   Customer
**   Location of production subsidiaries

Table 15.4   The most important customers for existing production bases (FY 1992 survey) (unit: %)

** \ *	Japan	NIEs	ASEAN	Other Asian Countries	USA/ Canada	EU	Latin America	Total number of firms
NIEs	14.7	72.9	3.6	0.3	6.6	1.9	0.0	361
ASEAN	15.5	7.4	63.6	1.0	10.4	2.0	0.0	393
Other Asian Countries	35.4	3.1	0.0	57.3	4.2	0.0	0.0	96
USA/Canada	3.6	0.6	1.1	0.4	93.8	0.2	0.2	466
EU	1.9	0.4	0.0	0.4	2.6	94.8	0.0	267
Latin America	9.2	0.0	0.8	0.0	12.3	4.6	73.1	130

Notes:
*   Customer
**   Location of production subsidiaries

Table 15.5   The most important customers for existing production bases (FY 1993 survey) (unit: %)

***** / ******	Japan	NIEs	ASEAN	China	Other Asian Countries	USA/ Canada	Latin America	EU	Total number of firms
NIEs	9.44	73.85	3.87	0.00	0.73	8.23	0.24	3.63	413
ASEAN	17.13	2.95	67.72	0.00	0.39	8.07	0.00	3.74	508
China	33.33	11.11	0.00	45.45	1.01	8.08	0.00	1.01	99
Other Asian Countries	9.62	0.00	0.00	0.00	90.38	0.00	0.00	0.00	52
USA/Canada	3.73	0.20	0.20	0.00	0.00	95.29	0.20	0.39	510
Latin America	5.10	0.00	0.00	0.00	0.00	13.38	80.25	1.27	157
EU	3.19	0.00	0.00	0.64	0.00	0.64	0.32	95.21	313
Subsidiaries in customer's country	–	85.90	85.47	–	95.74	89.30	96.03	79.53	1,393

Notes:
*   Customer
**   Location of production subsidiaries

Table 15.6   The most important customers for existing production bases (FY 1994 survey) (unit: %)

***** / ******	Japan	NIEs	ASEAN	China	Other Asian Countries	USA/ Canada	Latin America	EU	Total number of firms
NIEs	11.6	74.2	4.9	1.4	0.4	5.9	0.2	1.4	492
ASEAN	19.0	4.0	67.1	0.3	1.7	5.4	0.8	1.6	630
China	33.5	2.5	2.5	57.0	0.0	3.8	0.6	0.0	158
Other Asian Countries	6.8	0.0	0.0	0.0	93.2	0.0	0.0	0.0	44
USA/Canada	3.9	0.2	0.2	0.0	0.0	94.7	0.7	0.4	562
Latin America	5.6	0.0	0.0	0.0	0.0	17.9	75.9	0.6	162
EU	1.6	0.0	0.3	0.0	0.0	0.0	0.0	98.1	322
Subsidiaries in customer's country		80.5	87.5		97.6	91.7	92.7	80.7	

Notes:
*   Customer
**   Location of production subsidiaries

Table 15.6 (based on the Tejima 1994 survey) shows that in the case of 492 production companies in Asian NIEs, 7.3% are mainly oriented toward the USA/Canada and the EU and 11.6% are mainly oriented toward Japan. In the case of 630 production companies in ASEAN countries, 7% are aimed at the USA, Canada and the EU and 19.0% are aimed at the Japanese market. Finally, in China, 3.8% of 158 production companies are targeted at the USA, Canada and the EU and 33.5% are targeted at Japan.

If we overview Tables 15.3–15.6 we can see most clearly that Japanese companies' production subsidiaries in ASEAN countries have gradually changed their role from export bases to the USA, Canada and the EU to export bases to Japan in the period between 1991 and 1994. Production companies in Asian NIEs have also changed their role in the same direction as in ASEAN, although the result is more unstable than is the case in ASEAN. China is very popular as a supply base for Japanese markets, and less important for the USA/Canada and the EU.

Therefore, we have to move to the third category of Japanese FDI. The importance of constructing Asian supply bases for Japan is clear in Tables 15.3–15.6. If we go back to Table 15.2, we see clearly that the motivations have been strengthened in FYs 1993 and 1994. Now, Japanese companies are, eager to transfer further products from domestic networks to Asian networks as soon as the products mature and their production processes are established, because the shift is urgently required to compete against severe price competition in foreign and domestic markets.

The fourth category of FDI has become more and more important recently. High economic growth among Asian countries has stimulated the rapidly expanding Asian market. For example, it is said that the most popular consumer goods among Chinese living in large coastal urban area are colour televisions, air conditioners and electric ovens, while ten years ago they were bicycles, watches and radios. The Chinese automobile market is expected to reach about 3 million units per annum at the beginning of the 21st century, three times the current size.

Again, in Tables 15.3–15.6, Asian local markets are regarded as the most important by more than half of the Asian production subsidiaries of Japanese companies.

In addition, if we consider the medium-term (next three years) and long-term (next ten years) strategies of Japanese companies for Asian countries, many of them recognize that it is most important to empower production and sales facilities in Asia to correspond to the growing local market of Asia (based on Tejima 1993 survey).[3]

With those four categories of Japanese FDI in Asia, we can analyze FDI trends in Asia in the 1980s and 1990s (see again Table 15.1). Roughly speaking, the potential motivation of category 1 to invest in Asia has been prevailing through all periods of the 1980s and 1990s.

However, the surge of Japanese FDI was realized only by the push of the second category of FDI, especially after 1985. Japanese firms have to recognize that even an effective domestic production and export system was no longer most appropriate to serve foreign markets, so they activated overseas production in North America, Western Europe and Asia. The appreciated yen made it easier to buy foreign properties. Additionally, the Japanese economic boom in the late 1980s prompted the expansion of Japan's FDI, because the boom in stock markets enabled Japanese parent companies to collect low-cost money to invest in foreign countries. The economic boom also improved the business performances of Japanese parent companies and encouraged them to adopt aggressive globalization policies. The stable growth of Japanese, US, Canadian and EU economies persuaded them to establish and expand supply bases in Asian countries to serve those developed countries. In the late 1980s, the first, second and third categories of FDI worked well because of the expanding demand of developed countries, low financial cost and appreciated Japanese yen.

At the beginning of the 1990s, the major economic conditions for FDI changed from supportive to suppressive. The changes included, first, the economic slowdown of Japan, the USA, Canada and the EU; second, increasing capital costs for Japanese parent companies caused by shrunken stock markets; and third, the deteriorating business performances of Japanese parent companies facing a stagnant domestic economy.

The drastic changes in those conditions caused a major change in Japanese FDI, from the upward trend in the late 1980s to the downward trend in the beginning of the 1990s. However, FDI in Asia has been relatively stable in comparison with FDI in the USA, Canada and the EU (see Table 15.1 again). In fact, the four categories of Japanese FDI in Asia have even been strengthened under these deteriorating conditions. The motivation to build Asian export bases for the USA/Canada and the EU has been weakened, while the motivation to build supply bases for local Asian countries and Japan has been strengthened since 1993.

As I pointed out at the beginning of this section, Japanese FDI turned again to an upward trend in the FY 1993 (see Table 15.1). This new trend was caused by two prominent factors, that is, FDI increase in Asia and in the USA/Canada.

The FDI increase in Asia, especially in the manufacturing sectors, was in exactly the same direction as the medium term (1994–1996) prediction of the Tejima 1993 survey.[4] The prediction said that Japanese FDI would be increased for the next three years (1994–1996) for two reasons.

The first reason is Japanese companies' strategies in Asia to create or expand production bases under the accelerated yen appreciation, in order to maintain international competitiveness by utilizing lower production costs in Asia. In other words, they wanted to supply the Japanese market, the local Asian markets and markets in Western countries, from Asian production bases instead of Japanese production facilities.

The second reason was the almost two digit growth rate of Asian local markets, which attracted foreign investors.

Actual FDI in Asia in 1993 exactly indicated the increase in FDI for the electric/electronic, machinery and transportation industries in China, Thailand, Malaysia, Singapore and the Philippines, many of which were intended to construct and/or expand production bases serving markets in Japan, and Asian and Western countries (see Table 15.2).

The resurgence of FDI in the USA, Canada and the EU in the FY 1993 is different from that in Asia, because many of the increases in the western countries are to provide financial support for poorly performing projects implemented in the real estate, construction and manufacturing industries in those countries. We can, however, expect more positive FDI, including R&D to be increased in the future.

All four categories will stimulate Japanese FDI in Asia. It should be noticed that the four categories of FDI have been basically intended to strengthen the international competitiveness of Japanese companies and their production and sales networks. In the next section, I will analyze the mechanism of Japanese production systems and FDI with a simple model, using the concept of J. Dunning's (1993) 'I' (internalization) advantage, 'O' (ownership) advantage and 'L' (location) advantage.

FROM DOMESTIC NETWORKS TO INTERNATIONAL NETWORKS

Many people argued about Japanese companies' competitive advantages, especially about their flexible production system, 'Kaizen', which improves each part of the production process with daily step-by-step efforts and effective networks between assemblers and parts suppliers.

In this section, I focus on the production networks between assemblers and parts suppliers.

R. Coase (1988), O. Williamson (1986) and other authors introduced the concept of 'transaction cost'. I shall try to show, with a little expansion of this concept, that Japanese companies' flexible and close networks between assemblers and parts suppliers can be more effective than transactions in a completely competitive market or completely internal production.

First, the concept of transaction cost and internalization cost are introduced. Second, I assume that regarding intermediate product 'XP', that is a part or a bundle of parts to produce final goods 'X' in the automobile or electric/electronic industries, there are three cases: the completely competitive market for intermediate products in one pole, completely internal production of parts on the other and, in between, Japanese firms' flexible networks between assemblers and parts suppliers.

In Figure 15.1, the competitive market for 'XP' goods is presented at point O, completely internal production is presented at point M and Japanese networks at point J. The horizontal axis measures the degree of vertical integration (V) of 'XP' goods for each assembling firm.

$$\text{At point O, V} = 0$$
$$\text{At point M, V} = \text{V max.}$$

The vertical axis measures transaction cost and internalization cost.

By definition, the transaction cost (TAC) will be maximum at point O and zero at point M. The TAC curve will have a steadily decreasing slope from O to M. Therefore,

$$\text{max. TAC (V)} = \text{TAC (O)} \tag{1}$$
$$\text{min. TAC (V)} = \text{TAC (M)} = 0 \tag{2}$$

differentiation of TAC (V) to V
$$\text{dTAC (V) / dV} < 0 \tag{3}$$

differentiation of (3) to V
$$\text{dTAC}^2\text{ (V) / dV}^2 < 0 \tag{4}$$

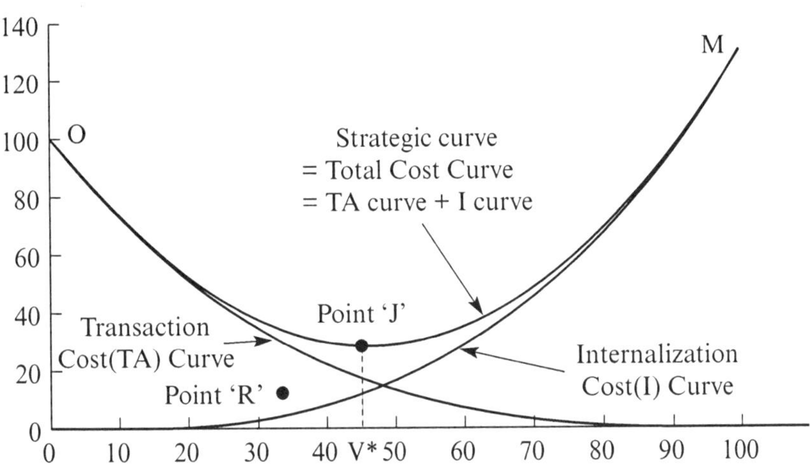

Note: TA and IC are in terms of average cost.
Transformation cost is assumed to be constant for simplification.

Figure 15.1   Transaction cost and internalization cost (convex: TAC max < ICC max)

Here we assume that when assemblers and parts suppliers prefer long-term transactions, the assembler (buyer) has a stronger bargaining power with its parts supplier when the buyer increases a little in size; however, this power diminishes progressively as the increase goes on.

Transaction costs can be equal to negative internalization benefit (IB).

However, we have to consider Internalization Cost (IC), which means that internal management and co-ordination costs, will be increased if Japanese companies enlarge groups of companies in order to move market transactions into intra-firm transactions.

By definition, IC shall be zero at point O and maximized at point M. We are now introducing one important assumption, that IC will be progressively increased if the groups of companies arc enlarged. It seems natural that bureaucratic ineffectiveness becomes progressively more serious when a companies' organization is enlarged more and more.

Therefore,

$$\text{min. IC (V)} = \text{IC (O)} = 0 \qquad (5)$$
$$\text{max. IC (V)} = \text{IC (M)} \qquad (6)$$

differentiation of IC (V) to V

$$d\text{IC (V)} / dV > 0 \qquad (7)$$

differentiation of (7) to V

$$d\text{IC}^2 \text{ (V)} / dV^2 > 0 \qquad (8)$$

The companies choose V in order to minimize IC (V) + TAC (V) = ST (V). ST is named as the strategic curve.

$$\text{ST (V)} = \text{TAC (V)} + \text{IC (V)} \qquad (9)$$

differentiation of ST (V) to V

$$d\text{ST (V)} / dV = d\text{TAC (V)} / dV + d\text{IC (V)} / dV = 0 \qquad (10)$$

Japanese companies choose $V = V^*$ for $d\text{ST (V}^*) / dV = 0$. It should be noticed that there are three possibilities now. If TAC (V) max. is assumed to be small enough to be neglected in comparison with IC (V), V^* shall be O; in other words, a completely competitive market, for example, between assemblers and primary parts suppliers, will be chosen (see Figure 15.2).

However, the assumption of a negligible TAC (V) is not appropriate for the Japanese automobile industry, or for electric/electronic industries which have less than 50 huge scale assemblers and large numbers of parts industries.

On the contrary, if IC (V) is assumed to be small enough to be neglected in comparison with TAC (V), V^* shall be M. In other words, complete intra-firm trade will be chosen (see Figure 15.3).

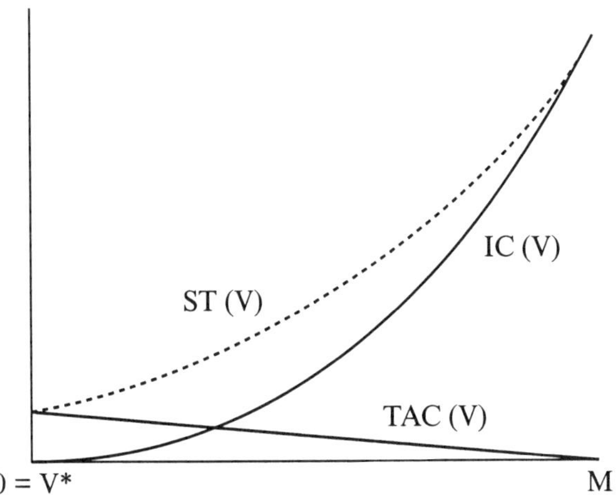

*Figure 15.2   Transaction cost and internalization cost (convex: TAC max <<
ICC max)*

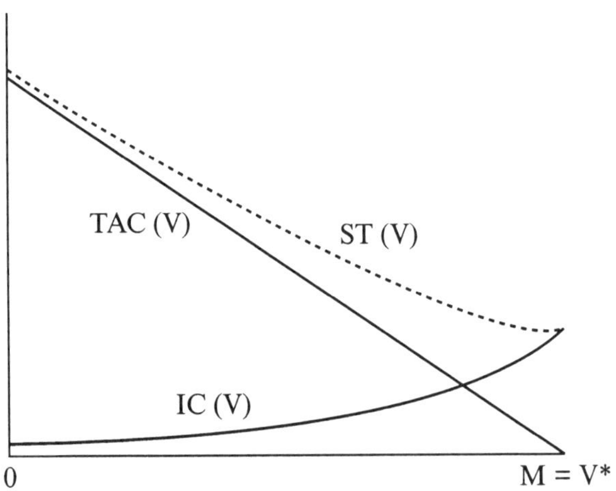

*Figure 15.3   Transaction cost and internalization cost (convex: TAC max >>
ICC max)*

In reality, if we consider substantially large organizations of Japanese automobile and electric/electronic assemblers, the second assumption also seems to be unrealistic. Roughly speaking, American car makers who have several hundred thousands employees seem to accept a larger IC (V) than Japanese car makers, who maintain about one tenth the employees of their American counterparts, keeping effective production networks with many parts suppliers.

The third possibility is indicated in Figure 15.1, where the point of lowest cost, that is, V* is expressed in between O and M. It seems to me that one of the origins of Japanese companies' international competitiveness is the choice of this point V*. Therefore, J = V*. The implicit assumptions of this possibility are that both TAC (V) and IC (V) are substantially high and that both TAC (V) and IC (V) are convex to the horizontal axis, as described in equations (4) and (8). This first assumption seems to be realistic for automobile and electric/electronic companies which require large-scale supporting industries.

Now, we turn to the international transactions. Figure 15.4 shows similar TAC (V) and IC (V) but now point O means export to a foreign country (named A country) and point M is a subsidiary located in country A, where all parts and materials are produced internally. The horizontal axis of Figure 15.4 measures the degree of vertical integration of overseas affiliates in their international networks. Figure 15.4 shows that ST (O) in point O is smaller than ST (M = 100) in point M because the domestically effective production system explained in Figure 15.1 exists behind point O in Figure 15.4. Their total production costs, including TAC, IC and physical manufacturing cost for assemblers, are higher

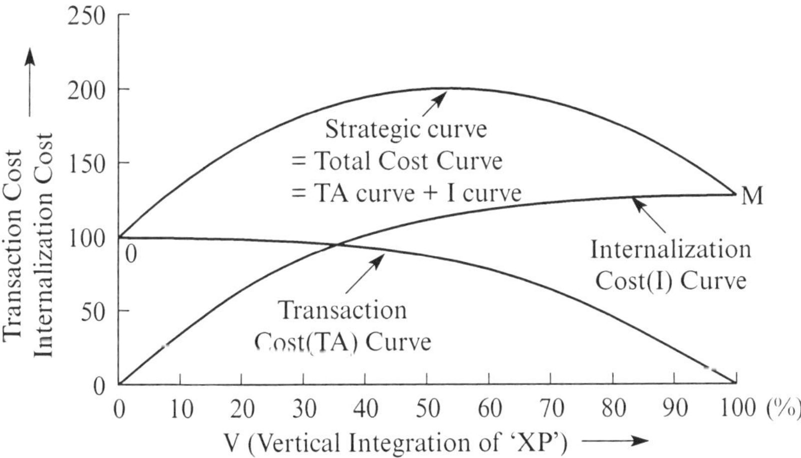

Figure 15.4   Transaction cost and internalization cost (concave: TAC max < ICC max)

in foreign countries than in Japan, in spite of that the average physical manufacturing cost is assumed to be equal for both in point O and M under the assumption of constant rate of return. Total production cost is higher even in the case of Asian countries, where labour cost itself is lower than Japan.

The reason is that they could not find qualified human resources and effective parts suppliers outside Japan. It is noteworthy that the TAC (V) curve and IC (V) curve and, therefore, ST (V) curve are concave to horizontal axis because foreign assemblers and parts suppliers prefer shorter term transactions than Japanese players.

Saying precisely, a Japanese firm at point O, which is producing domestically, are facing transaction costs for exporting final goods 'X' instead of transaction costs for procuring intermediate product 'XP'. To simplify the figure 15.4, however, we assume that the transaction cost curve for Japanese parent companies of exporting X and the transaction cost curve for their affiliates in country A, which procure XP, is an identical TAC curve in Figure 15.4.

Japanese automobile and electric/electronic firms had clearly I (internalization), O (ownership) and L (localization) advantages in Japan, but not in foreign countries.

Because of smaller ST (O) than ST (M), many Japanese firms preferred to take domestic production plus export strategy instead of overseas production, assuming that transaction cost for export was negligible, before facing the issues of trade frictions and Yen appreciation.

However, if TAC (V) is dramatically increased from TAC1 to TAC2 for Japanese parent companies, the choice of production will be shifted to point P2 at M from point P1 at O in Figure 15.5 because, now, ST (M) is smaller than ST (O2), where O2 is a new domestic production point under the TAC2 curve. An increase in TAC (V) for parent companies will be caused by trade frictions with the USA, Canada and EU and dramatic appreciation of the Japanese Yen. In fact, the situation happened in the late 1980s, as explained earlier. Dunning's I, O, L advantages as a total have become effective in the USA, Canada, the EU and Asian countries because of the large increase of TAC (V) for Japanese parent companies although I and O advantages are substantially lost in overseas production.

Japanese FDI in Asia was relatively more successful than FDI in the USA, Canada and the EU because of the FDI category 1 in Asia as explained above. Notably, still ST (M) in Figure 15.5 is larger than ST (O) in Figure 15.5 or ST (V*) in Figure 15.1 because overseas subsidiaries cannot have production networks as effective as Japanese networks. However, overseas subsidiaries owned by Japanese assemblers have started to acquire more effective production networks with newcomers or other unfamiliar Japanese suppliers, their overseas subsidiaries, and local companies, as well as conventional well-known parts suppliers and their overseas subsidiaries. Therefore, in the future, in Figure 15.5, the TAC (V) curve and IC (V) curve for overseas subsidiaries will turn to convex

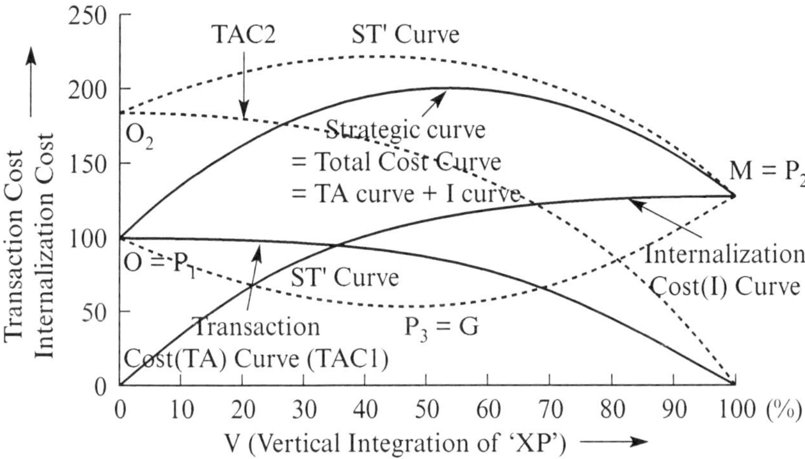

Figure 15.5   Transaction cost and internalization cost (concave: TAC max > ICC max)

from concave against the horizontal axis and, therefore, ST (V) curve will turn to convex from concave, too. Moreover, the TAC (V) curve for Japanese parent companies will shift back from TAC2 to TAC1 because increasing overseas production generally decreases the risk of Yen appreciation and trade frictions. Those mean that the most effective (optimum) point will move from point P2, where ST (M) is achieved, to point P3 at G to achieve ST (G). In other words, it means that if Japanese parent companies intend to have international (Global or Asian regional) networks, they can finally reach the point 3 to achieve ST (G), which may be lower than ST (O) in Figure 15.5 or ST (V*) in Figure 15.1 because Japanese companies can make networks with wider range of candidates, including foreign companies.

The recent trend of Japanese FDI in the USA, Canada, the EU and Asia appear to proceed in this direction, toward point G. This is described as the movement from conventional domestic networks to international open networks, or one new form of Japanese 'Globalization'.

ASIAN NETWORKS OF PRODUCTION SUBSIDIARIES OWNED BY JAPANESE COMPANIES

Several articles argue that intra-industry trade between Japan and other Asian countries has dramatically increased in recent days using the index of Grubel and Lloyd.[5] This type of argument frequently says that more prevalent intra-firm trade means more prevalent horizontal trade and more horizontal division of labour in intra-regional trade between Japan and other Asian countries.

For example, some companies are producing microchips of semiconductors in ASEAN countries, importing silicon wafers made in Japan; and other companies are producing some types of camera and medium-sized colour television sets in ASEAN and China while their parent companies are producing colour copy machines and high-definition television sets in Japan. The former example can be regarded as a case of vertical division of labour and the latter as horizontal division of labour.

In recent days, under the high pressure of the appreciated yen, horizontal division of labour can become more prevalent because production of more and more relatively labour-intensive goods cannot be maintained in Japan. As soon as products mature and production processes are firmly established, they are shifted to production bases in Asia. Apparently, the horizontal division of labour between Japan and other Asian countries seems to be becoming popular.

On the other hand, vertical division of labour is also prevailing with countries which offer large-scale labour pools, such as China, India, Indonesia and Vietnam. In such huge labour-surplus countries, downward pressures on wages always function very effectively because of undiminished labour supply and gradually relaxed restrictions on domestic labour mobility. Therefore, those countries can maintain their comparative advantages in labour-intensive industries when they have high economic growth.

All these factors seem to indicate now that both horizontal and vertical division of labour are prevailing.

However, I would like to point out that the definition of 'vertical' and 'horizontal' should be clarified first.

Traditionally; we use the word 'vertical' in two ways, that is, 'inter-industry' and 'different intensity of production factors'. One classical example is the international trade between the (relatively capital-intensive) textile industry of England and the (relatively labour-intensive) wine industry of Portugal. In my sense, the second nature of the word 'vertical', that is, factor intensity, is more meaningful in international economics than the first. Now, as I pointed out at the beginning of this section, intra-regional trade in Asia is frequently regarded as horizontal trade, because intra-industry trade in Asia is more important than before.

However, in many cases, labour-intensive goods are imported to Japan and capital-intensive goods are imported to other Asian countries in the same industry. I argue that intra-industry trade between final goods which have different factor intensities should be regarded as a 'vertical trade' and, if this is so, there now exists a large-scale vertical division of labour in Asia. Generally speaking, 'horizontal trade' or 'horizontal division of labour', which exist, at the moment, between Japan, the USA, Canada and the EU, have not yet been formed in the Asian region. 'Horizontal trade' is defined as trade at the same level of high value-added and sophisticated goods, oriented toward other countries' sophisticated and changeable demands. One big prerequisite of 'horizontal trade' and 'horizontal division of labour' is the existence of the capability of research and development to create new products with high value-added (on the supply side) and the large scale markets for those goods (on the demand side). At present, many Asian countries still have not satisfied the criteria, although some of them, for example, Korea and Taiwan, may catch up with them soon.

The motivations of Japanese FDI have very strongly supported the vertical division of labour, as explained earlier. The first three motivations have been strongly related to vertical trade and vertical division of labour between Japan and other Asian countries.

Only the fourth motivation may lead to horizontal trade and horizontal division of labour in future, if the local market can become more sophisticated.

Furthermore, in Figures 15.1–15, as I explained the vertical integration of a production process of goods X can be an accelerator of FDI in Asia. In fact, parts suppliers' FDI has been increased in Asia since 1993 (Table 15.2).

Empirically, the importance of vertical division of labour can be shown in the results of the Tejima 1992 survey.

Table 15.7 shows the content of products by production subsidiaries in major regions. The products are classified in three categories of completion, that is, raw materials, spare parts and final goods. The products are also classified in three degrees of quality, that is, commodity goods, intermediate goods and high value-added goods. The important two aspects are the share of high value-added goods and the share of spare parts. If the share of high value-added goods in Asian production companies is as high as the share in the production companies in the USA, Canada and the EU, it will indicate that subsidiaries in Asia are in a similar position related to the horizontal division of labour, as those in America and Europe. If the share of spare parts is higher in Asia than in America and Europe, it will indicate that the vertical division of labour is more popular in Asia than in Europe and America.

Tables 15.7 and 15.8 show that the production share of high value-added goods is still lower in Asian NIEs, ASEAN countries and other parts of Asia (including China) than in the USA, Canada and the EU for all industries, and especially for the electric/electronic industry. The same tables show that the production share of spare parts is higher in Asian NIEs, ASEAN countries and other parts of Asia (including China) than in the USA, Canada and the EU for all industries, and especially for the electric/electronic industry.

Tables 15.11–12 show more detailed results than Tables 15.7–15.10 regarding the content of the products of production subsidiaries by each major sales market.

Table 15.7   Contents of products of existing production bases for all industries (unit: %)

Important market	NIEs	ASEAN	Other Asia	USA/ Canada	EU	Latin America
Commodity goods	32.9	39.9	39.2	20.5	19.9	37.1
Intermediate goods	46.6	43.5	46.8	39.7	38.2	41.2
High value-added goods	20.5	16.6	13.9	39.7	41.9	21.6
Raw materials	17.9	21.6	15.2	21.5	17.3	25.8
Spare parts	36.8	35.2	38.0	28.1	26.7	23.7
Final goods	45.3	43.2	46.8	50.5	56.0	50.5

Table 15.8   Contents of products of existing production bases for electrical machinery (unit: %)

Important market	NIEs	ASEAN	Other Asia	USA/ Canada	EU	Latin America
Commodity goods	28.2	38.5	29.2	17.3	16.3	28.6
Intermediate goods	54.1	47.4	50.0	50.0	48.8	35.7
High value-added goods	17.6	14.1	20.8	32.7	34.9	35.7
Raw materials	1.2	6.4	0.0	3.8	2.3	0.0
Spare parts	61.2	50.0	79.2	40.4	44.2	50.0
Final goods	37.6	43.6	20.8	55.8	53.5	50.0

Table 15.9   Contents of products of future investment plans for all industries (unit: %)

Important market	NIEs	ASEAN	Other Asia	USA/ Canada	EU	Latin America
Commodity goods	28.6	37.4	41.0	19.0	22.6	37.5
Intermediate goods	45.1	38.9	32.1	32.5	28.6	40.6
High value-added goods	26.4	23.7	26.9	48.4	48.8	21.9
Raw materials	14.3	22.1	20.5	23.8	16.7	21.9
Spare parts	37.4	27.5	34.6	25.4	23.8	34.4
Final goods	48.4	50.4	44.9	50.8	59.5	43.8

Table 15.10   Contents of products of future investment plans for electrical machinery (unit: %)

Important market	NIEs	ASEAN	Other Asia	USA/ Canada	EU	Latin America
Commodity goods	22.6	27 8	54.5	20 0	22.7	36.4
Intermediate goods	54.8	52.8	36.4	45.0	45.5	45.5
High value-added goods	22.6	19.4	9.1	35.0	31.8	18.2
Raw materials	3.2	5.6	0.0	20.0	4.5	0.0
Spare parts	51.6	36.1	59.1	40.0	36.4	45.5
Final goods	45.2	58.3	40.9	40.0	59.1	54.5

Table 15.11 shows that, for Asian production subsidiaries, spare parts production sold to Asian countries is more important than their sale to the USA, Canada and the EU. If we look at Japanese companies' Asian production subsidiaries in the electric/electronic industry, we find more clearly that their transactions with Asian regions are biased to spare parts (see Table 15.12) while their transactions with the USA, Canada and the EU are weighted towards final goods. For example, in the case of production subsidiaries in NIEs, spare parts share 70% of sales to Japan, 71.9% of sales to NIEs, and 66.7% each to ASEAN and other Asian countries, while the share was 28.6% sales to the EU and 41.2% to the USA and Canada.

To give another example, in the case of production subsidiaries in ASEAN, spare parts share 58.8% of sales to Japan, 68.8% of sales to NIEs, and 52.0% to ASEAN, while the share was 14.3% of sales to the EU and 30.8% to the USA and Canada. The above tables indicate that Japanese companies' subsidiaries' networks in Asia play an important role in the vertical division of labour.

In addition to that, we concluded that more than 50% of the trade of Japanese subsidiaries in Asia is transacted with related companies[6]. This means that about a half or more of the transactions reported in Tables 15.7–15.12 are realized as intra-firm trade.

All these things suggest that the vertical division of labour is more important in Japanese production networks in Asia than in the USA, Canada and the EU. Horizontal division of labour and horizontal trade, symbolized as the trade of high value-added final goods, is still not so popular among Japanese parent companies and their subsidiaries in the Asian region. However, the same Tejima 1992 survey suggests that in future, the share of spare parts production will be decreased in all industries, including in the electric/electronic industry. If we consider the planned production subsidiaries to be established in the

Table 15.11 Contents of products of each existing production base by market (unit: %)

Location of production bases	NIEs							ASEAN						
Location of purchaser	Japan	NIEs	ASEAN	Other Asia	EU	USA/ Canada	Latin America	Japan	NIEs	ASEAN	Other Asia	EU	USA/ Canada	Latin America
Commodity goods	34.0	27.7	41.4	53.8	27.8	46.4	0.0	45.3	26.3	40.3	50.0	44.4	35.7	100.0
Intermediate goods	52.8	47.6	41.4	30.8	38.9	46.4	0.0	34.4	52.6	45.1	37.5	38.9	50.0	0.0
High value-added goods	13.2	24.7	17.2	15.4	33.3	7.1	0.0	20.3	21.1	14.6	12.5	16.7	14.3	0.0
Raw materials	17.0	18.1	37.9	30.8	5.6	0.0	0.0	28.1	26.3	19.4	50.0	22.2	3.6	0.0
Spare parts	45.3	38.0	24.1	53.8	22.2	28.6	0.0	40.6	52.6	31.9	12.5	16.7	35.7	0.0
Final goods	37.7	44.0	37.9	15.4	72.2	71.4	0.0	31.3	21.1	48.6	37.5	61.1	60.7	100.0

Location of production bases	Other Asia							USA/Canada						
Location of purchaser	Japan	NIEs	ASEAN	Other Asia	EU	USA/ Canada	Latin America	Japan	NIEs	ASEAN	Other Asia	EU	USA/ Canada	Latin America
Commodity goods	40.0	33.3	0.0	35.7	0.0	80.0	0.0	25.0	33.3	75.0	50.0	16.7	18.9	14.3
Intermediate goods	40.0	66.7	100.0	50.0	0.0	20.0	0.0	27.8	16.7	25.0	0.0	44.4	41.0	85.7
High value-added goods	20.0	0.0	0.0	14.3	0.0	0.0	0.0	47.2	50.0	0.0	50.0	38.9	40.2	0.0
Raw materials	20.0	16.7	100.0	11.9	0.0	0.0	0.0	27.8	50.0	25.0	100.0	27.8	18.9	14.3
Spare parts	40.0	83.3	0.0	31.0	0.0	40.0	0.0	25.0	16.7	25.0	0.0	22.2	30.3	0.0
Final goods	40.0	0.0	0.0	57.1	0.0	60.0	0.0	47.2	33.3	50.0	0.0	50.0	50.8	85.7

Location of production bases	EU							Latin America						
Location of purchaser	Japan	NIEs	ASEAN	Other Asia	EU	USA/ Canada	Latin America	Japan	NIEs	ASEAN	Other Asia	EU	USA/ Canada	Latin America
Commodity goods	18.2	50.0	0.0	0.0	20.6	8.3	0.0	57.1	0.0	0.0	0.0	57.1	16.7	39.1
Intermediate goods	27.3	0.0	0.0	0.0	40.0	33.3	0.0	14.3	0.0	100.0	0.0	42.9	55.6	39.1
High value-added goods	54.5	50.0	0.0	100.0	39.4	58.3	0.0	28.6	0.0	0.0	0.0	0.0	27.8	21.9
Raw materials	18.2	0.0	0.0	100.0	16.4	25.0	0.0	71.4	0.0	0.0	0.0	57.1	27.8	17.2
Spare parts	18.2	50.0	0.0	0.0	27.3	25.0	0.0	14.3	0.0	0.0	0.0	14.3	33.3	23.4
Final goods	63.6	50.0	0.0	0.0	56.4	50.0	0.0	14.3	0.0	100.0	0.0	28.6	38.9	59.4

Table 15.12   Contents of products of each existing production base by markets (electrical machinery industry) (unit: %)

Location of production bases	NIEs							ASEAN						
Location of purchaser	Japan	NIEs	ASEAN	Other Asia	EU	USA/ Canada	Latin America	Japan	NIEs	ASEAN	Other Asia	EU	USA/ Canada	Latin America
Commodity goods	5.0	34.4	33.3	33.3	28.6	41.2	0.0	29.4	12.5	60.0	0.0	57.1	30.8	0.0
Intermediate goods	75.0	50.0	50.0	33.3	42.9	47.1	0.0	41.2	68.8	32.0	0.0	42.9	61.5	0.0
High value-added goods	20.0	15.6	16.7	33.3	28.6	11.8	0.0	29.4	18.8	8.0	0.0	0.0	7.7	0.0
Raw materials	0.0	3.1	0.0	0.0	0.0	0.0	0.0	5.9	12.5	8.0	0.0	0.0	0.0	0.0
Spare parts	70.0	71.9	66.7	66.7	28.6	41.2	0.0	58.8	68.8	52.0	0.0	14.3	30.8	0.0
Final goods	30.0	25.0	33.3	33.3	71.4	58.8	0.0	35.3	18.8	40.0	0.0	85.7	69.2	0.0

Location of production bases	Other Asia							USA/Canada						
Location of purchaser	Japan	NIEs	ASEAN	Other Asia	EU	USA/ Canada	Latin America	Japan	NIEs	ASEAN	Other Asia	EU	USA/ Canada	Latin America
Commodity goods	33.3	20.0	0.0	22.2	0.0	100.0	0.0	0.0	0.0	0.0	0.0	0.0	19.6	0.0
Intermediate goods	55.6	80.0	0.0	33.3	0.0	0.0	0.0	50.0	0.0	0.0	0.0	100.0	47.8	100.0
High value-added goods	11.1	0.0	0.0	44.4	0.0	0.0	0.0	50.0	100.0	0.0	0.0	0.0	32.6	0.0
Raw materials	0.0	0.0	0.0	0.0	0.0	0.0	0.0	0.0	100.0	0.0	0.0	0.0	2.2	0.0
Spare parts	100.0	100.0	0.0	44.4	0.0	100.0	0.0	100.0	0.0	0.0	0.0	0.0	41.3	0.0
Final goods	0.0	0.0	0.0	55.6	0.0	0.0	0.0	0.0	0.0	0.0	0.0	100.0	56.5	100.0

Location of production bases	EU							Latin America						
Location of purchaser	Japan	NIEs	ASEAN	Other Asia	EU	USA/ Canada	Latin America	Japan	NIEs	ASEAN	Other Asia	EU	USA/ Canada	Latin America
Commodity goods	0.0	0.0	0.0	0.0	17.1	0.0	0.0	0.0	0.0	0.0	0.0	0.0	0.0	40.0
Intermediate goods	100.0	0.0	0.0	0.0	46.3	100.0	0.0	0.0	0.0	0.0	0.0	0.0	25.0	40.0
High value-added goods	0.0	0.0	0.0	0.0	36.6	0.0	0.0	0.0	0.0	0.0	0.0	0.0	75.0	20.0
Raw materials	0.0	0.0	0.0	0.0	2.4	0.0	0.0	0.0	0.0	0.0	0.0	0.0	0.0	0.0
Spare parts	100.0	0.0	0.0	0.0	41.5	100.0	0.0	0.0	0.0	0.0	0.0	0.0	50.0	50.0
Final goods	0.0	0.0	0.0	0.0	56.1	0.0	0.0	0.0	0.0	0.0	0.0	0.0	50.0	50.0

future (see Tables 15.9 and 15.10), the share of final goods and high value-added goods will be increased in production subsidiaries planned for the future.

Moreover, the Tejima 1993 survey indicated that the acquisition of markets in the light of their future growth potential is the most important target for production subsidiaries in China and the second most important target for production subsidiaries in Asian NIEs and ASEAN countries over the long term. To achieve the target, they are very eager to produce higher value-added products over the long term in Asia, especially in Asian NIEs and ASEAN countries[7].

Finally, the Tejima 1994 survey indicates that the most important medium-term (next three years) strategies for production bases in Asia were, first, to establish commodity goods production for local markets, the world markets and the Japanese market; second, to establish sales bases; third, to establish parts procurement bases; and fourth, to produce higher value-added products for local markets.

On the other hand, the most important long-term (next ten years) strategies for production bases in Asia were first, to produce commodity goods for local markets and the world markets; second, to produce higher value-added goods for local markets and the world markets; third, to establish parts procurement bases; and fourth, to make strategic alliances with foreign companies to exchange technology, information and human resources.

No doubt, high value products will be produced more popularly in Asia for local markets than at present. A horizontal division of labour will become more realistic within ten years. Especially, the electric/electronic assembling industry and the automobile parts industry are eager to proceed with research and development in Asia as well as the production of high-value added goods. Asian countries will improve their capability of creating new products at a very rapid pace, partly with the contribution of Japanese multinational firms. They may not take a long time to satisfy supply-side requirement (that is, the capability of R&D to create new products) and demand-side requirement (that is, large-scale domestic demand for high value-added goods) in order to start true horizontal trade and true horizontal division of labour.

CONCLUSION

Japanese FDI in Asia has been one of the most successful results of Japanese globalization since the late 1980s.

They have enhanced their international competitiveness through the construction of intra-regional networks of production, sales, procurement, financing and R&D subsidiaries. In future, the role of newcomers will be more important when local companies, other Japanese companies and western multinational companies join the international networks. Japanese international networks will be able to enjoy more competitive advantages than conventional domestic networks.

Japanese FDI in Asia has also contributed to the development of Asian countries' economies through higher wage rates, technology transfer and an increasing export capability mainly through the mechanism of vertical division of labour.

In future, its contribution will be accelerated through the development of supporting industries and a gradual increase of R&D activities in Asian countries, which means that there will be a potential for truly horizontal division of labour in Asian regions. Ironically, Japan is now facing the problem of the so-called 'hollowing out' of the Japanese economy caused by the drastic shift of manufacturing facilities to Asian countries. Japanese companies have to find a fine balance to maintain both international competitiveness and domestic employment levels. Asian-made parts produced by Japanese affiliates are increasingly imported to Japan, with the effect of lowering the production costs of Japanese parent companies. Some of them will again increase FDI in the USA, Canada and the EU in order to enhance R&D capability and the production of high value-added goods in the near future. For Japanese companies to find the best solution is not easy in this transitional period, but it is clear over the long term, that Japan needs to achieve a horizontal division of labour with Asian countries. These countries will then gain a high income, large enough to become a market for high value-added goods, and will obtain qualified human resources with a high capability of R&D in the near future. This is one of the best solutions for Japanese prosperity.

NOTES

1. This regular annual survey (with questionnaire) of Japanese manufacturing companies has been carried out by myself and my staff since 1991. The results can be found in Tejima (1992) (for 1991); Tejima (1993) (for 1992); Tejima et. al (1994) (for 1993).
2. See Tejimi (1992), pp. 36–45.
3. See Tejima et al. (1994) pp. 58–65. 'Acquisition of market in light of future growth potential' is an extremely important target for Japanese manufacturing companies throughout all Asian regions.
4. Tejima et al. (1994), pp. 14–19.
5. See Hoosen (1990).
6. See Tejima (1993), pp. 80–81.
7. See Tejima et al. (1994), pp. 58–65.

BIBLIOGRAPHY

Aoki, Masahiko (1988) *Information, Incentives and Bargaining in the Japanese Economy*, Cambridge: Cambridge University Press.
Buckley, P.J. and M. Casson (1976) *The Future of the Multinational Enterprise*, London: Macmillan.

Coase, Ronald H. (1988) *The Firm, The Market, and The Law*, University of Chicago.

Dunnings, John H. (1993), *Multinational Enterprises and the Global Economy*, Wokingham: Addison-Wesley.

Encarnation, Dennis J. (1992) *Rivals beyond trade: America versus Japan in global competition*, Cornell University Press.

Graham, Kruguman (1989) *Foreign Direct Investment in the United States*, Institute for International Economics.

Hoosen, M. (1990 *Kaigai Tooshi Kenkyuu Sho Hoo* (Monthly Report of the Research Institute for International Investment and Development, Export-Import Bank of Japan) **17** (11).

Julius, DeAnne (1990) *Global Companies and Public Policy*, Royal Institute of International Affairs.

OECD Development Center, *Technical Papers* Nos 57, 64, 65.

Oman, Charles (1994) *Globalization and Regionalization: The Challenge for Developing Countries*, OECD Development Center.

Porter, Michael E. (1990) *The Competitive Advantage of Nations*, Macmillan.

Tejima, Shigeki (1992) 'Japanese Foreign Direct Investment in the 1980s and its Prospects for the 1990s', *EXIM Review* **11** (2), pp. 25–51.

Tejima, Shigeki (1993) 'Future Prospects of Japanese Foreign Direct Investment in the 1990s, Based on the Trend and Features of Japanese FDI in the 1980s', *EXIM Review* **13** (1), pp. 43–95.

Tejima, Shigeki (1996) 'Japanese Foreign Direct Investment at the New Stage of Globalization and its Contribution to the Asian Pacific Region', *Research in Asian Economic Studies* **7** (B), pp. 369–89.

Tejima, Shigeki et al. (1994) 'The Recent Trends of Japanese Foreign Direct Investment and Prospects for Japanese FDI in the 1990s based on the Japan EXIM Bank's Survey Implemented in FY 1993', *EXIM Review* **14** (1), pp. 1–82.

Thomsen, Nicolaides (1991) *The Evolution of Japanese Foreign Direct Investment in Europe*, New York: Harvester Wheatsheaf.

United Nations (1991–1994) *World Investment Reports*, United Nations.

Vernon, Raymond (1993) 'Transnational corporations; where are they coming from, where are they headed', UNCTAD, *Transnational Corporations*, **1** (2).

Williamson, Oliver E. (1986) '*Economic Organization: Firms, Markets and Policy Control*', Wheatsheaf Books.

World Bank (1991–3) *World Debt Tables*, World Bank.

16. Taiwanese outward FDI: the response to regionalization

Michael McDermott

INTRODUCTION

Taiwan's achievements at the macro level have been well documented (eg. Elegant, 1990; Gold, 1986; Li, 1988). It has the world's largest foreign reserves (US$90.4bn in July 1994), is the world's eleventh leading export nation (exports of $85.0bn in 1993), the 14th largest trading nation (two-way trade of $160bn); it is one of the world's 25 richest countries (per capita income $11 300 in 1994), and still enjoys impressive Gross Domestic Product (GDP) growth (more than six per cent in 1994).

In contrast, relatively little has been written with a focus on the meseo and micro level, namely Taiwan's industrial structure and corporate sector, respectively. Basically, the composition of Taiwan's industrial structure on a sectoral basis has changed dramatically, and thus so too has the nature of its exports. Where textiles, footwear and plastics were once the mainstay of the economy, today electronics, strongly focused on information products, is the island's main industry and major export earner.

At the micro level, little has changed, in that the economy is still dominated by a huge array of small and medium-sized enterprises. Their success in international markets has been achieved largely through original equipment manufacturers (OEM) sales to US and European multinationals. This successful pursuit of a low cost generic strategy through international subcontracting has tended to conceal from end users the fact that Taiwan is a world-class manufacturer of a widening range of products that are increasingly technology-intensive. Few Taiwanese companies have emerged as world-class marketers, able to differentiate their products.

However, as will be seen in this paper, Taiwanese companies are remarkably flexible, and perhaps this is their greatest strength. In less than ten years, they have changed their priority international market on no fewer than three occasions. Similarly, unrelated product diversification has not resulted in the disastrous consequences which so many western companies in declining industries experienced when they sought security in more dynamic sectors.

Undoubtedly, the global interlinked economy appears to be moving towards a series of regional trading blocs. This trend has resulted in a plethora of acronyms for such blocs. It is not the purpose of this paper to review these. However, one thing is certain, and that is that throughout Asia there is a widespread perception that the USA especially, and the EU, regard the emerging Asian economies as a major threat rather an unprecedented opportunity. A variety of measures (such as anti-dumping duties, local content rules, quotas, and voluntary restraint agreements) have been used by western countries to protect their non-competitve industries, but without any conspicuous success. Now other issues (such as human rights) are being introduced to trade relations discussions.

In the light of these trends, Asian companies have not surprisingly found new outlets for their products. Fortuitously, China's 'open door' policy, introduced in 1978–79, has now rendered the world's largest market also the most attractive one, especially to the overseas Chinese. In 1993 China attracted more inward investment ($23bn) than all developing countries attracted in 1989. The bulk of this was invested by overseas Chinese in Hong Kong, Macau, Singapore and, of course, Taiwan. However, these overseas Chinese have also emerged as major investors in the ASEAN region and in Vietnam, where the economic reforms, or 'doi moi' policy, introduced in 1986, are beginning to bear fruit. Perhaps, paradoxically, the world's star economies in the 1990s are likely to be East Asia's two socialist economies, namely China and Vietnam.

Therefore in order to appreciate the opportunities presented by East Asia today, it is worthwhile providing a historical perspective before focusing on the specifics of Taiwanese outward FDI.

FREE TRADE AND GATT: GROWTH IN INTERNATIONAL TRADE AND INVESTMENT

In recent years, a rapidly changing economic and political environment has resulted in multinationals (MNEs) increasingly abandoning a decentralised, country-centred perspective, and instead adopting a regional focus, with high levels of centralized co-ordination and integration of activities. It is important to appreciate the factors which have enabled MNEs to pursue such policies and strategies.

Worldwide economic depression during the 1930s led to the abandonment of free trade, and the imposition of protectionist policies as nations sought to safeguard domestic industries. This resulted in a large increase in outward FDI from the USA, bound mainly for developed markets in Europe, previously served either by exports from the USA or by exports from an existing operation elsewhere in Europe. It led in essence to country-centred strategies, accelerating the eventual decline of plants established originally to cater for the entire European market (Hood and Young, 1982; McDermott, 1989).

The end of World War II saw the international community agreed on the need to avoid the mistakes of the inter-war years. Top priority was a return to the free-trade policies which had enabled the major economies of Europe and North America to grow so rapidly in the period 1870-1914, and which also coincided with the zenith of economic imperialism. Hence a number of facilitating organizations were established. These included the International Monetary Fund (IMF) and the General Agreement on Tariffs and Trade (GATT). The former was established to provide financial stability on a worldwide basis, and the latter to foster an environment compatible with the growth of international trade.

Enthusiam for free trade was restricted though, to developed nations, and as the economies of Europe recovered, the west was indeed 'the affluent society'. In Japan the war-torn economy also reported impressive growth, and with its cost advantages, its companies began to penetrate western markets.

By the early 1960s Asia's four 'tigers' recognised that in an era when developed nations were committed to free trade, an outward-oriented economic development strategy held great promise. After all, western MNEs could establish assembly or manufacturing operations in these low cost locations and then import components or final products without penalty. Moreover, products from developing countries qualified for the Generalized System of Preferences status, a form of positive discrimination favouring products imported from developing nations.

During this period, very few developing countries were receptive to inward investment. Thus, instead of investing in neighbouring Mexico, US firms had to incur the transportation costs in shipping components and finished products to the few developing country economies in Asia that were favourable to inward FDI. Similarly, in Europe the political environment dissuaded or prevented firms from investing in low-cost Eastern Europe, and even some of the southern European countries.

In the absence of intense competition to attract cost-driven mobile investments, Asia's four 'tigers' outperformed other developing economies during the 1960s and 1970s. This trend continued in the 1980s, but by the end of the decade virtually all developing countries had abandoned their import-substitution policy and embraced an export-oriented economic development strategy. In retrospect, the most significant policy transformation was initiated voluntarily in China in 1978. However, many developing countries in Africa and Latin America, and some in Asia, switched to an outward-oriented strategy only under pressure from the IMF.

IMF: ITS IMPACT UPON INWARD INVESTMENT POLICY IN DEVELOPING COUNTRIES

The 1980s debt crisis arising from developing countries' inability to maintain their repayments on massive foreign borrowings, threatened the entire capitalist economic system. The banking system of developed countries was on the brink of collapse due to their imprudent lending. Intervention was necessary and debts were rescheduled by the IMF on condition that governments of debt-torn economies agreed to introduce policies favoured by the IMF. These countries included most of Latin America, many countries in Africa, and some in Asia (such as the Philippines). These developing countries were advised to 'earn more, and spend less' so that they could maintain debt repayments.

If such nations were to 'earn more', they had to reduce their dependence on commodities, the price of which could fluctuate dramatically, and which were exposed to climatic vagaries. Creating an export-oriented manufacturing sector became a priority, and worldwide for the first time, developing countries in large numbers entered the global 'lottery' for FDI. Did it really matter much to the MNEs if components were sourced in Malaysia or Thailand? From the host country's perspective, there were no jackpot winners, but the prize of steady growth appeared to justify the stake of incentives, tax holidays and so on, which invariably accompany the formation of Export Processing Zones to attract multinationals.

This switch in FDI policy was generally accompanied by a market liberalization and privatization policy. Thus, the role of developing countries was changing. As well as being attractive production bases, they emerged as potentially massive sources of consumption of foreign products (for example, 1.2bn consumers in China alone with rapidly growing disposable income). This watershed could not have arisen at a more opportune moment for companies based in Japan and Asia's NIEs.

ASIA'S CHAMPION EXPORTERS: PROTECTIONISM IN THE WEST AND COMPETITION AT HOME

Where Asia in the 1950s–1970s merely represented a source of low-cost suppliers with little bargaining power, and Japan, Korea and Taiwan relied heavily upon the USA for aid and trade, this relationship soon changed as Japan and then the four 'tigers' grew rapidly and challenged the dominance of US companies. By the mid 1980s, the USA had a massive trade deficit problem due almost entirely to these economies. A variety of measures were implemented to reduce imports from these countries.

First, Japanese firms bore the brunt of US protectionism, and they adjusted their international marketing and production strategies. Replacement export markets were found, and 'transplants' established to circumvent protectionist barriers. Then, the large South Korean *chaebols* became the targets of successive US administrations, and when they turned their attention to Europe, their dramatic sales growth saw the European Commission impose anti-dumping penalties upon their major exports (colour televisions, microwave ovens, video cassette recorders, and audio/video tapes).

At the same time, the US had continued to take a firm stance with Japan, South Korea and Taiwan. This resulted in the rapid appreciation of the Yen, the Won and the New Taiwan dollar, respectively, rendering their exports to the USA less competitive. The US also negotiated the liberalization of these economics' domestic market. However, along with the EU, it brought pressure to bear on other developing countries to remove import barriers. Thus, while Japan, South Korea and Taiwan found it more difficult to penetrate their traditional export markets, and at home faced foreign competition often for the first time, this was ultimately compensated for by the opening up of developing country markets in Asia and elsewhere.

REGIONALIZATION AND THE TWIN BENEFITS: EXPANDING MARKETS, SHRINKING COSTS

By the late 1980s, a large number of developing countries were pursuing an economic development strategy broadly similar to that selected by Asia's four 'tigers' two decades earlier. For the first time, MNEs based in developed, high-cost, low-growth countries had access to low-cost, high-growth markets.

US MNEs only had to look to Mexico and the other main Latin American economies to find an hospitable and stable economic environment. With its unique location-specific advantage of bordering the USA, *and* cheap labour, FDI flooded into Mexico. In 1989 it accounted for 17 per cent of the total of $24bn invested in developing countries. But such is the pace of change that four years later, China alone attracted more FDI than the total FDI in developing countries in 1989!

In Europe the enlargement of the EC saw low-cost economies (Greece, Portugal, Spain) become member countries. The Iberian countries saw inward investment soar. Moreover, the reunification of Germany, and the collapse of communism in eastern Europe transformed the investment and trading environment in Europe. Similarly in Asia, Japan and Asia's NIEs have the next generation of 'tigers', as well as China and Vietnam, offering huge markets and low-cost locations.

As a consequence of all these changes, MNEs from any country can obtain in their own regional backyard a large market *plus* a cheap source of production. In the past, trans-regional trade and investment had been necessary to satisfy these conditions. Western firms had to source from, or invest in, the Far East to gain crucial cost advantages, and Asian producers had to export to or invest in either the USA or the EC. This is no longer the case, and this perhaps more than anything has lulled policy makers and business leaders into what may prove a false sense of security based upon the belief that membership of a large regional bloc compensates for the demise of free trade on a global basis. The rest of this paper focuses on the response of Taiwanese enterprises to this trend.

TAIWAN: CHANGING DIRECTIONS IN GLOBAL MARKETS

Japan is well prepared for an era of protectionist trading blocs. After the rapid appreciation of the Yen in the mid-1980s, Japanese outward FDI increased dramatically. Its main MNEs have all transferred their complete value chain activities to North America, the EU, and other countries in Asia.

South Korean FDI in North America and the EU was until recently mainly defensive – a response to protectionism. Its main three consumer electronics companies (Goldstar, Samsung and Daewoo) all have several plants in the two regional trading blocs of the developed countries. In 1994, Samsung announced a $1.0bn investment in a greenfield site in north-east England to produce its brown goods. This offensive investment is the first really significant case of FDI by a Korean *chaebol* in the EU. Past experiences involving Japanese and Korean MNEs in the EU suggest that this investment will trigger a similar response by major rivals, notably Goldstar. The Korean pattern is likely to follow that of Japan. A wave of FDI in electronics will be followed by one in autos.

Unlike these East Asian rivals, Taiwanese investment in the EU remains weak, and in the USA annual inflows are declining. This is in sharp contrast to rapid increases in investment levels in East Asia, where Taiwan has emerged in recent years as the single largest investor in a number of second and third generation 'tigers', as an array of Small and Medium-Sized Enterprises (SMEs) transfer labour-intensive activities to lower cost locations.

Between 1987 and 1993, the value of Taiwan's outward FDI was almost $31bn, making it the sixth largest source of FDI during this period. In terms of Taiwan's outward foreign direct investment, official home country statistics grossly understate the actual number and value of projects They do indicate though that the USA and Asia have accounted for the vast bulk of outward FDI, with Europe having an insignificant share. Asia's emerging economies will attract the lion's share of Taiwan's outward FDI during the rest of the decade. Moreover, this emphasis on East Asia is recent and reflects two factors: (1) this region probably offers an unprecedented magnitude of marketing opportunities: (2) protectionism in the west.

A chronological review of Taiwan's international marketing activities suggests that three phases can be identified. These are discussed briefly below.

Phase 1: Focus on USA through International Subcontracting, 1960–86

Traditionally, the USA has been Taiwan's main export market and also the main destination for outward foreign direct investment. Its prominence has been substantially reduced. As recently as 1984 it absorbed more than 48 per cent of its total exports, but this had shrunk to 32.4 per cent in 1990. Moreover, the nature of these exports tended to be labour-intensive products, and since Taiwanese companies had transferred their production of these to lower cost locations, exports to the USA now account for just over one quarter of Taiwan's total exports. Similarly, the USA, which had accounted for more than half of Taiwan's outward foreign direct investment during the period 1959–90, has seen its share fall to less than 10 per cent of recent outflows. In the first half of 1994, total Taiwanese outward FDI amounted to just less than $1.0bn (£936m), and the USA accounted for a mere $77m, a 79 per cent fall on 1993 levels.

Phase 2: Target Europe with OEM and and Own Brand Manufactures (OBM), 1986–1992

Taiwan's largest companies have already established a manufacturing presence in the USA and thus have a presence within NAFTA. During the second half of the 1980s Taiwan had succeeded in diversifying its export base, and Asia and Europe emerged as much more significant markets. Indeed, in information products, its fastest growing export industry, Europe emerged as the largest export market, accounting for more than half (51 per cent) of Taiwan's total personal computer (PC) exports; Taiwan is the world's third largest PC producer. However, fears of protectionism and the need to produce within the EU to be competitive, were already driving Taiwanese firms to focus on markets closer geographically and with lower cultural distance.

With the exception of Tatung, Taiwanese firms only began to establish marketing subsidiaries in the EU in the late 1980s, but many appreciate the threat of a protectionist Europe, and are well-advanced in their selection of plant site. There would appear to be a strong reluctance to commence production in the EU, until it proves economically compelling (for example, Delta Electronics selected a site in Glasgow but decided against opening the plant). At the moment the prospect of a wave of Taiwanese investment in the EU appears to be receding.

In 1990 Taiwanese companies appeared preoccupied with Europe and the impact of 1992. Many indicated that they were on the brink of establishing a manufacturing presence on a greenfield site in the EU. This has not materialized and its likelihood has receded.

Phase 3: Focus on East Asia's Emerging Nations, 1990–

During the first half of the 1990s, Taiwan has once again re-oriented its economy to another major regional market, namely Asia's emerging economies (the ASEAN countries, Vietnam and mainland China/Hong Kong). Hong Kong (22 per cent of total exports in 1994) is now likely to replace the USA as the single largest export destination, despite a significant slowdown in indirect exports to mainland China.

In general, East Asia is clearly a priority for Taiwanese companies, but clearly the US and European markets remain of utmost importance, and for some companies they remain the key markets. There now follows a review of regionalization and its impact on Taiwanese companies in each of these three large regional markets.

TAIWANESE FOREIGN DIRECT INVESTMENT IN THE USA: THE IMPLICATIONS OF NAFTA

The earliest investors in Taiwan were US MNEs and they also were the first to use indigenous Taiwanese companies as major subcontractors. These two trends had a crucial role in determining the destination of Taiwan's exports. Not surprisingly then, the first ever Taiwanese overseas manufacturing plant was established in the USA in 1974 at Los Angeles, when Tatung opened an electric fan producing facility.

In 1981 Tatung opened its second US plant, in Atlanta, to produce colour televisions and home appliances. Its arch-rival Sampo had also selected Atlanta, when in 1980 it established its first overseas plant, which also produced colour televisions. These early Taiwanese greenfield investments in the USA were motivated by a desire to serve the investors' largest export market. These plants are now competing with the numerous TV-producing plants which are already to be found in Mexico's maquiladores.

Between 1959 and 1990, the USA, according to home country statistics, accounted for around half of Taiwan's total outward FDI. In terms of future flows, then clearly NAFTA may well divert investments from the USA to Mexico.

Taiwanese government officials responsible for advising firms on outward FDI, are promoting heavily the attractions of Mexico for greenfield investments. Thus, Mexico is likely to gain at the expense of the USA. Foreign divestment from the USA by these early Taiwan investors should therefore not be discounted, and the formation of NAFTA could trigger such action.

In June 1994, the Mexican government revealed that a five-hectare 'Taiwan industrial park' would open in 1995, based in the city of Mexicali, which borders California. According to a senior Mexican official, 'The most important incentive for the Taiwan business community to invest in Mexico is that they can enjoy NAFTA privileges in exporting goods to the United States without facing quota restrictions' (Taiwan Industrial Panorama, August 1994).

The more recent cases of Taiwanese investment in the USA have been geared towards access to key technologies and distribution channels. These have taken the form of acquisitions and have often been relatively insignificant in terms of their monetary value, but potentially of enormous strategic importance. In the case of Acer, post-acquisition integration has been traumatic, resulting in heavy losses and the resignation of the President of Acer America. NAFTA is unlikely to influence the management of these businesses.

Future cases of Taiwanese FDI in the USA are much more likely to involve acquisitions and joint ventures, as the Taiwanese endeavour to develop world class status in high-tech sectors such as advanced materials, aerospace, automation, biotechnology and so on.

TAIWANESE FOREIGN DIRECT INVESTMENT IN THE EU: THE IMPLICATIONS OF '1992'

Hood and Truijens (1992) and McDermott (1990) demonstrate that Japanese and Korean plant openings have often been a direct response to the imposition of anti-dumping penalties. The establishment of these 'screwdriver' plants led the EC to insist upon minimum local content levels to minimise the fear of imported components. The current local content ruling is deterring a number of Taiwanese firms (such as Delta Electronics) from proceeding with their EU investment plans.

Between 1990 and 1993 the author interviewed parent company executives of a number of Taiwan's leading electronics companies: in consumer electronics (Sampo, Tatung, and Tcco) and in information products (Acer, Caf, Kunnan, Mitac, and Microtec). Most of these firms said they were in the process of looking for an appropriate plant location site or sites in the EU. More recently, some further interviews have been conducted at the subsidiary level. In 1994 Hualon, a man-made fibre producer, announced its plans to proceed with an $800m investment in Ulster. This serves as a timely reminder that potential sources of

Taiwanese investment in the EU extend beyond electronics to sectors such as machine tools, and food and beverages.

McDermott (1991a) discusses in detail the potential investors and offers a plant-location decision model. Put simply, Taiwanese companies are seeking low-cost, productive labour in locations where English is widely spoken and which offer a sound base for distribution throughout the EU. This model was derived from interviews with producers of finished products, especially computer manufacturers such as Acer, and it must be stressed that an English-speaking location was crucial. As consumer goods producers, these companies enjoyed a freedom of choice in their plant location decision-making denied to suppliers of industrial information products (such as monitors, tubes and other computer peripherals), which are obliged by competitive imperatives to locate in close proximity to their largest industrial customers (such as Compaq and IBM). In the EU, the greatest concentration of information products producers is in the UK, and in Scotland in particular. Thus, even in 1991, it was apparent that future Taiwanese investment in the EU was likely to be concentrated in the UK, especially Scotland (see McDermott, 1991a; 1991b).

In 1990, Tatung was the only Taiwanese company with a manufacturing presence in the EC, having had a facility at Telford in the UK since 1981, which produces 1500 colour televisions and 800 computer monitors daily (McDermott, 1992). The Telford facility produces 95 per cent of its component needs and is thus unlikely to be adversely affected by any move towards a more protectionist EU.

Acer, Taiwan's leading PC manufacturer, is untypical of Taiwanese firms in that it has very quickly sought to become a global organization, with a global production and operations strategy. Thus its Malaysian plant (opened in 1990) supplies parts to its domestic operation, but also to its plants in the USA and the EU. Regional protectionism would thus require Acer to dismantle its loosely integrated production system.

In 1990, Acer was unsuccessful in its bid for Apricot Computers, having been outbid by Japan's Mitsubishi. Shortly afterwards it gained a foothold in the EU through the acquisition of Holland's Kangaroo N.V.

Since 1990, Acer had been acutely aware of the importance of establishing a significant manufacturing base in the EU. However, it was not until 1997 that Acer was publicly reported to be involved in the final stages of the plant location decision. The delay in this process was surprising; the selected country was entirely predictable – the UK. Perhaps the element of risk in undertaking the investment had been significantly reduced by winning a massive contract to supply IBM with notebook computers. The proposed 1000 job facility aroused controversy in the UK over allegations of job poaching by rival regional development agencies in the UK. Wales and the north east of England are tipped as the most likely locations. Needless to say this will disappoint Ireland's IDA, the first European inward investment agency to target Acer (1985), and locate in Scotland, which had enjoyed significant success in attracting Taiwanese investments.

Yuen Foon Yu, one of Taiwan's top 10 business groups and the parent company of Caf Computer, is believed to have purchased a 50 acre site at Cork in the Republic of Ireland. It hopes to develop the site as a science park for Taiwanese electronics companies, based on the model of Hsinchu science park, Taiwan's equivalent of Silicon Valley (McDermott, 1991b; 1992).

Mitac, which relies on the EU for 60 per cent of its total sales, has selected Telford as its EU manufacturing base. Having narrowed the number of possible host nations down to three (the UK, Ireland, and the Netherlands), it employed ten criteria to evaluate these countries: language, quality of outputs, government incentives, national characteristics, education, technological level, production costs, component supply, geographical location, and market attractiveness.

Microtec, one of the leading colour desktop scanner manufacturers, has been focusing on expanding OEM sales since mid-1993, and is focusing mainly on the European market. Its main client is the German firm, Vobis.

It would appear that all of Taiwan's leading producers of finished information products regard '1992' as a barrier to trade and have already, or are in the process of, adjusting their international market supply mode.

By far the two largest Taiwanese investments in the EU have both been in Scotland, in Lanarkshire, and involved producers of components. Lite-on and Chunghwa make monitors and tubes respectively. Their mobility and choice of location was determined largely by their largest industrial buyers (such as Compaq and IBM), both of which are located in nearby Renfrewshire. These companies are emerging as global suppliers to their main customers by establishing facilities in key locations in other regional markets (such as Mexico, to cater for NAFTA).

TAIWANESE FOREIGN DIRECT INVESTMENT IN EAST ASIA'S EMERGING ECONOMIES

All emerging economies are developing countries, but not all developing countries are emerging economies. East Asia's emerging economies include the four 'tigers', the ASEAN countries, China and Vietnam. South Korea is excluded from the analysis because levels of Taiwanese FDI are very low. Hong Kong and Singapore are high-cost, resource-dependent, small markets but their world-class infrastructure renders them important locations for regional headquarters for MNEs, including those from Taiwan. For example, Acer invested $12m to establish its ALAP (Africa, Latin America and Asia Pacific) headquarters in Singapore. Acer ALAP oversees more than 70 subsidiaries and distributors in the regions under its remit. In terms of Taiwan's outward FDI, the focus is on the ASEAN countries and Vietnam and, of course, China.

Clearly, East Asia offers quite different location-specific advantages from North America and the EU. Due to cultural and geographical proximity, clearly many Taiwanese firms, have been attracted across the Straits to the mainland. However, many Taiwanese firms encouraged by the government's 'Go South Investment Policy' have transferred labour intensive production processes to ASEAN in order to achieve cost reductions by utilizing the supply of cheap labour which countries such as Indonesia, Malaysia, and Thailand offer. This policy reflects the political imperative to avoid economic dependence on the mainland. Indeed, in recent years Taiwan has emerged on a stock basis as the single largest investor in Vietnam, number two in Malaysia and China, and number three in Indonesia and Thailand. However, the investments in south east Asia have had disappointing results compared to those in mainland China. Those in South East Asia have recorded a return on investment of 8.31 per cent on average paid-in capital of $9.7m, compared to 17.18 per cent on $4.5m in mainland China.

During the first half of 1994, all ASEAN countries, with the exception of Indonesia, recorded sharp increases in inward FDI from Taiwan. In Malaysia, Singapore and Thailand it was up more than 100 per cent on the 1993 level. In June 1994, the Indonesian government removed various disincentives to investors, such as the ban on 100 per cent foreign ownership. Taiwanese investors are likely to respond positively to such changes, but the world's largest Islamic country and the fourth most populous perhaps poses the highest risk in the region.

In common with most foreign investors in China, Taiwan's FDI in China is concentrated on the coastal provinces and cities. With the exception of the food and beverage sector, virtually all cases of indirect investment in the mainland in the first half of 1994 went into high value-added or high-tech manufacturing.

In ASEAN and China, President Enterprises has undertaken a large number of investments. Although largely unknown in the west, this company aims to become the world's largest food processing company. In Taiwan it holds the franchise from Southland of the USA for 7-Eleven. It hopes to secure similar rights for the mainland, but faces fierce competition (for example, Hong Kong's Daily Mart already has the franchise for the Shenzen region).

There is growing concern that investments in ASEAN lead to a hollowing out of the Taiwanese economy. However, often the critical components continue to be made in Taiwan, with the ASEAN plant simply undertaking assembly. For example, Cal-comp the fax producer, had output of 300 000 units in 1993, giving it a 3.4 per cent share of the global market. In 1994 it established a plant in Thailand with an annual production capacity of 240 000 units, or 30 per cent of the firm's total capacity. However, Taiwan will supply 90 per cent of the Thai plant's components.

From the host country's perspective, the high level of imported components utilised by Taiwanese electronics plants is offset by at least equally high levels of exports. For example, each year Tatung's plant in Thailand exports all its output. The finished products (400 000 colour televisions and 350 000 satellite receivers) are destined mainly for the EU market, while one million printed circuit boards are shipped back to Taiwan.

Similarly, Acer and Mitac also use their plant in Malaysia to serve developed country markets, and in the case of the former, to feed the manufacturing plant in the EU. Protectionism in terms of import tariffs and local content regulation represent a major threat in the short term to those facilities which rely heavily on the EU market.

These rationalized manufacturer subsidiaries need to identify and develop substitute markets or see their status being reduced to simple marketing satellites. Fortunately, rapid economic growth in South East Asia is resulting in sales growth in the region, and thus changing location-specific advantages. Apart from the cost dimension, market access will become a prime motive for maintaining existing investments in the region, and expansion appears likely, even without the prospect of protectionism in the ASEAN region. For example, Sampo, which already has a plant in China and Thailand, is planning to open a second plant in Thailand, and possibly one in Indonesia.

As noted above, the Taiwanese authorities are establishing industrial parks for Taiwanese companies venturing overseas. A recent case involves a joint venture between them and their counterparts in the Philippines, to develop an industrial park at Subic Bay, the former US naval base. Work on the first phase, a 294 acre site, began in August 1994, and already 100 Taiwanese companies have sent letters of intent stating an interest at Subic, which offers one of Asia's best natural harbours and a US-trained workforce.

SUMMARY

Irrespective of regionalization, Taiwan may be expected to emerge as a higher profile home country to multinationals. Its firms need access to lower costs, markets, and resources, especially technology. In order to reduce costs they have already transferred production to China and south east Asia. Investments have been made in the USA and the EU in order to serve the local markets, albeit in terms of the latter, they are only beginning to build a distribution network. Key technologies have and will continue to be gained through internal and external development, in the form of acquisitions, joint ventures, and licensing agreements.

In the west, the importance of relationships is now acknowledged. Taiwanese companies and the overseas Chinese have a huge advantage over non-Chinese businesses, in that they have the relationships and cultural understanding so vital for business success in the mainland and other economies, where business is dominated by the Chinese. The Taiwanese will thus concentrate more in future on economies which are close culturally and geographically.

During the early 1990s, Taiwan's producers of finished electronics, especially information products, appeared to be the firms most likely to be affected by regionalization. It was firms such as Acer and its smaller rivals that appeared the most likely foreign investors, and also the most significant. Perhaps this was because these firms were engaged in consumer marketing and were thus highly visible, whereas component manufacturers were low-profile.

The internationalization process of Taiwan's computer manufacturers has displayed almost a reluctance to switch from exporting to foreign direct investment. Certainly Acer set a blistering pace in the late 1980s, but its plunge into the US market highlighted the difficulties in managing international operations. Its poor results there appear to have led to a much more cautious approach in the European market, and its status as the industry leader and symbol of national achievement probably rubbed off on its smaller rivals. The expected wave of Taiwanese investment in computer production, especially in Europe, has not materialised.

Perhaps somewhat surprising is that Taiwanese component manufacturers appear to be recognized as truly world-class and preferred suppliers to the most demanding of customers, the electronics giants from the USA and Japan. They have formed global networks to meet the regional needs of their companies and undertaken massive investments in Mexico and the EU to cement their vital relationships.

In Asia, Taiwan has emerged as one of the largest investors in all ASEAN countries save Singapore. These countries provide attractive offshore production locations and the operations are export-oriented. The devaluation of the currencies of ASEAN countries will enhance the competitive advantage of those facilities which rely on local sourcing rather than imported parts and components.

REFERENCES

'Taiwan's Acer-Inferiority Complex', *The Economist*, 1 February 1992.
Elegant, R. (1990) *Pacific Destiny: The Rise of the East*, London: Hamish Hamilton.
Gold, T. B. (1986) *State and Society in the Taiwan Miracle*, New York: M.E. Sharpe.
Hood, N. and Truijens (1992) *European Locational Decisions of Japanese Manufacturers: Survey Evidence on the Case of the UK*, SIBU Working Paper, 6.

Hood, N. and Young, S. (1982) *Multinationals in Retreat: the Scottish Experience*, Edinburgh: Edinburgh University Press.

Hwang, L.J. (1992) *The Internationalization of Taiwan Computer Industry*, Individual Research Project submitted in partial fulfilment for the Degree of Master of Science in International Marketing, University of Strathclyde.

Industrial Development and Investment Centre (1994) *Taiwan Industrial Panorama*, various issues.

Li, K.T. (1988) *The Evolution of Policy Behind Taiwan's Development Success*: New Haven: Yale University Press.

McDermott, M.C. (1989) *Multinationals: Foreign Divestment and Disclosure*, Maidenhead: McGraw-Hill.

McDermott, M.C. (1990) *The Internationalisation of South Korea's Electronics Firms*, European International Business Association Annual Conference, Madrid.

McDermott, M.C. (1991a) *Taiwan's Industry in World Markets: Target Europe*, Special Report No. 2111, Economist Intelligence Unit, London.

McDermott, M.C. (1991b), 'Taiwan's Electronic Companies are Targetting Europe', *European Management Journal*, **9** (4), December, pp. 466–74.

McDermott, M.C. (1992) 'The Internationalization of the South Korean and Taiwanese Electronics Industries: The European Dimension', in S. Young and J. Hamill (eds) *Europe and the Multinationals: Issues and Responses for the 1990s*, Aldershot: E. Elgar, Chapter 9.

17. The characteristics of successful firms in strategic alliances: a study of the Notebook PC Consortium in Taiwan

Po-Young Chu, Charles Trappey and David Lee

INTRODUCTION

The trend towards an integrated global economy forces businesses to cope with larger and more competitive businesses. Companies must continuously make technological changes, formulate strategies, and learn from their mistakes in order to survive. Businesses which attempt to restrain adaptation and change are likely to fail in the new integrated marketplace. Many Taiwan firms have asked the question 'If the resources of our single business are limited, how can we reduce the constraints and participate in the global market?' Strategic alliances have emerged as one solution that provides business managers with a flexible method to integrate resources. The formation of strategic alliances allows businesses to build competitive advantages.

Since the Taiwan economy relies greatly upon the contributions of small businesses, strategic alliances are of great interest to a variety of industries. The Economic Bureau and Economic Development Committee lead the promotion of strategic alliances. Their 1990 report recommended that under the present conditions of industry development, the Taiwan government should engage in three developmental strategies: (1) nurture the technological capability of industries; (2) develop the markets of high-technology products; and (3) build up international strategic alliances.

The third strategy, the development of strategic alliances with large multinational enterprises, has been pursued by numerous companies, especially in the electronics industry. Alliance formation has included technology licensing to enhance market competitiveness, the reduction of protectionist constraints, and the distribution of products in foreign markets through the partners' channels (Shang, 1991). Taiwan's strategic alliances have helped small businesses reduce the constraints of insufficient capital, personnel, and technology. Since small businesses are vulnerable to environmental changes, the alliance is often the only choice for survival and growth.

The strategic alliance challenges the concept that a single business enterprise is the most competitive structure. The changing global economy has created a need for more businesses to form alliances. However, academic research focusing on strategic alliance issues is limited, and many topics remain either unexplored or untested. For example, the characteristics of successful participants in strategic alliances are conceptually described in several articles, but there is little research that provides empirical data about the characteristics of strategic alliances. The data collected and analysed in this paper provide detailed information about the characteristics of participants that have collaborated in strategic alliances. The study investigates the characteristics of firms which benefit from strategic alliances. The goal of the study is to identify and to confirm significant relationships between the attributes of alliance participants and the success evaluations of the participants.

LITERATURE REVIEW

A large portion of the strategic alliance literature focuses on practical managerial issues without integrating the knowledge as theories. The alliance literature can be roughly classified into four major categories: managerial issues, conceptual research, case studies, and empirical research. The managerial issues focus on the success factors of strategic alliances and include strategic planning issues and organizational learning (Devlin and Bleackley, 1988; Pucik, 1988; Hamel, Doz and Prahalad, 1989; Lorange and Roos, 1991; and Lei and Slocum, 1991). Descriptions of the formation of strategic alliances are covered in the literature of James (1985), Harrigan (1987), and Ohmae (1989), whereas Souder and Nassar (1990a, 1990b) discuss the managerial problems of a research and development consortium.

The conceptual research of Contractor and Lorange (1988) explores the motivation of a strategic alliance based upon an analysis of costs and benefits. Killing (1988) studies the role of task complexity and organizational complexity in alliance decision making. Parkhe (1991) compares the characteristics of alliance partners and develops several hypotheses to describe how differences may affect the longevity of alliances. Finally, Harrigan (1987) develops a conceptual framework for joint ventures formed under different competitive environments.

Case studies have been used to describe strategic alliance issues. Niederkofler (1991) provides six cases which describe the evolutionary patterns of strategic partnerships, and Hamel (1991) focuses on cases reporting the relative learning capability of firms in an alliance. Wang (1991b) analyses the Notebook PC

Consortium in Taiwan, and Wang (1991a) also discusses the formation of alliances, the organizational design, and the management problems of the consortium.

Most of the empirical research addresses issues concerning the performance of alliances and the constructs used to measure and evaluate alliances. For example, Wu's (1987) empirical research of communications and computers industries in six developed countries provides a useful framework to study international strategic alliances. At the macro level, the relationships between alliance strategies and environmental factors are described. At the micro level, the relationships between firm characteristics, alliance strategies, and the firm's performance are described. Wu (1991) extended this micro level analysis to study the strategic alliances of communication, computer, and electrical component industries of Taiwan. The categories used to measure alliance structure include the characteristics of the firms, the position in the value-added chain, the objectives of the alliance, the participation of government agencies or academic institutes, and the structure of the alliance management. The alliance performance measures include the degree of achieving alliance objectives and the general satisfaction with alliance operations.

Harrigan's (1988b) empirical research explores whether or not the partner asymmetries would affect the performance of the alliance. Harrigan argues that joint ventures are more likely to succeed when partners possess complementary missions, resource capabilities, managerial capabilities, and other attributes that create a balanced strategic fit. The partner asymmetries of Harrigan's study include relative asset size, national origin, and joint venture experience levels. The venture performance indicators used in the analysis were venture survival, duration, and sponsor-indicated assessments of success. The results suggest that ventures last longer between partners of similar culture, asset size, and experience level. However, the alliance partners' traits did not offer much explanatory power in models of venture survival, duration, and success. The conclusions of the study imply that industry traits are more important than partner's traits in determining co-operative strategies.

In summary, the literature review indicates two areas of research critical to the further understanding of strategic alliances. First, the empirical research does not explore the characteristics of successful firms in alliances. There is no analysis of the relationships between the firms' attributes and the alliances success. Second, the measurement of alliance success is inadequate or is incomplete in the present research. For example, Harrigan (1988b) used duration as an indicator of alliance performance, while Parkhe (1991) proposed hypotheses concerning the longevity of alliances. These measures are implicitly regarded as positive indicators of alliance performance. However, Hamel (1991) criticized these measures, since alliances do not need to last forever. Hamel's viewpoint is that once the strategic objectives are reached, the alliance can be terminated.

This study addresses these two issues through the collection and analysis of empirical data. In the next section, the methodology of the study is described.

METHODOLOGY

The analysis framework for our study of the characteristics of successful firms in alliance is shown in Figure 17.1. This framework is different from Wu's framework (1987, 1991) in three ways. First, instead of focusing on the differences between alliances at the macro level, this study focuses on the differences between firms in alliances at the micro level.

Second, in addition to structural attributes, the study includes the alliance attributes as well as the characteristics of the firms. Third, since the alliance operating performance cannot be objectively measured and must be subjectively judged by the alliance participants, this study replaces the alliance operating performance with the alliance success evaluation.

Forty-six firms participated in the study. The sample data were collected after the alliance was terminated, and the results of empirical tests were then compared with the actual achievements of the alliance. Respondents were contacted by telephone and were asked to participate in the study. Thirty-two of the original 46 firms completed the survey sent via fax or mail, yielding a return rate of 84.2%. This sample represents almost 70% of the members of the PC Notebook consortia in Taiwan.

The variables used in the research are divided into two parts – the firm's attributes and the alliance success evaluations. The firm's attributes include structural attributes and alliance attributes. The specific attributes measured are shown in Table 17.1.

Four dimensions are used to measure alliance success. The dimensions are the individual achievement objectives of the firms, satisfaction with alliance

Attributes of the firm

Figure 17.1   The Notebook PC Consortium analysis framework

Table 17.1   Detailed list of firm's attributes

Structural Attributes	Alliance Attributes	

Operating Domain
• industry
• position in value chain
• portion of NBPC sales
• experience in NBPC
R&D Capability
• R&D expenditures
• relative ability
Age
Co-operative Experience
Scale
• sales
• number of personnel
• assets
• grade of association
	Self Management
	• commitment from
	  top managers
	• operating rules
	Basic Objectives
	• R&D components
	• develop prototype
	• negotiate with
	  foreign firms
	Strategic Objectives
	• reduce risk
	• reduce R&D cost
	• learn technology
	Consensus in Alliance
	Objectives
	• develop common type
	• help market products
	• differentiate products
		Co-operation Evaluation
		• task evaluation
		• dispute handling
		• input equality
		• output equality
		• common recognition
		Cadre of Committee
		Recognition of Alliance
		• technology / market
		  orientation
		• competitive /
		  noncompetitive

functional groups, achievement of alliance objectives, and overall satisfaction with the alliance. The derived factor scores from these four dimensions are used as weights to form the total score of alliance success. The statistical analysis includes all five of the success evaluations, but the test of the hypotheses only considers the total score of the alliance success evaluation variable.The hypotheses of this study are:

H1: The evaluation of alliance success varies according to the differences of the firm attributes.

H2: If a firm possesses high levels of an attribute, then it is more likely that the firm will rate the alliance as successful.

A three step statistical analysis process was used to test the hypotheses. The first step taken was to study the relationship between the firm's attributes and success evaluation of the alliance. The firm's nominal scale attributes were analyzed using ANOVA, whereas the ordinal or interval scale attributes were analyzed using statistical correlation.

The second step of the analysis was to group the firms by their structural attributes and their alliance attributes, and then determine whether the success evaluations were significantly different between groups. Thus, cluster analysis was used to separate firms into two groups according to the firm's non-nominal attributes. An ANOVA was then used to compare the success evaluations of the two groups.

Contrary to the approach taken in the second step, the third step of the statistical analysis required that the firms be grouped by their alliance success evaluations. The third step is intended to confirm the results of the second step and to provide a more robust confirmation of the differences. Thus, cluster analysis was used to separate the firms into two groups according to the firm's success evaluations. An ANOVA was then used to compare the attributes of the two groups.

RESULTS

From the analyses of structural attributes and success evaluations, the data support the argument that most of the structural attributes are not significantly related to the success evaluations. Only two of the structural attributes, industry and the portion of notebook PC (NBPC) in sales, are significantly related to the success evaluations ($p < 0.05$). The posterior analyses of the attributes by industry category shows that firms in the PC industry have higher success evaluation scores than firms in other industries (like PC peripherals, electrical components, terminals, communications, and consumer electronics). Furthermore, the firms which have highest portion ($> 1\%$) of NBPC in sales also have the highest success evaluation scores. The former may result from a preoccupation with the potential advantages that can be gained from an alliance. The latter may result from the increased profits generated from NBPCs and partly from the increased commitment of firms. Scale, age, and research and development capability are not significantly related to success evaluations ($p < 0.1$). However, when firms do possess NBPC experience (research, development, production, or marketing of NBPCs), then their relative R&D ability and age are significantly related to the success evaluation scores. In other words, when firms may have a higher portion of NBPC in sales, their age and scale attributes are also significantly related to success evaluation scores. Thus, R&D ability, age, and scale attributes are most beneficial to firms that are already established in the field of NBPC.

The results show that alliance attributes are significantly related to success evaluations, providing support for the first hypothesis. Attributes like commitments from top managers, basic objectives, strategic objectives, beliefs in alliance objectives, clarity of task allocation, alliance recognition, and technological orientation, are significantly related to the success evaluations. These results support hypothesis two, indicating that, if the firm possesses high levels of the attributes, then it is more likely that the firm will rate the alliance as successful. These findings show that the attitudes, recognition, and behaviours influence the evaluations of alliance success. A greater degree of commitment from top managers also led to higher success evaluations. Thus, if a new firm is more focused on the basic objectives of the alliance (for example, to introduce the NBPC), then it is more likely to develop its competitive advantages at the corporate level. The alliance participants with higher reporting levels for the clarity of task allocation also tend to give higher success evaluations.

The common model of Taiwan NBPC was introduced to the market in the later stages of the product life cycle. While many of the alliance participants began to receive orders for production, other firms started to cut prices. This situation degraded the relationship among members of the alliances. If the participants thought that the alliance was market-oriented (that the purpose of alliance focused on co-operation in marketing products), then price reduction in the market place undoubtedly downgraded the alliance success. However, if the participants thought that the alliance was technology-oriented (that the purpose of alliance was to foster R&D co-operation), then the success evaluations were affected by changes in the marketplace. Thus, the firms with a technology-oriented view of the alliance would give higher success evaluation scores. This finding reveals that participants' recognition of the mission of the alliance does influence its success evaluations.

There are two parts to the second stage of the analysis. First, cluster analysis is utilized to separate the firms into two groups based upon the firm's structural attributes. Then, an ANOVA is used to test whether the success evaluation scores are significantly different between the two groups. The results show that the firms can be divided into two distinct groups based upon their structural attributes. The major significant differences between the two groups are R&D expenditures, age, and scale attributes. The R&D expenditures, age, and scale attributes of Group 1 are all larger than Group 2, so Group 1 is labelled as the 'large scale' and Group 2 is labelled as the 'small scale'. However, further investigation reveals that the success evaluation scores between these two groups are not significantly different.

The differences among alliance attributes (as well as the success evaluation scores between the two groups) were tested using an ANOVA. Results of the analysis indicate that the major differences between these two groups are the attributes, including self management, basic objectives, strategic objectives, consensus in alliance objectives, clarity of task allocation, and committee cadre[1]. The structural attribute differences between the two groups are highly significant ($p < 0.001$), meaning that alliance attributes (not structural attributes) determine whether the participants will gain success in the positions in the consortium.

The third stage of analysis investigates the major differences between groups partitioned on the basis of success evaluations. Cluster analysis was used to classify the firms as high and low success evaluation groups, and the differences among firms' attributes were analyzed using ANOVA. The analysis shows that group differences based on success evaluation scores are significant. The following attributes are also significantly different: the portion of NBPC sales, the basic and strategic objectives, the consensus in alliance objectives, and the cadre of alliance committee. Few of the items belonging to the list of structural attributes were significantly different between the two groups. The findings reconfirm that alliance attributes have greater impact on the success evaluations than structural attributes (hypothesis one). In addition, members in the high success evaluation group possess more positive attitudes, more active behaviours, and deeper involvement than their counterparts in the low success evaluation group (hypothesis two). The three steps of analysis cross-validate the findings at each stage, and confirm that the alliance attributes play the dominant role in influencing the evaluations of alliance success.

MANAGERIAL IMPLICATIONS

Based upon the responses of the alliance participants, several managerial implications are derived. First, the objectives of the alliance must fit the strategic goals of the firm. Any firm intending to form an alliance should have a clear understanding of the objectives and natures of the alliance, since alliances have limitations (Devlin and Bleackley, 1988). Prior to its formation, alliance participants should also try to predict the costs and benefits of the endeavour. A number of firms participating in the Taiwan NBPC alliances rated the consortium negatively because the members' expectations exceeded the realized benefits. These firms also had a low consensus of alliance objectives and low evaluations of alliance success. Participants that form alliances with companies whose characteristics are not well known should be conservative in their expectations, since organizational learning is required.

Second, participants should commit themselves to the alliance and conscientiously manage the operations. Once a firm enters an alliance, it should understand that the co-operative benefits are created by the members of the alliance, and participants should set priorities to resolve alliance issues (Devlin and Bleackley, 1988). Systematic arrangements should be made to accommodate organizational learning (Pucik, 1988) and if possible, a special monitoring unit and operation rules should be established to supervise the progress and operations of an alliance. For large scale alliances, careful supervision can prevent the loss of competitive advantages. Involvement and commitment of top managers is critical to alliance success. Top managers should help the alliance personnel assign the resources of a firm with autonomy, so that the firm can cope with the volatile alliance situations efficiently (Souder and Nassar, 1990b).

Third, clear objectives must be set by all participants of the alliance. Although the alliance members seek common benefits, conflicts naturally arise that complicate the relationships among members. The setting of clear objectives encourages the alliance participants to seek and guard individual benefits. However, the search for organizational self-benefits should not jeopardize the common interests of alliance members. The essence of the alliance is 'You win and I win' (Lorange and Roos, 1991) and any self-benefiting behaviours that hurt the partnership will damage the consensus of co-operation.

In conclusion, the alliance must establish the mutual benefits. Alliance members should protect the benefits together and pool scarce resources. Mutual trust and co-operation is the foundation of long term alliances. Anything which is harmful to this foundation should be resolved by the consensus of members. The alliance agreement, including the rights and obligations of the members, must be concisely specified in a written document (Devlin and Bleackley, 1988). Therefore, the alliance committee will have the real power to restrain the members according to written rules. The composition of alliance members is also a critical issue. If the members are too homogeneous, then conflicts in benefits are more likely to arise. On the other hand, if the members are too heterogeneous, then consensus is harder to achieve. The best approach is to ensure that the members have common interests, but contribute their resources in a complementary way and receive their benefits in different areas (Killing, 1988). The number of alliance members should be constrained to the minimum level that matches the economic scale of the project. Thus, the complexities of communication, consensus building, and management can be reduced and the probability of success increased. As Niederkofler(1991) proposed, strategic alliances should be designed according to the strategic fit and the operating fit.

CONCLUSIONS

This study reveals that the attitudes, recognition, and behaviours of alliance participants are critical factors that affect the alliance success evaluations. The key findings of the study are outlined below:

1. The evaluations of alliance success are significantly different among firms.
2. The differences of success evaluations due to alliance attributes are more common and significant than those due to structural attributes.
3. The structural attributes significantly related to the success evaluations are the industry and the portion of NBPC in sales.
4. The alliance attributes significantly related to the success evaluations are the commitments from top managers, the basic and strategic objectives, the

consensus of alliance objectives, the clarity of task allocation, and technology-oriented recognition of the alliance.

5. The success evaluation scores for large scale firms with high R&D expenditure and greater tenure are not significantly different from small scale firms with low R&D expenditure and lesser tenure.
6. When the firms are classified by their alliance attributes, we find that the firms with greater involvement, stronger objectives, better self management, and higher consensus of alliance objectives have higher success evaluation scores than those of firms with negative attitudes and passive behaviours.
7. When the firms are classified by their success evaluations, we find that the group with higher success evaluations are characterized by a higher portion of NBPC sales, stronger objectives, higher consensus of alliance objectives, cadre of alliance committee, and non-competitive recognition of the alliance nature.

From the above findings, we conclude that the evaluations of alliance success in the same strategic alliance will not be identical. The major differences in the success evaluations come from the behavioural factors (behaviours, attitudes, and cognition) of the participants. Structural factors are not dominant. Furthermore, the success of an alliance is not inherently determined by the objective conditions, which are described as structural attributes. Subjective conditions, which are described as alliance attributes, play the dominant role in the alliance success. Thus, the alliance participants which are weak in the objective conditions are likely to gain success if they possess positive attitudes and actively co-operate in the alliance. Those firms with expertise different from the alliance should be careful not to lose their competitive advantages because of the additional requirements for organizational learning.

NOTE

1. Committee cadre means the firm is a key member in the consortium.

REFERENCES

Chinese

Shang, S.H. (1991) 'Foreword to the Special Issue of Strategic Alliances,' *Finance Monthly*, 15 August.

Wang, C.C. (1991a) 'The Discussions and Suggestions for the Notebook PC Consortium,' *Economic Forecasts*, 4 July.

Wang, H.C. (1991) *The Case Study of the Notebook PC Consortium in the R.O.C.: Analysis of the Demands of its Post Participants*, Unpublished MBA Thesis, National Chiao Tung University.

Wu, C.S. (1991), *The Structure of Strategic Alliances and the Evaluation of Alliance Performance*, The Symposium of the R&D Management of Industrial Technology in Taiwan.

English

Contractor, F.J. and P. Lorange (1988) *Cooperative Strategies in International Business*, Lexington: Lexington Book, pp. 3–28.

Devlin, G. and M. Bleackley (1988) 'Strategic Alliances – Guidelines for Success', *Long Range Planning*, **21** (5), pp. 18–23.

Evan, W.M. and Polk, (1990) 'R&D Consortia: a New Organizational Form,' *Sloan Management Review*, Spring, pp. 37–46.

Hamel, G. (1991) 'Competition for Competence and Interpartner Learning within International Strategic Alliances', *Strategic Management Journal*, **12**, pp. 83–103.

Hamel, G., Y.L. Doz and C.K. Prahalad (1989) 'Collaborate With Your Competitors – and Win,' *Harvard Business Review*, Jan/Feb, pp. 133–39.

Harrigan, K.R. (1987) 'Strategic Alliances: Their New Role in Global Competition,' *Columbia Journal of World Business*, **22** (2), pp. 67–69.

Harrigan, K.R. (1988a), 'Joint Ventures and Competitive Strategy,' *Strategic Management Journal*, **9**, pp. 141–58.

Harrigan, K.R. (1988b) 'Strategic Alliances and Partner Asymmetries,' *Management International Review*, pp. 53–72.

James, B.G. (1985) 'Alliance: the New Strategic Focus,' *Long Range Planning*, **18** (3), pp. 76–81.

Killing, F.P. (1988) 'Understanding Alliance: the Role of Task and Organizational Complexity', in: F.J. Contractor and P.J. Lorange (eds) *Cooperative Strategies in International Business*, Lexington Books, pp. 55–67.

Lei, D. and J.W. Slocum, Jr. (1991) 'Global Strategic Alliances: Payoffs and Pitfalls,' *Organizational Dynamics*, **19** (3), pp. 44–62.

Lorange, P. and J. Roos (1991) 'Why Some Strategic Alliances Succeed and Others Fail,' *Journal of Business Strategy*, Jan/Feb, pp. 25–30.

Lynch, R. P. (1989) *The Practical Guide to Joint Ventures and Corporate Alliances*, Wiley.

Niederkofler, M. (1991) 'The Evolution of Strategic Alliances: Opportunities for Managerial Influence,' *Journal of Business Venturing*, **6**, pp. 237–57.

Ohmae, K. (1989) 'The Logic of Strategic Alliances,' *Harvard Business Review*, Mar/Apr, pp. 143–54.

Parkhe, A. (1991) 'Interfirm Diversity, Organizational Learning, and Longevity in Global Strategic Alliance', *Journal of International Business Studies*, fourth quarter, pp. 579–601.

Pucik, V. (1988) 'Strategic Alliances, Organizational Learning and Competitive Advantage: the HRM Agenda,' *Human Resource Management*, **27** (1), pp. 77–93.

Souder, W.E. and S. Nassar (1990a) 'Choosing an R&D Consortium,' *Research-Technology Management*, Mar/Apr, pp. 36–41.

Souder, W.E. and S. Nassar (1990b) 'Managing R&D Consortia for Success,' *Research-Technology Management*, Sep/Oct, pp. 44–50.

Wu, C.S. (1987) *Strategic Alliances in Global Technological Competition: Case of Computers and Telecommunications Industries*, Ph.D. Dissertation, University of California, Los Angeles.

18. The opening of Taiwan's financial markets in the current period of protectionism

Henry Lo

INTRODUCTION

The North American Free Trade Area and the creation of a European Single Market constitute a serious threat to countries like the Republic of China (Taiwan), which rely heavily on trade. Taiwan is particularly vulnerable on account of its lack of bargaining power. Countermeasures have been proposed, although they are hardly feasible. However, it would seem that the rapidly-developing Pacific Basin countries, particularly those of East Asia, have a favourable enough development environment to continue to outperform the rest of the world. Taiwan can rely on its abundant foreign exchange reserves and use its valuable experience with financial reform to help its less fortunate neighbours to catch up with the developed world. This means that Taiwan should further open its financial markets to the world in general and to the region in particular.

This study examines the prospects for Taiwan as a regional financial centre in the light of its own financial reform. It covers the following topics: an overview of the basic characteristics of the Taiwan economy; a description of the history of financial reform and the early attempts to open up domestic financial markets; a consideration of the impact on Taiwan of the formation of regional economic blocs and an evaluation of the proposed alternatives; a description of the acceleration of financial reform after the 1986 European Single Act; a look at the efforts to establish a regional financial centre and their feasibility; and finally, a brief conclusion.

CHARACTERISTICS OF THE TAIWAN ECONOMY

The Republic of China (Taiwan) is about the size of the Netherlands, but two-thirds of its area consists of mountains which make agricultural development difficult. Furthermore, the scarcity of natural resources and a limited domestic market seriously hampered economic development.

Taiwan's foreign trade did not get off the ground until the 1970s, but since then the island has recorded massive export surpluses, a high savings rate, and so on. In the last 40 years, Taiwan has developed one of the world's most dynamic economies, and per capita GNP has risen from US$70 in the 1950s to US$8815 in 1991. Real GNP grew at an average rate of 8.9% per annum. Rapid industrialization caused substantial changes in the economic structure, as the centre of gravity shifted from agriculture to industry. Within industry, there was a shift from labour-intensive light manufacturing to more capital- and skill-intensive industries. Economic development in Taiwan has been characterised by rapid growth, export expansion, stable prices, and so on. In the course of this development, the economy underwent significant long-term changes with respect to production, trade and employment. The first stage of development, from 1949 to about 1961, was an import-substitution stage. It was followed by a period of export-expansion to about 1979, during which exports of such labour-intensive manufactures as textiles, garments and shoes grew rapidly. The current stage began in 1980, when Taiwan started to climb up the technological ladder.

Taiwan's economic structure is still in transition, moving toward a more open economy. Taiwan's industry is shifting toward such high-tech products as computers and fibre optics. For modernization, it needs advanced technologies and equipment, efficient management, automation, technological upgrading, more technical training, improved product quality, and better industrial design capability. According to this scenario, Taiwan manufacturers are likely to co-operate with foreign companies to develop new technologies and to explore new horizons.

FINANCIAL DEREGULATION PRIOR TO 1985

Recent financial reform in the Republic of China (ROC) has been motivated by several concerns (Liang 1991). First, while the ROC's manufacturing sector and exports have grown vigorously, making Taiwan a major participant in world trade, its financial system has remained relatively unsophisticated and out of step with the pace of industrial development. Second, the ROC's excessive foreign exchange reserves, resulting from a large trade surplus, led the United States, whose trade deficit with the ROC has been larger than that of any other trading partner, to urge Taipei to open its financial markets further to foreign institutions and investors. Third, computerized trading and other innovations in world financial markets make it essential that the ROC deregulate its domestic financial markets if it is to remain financially competitive both at home and abroad.

Historically, Taiwan has always enjoyed price stability and a balanced fiscal budget, and these are essential if a country is to avoid the adverse effects and externalities of liberalization (McKinnon, 1981). By far the most significant aspect of the liberalization process has been price deregulation, particularly interest rate and exchange rate deregulation.

Interest Rate Liberalization

The phasing out of interest rate controls began in the money markets and then proceeded to the banks, where controls were lifted first on large deposits and then on small deposits. The first step was the establishment of a money market in 1976, which provided a major source of short-term business financing outside the banking sector. The market rates have been a useful barometer for gauging money market conditions. Then, in 1980, interest rate restrictions were removed on banks' negotiable certificates of deposit and debentures. Banks and credit co-operatives were permitted to set their own bill discount rates. Foreign currency loans by foreign bank branches and accommodations for usance credit made by domestics banks on the basis of borrowing abroad were exempted from interest rate restriction. Banks were thereupon allowed greater flexibility and freedom in their operations. Moreover, the banks were allowed in 1985 to set their own rates on foreign currency deposits. This reform helped keep the rates in line with those on international financial markets and encouraged foreign currency earners to hold foreign currency deposits.

Foreign Exchange and Capital Flow Deregulation

The New Taiwan (NT) dollar was officially pegged to the US dollar. Under this regime, firms faced less uncertainty in conducting trade and making investments. This practice, however, impeded the automatic adjustment mechanism in financial instability. The foreign exchange system was converted from a fixed-rate system to a floating-rate system upon the establishment of a foreign exchange market in 1979. The value of the NT dollar has fluctuated. But as the trade surplus swelled, the build-up of the Central Bank's foreign exchange reserves began to cause a natural appreciation of the NT dollar against the US dollar. The Central Bank was unable to prevent this appreciation completely, and anyway, an appreciation of the domestic currency would help offset the serious disequilibrium of trade. Therefore, the NT dollar was allowed to appreciate. Capital movement was not prohibited altogether prior to 1985, as importers were allowed to borrow foreign currency through commercial banks and sell it on the foreign exchange markets. Also, commercial banks were allowed to borrow foreign currency from abroad.

It was a significant step toward liberalization, when foreign exchange controls were largely relaxed to allow direct capital outflow by the non-bank private sector, and to allow ROC residents to hold and use foreign currencies freely. The limits on purchases of foreign currency for outward remittance were raised gradually to a maximum of US$5 million per adult per year.

The relaxation of foreign exchange controls has made it possible for ROC residents to invest, acquire real estate or securities, or just deposit in banks overseas. Additionally, specific channels have been set up through which people can invest in foreign securities. The transactions conducted through these channels are not subject to the US$5 million limit on outward and US$50 000 limit on inward remittances. Investors can now build up a more diversified portfolio and enjoy a potentially higher rate of return.

Geographical and Operational Deregulation

Foreign banks face two basic types of restrictions on their activities in a host country: those governing their entry into a domestic market and those shaping the nature and extent of their operations once they are established. Foreign banks, which had an almost negligible presence in Taiwan in the 1960s, have grown to become a significant force in domestic financial markets. There are currently 51 local branches of foreign banks and 21 representative offices, of which 15 branches and 5 representative offices are European. Their growing presence contributes to greater competition in Taiwan. Banks with branches in Taipei have been granted the right to establish a second branch in Kaohsiung, an industrial centre in southern Taiwan and the world's fourth largest container port. However, only six banks have taken advantage of this privilege so far.

Until 1985, foreign banks were allowed to conduct exactly the same operations as domestic commercial banks, except that they were not permitted to set up savings and trust departments, to accept passbook savings and time savings, to extend long-term loans, or to conduct certain types of trust business which domestic banks could do with the approval of the Ministry of Finance. Foreign banks were allowed to offer pre-export loan finance by borrowing from abroad.

THE THREAT OF REGIONAL ECONOMIC BLOCS AND ITS IMPLICATIONS FOR TAIWAN

North American Free Trade Area

The USA has been a major export market for Taiwan and a major source of capital as well as technology. Bilateral trade with the United States amounted to

US$34.3 billion in 1990; of this figure, imports accounted for US$12.6 billion (or 32.4% of the total). Taiwan's trade surplus of US$9.1 billion (or 23% of Taiwan's total) and exports of US$21.7 billion with the United States, represented 73.1% of the nation's total trade surplus. Recent efforts to improve the trade imbalance and to diversify Taiwan's export markets began to show progress in 1991. The Americans are determined to solve the long-term trade deficit problem in order to protect their domestic industries. Hence the levying of anti-dumping tariffs and countervailing duties, and the adoption of trade quotas. In another protectionist move, Washington has established a North American Free Trade Area (NAFTA) with Canada and Mexico, and this will have a potentially significant impact on Taiwan.

Taiwan's exports to the US are concentrated on clothing, wood and rubber products, electrical and non-electrical machinery, transportation equipment, and so on. Canadian exports to the US do not present a substantial substitution problem for Taiwan as they consist mainly of food, raw materials, fabricated materials and motor vehicles. However, there is a material overlap between Taiwan's exports to the US and those of Mexico, which include fish, fruit, coffee, petroleum, chemicals, metal products, clothing, electrical and non-electrical machinery, and transportation equipment. Mexico, with its developed industrial base, cheap labour and cheap land, could well offer Taiwan strong competition after the formation of the US Mexico Free Trade Area. Moreover, foreign direct investment in the FTA is usually given national treatment. Therefore, US capital may well be diverted from other countries toward Canada and Mexico. That will have a further negative impact on US direct investment in, and technology transfers to, Taiwan.

The Single European Market

Taiwan's export diversification strategy has worked well, as can be seen from the growth in two-way trade with Europe. In recent years, the increase in trade has prompted European countries to adopt a more realistic attitude toward the ROC, encouraging informal contacts and dialogue between government officals. European technology symposia, technology exhibitions, and investment seminars have been held regularly and frequently in Taipei, giving Europe a strong presence. It was expected in some quarters that trade with Europe would surpass that with the US by the mid-1990s, but this expectation may have to be revised in view of moves toward a single market in the European Community (EC) and the possible creation of a 'Fortress Europe'. This fear is exacerbated by several factors. First, Taiwan is excluded from the EC special preference arrangements with developing countries. Second, EC member countries like Portugal, Greece, and Spain, which share similar comparative advantages with Taiwan, will become tough competitors of the ROC. Third, the EC, the EC-EFTA

(European Free Trade Association) linkage, and the EC-Eastern Europe Co-operation will divert investment resources from Taiwan.

This possibly marks the beginning of a regional trading bloc. Generally speaking, protectionism is not a desirable strategy, because it both inflicts direct losses on consumers and weakens incentives to manufacturers to improve quality and control prices. These regionalization developments will inevitably divert some trade from outsiders, and by so doing, could have a substantial impact on Taiwan's economy. As Taiwan is heavily dependent on trade, it is important for Taipei to conduct non-discriminatory and open trade. Although the European Commission meeting in 1988 indicated that future European trade policy would emphasize world partnership based on the principle of 'reciprocity', Taiwan's concern was that in trade matters it is in a weak bargaining position, because Europe does not attach so much importance to Taiwan as Taiwan does to Europe. Statistics revealed that Taiwan's exports to Europe were only 0.5% of Europe's total imports, and Taiwan's imports from Europe were only 0.9% of the latter's total exports in 1990.

In contrast, 17.3% of Taiwan's total imports were from Europe and Europe accounted for 18% of its total exports. Furthermore, Taiwan's current non-diplomatic channels of communication with Europe are particularly vulnerable to being used to force Taiwan into trade concessions. It is also doubtful how far Taiwan can make its opinions on trade and investment heard through existing channels.

Possible Measures Taiwan Could Adopt

One response open to Taiwan is to form a bilateral FTA with the US. There are benefits and disadvantages to this proposal. It would improve US access to Taiwan's markets and help rectify the US trade deficit, but whether Taiwan is strong enough to absorb the high cost involved in the adjustment of its agriculture, finance and other services as a result of the opening of its internal markets remains in question. The most important concern is probably the politically sensitive US–Mainland China relationship, and for this reason a Taiwan–US FTA seems to be a remote possibility.

Another possibility is to increase direct investment in the EC in order to circumvent the protectionist barriers. This would mean competing for a piece of the single market pie, and it would be important to act appropriately to maintain a market share. Taiwan's direct investment in Europe has grown since 1987, but not on the expected scale. This hesitation may be due to a lack of knowledgeable consultants, as there can be no confidence without guidance in an unfamiliar environment. It is probably difficult, at this stage, to form an overall strategic plan, and it would be more feasible to develop the competitiveness of individual products on a trial basis. In the meantime, investment in Mainland China, a more familiar environment, is enjoying rapid growth.

Some people have proposed that Taiwan should form its own free trade area – a Pacific Free Trade Area or a Chinese Area – in response. The Pacific Basin countries have the world's fastest growing economies, and they account for more than half of the world's production and over one-third of the world's trade. If these countries could form a free trade area, intra-regional trade and investment would expand immediately, with much faster economic growth. If the FTA were open to outsiders, it would promote global free trade and investment.

Whether this FTA could be formed on the basis of any of the existing co-operative arrangements would depend on the resolution of difficulties such as protectionist barriers against imports and foreign investment, historical antagonism against Japan, and so on. Significant differences in language, culture, religion, social systems, industry policies, political security and economic structure also add to the difficulties of close economic co-operation. It would require huge and long-term efforts to reach an agreement on how to share the burdens and benefits of integration. Besides, the EC has taken about 40 years to come this far; is Taiwan prepared to wait that long?

A Chinese Area

The rapid increase in cross border commercial activity involving Taiwan, Mainland China and Hong Kong has prompted discussion of a Chinese area. The basis for this integration is potential factor complementarity: Taiwan has a relative abundance of capital and commercial technology, whereas the Chinese Mainland has natural resources and labour. From a Chinese (Taiwan or Mainland) point of view, therefore, this would certainly be a welcome development. However, barriers against the integration of these economies abound, and the most basic one is political. At present, trade and investment between the two sides of the Taiwan Strait are conducted in a very complicated manner. Forbidden from trading directly with the Mainland, Taiwan businessmen have to ship goods through a third region (Hong Kong or another country). There are also restrictions on the categories of goods that may be imported from the Mainland to Taiwan, and on investment activities. These restrictions have been imposed on the grounds of national security, as well as the need to avoid legal disputes and possible economic control by the Mainland. It is doubtful whether economic integration could take place before political differences are resolved. Given the weak political position of Taiwan in the international arena, the above-mentioned measures are not feasible in the foreseeable future. Taiwan has to take other measures to look after its own interests.

FURTHER ACCELERATING FINANCIAL LIBERALIZATION

Foreign Exchange Market

The foreign exchange market established in 1979 enabled the NT dollar to float freely within the Central Bank's centralized 'mid-rate' exchange rate transaction system. The rate of the US dollar against the NT dollar was set daily on the basis of a weighted average rate of inter-bank transactions in US dollars on the previous business day. One of the weaknesses of this system was that it did not allow the exchange rate to react quickly to changing supply and demand conditions in the bank-customer market. The Central Bank of China (Taiwan) therefore established a new exchange rate system in 1989 based on free price negotiation for transactions over US$30000. In 1990, the Central Bank of China went a step further by allowing each individual bank complete freedom to determine its own transaction exchange rates in the bank-customer market. It is the spot rate system which applies to foreign exchange transactions.

In 1991, banks were allowed to manage foreign currency swaps and margin trading. In November that year, the forward foreign exchange market was re-established, and authorized foreign exchange banks were allowed to use an accrual basis rather than a cash basis to calculate their foreign exchange position limit. The initial objective of the forward market was to provide a hedging device only for underlying trade transactions. This device will be considered for capital account transactions if the forward market operates smoothly for a period of time.

Offshore Banking Operations

In late 1983, the Central Bank of China promulgated various regulations concerning offshore banking services. These allowed banks located within the national boundaries to establish offshore banking units (OBUs) as a means of strengthening international financial activities. OBUs are business units of banks which accept deposits and make loans in foreign currencies at free market interest rates. They maintain accounts separate from the domestic unit. In March 1992, a total of 32 banks, half local banks and the other half foreign banks, participated in the OBU market. Total assets of OBUs in the meantime amounted to US$23 billion. Geographically, Asia was the largest source of funds (82% of the total) and the major utilizer (90%).

Banks

State-controlled banks are still the mainstay of Taiwan's banking system, with privately owned banks accounting for only a small fraction of banking activities.

Relatively slow progress has been made in privatising these banks and in allowing them more freedom in managing their own operations, but a number of state-controlled banks are scheduled for privatization soon. Moreover, following the recent entry of 15 private banks into the local market, competition in the Taiwan banking sector is becoming increasingly intense. The Banking Law was revised in 1989, and all the former controls over interest rates were completely abolished. Since then, banks have been free to set their own rates of interest and, as a result, short-term interest rates are principally determined by the supply of, and demand for, funds. The Law also provides national treatment for foreign banks, enabling them to accept savings deposits, extend long-term credits, and engage in some investment banking activities. The scope of foreign banking operations will expand considerably and foreign banks will have more opportunities to introduce new financial products and provide better services to customers.

The Law also granted licences to new private commerical banks. Minimum paid-in capital has been set at NT$10 billion (approximately US$36 million), at least 20% of which may be raised through public share subscription. In addition, new banks must recruit senior staff whose banking experience is commensurate with their new responsibilities. There are now 15 new commercial banks in operation, and applications for other new banks are being reviewed. The entry into the market of these new banks has ended the monopoly of the banking industry, and there are clear indications that the prices of financial services, such as service charges and interest rates on deposits and loans, are becoming more reasonable due to the strong competition.

As the banks' role in the current stage of economic development has already grown beyond mere financing for local exporters and importers, domestic banks are being urged to establish an extensive network of foreign branches and overseas subsidiaries to boost their international connections and to accelerate voluntary innovations. The expansion of outward foreign direct investment (FDI) provides good opportunities for linking up with the global arena. Outward FDI enables the ROC to share the fruits of its economic achievement with other developing countries, by helping them to expand their export markets for unskilled labour-intensive products. To facilitate this process, it must establish a globalized commercial banking system with a network of foreign branches and overseas subsidiaries that will provide Taiwan investors with the financial services they need. Then Taiwan will be able to increase its share of expanding international financial markets and help accelerate the industrialization of the economies in which it has invested.

The restrictions on the establishment of foreign branches and subsidiaries were lifted in 1988. As of the end of March 1992, 10 domestic banks had established a total of 26 branches, 14 representative offices, and five subsidiaries overseas.

Capital Markets

In 1991, Merrill Lynch and Shearson Lehman Brothers were granted permission to establish branches in Taipei. Now the public can trade in securities on the New York, London and Tokyo stock exchanges through these two foreign securities firms. Of particular note is the US$100 million worth of Dragon Bonds that were issued in Taiwan in December 1991 by the Asian Development Bank. These Dragon Bonds are the first foreign currency bonds to have been directly issued in Taiwan.

The process of financial liberalization is not yet complete. The range of financial products available is not yet adequate, the market mechanism has not been fully brought into play, and the rules of the game have not yet been thoroughly established and effectively enforced. The development of the stock market has preceded that of other markets, but the stock market is still basically a place for playing the money game.

A REGIONAL FINANCIAL CENTRE IN ASIA

It is estimated that the ROC's per capita Gross National Product (GNP) will reach US$14000 by 1996. The development of Taipei into a regional financial centre has already been incorporated into the Six-Year National Development Plan. The plan puts heavy emphasis on improvements in the quality of life in the ROC, upgrading industry, protecting the environment, and extending and improving health care.

The conditions for the establishment of a regional financial centre in a city like Taipei are both objective and subjective. Taiwan enjoys political and social stability and rapid economic growth. Orderly financial liberalization, flourishing foreign trade and well-developed telecommunications facilities make it clear that Taipei already posesses some of the qualifications necessary to become a regional financial centre. Liberalization measures have freed the interest rates markets, foreign banks have been permitted to expand their types of business, and those with branches in Taiwan have been given permission to establish a third branch. Restrictions on new domestic securities companies have been lifted, foreign securities houses have been encouraged to enter the local markets, and new insurance companies are being set up. All these have served to encourage domestic financial competition and improved the quality of financial services.

With regard to the foreign exchange market, Taiwan has a spot rate system for foreign exchange transactions. Thirty-two offshore banking units with total assets of US$23 billion provide a foundation for the foreign currency call-loan market. Each individual bank in the bank-customer market is free to set its own exchange rate. ROC residents are free to hold and utilize foreign exchange for the purpose of trade. The controls on capital account transactions have also been relaxed. With funds now free to move across national boundaries, changes in international interest rates are exerting an increasingly important influence on domestic rates. These developments have helped speed the internationalization of the domestic financial market.

Well-developed financial centres like London and New York evolved under very strong economic and commercial conditions and a sound financial system. Others, like Singapore, are principally the result of vigorous government promotion. The preparations required for such a centre in Taipei include: (1) attracting international brokerage houses to Taiwan so as to establish links with the international market and thus enhance the efficiency of Taiwan's financial markets; (2) staff training and development in both languages and other specialities, initially to be carried out abroad; (3) improving telecommunications services and lowering the standard charges for long distance telephone calls and telex messages, so as to make Taipei financial services more price-competitive; (4) the construction of an international financial building equipped with first-rate telecommunications facilities to be leased to international financial organizations; (5) establishing an organized gold market; and (6) introducing new products.

The Rationale

Until recently, Japan and West Germany were the major suppliers of funds on the international markets. However, Japanese domestic investment rose sharply in 1990, and a bearish stock market, falling real estate prices, and more stringent capital lending ratios set by the Bank for International Settlements weakened the lending abilities of banks in Japan. At the same time, reunification markedly increased the financial burden on the German government, requiring the issuance of government bonds. For these reasons, the supply of funds on international markets has not kept up with surging demand, resulting in a tightening of international credit. Against this backdrop, the ROC has continued to record a trade surplus and accumulate foreign exchange reserves. It will therefore remain a major supplier of funds to international financial markets in the future. Apart from the fund supplier aspect, there is a need for a new regional financial centre to accommodate the financial demand within the region (see the following section), as the existing financial centres have their own problems.

Financial Markets in the Pacific Basin

Generally speaking, the financial markets of the Pacific Basin region segregate credit and engage in specialised financial activities. Indirect finance is more developed than direct finance, and there is a relatively high degree of control over prices, market participation, the scope of securities, foreign exchange, and the transfer of capital. In recent years, in response to the impact of computer and telecommunications technology and financial globalization, Pacific Basin countries have carried out some degree of financial reform in the expectation that their financial systems will be integrated with international markets.

In the Asian region of the Pacific Basin, Taiwan and Korea both entered a phase of stable growth in 1990 after having experienced some overheating. Indonesia, Malaysia and Thailand, enjoyed high growth rates as the result of large amounts of investment from Japan and the Asian newly industrialized countries (NICs) attracted by their low labour costs and abundant resources. The Philippines suffered due to internal political turmoil. Stable economic growth depends on a continuous stream of investment and capital accumulation, and there must also be a healthy financial market and effective financial intermediation in order to mobilize national savings.

The financial markets of Tokyo, Hong Kong and Singapore have long been established as global financial centres, while the Toyko market is second to none in terms of transaction volume. However, it still lags behind New York and London with respect to market deepening, the variety of financial investment, financial expertise and operational efficiency. What is more, the Toyko market maintains various controls and traditional practices which have been abolished in New York and London.

The Hong Kong and Singapore financial markets have developed from free trading port cities. Their major difference is one of financial control. The Hong Kong financial market is completely directed by market forces, whereas that of Singapore is subject to heavy government involvement in its day-to-day operations and development. These markets are free and open and have reached an advanced stage of liberalization and internationalization. However, in the new environment of financial globalization and the growth of electronic banking, they find it difficult to supervise their financial institutions adequately and to cope with operational crises.

The ROC and Korean economies share a similar pattern of development, but they have adopted different approaches to financial deregulation. Taiwan began by deregulating interest rates, starting with money market interest rates and then gradually progressing to deposit and loan market interest rates. Korea, on the other hand, began by easing restrictions on the establishment and activities of financial institutions. As a consequence, Korea's interest rate deregulation is still at an early stage of development. Because Korea has regulated interest rates for an extended period, Korean banks really lack experience in managing interest rate risk. How to deregulate interest rates is now a major challenge facing Korea.

The Southeast Asian countries have not achieved a high level of development in either direct or indirect financing. Their securities markets are especially backward, the degree of financial deepening is very limited, the governments exercise a high degree of control and capital outflows are tightly restricted. Because these countries generally register balance of payments deficits, they vigorously encourage foreign direct investment as a means of promoting economic growth and technology transfers without increasing their interest rate burden.

The reform and modernization of their financial systems, as well as the opening of their domestic financial markets to foreign institution participation, have become extremely important to them. In fact, intra-regional investment has risen as some labour-intensive manufacturers in Japan and the NICs (especially South Korea and Taiwan) have relocated their operations to Thailand, Malaysia, the Philippines, Indonesia and China to maintain their competitive edge.

Additionally, as European economic integration approaches, some multinational enterprises may want to shift their investment from here to Europe. In these circumstances, the Southeast Asian countries would have to rely even more heavily on investment from Japan and the NICs.

CONCLUSIONS

The emerging European and North American economic blocs threaten the Taiwan economy with a diversion of trade and investment. The best way to alleviate or even remove this threat would be for Taiwan to be treated essentially as a member of these trade blocs with regard to trade and investment. Taiwan is fully aware of its position and realises that free trade would be the best policy, as it might invite reciprocity. The best course of action would be to open up domestic markets, prepare for competition, adopt macroeconomic policies that would help to restore equilibrium in the balance of payments, adjust the industrial structure, improve living standards, and promote regional integration.

Liberalization policies should be pursued further. The essential task at the moment is to create a new financial environment that is both more dynamic and more secure by (1) permitting greater foreign access to the local financial market; and (2) formulating up-to-date laws and regulations and enforcing them strictly and consistently, in order to foster and strengthen confidence in financial institutions.

The process of market restructuring and of reorganising the regulatory framework has yet to be completed. Further financial deregulation and financial reform are imperative if the ROC is to establish Taipei as a regional financial centre.

REFERENCES

Chang, Chicheng (1990) 'Financial Liberalization in the Republic of China' in S.G. Rhee and R.P. Chang (eds) *Pacific Basin Capital Markets Research* North-Holland.

Cheng, Hangsheng (1989) 'Financial Policy and Reform in Taiwan', in H.Cheng (ed.) *Financial Policy and Reform in Pacific Basin Countries*, Lexington Books.

Cole, D.C. and R.F. Slade (1987) 'Reform of Financial Systems' in Dwight Perkins & Michael Premes (eds) *Reforming Financial Systems in Developing Countries* Harvard Institute of International Development.

Khouty, S.J. (1990) *The Deregulation of the World Financial Markets*, Pinter Publishers.

Kuo, S. W. (1990) 'Liberalization of the Financial Market in Taiwan in the 1980s' in S.G. Rhee and R.P. Chang (eds) *Pacific Basin Capital Market Research*, North-Holland.

Li, K.T. (1990a) 'New Trends in Pacific Rim Trade and Investment', *Industry of Free China*, **LXXIV**, No. 4.

Li, K.T. (1990b) 'The Taiwan Experience and Taiwan's Political and Economic Prospects', *Industry of Free China*, **LXXIV**, No. 5.

Liang, K.S. (1991) 'Background and Lessons of Financial Reform in the Republic of China', *Industry of Free China*, **LXXVI**, No. 4.

Liang, K.S. & C.H. Liang (1990) 'Taiwan's Economic Development and Its Implications for the Pacific Asian Region', *Industry of Free China*, **LXXIV**, No. 3.

Lin, C.C.S. (1991) 'Toward the Emergence of Taipei as an International Financial Centre', *Industry of Free China*, **LXXV**, No.5.

McKinnon, R.J. (1973) *Money and Capital in Economic Development*, Brookings.

McKinnon, R.J. (1981) 'The Order of Economic Liberalization: Lessons From Chile and Argentina' in Karl Burnner & Alan H. Meltzer (eds) *Economic Policies in a World of Change* North-Holland.

Siew, V.C. (1991) 'Trade Policy and Protectionism', *Industry of Free China*, **LXXVI**, No. 5.

Stigler, G.J. (1971) 'The Theory of Economic Regulation', *Bell Journal of Economics and Management Science*, **2**, Spring.

Walter, Ingo (1988) *Global Competition in Financial Services*, Ballinger Publishing Co.

Wang, Jiann-chyuan (1991) 'The Changing Role of Taiwan in Pacific Rim Regional Development', *Industry of Free China*, **LXXV**, No. 2.

19. Political risk management: a case study of Turkish companies in Central Asia and Russia[1]

**Mehmet Demirbag, Recep Gunes
and Hafiz Mirza**

INTRODUCTION

The Central Asian Republics are among the most unexplored parts of the world with regard to foreign direct investment climate and the political risk perception of foreign multinational corporations (MNCs). With the opening up of the Central Asian and Russian markets, the subject gained a dramatic importance not only for Turkish companies, but also for foreign MNCs based in Turkey and planning to use their Turkish operations as a springboard for entering these markets. Despite many unfavourable political events in the Russian Federation and the Central Asian Republics (or the so called Turkic Speaking Republics) there seems to be an increasing interest by MNCs in these resource-rich markets. Data provided by TIKA (Turkish Co-operation and Development Agency) indicates that there is an ever-growing interest, not only by Turkish companies, but also by Western and Japanese MNCs, to enter into co-operation and gain a market share despite all the economic and political turbulence.

The political dimensions of foreign direct investment decisions include the actions or strategies that attempt to obtain or sustain a competitive advantage from non-economic actors. As Boddewyn (1986 p. 4) puts it 'if a firm cannot be a cost differentiation or focus leader, it may still beat the competition on another ground, namely, the non market [political] environment'. Political risk is the possibility of a multinational company being significantly affected by political events in a host country or by a change in the political relationships between a host country and one or more other countries. Early studies in the USA by Aharoni (1966), Root (1972), Van Agtmael (1976), and La Palombara and Blank (1977) found that although political risk is perceived by MNCs to be one of the dominant factors in foreign investment decisions, few companies engaged in a systematic evaluation of political risks which considered their likely incidence and their specific consequences for the company.

In the international business literature, four different approaches to political risk and political risk management have been researched. The first group deals with the subject from the forecasting point of view in assessing international political risks faced by MNCs (Boddewyn, 1986; Kobrin, 1982; Moran 1985; Poynter, 1982; Sethi and Luther, 1986). The second approach to international political risk management is mainly concerned with lobbying for favourable treatment from the host government (Boddewyn, 1986; Doz, 1986; Pfeffer, 1987; Prahalad and Doz, 1987). The third approach, however, focuses more on home country assistance rather than the host country (Caves and Jones, 1985; Czinkota and Ricks, 1981). The fourth cluster of studies dealing with international political risk management aim to design strategies protecting local operations from host government intervention (Encarnation and Wells, 1986; Kogut, 1985; Porter and Fuller, 1986; Preble, Rau and Reichel, 1988).

The main objective of this paper is to examine the political risk perception of companies operating in Central Asian and Russian markets from top managers' points of view. Therefore the study is exploratory in nature and involves exploration of executives' perception of political risk and their assessment methods. In doing so, the researchers aim to uncover the importance of factors associated with political risk assessment for sample firms in these markets, and the significance of political risk factors in their foreign direct investment decisions. The paper also examines the question whether there is any linkage between political risk perception and the strategies of Turkish MNCs in entering the above-mentioned markets.

The paper contains four main parts. The first section describes the subject and provides a description of the current state of the countries examined, and some background information. The second section deals mainly with the sample and the methodology used for data collection and treatment, and the third section discusses the empirical findings of the study. The last section is the conclusion. This section also discusses the limitations of the study and possible implications of the empirical findings for managers.

RECENT DEVELOPMENTS IN CENTRAL ASIAN REPUBLICS AND TURKISH FOREIGN DIRECT INVESTMENTS

The purpose of this section is to provide a brief overview of Turkish Foreign Direct Investment trends and to focus on development of Turkish FDI in

Central Asian Republics and Russia. The overview focuses on the main features and is not comprehensive.

Recent Developments in Central Asian Republics

After the collapse of the Soviet Union, the 'nationalization' process first started in the Baltic states. A similar approach was followed by the newly independent states of the Central Asian Republics. Political uprisings were first seen in Alma Ata, the capital of Kazakhstan, followed by the Baku events in Azerbaijan. Although the western countries turned their attention to the Baltic states, which were never accepted as Soviet satellites by the west, a similar wind of independence was blowing in the Central Asian Republics. The world witnessed announcements of independence by a series of Central Asian Republics. Some of these newly independent states, namely Azerbaijan, Turkmenistan, Uzbekistan, Kazakhstan, and Kyrgyzstan are populated by peoples of Turkic origin, and Turkic dialects are widely spoken. Thus, the cultural, religious, and linguistic proximity attracted Turkey's attention, and she was the first country to develop political and economic relations with them. Turkey tried to take the opportunity not only for cultural reasons, but also for economic and political reasons. With a population of approximately 60 million people living in six million sq. km, these newly independent states seem to supply some good market opportunities, albeit with political and economic risks.

Although the process of restructuring the economies of these newly independent republics, which were previously state controlled, remains in the first stage, Turkish investors seem to play an important role in the transformation process. To some extent, the Turkish Eximbank also seems to contribute to the restructuring of these fragile economies. Table 19.1 indicates the distribution of credits opened for the newly independent states of Central Asia by the Turkish Eximbank in 1993.

Since the 1980s, Turkey has changed her inward looking, autarchic political economic system, and capital inflow and outflows became more apparent. Between 1992 and 1994, as can be seen from Table 19.2, an increasing interest in Turkish FDI is witnessed. Although most Turkish FDI still goes to European countries, the Central Asian Republics and Russia seem to have become an alternative market. This development also appears to match Turkey's trade patterns and the configuration of foreign direct investment by Turkish companies.

An examination of Turkish FDI in the subject countries indicates that Russia seems to receive the largest number of companies, although firms operating in Kazakhstan are relatively larger in size. Azerbaijan, however, seems to be preferred by smaller size companies. This may be due to the geographical proximity between Azerbaijan and Turkey, and the size of the Azerbaijani market is relatively small as compared with other Republics such as Kazakhstan.

These statistics, however, exclude the many companies which are not registered by the Under Secretariat of the Treasury, and also exclude contractors and subcontractors operating in the region.

Table 19.1   Turkish Eximbank credits for C.A.R. (31 August 1993) (1000 US$)

Countries	Credit Limit (Goods)	Credit Limit (Project)	Credit Limit (Project + Goods)	Used amount
Uzbekistan	125 000	125 000	250 000	L/C amounting US$175m (US$50m for projects) has been opened and US$124.6m has been used in the transfers.
Kazakhstan	50 000	150 000	200 000	L/C amounting US$10.06m has been opened and US$5.7m has been used in the transfers.
Turkmenistan	75 000	15 000	90 000	L/C amounting US$63.93m has been opened and US$23.0m has been used in the transfers.
Kyrgyzstan	25 000	50 000	75 000	L/C amounting US$6.32m has been opened. US$1.58m has been used in the transfers for agricultural medicine.
Azerbaijan	50 000	200 000	250 000	L/C amounting US$10.09m has been opened and US$4.75m has been used in the transfers.
Nahcivan	10 000	–	10 000	US$9.65m has been used in the transfers.
Tajikistan	50 000	–	50 000	
Georgia	50 000	–	50 000	L/C amounting US$11.14m has been opened.
1) Total financing of exports	435 000			L/C amounting US$276.54m has been opened and US$163.24m has been used.
2) Total financing of projects		541 000		
3) Total financing			975 000	

Note: L/C = Lines of Credit

Source: Report Presented to the Turkish President by TIKA (September 1993)

Table 19.2   Turkey's direct investment by country

Country	Cumulative to 1989		1990		1991		1992		1993		1994		Total to 1994	
	No. of E'prises	Amnt of Capital Exp'ted	No. of E'prises	Amnt of Capital Exp'ted	No. of E'prises	Amnt of Capital Exp'ted	No. of E'prises	Amnt of Capital Exp'ted	No. of E'prises	Amnt of Capital Exp'ted	No. of E'prises	Amnt of Capital Exp'ted	No. of E'prises	Amnt of Capital Exp'ted
Germany	40	33 995	4	12 894	5	10 907	8	39 300	5	9 376		17 347	62	123 819
Switzerland	38	18 775	3	12 479	–	3 788	2	2 047	1	12 170	1	384	45	49 643
UK	23	66 110	7	58 278	1	6 461	1	15	4	7 244	3	21 835	39	159 943
Netherlands	6	3 263	1	5 319	–	–	1	20 638	1	17 884	1	31 383	10	78 487
France	5	9 147	1	390	2	5 804	4	633	1	7 272	–	–	13	23 246
USA	11	12 965	7	77 858	3	559	4	3 083	2	3 207	3	650	30	98 322
S. Arabia	2	707	–	–	–	–	1	1 200	–	391	–	–	3	2 298
Luxembourg	2	20 694	1	4 900	–	–	2	10 250	1	5 000	1	2 850	7	43 694
Austria	1	10 012	1	9 180	–	–	–	–	1	1 141	–	–	3	20 333
Spain	1	500	1	201	–	–	–	–	–	–	–	–	2	701
Italy	5	558	–	–	–	–	1	12	–	–	–	–	6	570
Taiwan	1	100	–	–	–	–	–	–	–	–	–	–	1	100
Jordan	2	900	–	–	–	–	–	–	–	–	–	–	2	900
Tunisia	–	–	–	–	–	–	1	210	1	49	–	310	2	569
Algeria	–	–	–	–	–	–	1	285	–	–	–	–	1	285
Japan	1	78	–	–	–	–	–	–	–	–	–	–	1	78
Hungary	1	10	1	15	–	–	1	163	2	852	1	82	6	1 122
Poland	1	135	–	–	2	111	–	–	1	76	1	3	5	325
Belgium	1	37	1	2 000	2	316	4	172	1	594	1	17 889	10	21 008
Finland	1	66	–	–	–	–	–	–	–	–	–	–	1	66
Bahrain	1	15 000	–	–	–	–	–	–	–	–	1	3 000	2	18 000
Pakistan	2	359	–	–	–	–	–	–	–	–	–	–	2	359
Bangladesh	–	–	–	–	–	–	–	–	–	–	1	59	1	59
Denmark	1	20	–	–	–	–	1	40	–	309	–	149	2	518

Table 19.2   continued

Country	Cumulative to 1989		1990		1991		1992		1993		1994		Total to 1994	
	No. of E'prises	Amnt of Capital Exp'ted	No. of E'prises	Amnt of Capital Exp'ted	No. of E'prises	Amnt of Capital Exp'ted	No. of E'prises	Amnt of Capital Exp'ted	No. of E'prises	Amnt of Capital Exp'ted	No. of E'prises	Amnt of Capital Exp'ted	No. of E'prises	Amnt of Capital Exp'ted
Nigeria	1	3 231	–	–	–	–	–	–	–	–	–	–	1	3 231
Malaysia	1	4	–	–	–	–	–	–	–	–	1	50	2	54
Iraq	1	10	–	–	–	–	–	–	–	–	–	–	1	10
Czechoslovakia	–	–	1	3	1	97	–	–	1	7	–	–	3	107
TRN Cyprus	32	2 784	1	10	1	20	1	351	6	3 895	3	547	44	7 607
Bulgaria	2	167	–	–	6	519	6	134	1	83	–	–	15	903
Kuwait	1	50	–	–	–	–	–	–	–	–	–	–	1	50
Romania	–	–	–	–	4	214	9	1 966	6	5 937	4	4 129	23	12 246
Former USSR	1	6 958	2	2 542	–	–	–	–	–	–	–	–	3	9 500
Azerbaijan	–	–	–	–	7	291	13	2 127	11	6 811	5	285	36	9 514
Kazakhstan	–	–	–	–	–	–	1	3 654	12	59 526	3	66 787	16	129 967
Kyrgyzstan	–	–	–	–	–	–	2	70	4	14 099	1	9	7	14 178
Turkmenistan	–	–	–	–	–	–	3	102	1	250	3	3 338	7	3 690
Uzbekistan	–	–	–	–	–	–	3	80	2	1 030	3	323	8	1 433
Russian Federation	–	–	–	–	–	–	9	6 318	6	2 567	8	3 394	23	12 279
Lithuania	–	–	–	–	–	–	–	–	–	–	1	25	1	25
Moldova	–	–	–	–	–	–	–	–	1	10	–	–	1	10
Ukraine	–	–	–	–	–	–	2	186	6	1 468	2	103	10	1 757
Egypt	–	–	–	–	–	–	–	–	1	1 557	1	29	2	1 586
Thailand	–	–	–	–	–	–	–	–	–	–	1	16	1	16
Total	185	206 635	32	186 069	34	29 087	81	93 036	79	162 805	50	174 976	461	852 608

Note: Currency is Turkish Lira 000s

Source: Prime Ministry of the Republic of Turkey, Under Secretariat of Treasury, September 1995

METHODOLOGY AND DESCRIPTION OF SAMPLE

This study is based on the collection of primary data from Turkish companies operating in the Central Asian Republics and the Russian Federation. Management executives were interviewed directly. The authors used the executive interview method for data collection, and at the end of each interview, the interviewee was asked to fill in a questionnaire, which was later used for quantitative analysis. The triangulation technique, which involves the amalgamation of quantitative and qualitative results, will be used in reporting the findings of this study.

For the sample selection, four main criteria were employed: the size of the operation, the industrial sector, the percentage of equity shares held by local and foreign parent firms, and the countries hosting these operations. For the purpose of this study, foreign operations were defined as wholly owned subsidiaries, joint ventures (majority, 50%, and minority owned), construction contracts, management contracts including industrial co-operation agreements, and export trade and other commercial activities.

Approaches to Turkish companies operating in the Central Asian Republics and the Russian Federation resulted in the parents of 45 affiliates agreeing to participate in the research. Although the number of firms surveyed for data collection was relatively small, as the number of operations of the sample firms in the subject countries is considered, the representativeness of the sample seems to be satisfactory. The distribution of the sample firms' operations by country of operation is shown in Table 19.3. As can be seen from Tables 19.3 and 19.4, the participant 45 firms represent 100 operations, since many of the sample firms own more than one operation, in some cases in more than one of the countries included in the research design.

Table 19.3 Distribution of the sample firms' operations by country of origin

Country of operation	Number of operations	Percentage in the sample
Azerbaijan	20	20.0
Turkmenistan	10	10.0
Kazakhstan	21	21.0
Uzbekistan	9	9.0
Russia	35	35.0
Kyrgyzstan	3	3.0
Other Autonomous Regions	12	12.0
Total	100	100.0

Source: Parent Firm Interviews

Table 19.4   Distribution of the sample firms' operations by organization type

Organization type of operation	Number of operations of the sample firms	Per cent
Wholly Owned Subsidiary	11	11.0
Majority Owned Joint Venture	10	10.0
50–50 Owned Joint Venture	7	7.0
Minority Owned Joint Venture	14	14.0
Sales Subsidiary	12	12.0
Assembly	2	2.0
Construction	17	17.0
Licensing Agreement	2	2.0
Technological co-operation	1	1.0
Export activities	24	24.0
Total	100	100.00

Source: Parent firm interviews

EMPIRICAL RESULTS

The empirical findings of this study are analysed both quantitatively and qualitatively. Table 19.5 gives brief descriptions of the countries examined, which will be used for the elaboration of quantitative analysis results. Although the verbal statements reported in Table 19.5 may not seem to be directly related to the political risk perceptions of executives, they can be used to draw inferences when assessing the descriptive statistics presented in the following section of the paper. These verbal statements also indicate that there are no major differences in terms of the risk faced by foreign investors in the countries examined.

Risk Factors Related to Production and Distribution in Central Asian Republics and Russia

This section includes the results of the two types of data analysis carried out on the collected data. The descriptive statistics and principal component analysis of production and distribution related risk factors are depicted in Tables 19.6 and 19.7.

Table 19.6 analyses the frequency of risk factors related to production and distribution in the subject countries. As can be seen from the ranking of

Table 19.5   Problems faced by Turkish investors in Newly Independent Central Asian Republics (qualitative assessment)

All Newly Independent Central Asian Republics (Uzbekistan, Kazakhstan, Turkmenistan, Krygyzstan, Azerbaijan)	• Depreciation of the rouble • Problems faced in obtaining financial guarantees • Quality problems faced in marketing goods transacted through counter-trade arrangements with these countries. • Foreign language problems and difficulties in accessing the region through telefax and telephone. • Increased cost of land transport due to unsafe state of roads, which increases transportation time. • Licence barriers faced in importing goods from CIS. • Inadequate financial resources. • Frequent changes in rules and regulations and unsettled state of legislation. • Minimum requirements for establishing a company. • Frequent changes in responsible persons and governmental offices. • Difficulties in finding appropriate companies. • Problems faced in customs tariffs. • Time-consuming Turkish Eximbank administrative procedures and lack of financial guarantee support from Turkish government. • Lack of a guarantee system which would protect foreign investors against political risks.
Uzbekistan	• Infancy of banking sector and unsettled state of the state bureaucracy • Difficulties in foreign country transfers. • Lack of information. • Cash payment difficulties.
Kazakhstan	• Lack of a Turkish commercial office in the country. • Problems faced in monetary transfers due to undeveloped banking system. • Shortage of foreign currencies. • Difficulties faced by investors in getting resident permits.
Kyrgyzystan	• Underdeveloped state of banking activities.
Azerbaijan	• Problems faced in obtaining letters of credit due to lack of correspondence relationships between Turkish and Azerbaijani financial institutions.

Table 19.6   Risk factors related to production and distribution (number of responses)

	I	II	III	IV	V	Mean	SD	Rank
Requirement to use local components	1	3	15	11	6	3.500	0.866	9
Requirement to employ local managers	4	6	15	6	6	3.108	1.082	5
Price controls	4	9	11	11	3	3.000	1.044	4
Production constraints	5	8	9	5	9	3.139	1.245	6
Intervention on prices	2	6	17	4	8	3.270	1.036	7
Intervention on wages	12	3	10	4	8	2.811	1.395	2
Trend to fix higher wages	2	7	12	8	7	3.306	1.040	8
Restrictions on distribution	5	8	15	4	5	2.892	1.082	3
Requirement to export a certain percentage of production	3	4	8	11	10	3.583	1.115	10
Increased production costs due to inflation	15	9	12	–	2	2.079	1.008	1

Note: Valid cases = 45. Not all reasons were relevant to each case. (The instrument used a Likert type scale with 5 points ranging from very negative to very positive where I = very negative and V = very positive.)

variables, the most frequently cited variables by Turkish firms operating in Central Asian republics and Russia are 'increased production costs due to high inflation rates', 'price controls', 'restrictions on distribution', and 'production constraints'. Throughout interviews, respondents' verbal statements indicated that the lack of distribution networks in Central Asia and Russia caused great difficulties.

Although descriptive statistics highlight certain aspects of the risks involved in operations in the countries examined, principal component analysis was used in order to explore the underlying dimensions of production and distribution related issues. The requirements of factor analysis were closely observed. The statistical tests and criteria for factor analysis adequately satisfied the requirements of factor analysis.[2] Principal component factor analysis (Table 19.7), generated three underlying dimensions of production and distribution related issues. The authors have described these factors by trying to capture the overall meaning of their components.

Table 19.7   Factor analysis: underlying dimensions of production and distribution related risk factors

Risk Indicator	Principal components			Eigen value
	1	2	3	
Issues Related to Local Policies				
Intervention on wages	0.83101			4.213
Requirement to export certain percentage	0.76703			
Trend to fix higher wages for FDI	0.71960			
Restrictions on distribution	0.61518			
Requirement to use local components	0.56460			
Pressures to employ local managers	0.55428	–0.45455		
Pricing and production policies				1.537
Intervention on prices		–0.93017		
Price controls		–0.85966		
Production constraints		–0.62619	–0.48218	
Inflationary Effect				1.057
Increased production costs due to inflation			0.71483	

N = 45   KMO = 0.64568   Total Variance = 68.1%
Bartlett's Test of Sphericity = 149.21879   Significance = 0.00000

- **Factor 1: Issues related to local wage policies** This factor correlates highly with six variables and explains 42.1% of the total variance. Variables associated with this factor are: 'intervention on wages', 'requirement to export a certain percentage of production', 'trend to fix higher wages for FDI', 'restrictions on distribution', 'requirement to use local components', and 'pressures to employ local managers'.
- **Factor 2: Issues related to pricing and production policies** The second factor relates to host governments' policies concerning pricing of goods and services. This factor correlates with three variables, which relate to two main areas. The first area is 'intervention on prices', and 'price controls'; the second area is related to 'production constraints'. This factor explains 15.4% of the total variance, and variables associated with the factor display a mixed composition.
- **Factor 3: Inflationary effect** The third factor relates to 'increases in production costs due to high rate of inflation', and correlates only with

one variable. As the descriptive statistics indicated, this factor is ranked as the most negative aspect of operations in host countries. This factor explains a further 10.6% of the total variance.

The critical risk factors emphasized most by respondents in the financing aspects of operations and the macroeconomic management of the host countries, were variables related to host country economic performance, such as 'host government's ability to have international loans', 'host country balance of payments', 'foreign debts of the host country', 'policies of local banks and financial institutions', and 'growth trend of GNP in the host countries'. These quantitative findings were also supported by the qualitative statements reported in Table 19.8.

Table 19.8   Risk factors related to financing and macroeconomic management (number of responses)

	I	II	III	IV	V	Mean	SD	Rank
Requirement to have local partners	5	9	7	12	6	3.128	1.209	15
Local tax rates in transferring goods	7	12	12	7	3	2.683	1.116	10
Foreign exchange control regulations	9	8	16	5	2	2.575	1.063	6
Restrictions on license payments	7	5	15	6	4	2.865	1.228	12
Restrictions on remitting profits & dividends	9	8	9	6	9	2.951	1.397	14
Requirement to contribute local infrastructure	2	14	10	12	1	2.897	0.924	13
Policies of local banks	21	8	8	1	3	1.951	1.166	1
Host government's ability to have international loans	19	9	6	5	2	2.073	1.194	2
Foreign debts of host countries	11	5	10	3	1	2.200	0.958	4
Host governments' balance of payments	15	10	12	2	1	2.100	0.995	3
Growth trend of GNP in host countries	8	12	9	5	4	2.605	1.158	7
Duties and excises	3	15	14	5	3	2.750	0.971	11
Requirement to reinvest	3	9	10	13	5	3.200	1.091	16
Late payments for completed projects	13	7	9	3	6	2.526	1.326	5
Interventions on expatriate managers' salaries	3	8	7	10	11	3.462	1.221	17
Special taxes for FDI	6	16	9	4	5	2.650	1.158	9
Fixing transfer price to enhance local taxation	4	8	15	9	4	2.650	1.055	8

Note: Valid cases = 45. Not all reasons were relevant to each case. (The instrument used a Likert type scale with 5 points ranging from very negative to very positive where I = very negative and V = very positive).

During an interview, an interviewee stated that 'the main problem with these countries is the shortage of foreign currency and lack of adequate financial institutions and banks. When we approach them for a transaction, by and large, their first offer is a counter-trade arrangement. Since we sell only wood processing machinery, we can not swap machinery with timber. In my opinion their immediate need is Turkish or other foreign investors who would invest in those markets'.

Another interviewee also pointed out similar problems and stated that 'if we had had a financial institution which would provide loans to those countries, we could have increased our trade volume'.

Exploratory factor analysis was also performed on variables for which descriptive statistics were presented in Table 19.8. The factor solution, containing 15 variables, satisfied the assumptions of the technique. The results depicted in Table 19.9 are based on this factor solution and indicate four main factors. These were:

- **Factor 1: Macro economic indicators** The first factor relates to the macroeconomic management of host countries. This factor correlates highly with three variables, namely, 'growth trend of GNP in host countries', 'foreign debts of host countries', and 'balance of payments'. This factor explains 29.5% of the total variance.

- **Factor 2: Issues related to transfer pricing** The second factor correlates highly with three variables: 'reinvestment regulations', 'fixing transfer prices to enhance local taxation', and 'intervention on expatriate managers' salaries'. The factor explains a further 19.1% of total variance.

- **Factor 3: Financial credibility** The third factor relates to another dimension of financial and macroeconomic management related issues, and correlates highly with five variables, which are all about financial credibility. These variables are 'policies of local banks and financial institutions', 'abilities of host governments to access international loans', 'foreign exchange control regulations', 'late payments for completed projects and services', and 'restrictions on profit repatriations'. Variables associated with this factor seem to be highly important for foreign investors in assessing political risk in the subject countries, and this factor explains a further 9.8% of total variance.

- **Factor 4: Taxation policy** The last factor extracted through principal component analysis relates to taxation policy in the host countries. This factor correlates highly with four variables, namely, 'local tax rates', 'custom duties and excises', 'special tax rates for foreign investors' and 'requirements to align with local partners'; it explains a further 8.3% of total variance.

Table 19.9　Factor analysis: underlying dimensions of finance and macroeconomic management related factors

Risk Indicators	Principal components				Eigen value
	1	2	3	4	
Macroeconomic Indicators					4.429
Growth trend of GNP	0.88323				
Foreign debts of host countries	0.85528				
Balance of payments	0.72871				
Issues Related to Transfer Pricing					2.864
Requirement to reinvest		0.93467			
Fixing transfer price to enhance local taxation		0.68491			
Intervention on expatriate managers' salaries		0.57715			
Financial Credibility					1.465
Policies of local banks & financial inst.			0.86635		
Ability to have access to international loans			0.69440		
Foreign exchange control regulations			0.68236		
Late payments			0.48082		
Restrictions on remitting profits			0.45118		
Taxation Policy					1.244
Local tax rates in transferring goods				−0.76246	
Duties and excises				−0.75004	
Special tax rates for FDI				−0.59584	
Requirement to have local partners				−0.53652	

N = 45　　　　　KMO = 0.511539　　　　Total Variance = 66.7%
Bartlett's Test of Sphericity = 253.96122　　Significance = 0.00000

The results depicted in Table 19.10 are based on interviewees' assessment of risk factors related to the host countries' social and political aspects. As the Table indicates, although 'host governments' attitude towards foreign direct investment', 'continuity in the host governments' policies', 'export controls', and 'intervention on expatriate managers' salaries' ranked as very positive, 'religious and cultural groups', 'danger of expropriation of assets', and 'ethnic and religious conflicts' in the subject host countries were assessed as very negative. In many cases, interviewees emphasized highly the desperate state of the working class in the subject countries. Unsettled disputes in many parts of the old Soviet Union, namely conflicts between Azerbaijan and Armenia, the Chechnyan war, and border conflicts between other republics, were emphasized greatly.

Table 19.10   Risk factors related to the host countries' social and political aspects (number of cases)

	I	II	III	IV	V	Mean	SD	Rank
Danger of expropriation of assets	9	8	12	7	3	2.677	1.154	5
Political ideology of the host country	2	18	9	9	3	2.829	1.020	11
Constraints on transferring capital and goods	8	12	8	6	6	2.750	1.274	10
Export controls	4	6	13	10	7	3.250	1.143	21
Pressures from municipal authorities	3	13	13	8	3	2.857	1.004	13
Political polarization in the host country	6	7	17	5	4	2.846	1.077	12
Restrictive actions of government in order to hold power	6	11	5	11	5	2.947	1.223	16
Ethnic and religious conflicts	6	11	13	9	1	2.700	1.004	7
Regional conflicts	7	10	11	8	3	2.744	1.122	8
Level of class conflicts in the society	3	12	17	8	–	2.750	0.818	9
Religious and cultural grouping	14	6	16	4	–	2.250	0.865	2
Xenophobia	3	5	15	16	1	3.175	0.901	19
Nationalist trends	11	11	11	7	–	2.350	1.012	3
Radical left trends	5	4	20	3	3	2.875	0.932	14
Host government's attitude towards foreign capital	2	4	12	14	7	3.513	1.073	20
Political stability of the host country	14	5	11	1	9	2.650	1.454	4
Continuity in the host government policies	7	10	9	4	9	2.949	1.330	17
Attitude of the host country towards FDI in the past	17	5	9	7	1	2.231	1.266	1
Attitude of political opposites towards FDI	2	12	15	8	2	2.897	0.899	15
Quality of host government's international relations	3	16	12	8	1	2.700	0.909	6
Pollution regulations	5	8	10	12	4	3.051	1.213	18

Note: Valid cases = 45. Not all reasons were relevant to each case. (The instrument used a Likert type scale with 5 points ranging from very negative to very positive where I = very negative and V = very positive.)

The 21 selected variables for which descriptive statistics were presented in Table 19.10, were data-reduced by principal component analysis with an oblique rotation using the SPSS/PC+ program (Norusis, 1988). The aim was to identify the underlying dimensions of this aspect. Five main factors were generated. The factor solution seems to fit the data quite well as it accounts for 71.4% of the total variance. Factors generated by the principal component process are reasonably well grouped. Various criteria and tests that were used also appear to confirm the appropriateness of factor analysis for data. There was no instability in the pattern of component loadings, although the ratio of observations (45 cases) to 21 variables was lower than the 4.0 figure advocated by Hair et al. (1979).

Table 19.11   Factor analysis: underlying dimensions of social and political aspects

Risk indicators	Principal components					Eigen value
	1	2	3	4	5	
Political Climate of the Host Country						4.912
Political stability of the host	0.87761					
Continuity in the host government's policies	0.86054					
Attitudes of political opposites towards FDI	0.84710					
Quality of host government's international relations	0.76426					
Pressure from local authorities	0.72263					
Restrictive actions of host governments to hold power	0.58696					
Issues Related to Ideological Changes						4.402
Radical left trends		0.76372				
Nationalist trends		0.70691				
Regional conflicts		0.70176				
Ethnic and religious conflicts		0.60210				
Xenophobia		0.59337				
Religious and cultural groupings		0.55499				
Attitudes of host countries towards FDI in the past		0.52734				

Issues Related to Property and Trade			2.598
Constraints on transferring goods and capital	0.86640		
Export controls	0.73628		
Danger of expropriation of assets	0.67780		
Transfer pricing to enhance local taxation	0.54492		
Societal and Ideological Conflicts			1.898
Ethnic and religious conflicts		−0.83952	
Level of class conflicts		−0.72609	
Political polarisation in the host countries		−0.63045	
Religious and cultural grouping		−0.52224	
Governmental Ideology and Regime			1.174
Political ideology of host countries			−0.83309
Restrictive actions of host governments to hold power			−0.53774
Nationalist trends			−0.56621

N = 45 KMO = 0.57860 Total explained variance = 71.4%
Bartlett's Test of Sphericity = 418.65621 Significance = 0.00000

Thus, five main factors were generated (Table 19.11). These factors were:

- **Factor 1: Political climate of the host country** This factor is highly correlated with variables such as 'political stability of host governments', 'continuity in host governments' policies', 'attitude of opposite parties towards FDI', 'quality of host governments' international relations', 'pressures from local authorities', and 'restrictive actions of host governments to hold power'. This factor also correlates reasonably with another variable, 'quality of host governments' international relations'. The first factor is therefore labelled 'political climate of the host country' and accounts for 23.4% of the total variance. This factor, by and large, explains the most important aspect of political risk in host countries.

- **Factor 2: Issues related to ideological changes and ethnic conflicts** The second factor relates to another dimension of the societal and political aspects of the host countries, and correlates highly with seven variables. These variables are all about ideological and ethnic issues; they are 'radical left trends', 'nationalist trends', 'regional conflicts', 'ethnic and religious conflicts', 'xenophobia', and 'religious and cultural groupings'. Variables associated with this factor seem to be highly important for foreign investors in assessing political risk in the subject countries, and this factor explains a further 21.0% of total variance.

- **Factor 3: Issues related to property and trade** The third factor correlates highly with four variables. These variables are 'constraints on transfer of goods and capital', 'export controls', 'danger of expropriation of assets', and 'transfer pricing to enhance local taxation'. Variables associated with this factor seem to display a mixed composition, but the factor can be referred to as 'issues related to trade and property'. This factor explains a further 12.4% of total variance.

- **Factor 4: Societal and ideological conflicts** The fourth factor also correlates highly with four variables. These variables, as can be seen from Table 19.11, are all concerned with societal and ideological conflicts in host countries. These variables include 'ethnic and religious conflicts', 'level of class conflicts', 'severe political polarization', and 'religious and cultural groupings'. This factor accounts for a further 9% of the total variance.

- **Factor 5: Governmental ideology and regime** The last factor correlates moderately with three variables, concerning governmental ideology and regime. Variables associated with this factor also seem to be very important for foreign investors in assessing political risk in the subject countries, and this factor explains a further 5.6% of total variance.

Risk factors related to the host countries' legal and administrative aspects are reported in Table 19.12. The major risk factors associated with operations in newly independent Central Asian Republics and Russia, as perceived by the respondents in this research, were concerned with 'the level of bureaucracy', 'extent of corruption', 'effectiveness of government departments', and 'legal system of host countries'. A similar conclusion can be drawn from verbal statements reported in Table 19.5. Throughout interviews with executives, it has very often been stated that a dramatic shift in mentality was needed. As an interviewee stated:

'Although I drew a very pessimistic portrait of the host country, one should mention that this is the result of a regime which has been ruling the country for 70 years. Despite all this, we all believe that they will pick it up very soon. What they need is a change in mentality and a new management philosophy.'

Table 19.12 Risk factors related to the host countries' legal and administrative aspects (number of responses)

	I	II	III	IV	V	Mean	SD	Rank
Legal system of host countries	8	14	12	3	3	2.475	1.065	3
Level of bureaucracy	19	10	3	5	2	2.000	1.167	1
Agreements and alliances with other countries	3	8	14	7	7	3.179	1.105	6
Choice between socialist system and market economy	2	6	7	13	10	3.605	1.098	9
Management style of the government	–	8	17	9	5	3.282	0.877	8
Effectiveness of governments' administrative levels	5	13	12	5	4	2.744	1.081	4
Extent of corruption	17	10	10	2	2	2.073	1.095	2
Relations between government and army	4	5	14	11	6	3.250	1.102	7
Employee–employer–trade union relations	8	2	13	14	3	3.050	1.166	5

Note: Valid cases = 45. Note all reasons were relevant to each case. (The instrument used a Likert type scale with 5 points ranging from very negative to very positive where I = very negative and V = very positive).

Factor analysis was applied to nine variables (Table 19.13), all related to legal and administrative practices in countries under consideration, aiming to explore quantitatively the underlying dimensions of such practices. Principal component analysis identified three main factors. These were:

- **Factor 1: Legal and administrative practices** The first factor (see Table 19.13) relates to host governments' legal and administrative practices. This alone explains 36.9% of the total variance, so this, by and large, can be considered as the most important aspect of foreign investors' risk perception. Variables associated with this factor are 'extent of corruption', 'management style of host governments', 'level of bureaucracy', 'effectiveness of government administration', and 'legal system in host countries'.

- **Factor 2: Agreements and alliances** The second factor relates to host governments' international agreements with external forces. The factor loads highly on two variables and explains 25.1% of the total variance. The third variable, which seems to be a double loaded variable, is more related to Factor 3.
- **Factor 3: Effects of past ideologies and environmental issues** Although this factor loads negatively on the first variable 'ideological choice between socialist system and market economy', factor loadings on 'employee–employer–trade union relations' and 'environmental legislation' are positive and relatively high. This factor explains a further 11.8% of the total variance after rotation.

Table 19.13   Factor analysis: underlying dimensions of legal and administrative aspects

Risk Indicators	Principal components			Eigen value
	1	2	3	
Legal and Administrative Practices				3.69
Extent of corruption	0.81518			
Management style of host government	0.80732			
Level of bureaucracy	0.80463			
Effectiveness of government administration	0.79764			
Legal system of host countries	0.75106			
Agreements and Alliances				2.51
Relations between government and army		0.86157		
Agreements and alliances with other countries		0.82841		
Employee–employer–trade union relations		0.71231		
Effects of Past Ideologies and Environmental Issues				1.18
Ideological choice between socialist system and market economy			–0.57755	
Environmental legislation			0.79393	
Employee–employer–trade union relations			0.60665	

N = 45   KMO = 0.63698   Total explained variance = 73.9%
Bartlett's Test of Sphericity = 186.13598   Significance = 0.00000

Table 19.14 analyses the methods used for assessing political risk by Turkish companies operating in the subject countries. 'Grand tours' involve executives of the subject firms visiting the potential host country to see the conditions at first hand and to meet government officials and businessmen. Throughout the interviews conducted, respondents cited executive level visits to the potential host country as most frequently used, and a most important approach for assessing risk.

Table 19.14   Risk assessment methods used for operations in the Central Asian Republics and Russia by Turkish firms (number of responses)

	I	II	III	IV	V	Mean	SD	Rank
Executive level visits (grand tours)	2	4	4	12	19	4.024	1.193	1
Information gathered from experts (old hands)	1	2	10	13	16	3.979	1.024	2
Information given by government offices and institutions	4	6	17	11	3	3.073	1.058	3
Delphi techniques	8	9	8	8	8	2.976	1.423	4
Information from international institutions and agencies	7	6	12	11	4	2.975	1.250	5

Note: Valid cases = 45. Not all reasons were relevant to each case. (The instrument used a Likert type scale with 5 points ranging from very negative to very positive where I = very negative and V = very positive.)

The second preferred method, most important for supplementing information collected through 'grand tours', was to collect information from experts (old hands). Typically, businessmen and diplomats with prior experience of the host country were among the 'experts' used.

The analysis in Table 19.14 indicates that 'Delphi techniques', rank as the third most important method in assessing political risk prior to an investment decision by Turkish companies. 'Delphi techniques' generally combine the checklist approach with the use of outside experts. Information gathering from home country government offices, and the use of international institutions and agencies for information (such as the BERI index) ranked as the least utilised methods for political risk assessment by the sample companies.

All 45 firms in the sample responded to the question asking about their attitudes towards certain strategies for managing political risk in the Central Asian and Russian markets. The question, as can be seen from Table 19.15, included 12 variables, and the interviewee was asked to rank these variables on a scale from 1 to 5 where 1 indicated the least effective strategic choice, and 5 represented the most important strategic choice for managing political risk in the given environment.

Table 19.15   Assessment of strategies for management of political risk (number of responses)

	I	II	III	IV	V	Mean	SE	Rank
Joint venture with a third country firm	9	6	13	7	6	2.878	1.345	7
Close relations with host government officials	2	2	2	13	23	4.262	1.083	1
Getting support from Turkish high level officials	3	7	10	17	4	3.293	1.101	3
Providing participation for local partners	–	6	13	16	7	3.571	0.941	2
Increasing size of operation	2	9	19	8	3	3.024	0.961	6
Supporting host government's policies	2	6	20	9	4	3.171	0.972	4
Contributions to election campaigns	12	10	17	1	1	2.244	0.994	12
Selecting high level managers from host nationals	3	13	14	9	1	2.800	0.966	9
Not insisting on initial compromises	6	4	26	3	1	2.725	0.905	8
Stopping profit repatriation	11	14	11	3	2	2.293	1.101	11
Transfer of majority shares to local partners	14	6	9	9	1	2.410	1.272	10
Leaving management of operation to local partners after a certain duration	4	6	13	13	3	3.128	1.105	5

Note: Valid cases = 45. Not all reasons were relevant to each case. (The instrument used a Likert type scale with 5 points ranging from very negative to very positive where I = very negative and V = very positive).

The attitudes emphasised most were strategies such as 'close relations with host government officials', 'getting support from high level Turkish officials', 'including local partners in projects', and 'leaving management of operation to local partners after a certain duration'. 'Transfer of majority shares to local partners', and 'firm's contribution to election campaigns in the host country' were, however, amongst the least emphasized strategies to manage political risk in the region. Other strategies such as 'selecting upper level managers from host nationals', 'increasing size of operation', and 'supporting host government's policies' were seen as moderately important.

As indicated in Table 19.15, a list of 12 variables was used to match the strategic choices as closely as possible. Since the selected variables included some near-duplicates within the domains of interest, the degree of association between variables was also analysed. The correlation matrix indicated medium correlations, which is expected to some extent, because of the interrelatedness of all the strategic choices. Nevertheless, this pattern of correlations suggested that a factor solution is a feasible way of data reduction in order to identify the underlying dimensions of political risk management strategies in given environments. Therefore, the underlying dimensions of risk management

Table 19.16 Factor analysis: underlying dimensions of social and political aspects

Strategy clusters	Principal components				Eigen value
	1	2	3	4	
Support Strategies					4.268
Increasing the size of operations	0.83449				
Supporting host government policies	0.75451				
Leaving management of operations to local partners after a certain duration	0.57459				
Not insisting on initial compromises	0.54106				
Providing participation for local partners	0.54036				
Selection of high level executives from host nationals	0.50033				
Lobbying Activities in Host Countries					1.794
Close relations with host government officials		0.87451			
Participation of local partners		0.71474			
Stopping profit repatriation		–0.51801	0.51430		
Lobbying Activities at Home					1.179
Getting support of home government high level officials			0.76189		
Selection of high level executives from host nationals			0.57274		
Control Strategies					1.084
Joint venture with a third country firm				0.86797	
Transfer of majority shares to local partners				0.73821	
Contributions to election campaigns				0.56507	

N = 45 KMO = 0.62888	Total explained variance = 69.4%
Bartlett's Test of Sphericity = 184.50719	Significance = 0.00000

strategies identified in this section may provide further insights into factors affecting strategy formulation in transitional environments.

As indicated in Table 19.16, four main factors were generated to identify the underlying dimensions of political risk management strategies. These were:

- **Factor 1: Support strategies** The first factor (see Table 19.16) relates to support for host governments' policies and working in harmony with host governments. This factor explains 35.6% of the total variance. Variables associated with this factor are 'supporting host government policies', 'increasing the size of operation', 'participation of local partners', 'leaving management of operations to local partners', and 'selection of executives from host nationals'.

- **Factor 2: Lobbying activities in host countries** The second factor accounts for 15.0% of the variance of the rotated factors. The factor shows that this is the most important strategy by which foreign investors can manage the political risks faced in the subject countries. Variables associated with this factor are 'close relations with the host government officials', and 'providing participation for local partners'.
- **Factor 3: Lobbying activities at home** The third factor is related to foreign investors lobbying activities at home and executive selection issues. This factor explains a further 9.8% of the total variance. Two variables correlate highly with this factor. These are 'getting the support of home government high level officials', and 'selection of high level executives from host nationals'.
- **Factor 4: Equity control strategies** The last factor extracted through principal component analysis is also partly related to lobbying activities, but the main contributors to this factor can be described as equity control strategies. These variables are 'joint venture with a third country firm', and 'transfer of majority shares to local partners'. This factor accounts for a further 9% of rotated total variance.

As discussed in the introduction to this paper, five of these newly independent states are of Turkic origin, and Turkish dialects are spoken in these countries. In order to identify the proximities between these newly independent states and Turkey, respondents were asked to rank whether 'cultural', and 'linguistic', 'psychological' proximities had an impact on protecting against political risk. The main objective of this question was to explore the idea that managers accustomed to similar values might feel familiar with the environment of the host country, and therefore such a firm might have some advantages over its other foreign competitors.

The question analysed in Table 19.17 aims to explore whether cultural or other variables are more influential in managing political risk and operating effectively in given countries. As can be seen from the ranking of variables, respondents placed more emphasis on 'close relations between leaders of home and host countries' and 'bilateral agreements for the protection of investments'. Cultural, religious and linguistic proximity, however, seem to have a minimal impact. Therefore, this analysis implies that, although cultural familiarity is very important in managing day to day operations, the quality of government relations between home and host countries is much more influential in terms of managing political risk.

Table 19.17   Advantages perceived by Turkish firms in managing political risk (Central Asia only) (number of responses)

	I	II	III	IV	V	Mean	SD	Rank
Cultural proximity	2	5	7	15	13	3.762	1.165	3
Psychological proximity	4	4	8	13	13	3.643	1.284	4
Close relations between home and host countries (leaders)	–	7	6	10	19	3.976	1.137	2
Language similarities	3	4	14	7	13	3.561	1.246	5
Bilateral agreements to protect investments	–	2	9	17	13	4.000	0.866	1

Note: Valid cases = 45. Not all reasons were relevant to each case. (In measuring these variables a five point scale was used where I = Least important and, V = Most important advantages.)

SUMMARY AND CONCLUDING REMARKS

This paper has explored the political risk perceptions of Turkish direct investors and contractors in newly independent Central Asian Republics and Russia. Although the sample is small, tracking the perceptions of existing companies offers valuable insights on how to deal with political risk in these countries. Some explanations for the political risk management of Turkish companies have been offered, but further analysis is required before definitive conclusions can be drawn. There also seems to be some scope for using the experience of Turkish companies operating in Central Asian Republics to refine international business theory, so that political risk management strategies in less developed countries can be understood.

The major findings of this study are:

- Three main factors explain the financial risk perceptions of Turkish investors operating in subject countries. These factors are 'issues related to local policies', 'pricing and production policies', and 'inflationary effect'.
- The study also highlights risk factors attributable to the social and political aspects of the host countries. These factors are labelled 'political climate of host countries', 'issues related to changes in ideology', 'ideologies related to property and trade', 'societal and ideological changes', and 'governmental ideology and regime'.
- Risk factors attributable to macroeconomic management and the credibility of host government policies are labelled 'trends of macroeconomic indicators', 'issues related to transfer pricing', financial credibility of host governments', and 'taxation policies and taxation related issues'.

- The factor analysis used for analysing data quantitatively also revealed that political risk factors attributable to the legal and administrative regime of host countries can be clustered in to three main groups. These factors were 'legal and administrative practices', 'agreements and alliances', and 'effects of past ideologies'.

- The study also identified four main strategy clusters which might be used for managing political risk in the countries examined. These factors were 'support strategies', 'lobbying activities in host countries', 'lobbying activities at home', and 'flexible approach to control of operations'.

NOTES

1. This research has been partly funded by Inonu University research fund.
2. The correlation matrix indicated that more than half the coefficients were at a level greater than 0.4. Bartlett's test of sphericity, which indicates the relationship amongst variables, was computed at 149.21, with an associated significance level of 0.0000, which confirmed the relationship. The measure of sampling adequacy, Kaiser-Meyer-Olkin (KMO), was computed at 0.645, which is fairly adequate. The ratio of cases to variables is more than three to one, which indicates the adequacy of the sample for factor analysis. Communality of variables is satisfactorily high, which indicates that a great deal of variance is explained by common factors, and therefore variables have common dimensions.

BIBLIOGRAPHY

Aharoni, Y. (1966) *The Foreign Direct Investment Decision Process*, Graduate School of Business Administration, Harvard University.

Boddewyn, J. (1986) *International Political Strategy: A Fourth Generic Strategy?* Paper Presented at the Meeting of the Academy of International Business, London.

Boddewyn, J. (1988) 'Political Aspects of MNE Theory', *Journal of International Business Studies*, **19** (3) pp. 341–64.

Caves, R. and Jones, R. (1985) *World Trade and Payments*, Boston: Little, Brown & Co.

Czinkota, M. and Ricks, D.A. (1981) 'Export Assistance: Are We Supporting the Best Programs'. *Columbia Journal of World Business*, **16** (2) pp. 73–8.

Doz, Y. (1986) 'Government Policies and Global Industries', in M. Porter (ed.), *Competition in Global Industries*, Boston: Harvard Business School, pp. 225–66.

Encarnation, D. and Wells, L. (1986) 'Competitive Strategies in Global Industries: A View From Host Governments', in M. Porter (ed.), *Competition in Global Industries*, Boston: Harvard Business School, pp. 267–90.

Hair, J.F., Anderson, R.E., Tatham, R.L. and Grablowsky, B.J. (1979) *Multivariate Data Analysis*, Tulsa, Oklahoma: PPC Books.

Kobrin, S.J. (1979) 'Political Risk: A Review and Reconsideration', *Journal of International Business Studies*, Spring/Summer, pp. 67–80.

Kobrin, S.J. (1982) *Managing Political Risk Assessment*. Berkeley, CA: University of California Press.

Kogut, B. (1985) 'Designing Global Strategies: Profiting from Operational Flexibilities', *Sloan Management Review*, **26** (1) pp. 27–38.

La Palombara, J. and Blank, S. (1977) *Multinational Companies in Comparative Perspective*, The Conference Board.

Moran, T. (1985) 'International Political Risk Assessment, Corporate Planning, and Strategies to Offset Political Risk', in T. Moran (ed.), *Multinational Corporations: The Political Economy of Foreign Direct Investment*, Lexington, MA: Lexington Books, pp. 107–11.

Norusis, M.J. (1988) SPSS/PC +: *Advanced Statistics Guide*, V2.0, Chicago: SPSS Inc.

Pfeffer, J. (1987) 'Bringing the Environment back in: The Social Context of Business Strategy', in D.Teece (ed.) *The Competitive Challenge: Strategies for Industrial Innovation and Renewal*, Cambridge, MA: Ballinger Publishing, pp. 119–35.

Porter, M. and Fuller, M. (1986) 'Coalitions and Global Strategy'. In M. Porter (ed.) *Competition in Global Industries*, Boston: Harvard Business School, pp. 315–44.

Poynter, T.A. (1982) 'Government Intervention in Less Developed Countries: The Experience of Multinational Companies', *Journal of International Business Studies* **13** (1) pp. 9–25.

Prahalad, C. and Doz, Y. (1987) *The Multinational Mission: Balancing Local Demands and Global Vision*. New York : The Free Press.

Preble, J., Rau, P. and Reichel, A. (1988) 'The Environmental Scanning Practices of US. Multinationals in the late 1980s'. *Management International Review*, **28** (4) pp. 4–14.

Root, F.R. (1972) 'Analysing Political Risks in International Business', in Kapoor, A., and Grub, P. (eds), *Multinational Enterprise in Transition*, Darwin Press.

Sethi, S. and Luther, K., (1986) 'Political Risk Analysis and Direct Foreign Investment: Some Problems of Definition and Measurement'. *California Management Review*, **28** pp. 57–68.

Van Agtmael, A.W. (1976), 'How Business has Dealt with Political Risk', *Financial Executive*, **15** p. 27.

Wicks Kelly, M.E. and Philippatos, G.C. (1982) 'Comparative Analysis of Foreign Investment Evaluation Practices used by US Based Manufacturing Multinational Companies', *Journal of International Business Studies*, Winter, pp. 19–42.

PART 5

Integration Strategies

20. Integration within MNCs: from multidomestic to global and transnational firms?

Anne-Wil Harzing

Many of the contributions in this book refer to the role of multinational companies (MNCs) as important drivers of integration between countries. What is exactly meant by integration within MNCs often remains unclear, however. This chapter therefore explores the various ways in which MNCs integrate their activities across countries in somewhat more detail and differentiates between various types of MNCs in this respect. It also provides evidence as to the increase of MNC integration over the past decade.

INTEGRATION WITHIN MULTINATIONAL COMPANIES

A high level of integration of activities within MNCs implies a strong interdependence of various sub-units with the MNC with each other. According to Kobrin (1991), sub-units in an integrated firm should be seen as: '... incomplete economic entities [whose] value is, in large part, derived from relationships with others' (Kobrin, 1991, p. 19). Consequently, as Kobrin also indicates, a high level of integration should by necessity lead to a high level of intra-firm flows of resources, simply because the different sub-units cannot function without inputs from other sub-units. Integration within MNCs is therefore usually operationalized at the level of intra-firm resource flows.

Bartlett and Ghoshal differentiate these intra-firm resource flows into three main categories: raw materials, parts, components and finished goods; funds, skills and other scarce resources; and intelligence, ideas and knowledge (Bartlett and Ghoshal, 1987). Since only product data are available across a wide number of firms, intra-company trade (flows of raw materials, parts, components and finished goods) has become the standard way of measuring integration (see Kobrin, 1991 for a summary of studies which use this measure of integration). Knowledge, ideas and technology are then assumed to be embodied in products. There is one vehicle of intra-firm flows, however, which is consistently ignored in this way: the transfer of people within MNCs. Knowledge, skills, ideas and intelligence could easily be argued to be embodied in people rather than in products. It would therefore seem worthwhile to further explore the transfer of people within MNCs as a way of integration.

When thinking about the transfer of people within MNCs, the focus is usually on expatriation: the transfer of personnel from one part (usually headquarters) to another part of the MNC (usually one of the subsidiaries) for an extended period of time (usually 2–5 years). Expatriates can be sent out for quite a number of reasons. A major reason for expatriate assignments is the transfer of specific technological or managerial knowledge. In the author's research (Harzing, forthcoming), knowledge transfer was cited as the most important function of expatriation. The same result was found in a number of German studies over a substantial period of time (Pausenberger and Noelle, 1977; Kumar and Steinman, 1986; Groenewald and Sapozhnikov, 1990, Kumar and Karlhaus, 1992). Relatedly, expatriates are often sent out because no qualified local personnel is available. In this case the specific skills of the expatriate are transferred to the local subsidiary, often with the ultimate aim for local personnel to acquire these skills themselves. The transfer of knowledge and skills through expatriates would therefore seem to be a major integrative force across the different sub-units in the MNCs.

In addition, expatriates can be used to improve communication channels between different sub-units of the MNCs, so that the transfer of ideas and information becomes more effective and efficient. This is found to be especially important when cultural and linguistic barriers are high, as is the case in the interaction between Western/Japanese headquarters and Japanese/Western subsidiaries (Harzing, forthcoming). This function of expatriation is therefore likely to improve the functioning of the MNC as an integrated system.

Finally, expatriates can be seen as the bearers of corporate culture and can play a role in transferring this culture across different subsidiaries. In subsidiaries with an expatriate as a managing director and a higher number of expatriates in the top five jobs, managers were shown to be more likely to share the company's main goals and values (Harzing, forthcoming). Having a common corporate culture will undoubtedly facilitate the functioning of the MNC as an integrated system.

In sum, expatriates transfer managerial and technical knowledge, ideas, information and culture across the different sub-units of the MNC and intra-firm people flows should therefore be taken into account as an important addition to intra-firm trade flows when assessing the extent of integration within MNCs. The next section of this chapter will therefore look at the level of intra-firm flows with regard to *both* products (including parts and components) *and* people for different types of MNCs.

INTEGRATION WITHIN DIFFERENT TYPES OF MNCS

MNC Typologies

Within the field of international business or international economics, the terms multinational, global and transnational are often used interchangeably. The term transnational company (TNC) is usually preferred to indicate a company operating in different countries in a more or less integrated way. Within the field of international management however, these three terms have each come to represent a more specific meaning since the work of Bartlett and Ghoshal (1989, 1992). They offer a typology describing four types of MNCs (global, multinational, international and transnational) that vary in their (industry) environment, strategy, structure and processes. *Global* companies operate in industries with rather standardized consumer needs, which make the realization of economies of scale very important. Since price competition is very important, the dominant strategic requirement is efficiency, and these companies therefore integrate and rationalize their production to produce their standardized products in a very cost-efficient manner. *Multidomestic* companies are the complete reverse of global companies. Products or services are differentiated to meet differing local demands, and policies are differentiated to conform to differing governmental and market demands. Local demand is determined by cultural, social and political differences between countries. In *international* companies the critical success factor is the ability to transfer knowledge (particularly technology) to units abroad. It is a process of sequential diffusion of innovations that were originally developed in the home market, thus following the classic international product life cycle (Vernon, 1966). In a sense, a *transnational* company combines characteristics of the three previous types of companies, in that it tries to respond simultaneously to the sometimes conflicting strategic needs of global efficiency, national responsiveness and world-wide learning. In this type of company, expertise is spread throughout the organization, and subsidiaries can serve as a strategic centre for a particular product-market combination.

A review of 15, mostly prescriptive, typologies of MNC strategy/structure showed that all authors distinguished a global and a multinational type of MNC, all but two distinguished a third kind of strategy with elements of both global and multinational MNCs (called, for example, hybrid, dual, multifocal, or transnational); but only very few identified a type of MNC comparable to Bartlett and Ghoshal's international firm (see Harzing, forthcoming). Also an empirical test of the Bartlett and Ghoshal typology (Leong and Tan, 1993) showed that the international type of company did not differ significantly from the transnational type of company. In this chapter, we will therefore limit ourselves to the three most clearly distinguishable types of MNCs: global, multinational and transnational. We prefer, however, to replace the term multinational with multidomestic, and use the term multinational (MNC) as the generic term for a company operating in different countries.

Figure 20.1 portrays these three different types of MNCs visually and shows very clearly that the three models differ systematically with regard to their level and type of integration or interdependence. In multidomestic companies, the different sub-units of the MNC operate very independently from each other. Subsidiaries tend to operate as stand alone companies and their links with the local environment are much stronger than their links with the parent company. Headquarters do not play a dominant role in this type of MNC. In the global MNC however, there are very strong links between headquarters and subsidiaries, with subsidiaries being almost completely dependent on headquarters for resources. In this type of company, headquarters do play a dominant role and subsidiaries are seen as simple appendages of headquarters. In the transnational MNC, headquarters and subsidiaries all form part of an interdependent network; they are in a sense all dependent on each other. Headquarters does not necessarily play a dominant role, since subsidiaries can have strategic responsibility for particular product/market combinations.

Bartlett and Ghoshal assume a chronological development in these different types of MNCs, although this development should by no means be seen in a deterministic way. Between the two world wars, MNCs could predominantly be characterized as multidomestic, operating in an independent and loosely coupled way to cope with protectionism, high tariff and logistical barriers and

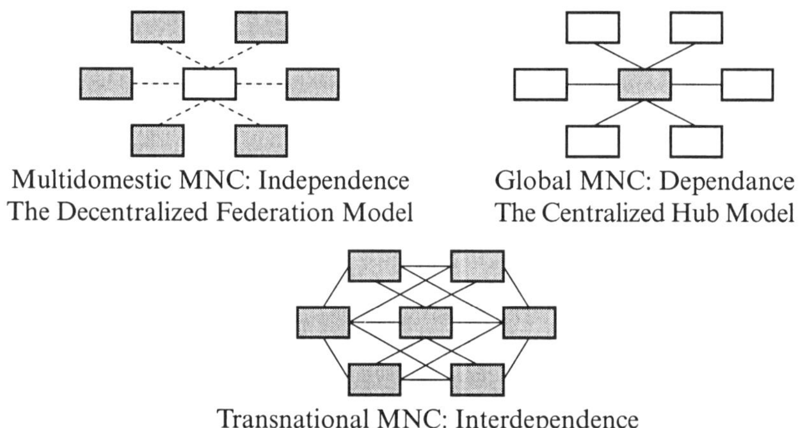

Source: Adapted from Bartlett and Ghoshal 1992

Figure 20.1   Three different organizational models of MNCs

differences in consumer preferences. In the fifties, American technological superiority led to more international types of MNCs following the international product life cycle. Successive reductions in trade barriers in the sixties and seventies, declining communication and transport costs and homogenizing consumer preference then led to the global era. In this era, global companies with their centralized structures and large-scale intensive production facilities dominated the scene. The eighties, however, saw an increasing concern on the part of host countries about the impact of MNCs on their balance of trade, national employment levels, and on the international competitiveness of their economies. Also, flexible manufacturing reduced the minimum efficient scale. These developments have therefore led to a need for transnational firms which comply with demands for global efficiency, local responsiveness and world-wide learning at the same time (Bartlett, 1986, Bartlett and Ghoshal, 1989).

Although Bartlett and Ghoshal's typology has been very influential in the field of international management, it combines prescriptive elements with the results of empirical research in a very limited number of MNCs. We have therefore empirically tested this typology on a larger scale and built configurations of MNCs which include a large number of headquarters and subsidiary characteristics, such as age, size, the type and role of the subsidiary, the use of various control mechanisms, the level of multinationality and diversification, the level of local production, R&D and product modification, intra-company sales and purchases, and the presence of expatriates. In this chapter, we will focus on the last two aspects of these configurations only: the level of intra-company sales and purchases (product flows) and the presence of expatriates (people flows).[1]

Data Collection

Data for the study were collected by means of a large-scale international mail survey. The survey involved mailing questionnaires to Chief Executive Officers and Human Resource Managers at the headquarters of 122 MNCs and to the managing directors of some 1650 wholly-owned subsidiaries of these multinationals in 22 different countries. This chapter only uses the data collected at subsidiary level. A complete description of the mailing procedures and response rates can be found in Harzing (1998a). The overall response rate at subsidiary level was 20%, varying from 7.1% in Hong Kong to 42.1% in Denmark. Table 20.1 summarizes the number of respondents by industry, country of location of headquarters and subsidiary country.

The total number of 287 subsidiary responses represents 104 different headquarters (85% of our population) and the number of responses per headquarters varies from one to eleven. With regard to the representativeness of our sample compared to the population of MNCs as a whole, we can remark that nearly two thirds of the Global Fortune 500 companies operate in the industries included in our sample. However, our population and our sample are

Table 20.1   Number of respondents by industry, subsidiary country and headquarters country

Industry	Number of respondents	Subsidiary country	Number of respondents
Electronics, electr. equipment	41	Argentina	4
Computers, office equipment	26	Austria	8
Motor vehicles and parts	30	Belgium	14
Petroleum (products)	20	Brazil	15
Food and Beverages	34	Denmark	16
Pharmaceutical	46	Finland	8
Paper (products)	25	France	14
Chemical (products)	55	Germany	16
Various	10	Hong Kong	5
		Ireland	11
Country of location of headquarters	**Number of respondents**	Italy	21
		Japan	16
		Mexico	10
Finland	23	Netherlands	25
France	26	Norway	13
Germany	32	Singapore	10
Japan	38	Spain	14
Netherlands	16	Sweden	11
Sweden	41	Switzerland	14
Switzerland	31	UK	25
UK	25	USA	13
USA	55	Venezuela	4

not completely representative of Global Fortune 500 firms with regard to headquarters countries. Although the percentage of American firms in our sample comes very close to the percentage of American firms in the Global Fortune 500, the percentage of Japanese firms in our sample is somewhat lower (17.3% versus 27%). Considerably higher is our percentage of European firms (52.9% versus 32%). This imbalance was created on purpose, however, in order to be able to analyse data at the level of the different European countries. With regard to subsidiary countries, we can remark that six of the eight commonly distinguished cultural clusters (see, for example, Ronen and Shenkar, 1985) are present in reasonable numbers in our sample (Anglo, Germanic, Nordic, Latin European, Far East and Latin American). Further, the 22 countries represented in our survey include a majority of the developed Western countries and a selection of Asian and Latin American countries.

Measures

Since no questions were readily available to measure the organizational model of MNCs, we created our own questions, based on the characteristics of the different types of firms as described in Bartlett and Ghoshal (1989, 1992b). Nine statements were constructed which measured aspects of organizational structure, the role of subsidiaries, the dominant competitive strategy, and so on. The organizational model of MNCs was – as most of the other concepts – measured at subsidiary level. Subsidiary managers, however, might not be fully informed of the organizational model applied by the MNC as a whole, and their opinions might be coloured by the specific circumstances of the subsidiary. The multi-rater reliability of the organizational model concepts was therefore first assessed. Since this multi-rater reliability was found to be acceptable for all but six companies, subsidiary scores for the remaining companies were aggregated at headquarters level. Subsequently, the nine items measuring specific elements of the organizational models were subjected to factor analysis and reduced to three factors which could be clearly interpreted as representing the different organizational models. Based on the factor scores for each of the three factors, each headquarters was thereafter assigned a dominant organizational model. To be accepted as a dominant organizational model, the factor score for this model had to be positive and higher than the scores for the two other models, while the difference from the next highest factor score had to be at least 10% of the spread in factor scores for the original factor. A further six companies were removed at this stage, because no dominant organizational model could be identified.

Product flows were operationalized using the percentage of intra-company sales and purchases (including parts and components) in relation to total sales and purchases. In order to be able to distinguish between *de*pendence and *inter*dependence as indicated in Figure 20.1 above, respondents were to differentiate between their purchases from or sales to *headquarters* on the one hand and *other subsidiaries* on the other hand. Three questions were used to assess the level of people flows, that is, the presence of expatriates in a given subsidiary. These questions asked respectively for the nationality of the managing director of the subsidiary, the number of top five jobs in the subsidiary held by expatriates and the total number of expatriates working in the subsidiary.

Results

Table 20.2 summarizes the results of our study with regard to the levels of intra-company product flows and intra-company people flows (expatriation) in different types of MNCs. Table 20.2 also shows that, as would be expected, multidomestic companies show the lowest level of product flows, while both

Table 20.2   Product and people flows in different types of MNCs

Organizational model	Multi-domestic	Global	Trans-national	Chi-square	Pairs significantly different at 0.05 (2-tailed)
Number of headquarters (92)	30	40	22		
Number of subsidiaries (247)	64	115	70		
Product flows					
• Total intra-company sales and purchases in this type of MNC as a percentage of total sales and purchases	27%	45%	40.7%	27.778, 0.000	G&T > M
• Intra-company sales and purchases between subsidiaries and headquarters in this type of MNC as a percentage of total sales and purchases	10.9%	24.3%	17.2%	25.017, 0.000	G > T > M
• Intra-company sales and purchases between subsidiaries in this type of MNC as a percentage of total sales and purchases	16.1%	20.7%	23.5%	5.335, 0.069	T > M
People flows					
• Total number of expatriates in subsidiary	3.5	11.8	12.3	15.527, 0.000	G&T > M
• % of subsidiaries having an expatriate as managing director	27%	42%	44%	4.320, 0.115	G&T > M
• Number of expatriates in top-5 subsidiary jobs	0.91	1.63	1.37	11.210,0 0.004	G&T > M

global and transnational companies have a level of product flows that is significantly higher. This is true for both product flows between subsidiaries and headquarters and for product flows between different subsidiaries, although the difference is larger for the former. Consistent with the models put forward above, transnational companies have the highest level of product flows between subsidiaries, while global companies have the highest level of product flows between headquarters and subsidiaries. People flows in terms of the level of expatriation are clearly higher in global and transnational firms. On all three measures of expatriate presence, subsidiaries of global and transnational firms score significantly higher than subsidiaries of multidomestic firms.

This section has shown that we can clearly distinguish different types of MNCs which depict different levels of both product flows and people flows. On each of the six measures, global and transnational MNCs show a higher level of intra-company flows and hence integration than multidomestic MNCs. Would these differences have any impact on the level of integration in the MNC population as a whole, and more specifically, can we distinguish a change in the level of MNC integration over the past decades? This is what we will discuss in somewhat more detail in the next section.

INCREASING LEVELS OF MNC INTEGRATION?

As was shown in the previous section, global and transnational MNCs show higher levels of intra-company resource flows and hence integration than multidomestic MNCs. According to Bartlett and Ghoshal (1989, 1992), multidomestic type of organizational models are most suitable for the environmental conditions which were dominant in the period between the two world wars. Recent developments in many industries would require a change to a global or preferably transnational type of MNCs. If MNCs followed these prescriptions, even if there were a time-lag effect in this, and changed their strategies, structures and policies to conform to a more global or transnational type of firm, we would expect an increasing level of intra-company flows and hence integration in the overall population of MNCs. This is a rather indirect way, however, of supporting the claim for an increasing level of integration. More directly comparable data for both product flows and people flows at different points in time would be preferable and will be discussed below.

For product flows a useful source of data on intra-firm trade is the Benchmark Survey on US Direct Investment Abroad published every four years by the Bureau of Economic Analysis (BEA).[2] These data are aggregated at the industry level. Kobrin (1991) used data from the 1982 Benchmark Survey to measure the level of what he called 'transnational integration'. To measure integration the affiliate sales to *foreign* affiliates, affiliate sales to parents, and parent exports to affiliates are calculated. This total is presented as a ratio to all foreign affiliate sales plus parent exports for majority owned non-bank affiliates of non-bank parents (Kobrin, 1991: 21).

$$\frac{\text{affil to affil} + \text{affil to par} + \text{par to affil}}{\text{affil sales} + \text{par exports}}$$

Applying exactly the same formula, we calculated the same figures for 1994, using the preliminary results from the 1994 Benchmark Survey.[3] Table 20.3 summarizes these data for the seven industries which were included in the study described above and for which data for both 1982 and 1994 were available.[4] As can be clearly seen, the level of intra-firm trade has increased in each of the seven

Table 20.3   Level of intra-firm trade in eight industries, 1982 and 1994

Industry	1982* Intra-firm trade[+]	1982 Rank	1994** Intra-firm trade[+]	1994 Rank	1982* Inter-sub trade[++]	1982 Rank	1994** Inter-sub trade[++]	1994 Rank
Household appliances	0.107	5	0.363	3	0.390	5	0.475	5
Computers and office machines	0.384	2	0.479	2	0.500	4	0.531	3/4
Motor vehicles and parts	0.435	1	0.491	1	0.330	7	0.391	7
Food products	0.090	7	0.194	6/7	0.590	1	0.646	1
Pharmaceuticals	0.212	4	0.348	4	0.560	2	0.610	2
Paper products	0.099	6	0.190	6/7	0.350	6	0.418	6
Industrial chemicals	0.258	3	0.301	5	0.520	3	0.530	3/4
Totals	0.226		0.338		0.463		0.514	

Notes:
*   Data for 1982 come from Kobrin (1991), based on the 1982 Benchmark Survey of US Direct Investment Abroad (published in 1985)
**   Data for 1994 come from the 1994 Benchmark Survey of US Direct Investment Abroad, Preliminary Results (published in 1997)
+   Intra-firm trade as percentage of total international sales
++   Inter-subsidiary trade as percentage of total intra-firm trade

industries. On average the level of intra-firm trade has increased by nearly 50%. In his article Kobrin (1991) made some very cautious comparisons between 1982 and 1986 and concluded that overall the level of intra-firm trade had risen by 16% between 1982 and 1986. He also indicated a marked increase in integration between 1967 and 1977 (according to Bartlett and Ghoshal the heydays of the global company), but relatively little change between 1977 and 1982.

Combined, these data therefore clearly indicate a continuous rise in intra-firm trade or integration. In the highly integrated computer and automobile industry, around 50% of international sales are now intra-company sales. Household appliances, pharmaceuticals and industrial chemicals form a second group with around a third of their international sales not crossing company borders. Remarkably, even in industries which used to be typical multidomestic industries (such as the food and paper industry) – in which subsidiaries operated very much as stand alone companies that produced for the local market only – a fifth of the international sales are now intra-company sales. It is remarkable that the rank-order in intra-company sales has changed very little over the years; only household appliances and industrial chemicals swapped places.

The second part of Table 20.3 shows that the level of trade between subsidiaries (as opposed to trade between subsidiaries and headquarters) became slightly more important between 1982 and 1994. In 1994 more than half of the intra-firm international trade was performed *between* subsidiaries of an MNC. The similarity in ranking between 1982 and 1994 is even more remarkable than in the case of overall intra-firm international trade. MNCs in all industries have increased their level of inter-subsidiary trade and the rank order for the different industries has virtually stayed the same.

Our own data on intra-company sales and purchases date from 1996. The way in which these data were gathered, however, differs considerably from the way they were gathered by the BEA. The BEA collected factual data from more than 2658 US MNCs and 21300 foreign affiliates. Our data were collected by asking the managing directors of some 280 subsidiaries for an estimate of the level of intra-company sales and purchases. Also, the location of the headquarters of these subsidiaries was not limited to the US, as can be seen in Table 20.1. Finally, the way in which the percentage of intra-company trade was calculated is slightly different (it omits the *par exports* in the formula, resulting in a denominator that is about 15%–20% smaller). Even so, the similarity in both the overall level of intra-company trade (39.7% or 31.8%–33.7% when the method of calculation is adjusted) and the rank-order for the different industries is remarkable (when compared to 1994 only the numbers 1 and 2 and numbers 3 and 4 swapped places, so no industry changed more than 1 place on the rank-order). The level of inter-subsidiary trade in our study lies between 52 and 53% and thus resembles the 1994 BEA data very closely.

Since our data were collected from MNCs headquartered in different countries, we can also make a comparison between the level of intra-company trade in MNCs originating in different countries. The level of intra-company trade in US MNCs (40.1%) lies very close to the overall average of 39.7%. This overall average, however, hides quite substantial differences between the other countries. Japanese (53.3%), Swiss (48.4%), and to a lesser extent German (44.7%) and Swedish MNCs (42.9%), score above the overall average, while the reverse is true for Finnish (18.9%), Dutch (24.1%), British (30.9%) and French (33.7%) MNCs. These differences are to a large extent caused by the fact that trade between headquarters and subsidiaries is much more intensive for the former group than for the latter. These differences are likely to be mainly due to an industry effect, however; for example, nearly 60% of the Japanese subsidiaries in the sample were operating in the highly integrated automobile or computer industry, while over 60% of the Finnish subsidiaries were operating in the paper industry. In this case, the common research practice of studying mainly US MNCs might not have been a major limitation, since they span a relatively large area of industrial activities.

With regard to product flows, increasing levels of integration seem to be clearly apparent from the data available. Unfortunately there is no official institution which systematically collects data on intra-company people flows, that is, expatriation. Since 1992, however, The American NFTC (National Foreign Trade Council), in collaboration with Windham International, publishes a yearly Global Relocation Trends Survey Report, which contains data on the expatriate practices of some 130–140 American and non-American MNCs. Each of the five reports published so far indicates an overall growth in the number of expatriates. Typically, about 50–60 of the companies report an increase in the number of expatriates each year, while only about 10% report a decrease. Also each year companies expect the number of expatriates to grow even further. Unfortunately, we cannot ascertain how much of this growth in expatriate numbers is caused by increased international activity. The number of expatriates may be increasing simply because companies set up new subsidiaries, which does not necessarily result in increasing levels of integration within the MNC as a whole, although this might tie additional countries to the MNC network. The fact, however, that in our own study the various measures of expatriate presence in a subsidiary were positively correlated with the level of intra-company trade portrayed by that subsidiary, might lead to the conclusion that both product and people flows within MNCs are becoming more intensive.

CONCLUSION

This chapter investigated the phenomenon of integration within MNCs. We discussed the various ways in which MNCs can integrate their activities and argued that flows of people might be as important as flows of products. Different types of MNCs, however, were shown to depict different levels of integration, both when measured as product flows and when measured as people flows. The general development of MNCs from multidomestic models to global and transnational models can be expected to lead to increasing overall levels of MNC integration. Statistical data at an aggregate industry level showed that intra-firm trade flows have increased over the past decade and that trade between subsidiaries has become somewhat more important as well. Although less exact figures were available on intra-firm people flows, in general the level of expatriation was shown to be on the increase as well. This chapter therefore allows us to conclude that MNCs are indeed becoming more integrated and will probably become even more so in the next century. The big question is, however, whether this will necessarily result in a higher level of integration between *countries* and what the effect on regionalization will be. This issue is discussed in other chapters of this book. It remains beyond any doubt however, that MNCs, and especially those of the global and transnational type, are crucial actors in the process of both globalization and regionalization.

NOTES

1. See Harzing, 1998b and Harzing, forthcoming, for a complete description of these configurations.
2. The sample for both 1982 and 1994 is restricted to American multinationals. Although the BEA publishes a report on FDI in the US, the type of data collected and the large incidence of missing values does not allow a similar calculation of transnational integration for non-US MNCs.
3. The numerator includes column 5 (affiliate sales to US parents) and column 8 (affiliate sales to other foreign affiliates) from Table III.F.9 (Sales by Affiliates, Industry of US Parent by Destination) and column 3 (parent sales to foreign affiliates) from Table II.O.1 (Sales by US Parents, Industry of US Parent by Type and Destination). The denominator includes column 1 (total affiliate sales to all destinations) from Table III.F.9 and columns 3 and 4 (parent sales to foreign affiliates and to other foreign persons) from Table II.O.1.
4. This meant that we had to exclude the petroleum industry since no data were available for this industry for 1982.

REFERENCES

Bartlett, C.A. (1986) 'Building and Managing the Transnational: The New Organizational Challenge', in Porter, M.E. *Competition in Global Industries*, pp. 367–401, Boston, Mass: Harvard Business School.

Bartlett, C.A. and Ghoshal, S. (1987) 'Managing Across Borders: New Organizational Responses', *Sloan Management Review* (Fall), pp. 43–52.

Bartlett, C.A. and Ghoshal, S. (1989) *Managing Across Borders: The Transnational Solution*, Boston, Mass.: Harvard Business School Press.

Bartlett, C.A. and Ghoshal, S. (1992) *Transnational Management: Text, Cases and Readings in Cross-Border Management*, Irwin.

Bureau of Economic Analysis (1997) *US Direct Investment Abroad: 1994 Benchmark Survey, Preliminary Results*, Washington DC: US Department of Commerce.

Groenewald, H. and Sapozhnikov, A. (1990) 'Auslandentsendungen von Führungskräften: Vorgehenweisen internationaler Fluggesellschaften', *Die Unternehmung*, **44** (1), pp. 28–42.

Harzing, A.W.K. (1998a) 'Response Rates in International Mail Surveys: Results of a 22 Country Study', *International Business Review*, **7** (1).

Harzing, A.W.K. (1998b) *Configuration Analysis in International Management: The Way Forward?* Paper presented at the 25th Annual Conference AIB UK Chapter, 3–4 April, London.

Harzing, A.W.K. (forthcoming) *Plans, Procedures and Bumblebees: an International Study into Control Mechanisms in Multinational Companies*, unpublished PhD thesis.

Kobrin, S.J. (1991) 'An Empirical Analysis of the Determinants of Global Integration', *Strategic Management Journal*, **12**, pp. 17–31.

Kumar, B.N. and Karlhaus, M. (1992) 'Auslandseinsatz und Personalentwicklung: Ergebnisse einer empirischen Studie über den Beitrag der Auslandsentsendung, *Zeitschrift für Personalforschung*, **6** (1), pp. 59–71.

Kumar, B.N. and Scheimann, H. (1986) 'Japanische Führungskräfte zwischen ensandten und lokalen Führungskräften in Deutschland', *Zeitschrift für Betriebswirtschaftliche Forschung*, **38** (6), pp. 493–516.

Leong, S.M. and Tan, C.T. (1993) 'Managing Across Borders: an Empirical Test of the Bartlett and Ghoshal [1989] Organizational Typology', *Journal of International Business Studies* (Third Quarter), pp. 449–64.

National Foreign Trade Council, (1992–1996) *Global Relocations Trends: 1992/3/4/5/6 Survey Reports*, New York: Windham International and NFCT.
Pausenberger, E. and Noelle, G.F. (1977) 'Entsendung von Führungskräften in ausländische Niederlassungen', *Zeitschrift für betriebswirtschaftliche Forschung*, **29** (6), pp. 346–66.
Ronen, S. and Shenkar, O. (1985) 'Clustering Countries on Attitudinal Dimensions: A Review and Synthesis', *Academy of Management Review*, **10** (3), pp. 435–54.
Vernon, R.G. (1966) 'International investment and international trade in the product cycle', *Quarterly Journal of Economics* (May), pp. 190–207.

Index

Abonyi, G. 193
Acer 251, 252–4, 255
Aharoni, Y. 283
air transport sector 108
Alcatel 140
alliance competition 20
alternative dispute resolution 106
Anderson, A. 120
antidumping measures 120, 122, 123
Appleyard, B. 12
application–adaptation dilemma model
    158, 163
Apricot Computers 252
Aquascutum 78
arbitration *see* dispute settlement
    procedure
Argyris, C. 55
Asahi Glass 81
Asia Pacific Economic Cooperation
    (APEC) 6, 100–101, 113, 188
Asian Development Bank (ADB) 8, 193,
    195
Association of South East Asian Nations
    (ASEAN) 4, 6, 8
    ASEAN Free Trade Area (AFTA)
        188, 199–212
        basic economic effects of 199–206
        exposure to regional competition
            and 205–6
        possible future scenarios 206–11
        regional sourcing/subcontracting
            and 203–4
        scale economies of 201–3
    ASEAN Industrial Complementation
        (AIC) 203–4
    ASEAN Industrial Projects (AIP) 203
    ASEAN Joint Ventures (AJV) 202,
        204
    ASEAN Preferential Trading
        Agreement (PTA) 205
    Growth Triangles 4, 8, 187–97
    Samsung and 22, 23, 24, 25

Australia 4
automobile industry *see* car (automobile)
    industry
Azerbaijan, study of Turkish companies
    in central Asia 283–308

Bairoch, P. 3
banks and banking 140, 246
    Taiwanese financial liberalization 271,
        272, 276–7, 278
    Turkish companies in central Asia and
        295
Bartels, F. 8
Bartlett, C.A. 30, 34, 35, 57, 313, 315,
    316, 317, 319, 321, 322
Baum, O. 81
Berlin, Japanese investment in 64–5, 66,
    67–9, 71–4, 75–6, 81–2
Blank, S. 283
Bleackley, M. 259, 265, 266
BMW 144
Boddewyn, J. 283, 284
Bonnenberg, H. 86
Böttcher, L.R. 33, 34, 35
Brabeck-Lemathe, P. 33
Brazil, Toyota car production in 144
Brunei, Asian growth triangles and 8,
    193, 195
Buckley, P.J. 12, 14, 16, 18, 19, 30, 32
Bulgaria 79
Bultmann, R. 18
Bush, G. 127

Caf 251
Cal-comp 254–5
Calori, R. 52
Calvo Doctrine 104
Cambodia 8, 193
Canada
    foreign direct investment by 98
    foreign direct investment in 98, 216,
        220, 231

Japanese car production in 144, 147,
        149, 155
    North American Free Trade
        Agreement (NAFTA) and
        investment provisions 98, 100,
        106–7, 108
        US trade actions 123–9
    Single European Market and corporate
        trade and investment strategies
        131, 132, 137–41
    US trade actions and 119–29
    US–Canada Free Trade Agreement
        (FTA) 98, 102, 103, 105, 110
        business implications of trade
            remedy laws 119–29
capital
    international capital market 12–13
    Taiwanese financial sector
        liberalization 271–2, 278, 279
    see also foreign direct investment
        (FDI)
car (automobile) industry 126–7
    Toyota Motor Corporation overseas
        production case study 147–55
Carriage House Foods 133
Casson, M. 14, 16, 19, 30
Caves, R. 31, 284
Cecchini Report 201, 202
Central Asian Republics, study of
    Turkish companies in 283–308
Ceraci, V.J. 6
Chandler, A.D. 54
Chapman, M. 19
Chia, S.Y. 6, 194
China 7, 18
    Asian growth triangles and 4, 8, 190,
        192, 193
    foreign direct investment in 244, 247,
        254
    Japanese electronics production in 160
    Taiwan and 275
Christensen, C. 30
Chunghwa 253
Clegg, J. 18
Clinton, B. 127
Coase, R. 16, 18, 225
Columbia Pictures 78
Commonwealth of Independent States
        (CIS) 24, 79, 86
    see also Central Asian Republics;
        Russia; Ukraine

communications infrastructure, in former
        East Germany 66, 85
Compaq 252, 253
compensation for expropriation of assets,
        North American Free Trade
        Agreement (NAFTA) provisions on
        102–3
competition policy in North American
        Free Trade Agreement (NAFTA)
        111, 112
competitiveness
    global 16–17
    government/state and 13–14, 16–17
    management of 15
    measurement of 15
    nature of 14–15
computer industry 249, 251, 252–3
    Notebook PC Consortium case study
        258–67
concept of globalization theory 29, 30,
        33–7
Contractor, F.J. 259
Cooke, K. 128
countervailing actions 120, 122, 123
Crawford, M. 125
culture 19
    cultural exemptions in North
        American Free Trade Agreement
        (NAFTA) provisions 107, 108,
        109
    cultural globalization 3
    integration of transnational companies
        and 314
    Japanese regional headquarters in
        Europe and 52, 54–60
    time aspect of 58–9
    Turkish companies in central Asia and
        305–6
customs union theory 200
Czechoslovakia, Japanese investment in
        70, 79
Czinkota, M. 284

Daewoo 248
Dalgety 133
Dearden, R.G. 123
debt problems 246
DeBusk, A. 124
Delta Electronics 249, 251
Denmark, integration of transnational
        corporations in 317

developing countries
  debt problems 246
  world system and 18–19
Devlin, G. 259, 265, 266
dispute settlement procedure
  in North American Free Trade
     Agreement (NAFTA) 103–6,
     112, 121, 122–3
  in US–Canada Free Trade Agreement
     (FTA) 121–3
Doern, G. 119, 120
double-loop learning 55–6, 57
Doz, Y. 30, 259, 284
Dragon Bonds 278
Dunning, J.H. 13, 31, 225

East Asian Caucus (EAC) 22, 25
Eastern Europe *see* socialist economies
eclectic paradigm 31
Eddy Match 125
effectiveness, competitiveness and 14
efficiency, competitiveness and 14
Egawa, Mr 91
electronics industry, Toshiba
    Corporation overseas production
    case study 157–73
Elegant, R. 243
Encarnation, D. 284
endogenous growth theory 19
environmental problems
  in former East Germany 67, 86, 89–90
  Turkish companies in central Asia and
    302
Ernst, A. 84
ethnic conflict, Turkish companies in
    central Asia and 300
European Free Trade Area (EFTA) 13,
    274
European Union (EU) 4, 6, 7, 13
  ASEAN Free Trade Area (AFTA) and
    201
  competition policy in 111
  corporate trade and investment
    strategies and 131, 132, 137–41
  global competitiveness strategies for
    European domestic market 29–46
    characteristics of 43–4
    empirical survey of 37–45
    influencing factors 42–3
    patterns of 37–41

    successful 36–7, 41–2, 44–5
    theoretical concepts of 29–30, 31–7
  integration of 7, 131
  internal investment 247
  Japanese corporate regional
    headquarters in 49–61, 146
  Japanese foreign direct investment in
    49–50, 77–9, 84, 216, 220, 231
    in former East Germany 64–76,
     77–91
  Japanese overseas production in 251
    Toshiba Corporation case study
     158–60, 163–4, 167–73
  Samsung and 22, 23
  South Korean foreign direct
    investment in 248, 251
  Taiwan and 251–3, 273–4
    Taiwanese foreign direct investment
     248, 249–50, 251–3, 255, 274
  US protectionism and 247
exchange rates 271, 276
expatriates, integration of transnational
    companies and 314, 319–20
expropriation of assets
  North American Free Trade
    Agreement (NAFTA) provisions
    on 102–3
  Turkish companies in central Asia and
    300

factor price equalization theorem 214
Fernmeldetechnik Nordhausen 80, 81, 83
financial market liberalization in Taiwan
    269–81
financial services sector 107, 140
Finland, integration of transnational
    corporations in 323
Fordism 146
foreign direct investment (FDI) 13
  characteristics of 43–4
  globalization and 29–30, 31–3, 42–5,
    46
  influencing factors 31–2, 42–3
  internalization advantages and 31, 32
  investment strategies in response to
    EU and North American Free
    Trade Agreement (NAFTA)
    131–42
  Japanese 77, 83, 215–16
    in Asia 71, 75, 214–41

in Europe 49–50, 64–76, 77–9, 84
in former East Germany 64–76,
    77–91
in North America 77, 78, 216, 220,
    231
location advantages and 31, 32
North American Free Trade
    Agreement (NAFTA) provisions
    on 97–113
    dispute settlement procedure 103–6,
        112
    national treatment provisions
        100–103, 109
    reservations and exceptions to 101,
        106–8
ownership of business-specific
    advantages and 31–2
ratio to domestic investment 3
strategic determinants 32–3
study of Turkish companies in central
    Asia and Russia 283–308
success factors 44–5
Taiwanese 243–56
theory of direct investment 29–30,
    31–3
Foster, G.M. 19
four-knows training 57–8
France 7
    foreign direct investment in 49, 50
    integration of transnational
        corporations in 323
    Japanese electronics production in
        160, 163, 169–70
Frankfurter Messeturm 79
free trade area theory 200
Freeman, A. 125
Fuller, M. 284

game theory 17
Garcia-Pont, C. 32
Garfield, C. 56
Geertz, C. 19
General Agreement on Tariffs and Trade
    (GATT) 97, 99, 103, 245
    future of 128–9
    Uruguay Round 101, 109, 110, 112
    US trade actions and 125, 127–8
General Electric (GE) 158, 171
General Motors 144, 150

Germany 7, 247, 279
    foreign direct investment in 50
        in former East Germany 64–76,
            77–91
    integration of transnational
        corporations in 323
    Japanese car production in 146
    Japanese electronics production in
        160, 163, 167–8
    survey of globalization strategies in
        37–45
Ghoshal, S. 30, 34, 35, 57, 313, 315,
    316, 317, 319, 321, 322
globalization
    concept of globalization theory 29, 30,
        33–7
    definition of 3
    foreign direct investment and 29–30,
        31–3, 42–5, 46
    government/state and 3
    gravity model of 7
    integration within transnational
        corporations 313–24
    labour market and 17
    regionalization and 4, 6–9
    strategies for 29–46
        characteristics of 43–4
        empirical survey of 37–45
        influencing factors 42–3
        patterns of 37–41
        successful 36–7, 41–2, 44–5
        theoretical concepts of 29–30, 31–7
    trends in 3
Goehle, D. 34
Gold, T.B. 243
Goldstar 248
government and the state
    competitiveness and 13–14, 16–17
    globalization and 3
    Japanese investment in former East
        Germany and 67–9, 86–7, 88–9,
        90
    labour market and 13, 17
    NAFTA's investment provisions and
        101
    origins and evolution of 16, 17–18
    protectionism and 127
    public procurement policies 140
    regionalization and 8–9
    state enterprises 107, 111
    Turkish companies in central Asia and
        300–302

gravity model 6–7, 9
Greater Mekong Subregional
    Cooperation 8, 193, 195
Greece 247, 273
  ancient, origin of the state in 18
  Japanese car production in 144
Griffiths, J. 52
growth pole theory 7
growth triangles 4, 8, 187–97
  characteristics of 194–5
  prospects and challenges for 195–7
  recent developments 187–94
growth zones 7

Haiss, P.R. 59
Hamburg, survey of globalization
    strategies in 37–45
Hamel, G. 259, 260
Hampden-Turner, C. 55
Hansen, N.M. 7
Harrigan, K.R. 259, 260
Harzing, A.W.K. 314, 315, 317
Herman, L. 124
Hickson, D.J. 59
Hiley, M. 8
Hilpert, H.-G. 84
Hinterhuber, H. 30
Hitachi 157
Hobbes, T. 18
Hofstede, G. 59, 61
Honda 78, 126–7, 144, 146, 154, 155,
    157
Hong Kong 4, 7, 18
  Asian growth triangles and 190, 194
  financial markets 280
  foreign direct investment in 250, 253
  integration of transnational
    corporations in 317
Hood, N. 245, 251
Horlick, G. 124
Hualon 251
Hugo Boss 78
Hungary 4
  Japanese investment in 70
Huntington, S.P. 3
Hymer, S. 30, 31, 32

IBM 158, 171, 173, 252, 253
Imada, P. 201
India 24

individualism 54–5
Indonesia 18
  ASEAN Free Trade Area (AFTA) and
    201, 203, 205, 211
  Asian growth triangles and 4, 8, 190,
    192–3, 195
  foreign direct investment in 254, 280
  international trade of 200
inflation, Turkish companies in central
    Asia and 293–4
information, access to 69, 88
Inkeles, A. 19
institutional economics, new 16
intellectual property, North American
    Free Trade Agreement (NAFTA)
    provisions on 99, 109
interest rates 13, 271
internalization costs 225–31
International Centre for Settlement of
    Investment Disputes (ICSID)
    Convention 103–4, 105
International Chamber of Commerce
    (ICC) 105, 106
International Monetary Fund (IMF) 3, 7,
    245
international trade
  ASEAN Free Trade Area (AFTA) and
    188, 199–212
  competitiveness and 12–13, 14
  gravity model of 6–7, 9
  intra-industry trade 231–2
  protectionism 127, 244–5, 247
  ratio to output 3
  strategies in response to EU and North
    American Free Trade Agreement
    (NAFTA) 131–42
  theories of 200
  US trade actions and 119–29
international transfer model 158
intra-industry trade 231–2
investment, direct *see* foreign direct
    investment (FDI)
Ireland, Taiwanese foreign direct
    investment in 253
Itoh 78

James, B.G. 259
Japan 18
  ASEAN Free Trade Area (AFTA) and
    201

Asian growth triangles and 192
competitiveness of 12
culture of 54–60, 61
economic development of 245, 246
financial markets 280
financial problems in 67, 74, 83–4,
    158, 279
foreign direct investment by 77, 83,
    215–16
  in Asia 71, 75, 214–41
  in Europe 49–50, 77–9, 84
  in former East Germany 64–76,
    77–91
  in North America 77, 78, 216, 220,
    231
integration of transnational
    corporations in 318, 323
Japanese corporate regional
    headquarters in Europe 49–61,
    146
North American Free Trade
    Agreement (NAFTA) and 128
overseas production 251
  horizontal division of labour and
    214–41
  Toshiba case study 157–73
  Toyota Motor Corporation case
    study 147–55
US protectionism and 247
Jenoptik 91
Jones, R. 284
Just-In-Time system 146

Kamei, M. 81
Kanda, M. 57
Kangaroo NV 252
Karlshaus, M. 34, 314
Karpotok-Tisza Agreement 4
Kazakhstan, study of Turkish companies
    in central Asia 283–308
Kidd, J.B. 50, 52, 54, 56, 58
Killing, F.P. 259, 266
Kito, S. 84
Kloeckner 78
Knickerbocker, F. 30, 32
Knight, F.H. 18
Kobrin, S.J. 11, 30, 284, 313, 321, 322
Kogut, B. 12, 30, 31, 284
Korea see North Korea; South Korea
Kozul-Wright, R. 3

Kumar, B. 33, 34, 314
Kunnan 251
Kyrgyzstan, study of Turkish companies
    in central Asia 283–308

La Palombara, J. 283
labour
  division of 8
    Japanese foreign investment and the
      horizontal division of labour
      214–41
labour market 13, 17
  in former East Germany 66–7, 87
Langewiesener Thermos 80, 81, 83
Langhammer, R. 203, 208
Laos 8, 18, 193
Laura Ashley 78
learning
  double-loop learning 55–6, 57
  four-knows training 57–8
  individual 54–5
  organizational learning, Japanese
    regional headquarters in Europe
    and 53, 54–6, 57
Lee, T.Y. 6
Lei, D. 259
Leong, S.M. 315
Leyton House 78
Li, K.T. 243
Liang, K.S. 270
linear view of time 58–9
Linnemann, H. 6
Lipsey, R.G. 120
Lite-on 253
local content rules 126–7, 141
location theory 7
Lorange, P. 259, 266
Louis Rayer cognac 78
Low, L. 201, 211
Luitpold-Werke 78
Luther, K. 284

McDermott, M.C. 245, 251, 252, 253
McGill, M.E. 55
Magnusson, P. 128
Mahathir, M. 22, 25
Malaysia 18
  ASEAN Free Trade Area (AFTA) and
    203, 205

Asian growth triangles and 190,
192–3, 195
electronics production in 160, 252,
255
foreign direct investment in 254, 280
North American Free Trade
Agreement (NAFTA) and 128
management
implications of strategic alliances for
259, 265–6
Japanese regional headquarters in
Europe and 50, 52–60, 61
Martin-Bower 133
Matsushita 8, 157
Maucher, H. 33
Meehan, S. 123
Meffert, H. 34, 35
MEI Japan 80, 81, 83
Melo, J.D. de 194
Mercedes-Benz 74
Mercosur 6, 8
Merrill Lynch 278
Mexico 4, 7
economic liberalisation in 98–9, 108,
112
foreign direct investment in 98,
250–51
intellectual property rights in 99, 109
Japanese electronics production in
160, 163, 167, 172
North American Free Trade
Agreement (NAFTA) and 128,
273
investment provisions 98–100, 103,
104, 106–8, 111
US trade actions and 123
state enterprises in 111
Microtec 251, 253
Mintzberg, H. 58
Mirza, H. 3, 8
Mitac 251, 253, 255
Mitsubishi 157, 252
Mole, J. 59
Mongolia 192
monopolies, state 107, 111
Montes, M. 201
Moran, T. 284
Motherwell, C. 126
Motorola 158, 171, 173

Multilateral Agreement on Investment
(MAI) 9
multinational corporations *see*
transnational (multinational)
corporations
Myanmar 8, 193

Nassar, S. 259, 265
national treatment provisions in North
American Free Trade Agreement
(NAFTA) 100–103, 109
Naya, S. 201
Netherlands, integration of transnational
corporations in 323
new institutional economics 16
New United Motor Manufacturing Inc
(NUMMI) 147, 149, 150–52
Niederkofler, M. 259, 266
Nippon Sanso KK 80, 81, 83
Nissan 144, 146, 151, 154, 155, 157
Noelle, G.F. 314
Nohria, N. 32
North American Free Trade Agreement
(NAFTA) 4, 6, 8
competition policy in 111, 112
corporate trade and investment
strategies and 131, 132, 133–7,
141–2
dispute settlement procedure 103–6,
112, 121, 122–3
implications for Taiwan 250–51,
272–3
intellectual property provisions in 99,
109
investment provisions of 97–113
dispute settlement procedure 103–6,
112
national treatment provisions
100–103, 109
reservations and exceptions to 101,
106–8
rules of origin provisions in 109–11,
112
Samsung and 22, 23
state monopolies and 107, 111
US trade actions and 123–9
North, D. 16
North Korea 4
Tumen Delta Development Area 4,
192

Norusis, M. 297
Notebook PC Consortium case study
    258–67

Ohmae, K. 259
oil industry 107
Oldag, A. 86, 90
Olsen, M. 16
Opel 74
Open Regionalism 4, 6
Organization for Economic Cooperation
    and Development (OECD) 97, 101,
    112
organizational learning, Japanese
    regional headquarters in Europe and
    53, 54–6, 57
origin *see* rules of origin
overseas production
    Japanese foreign investment and the
        horizontal division of labour
        214–41
    Toshiba Corporation case study
        157–63
    Toyota Motor Corporation case study
        143–55

Pakistan 4
Palmeter, D. 123
Panagariya, A. 194
Pante, F. 193
Parkhe, A. 259, 260
Pass, C.L. 12, 14, 32
Pausenberger, E. 314
PEMEX 111
Petri, P.A. 11
petroleum sector 107
Pfeffer, J. 284
Philippines 280
    ASEAN Free Trade Area (AFTA) and
        201, 203, 205
    Asian growth triangles and 8, 193
    foreign direct investment in 255
    international trade of 200
Philips 158, 171
Phillips, K.P. 127
Poland 4
political risk management, study of
    Turkish companies in central Asia
    and Russia 283–308
Porter, M.E. 12, 32, 220, 284

Portugal 247, 273
    Japanese car production in 146
Power-Distance Index (PDI) 59
Poynter, T.A. 284
Prahalad, C.K. 30, 259, 284
Pratten, C. 202
Preble, J. 284
Prescott, K. 12, 14, 32
President Enterprises 254
Prewo, W. 6
prices, Turkish companies in central
    Asia and 293, 295
production
    overseas *see* overseas production
    Turkish companies in central Asia and
        293
property rights
    in former East Germany 66, 85, 89
    intellectual *see* intellectual property
    Turkish companies in central Asia and
        300
public procurement policies 140
Pucik, V. 259, 265
Pugh, D.S. 59

quality checking 125
quality management 52, 55–6, 146

Rau, P. 284
Red Wing 133
regionalization
    Asia and
        ASEAN Free Trade Area (AFTA)
            188, 199–212
        growth triangles 4, 8, 187–97
        Japanese foreign investment and the
            horizontal division of labour
            214–41
        Notebook PC Consortium study of
            strategic alliances 258–67
        Taiwanese financial market
            liberalization 269–81
        Taiwanese outward foreign
            investment 243–56
        Turkish companies in central Asia
            and Russia 283–308
    competitiveness and 13
    definition of 7
    Europe and

global competitiveness strategies
for European domestic market
29–46
Japanese corporate regional
headquarters in Europe 49–61,
146
Japanese investment in former East
Germany 64–76, 77–91
Toshiba overseas production case
study 157–60, 162–3, 167–73
examples of 4, 5
globalization and 4, 6–9
government/state and 8–9
gravity model of 7
labour market and 17
North America and
business implications of US trade
actions 119–29
corporate trade and investment
strategies 131, 132, 133–7,
141–2
investment provisions of North
American Free Trade
Agreement (NAFTA) 97–113
Toshiba overseas production case
study 157–60, 162, 163–7,
170–73
Toyota overseas production case
study 143–55
Samsung Group and 22–6
spillover model of 7, 8
transnational corporations and 7–8
Reichel, A. 284
RHM 133
Ricks, D.A. 284
Rockefeller Centre 78
Romania 4, 79
Ronen, S. 318
Roos, J. 259, 266
Root, F.R. 283
Rover Group 144
Ruggiero, R. 4, 6, 9
Rugman, A. 120
rules of origin 125
provisions in North American Free
Trade Agreement (NAFTA)
109–11, 112
Rumania 4, 79
Russia 4
Japanese investment in 70

study of Turkish companies in
283–308
Tumen Delta Development Area 4, 192

safeguard actions 120
Sampo 250, 251, 255
Samsung Group 9, 248
estimated figures for 1995 25–6
regionalization and 22–6
structure of 22–5
Sankyo Pharmaceutical 78
Sanyo 157
Sauvé, P. 9
scale economies 8
Schott Glaswerke 81
Schreyögg, G. 30
Schwanen, D. 9
Sethi, S. 284
7-Eleven 254
Shang, S.H. 258
Shearson Lehman Brothers 278
Shenkar, O. 318
Shepherd, D. 18
Siemens 140, 173
Silberston, A. 18
Singapore 7, 18
ASEAN Free Trade Area (AFTA) and
201
Asian growth triangles and 4, 8, 190,
192, 194
financial markets 280
foreign direct investment in 253–4
international trade of 200
Japanese electronics production in
159, 172
Slocum, J.W. 55, 259
Slovakia 4
small and medium-sized enterprises
(SMEs), globalization and 46
Smith, D.H. 19
social anthropology 19
social instability
in former East Germany 88
Turkish companies in central Asia and
300
socialist economies
trading links between 86
transition to market economies 14, 86,
247
Japanese investment and 64–76,
77–91

Solzhenitsyn, A. 18
Sony 72, 91, 157, 169
Souder, W.E. 259, 265
South Asian Association for Regional
    Cooperation (SAARC) 188
South Asian Preferential Trading
    Agreement (SAPTA) 188
South Korea 4, 18, 280
    Asian growth triangles and 192
    financial liberalization in 280
    foreign direct investment by 248, 251
    US protectionism and 247
Southland 254
Spain 247, 273
    Japanese car production in 144
Späth, L. 91
spillover model 7, 8
standards 140
state *see* government and the state
Steinmann, H. 30
Strange, R. 18
strategic alliances 8
    literature on 259–61
    managerial implications of 259, 265–6
    Notebook PC Consortium case study
        258–67
strategic management 30
strategic planning 30
strategies
    globalization 29–46
        characteristics of 43–4
        empirical survey of 37–45
        influencing factors 42–3
        patterns of 37–41
        successful 36–7, 41–2, 44–5
        theoretical concepts of 29–30, 31–7
subsidies, North American Free Trade
    Agreement (NAFTA) provisions
    and 112
Sweden, integration of transnational
    corporations in 323
Switzerland, integration of transnational
    corporations in 323
synchronic view of time 58–9

Taiwan 4, 18
    Asian growth triangles and 190
    computer industry in 249, 251, 252–3
        Notebook PC Consortium case
            study 258–67

economic structure of 243, 269–70
financial market liberalization in
    269–81
    further acceleration of 276–8
    possible Asian regional financial
        centre 278–81
    prior to 1985 270–72
foreign investment by 243–56
    in Asia 248–9, 253–5, 256
    in Europe 248, 249–50, 251–3, 255,
        274
    in North America 248, 249, 250–51,
        255
international trade and 272–3
    US protectionism and 247
Japanese car production in 144,
        149–50, 153–4, 155
regionalization and
    EU Single Market 251–3, 273–4
    NAFTA 250–51, 272–3
Tan, C.T. 315
Tan, R. 193
Tang, M. 187, 196
Tatung 250, 251, 252, 255
taxation, Turkish companies in central
    Asia and 295
technical standards 140
technology, trade and 12
Teco 251
telecommunications sector 107, 140
Teramoto, Y. 50, 52, 54
Thai Glass Industry 210
Thailand 18
    ASEAN Free Trade Area (AFTA) and
        201, 203, 205, 208, 210
    Asian growth triangles and 4, 8,
        192–3, 195
    electronics production in 160, 255
    foreign direct investment in 254, 280
    international trade of 200
Thant, M. 196
Thomson 158, 172
time, cultural differences and 58–9
Tinbergen, J. 6
Toh, M.H. 201, 211
Tomlin, B.W. 119, 120
Toshiba Corporation 157–73
    overseas production by 158–60,
        170–73
    comparative analysis of 171–2

Europe 163–4, 167–70
future prospects 172–3
North America 162, 163–7
Toshiba America Consumer
        Products Inc 162, 164, 175–6
Toshiba America Electronic
        Components Inc 166, 178–9
Toshiba Consumer Products Europe
        GmbH 167–8, 180–82
Toshiba Consumer Products (UK)
        Ltd 168–9, 182–3
Toshiba Display Devices Inc 165–6,
        176–8
Toshiba Electromex 167, 179–80
Toshiba Systems France SA
        169–70, 183–4
Toyota Motor Corporation 143–55, 157
    application overseas of Toyota
        Production System 146, 147–55
        Kouzi (Taiwan) 149–50, 153–4,
        155
        New United Motor Manufacturing
        Inc (NUMMI) 147, 149,
        150–52
        Toyota Motor Manufacturing USA
        (TMM) 147, 149, 152–3, 155
    overseas expansion process 143–6,
        154
Trade Related Investment
        Measures/Procedures
        (TRIMs/TRIPs) 101, 109
trade *see* international trade
training
    four-knows training 57–8
    Japanese methods 152
transaction costs 225–31
transnational (multinational)
        corporations
    developing countries and 19
    economic theory of 16–17
    integration within 313–24
        different types of companies and
        315–21
        increasing levels of 321–4
    overseas production by
        Toshiba Corporation case study
        157–63
        Toyota Motor Corporation case
        study 143–55
    regionalization and 7–8

study of Turkish companies in central
        Asia and Russia 283–308
trade and investment strategies in
        response to EU and North
        American Free Trade Agreement
        (NAFTA) 131–42
see also foreign direct investment
        (FDI)
Treuhandanstalt 64, 68–9, 81, 85, 86, 87,
        88–9, 90
Trevor, M. 157
Trompenaars, F. 58
Truijens 251
Tumen Delta Development Area 4, 192,
        195, 196
Turkey, study of Turkish companies in
        central Asia and Russia 283–308
Turkmenistan, study of Turkish
        companies in central Asia 283–308

Ukraine 4
Uncertainty-Avoidance Index (UAI) 59
United Kingdom
    cultural view of time in 58–9
    foreign direct investment in 49, 50, 52,
        78–9, 248, 251–3
    integration of transnational
        corporations in 323
    Japanese overseas production in
        cars 144, 146
        electronics 159, 162, 168–9
    North American Free Trade
        Agreement (NAFTA) and
        corporate trade and investment
        strategies 131, 132, 133–7, 141
United Nations Commission on
        International Trade Law
        (UNCITRAL) 104, 105
United Nations Conference on Trade and
        Development (UNCTAD) 3, 8
United Nations Development
        Programme (UNDP) 192
United States of America 4, 7
    ASEAN Free Trade Area (AFTA) and
        201
    Canadian responses to US trade
        actions 119–29
    foreign direct investment by 50,
        244–5, 247, 250

foreign direct investment in 100
  Japanese 77, 78, 216, 220, 231
  South Korean 248
  Taiwanese 248, 249, 250–51, 255
integration of transnational
    corporations in 318, 323, 324
international trade and 272–3
  protectionism 127, 247
Japanese overseas production in
  cars 144, 147, 149, 152–3, 155
  electronics 159, 160, 162–6
North American Free Trade
    Agreement (NAFTA) and
    investment provisions 97, 100, 103,
      107, 108
  trade actions 123–9
US–Canada Free Trade Agreement
    (FTA) 98, 102, 103, 105, 110
  business implications of trade
      remedy laws 119–29
Uzbekistan, study of Turkish companies
  in central Asia 283–308

Van Agtmael, A.W. 283
Vernon, R. 30, 315
Vietnam 8, 18, 23, 188, 193, 244
  foreign direct investment in 254
Vobis 253
Volkswagen 74, 146

wages
  in former East Germany 66–7, 87
  Turkish companies in central Asia and
      293
Wang, C.C. 260
Wang, H.C. 259
Wang, J. 190
Weinschrott, D. 6
Welge, M. 33, 34, 35
Wells, L. 284
Wiechmann, U. 30, 34
Williamson, O.E. 16, 225
Wolf, C. 6
Woot, P. de 52
World Bank 103–4, 105
World Trade Organization (WTO) 4, 6,
    22, 113
Wu, C.S. 260, 261

xenophobia
  Japanese investment in former East
      Germany and 69–70, 88
  Turkish companies in central Asia and
      300

York, R.C. 120
Yoshihide, I. 128
Young, S. 245
Yuen Foon Yu 253
Yugoslavia 79